Gypsy Economy

The Human Economy
Series editors:
Keith Hart, London School of Economics
John Sharp, University of Pretoria

Those social sciences and humanities concerned with the economy have lost the confidence to challenge the sophistication and public dominance of the field of economics. We need to give a new emphasis and direction to the economic arrangements that people already share, while recognizing that humanity urgently needs new ways of organizing life on the planet. This series examines how human interests are expressed in our unequal world through concrete economic activities and aspirations.

Volume 1
People, Money and Power in the Economic Crisis:
Perspectives from the Global South
Edited by Keith Hart and John Sharp

Volume 2
Economy for and against Democracy
Edited by Keith Hart and John Sharp

Volume 3
Gypsy Economy
Romani Livelihoods and Notions of Worth in the 21st Century
Edited by Micol Brazzabeni, Manuela Ivone da Cunha and Martin Fotta

Volume 4
From Clans to Coops:
Confiscated Mafia Land in Sicily
Theodoros Rakopoulos

Volume 5
Money in a Human Economy
Edited by Keith Hart

Volume 6
Money at the Margins
Global Perspectives on Technology, Financial Inclusion and Design
Edited by Bill Maurer, Smoki Musaraj, and Ivan Small

Gypsy Economy
Romani Livelihoods and Notions of Worth in the 21st Century

Edited by
Micol Brazzabeni, Manuela Ivone Cunha
and Martin Fotta

berghahn
NEW YORK · OXFORD
www.berghahnbooks.com

Published in 2016 by

Berghahn Books

www.berghahnbooks.com

© 2016, 2018 Micol Brazzabeni, Manuela Ivone Cunha and Martin Fotta
First paperback edition published in 2018.

All rights reserved. Except for the quotation of short passages
for the purposes of criticism and review, no part of this book
may be reproduced in any form or by any means, electronic or
mechanical, including photocopying, recording, or any information
storage and retrieval system now known or to be invented,
without written permission of the publisher.

Library of Congress Cataloging-in-Publication Data

Names: Cunha, Manuela Ivone Pereira da. | Brazzabeni, Micol.
Title: Gypsy economy : Romani livelihoods and notions of worth in the 21st century / edited by Micol Brazzabeni, Manuela Ivone Cunha and Martin Fotta.
Description: New York : Berghahn Books, [2015] | Series: The human economy | Includes bibliographical references and index.
Identifiers: LCCN 2015007889| ISBN 9781782388791 (hardback: alk. paper) | ISBN 9781785338229 (paperback: alk. paper) | ISBN 9781782388869 (ebook)
Subjects: LCSH: Romanies–Europe–Economic conditions–21st century. | Romanies–Europe–Social conditions–21st century. | Community life–Europe. | Values–Social aspects–Europe. | Capitalism–Social aspects–Europe. | Marginality, Social–Economic aspects–Europe. | Europe–Ethnic relations. | Europe–Economic conditions–21st century.
Classification: LCC DX145 .G974 2015 | DDC 330.940089/91497–dc23
LC record available at http://lccn.loc.gov/2015007889

British Library Cataloguing in Publication Data

A catalogue record for this book is available from the British Library

ISBN: 978-1-78238-879-1 (hardback)
ISBN: 978-1-78533-822-9 (paperback)
ISBN: 978-1-78238-886-9 (ebook)

Contents

Figures	vii
Acknowledgements	viii
Introduction: Gypsy Economy Micol Brazzabeni, Manuela Ivone Cunha and Martin Fotta	1
Chapter 1. Usury among the Slovak Roma: Notes on Relations between Lenders and Borrowers in a Segregated *Taboris* Tomáš Hrustič	31
Chapter 2. New Redistributors in Times of Insecurity: Different Types of Informal Lending in Hungary Judit Durst	49
Chapter 3. A Way of Life Flowing in the Interstices: Cigano Horse Dealers in Alentejo, Portugal Sara Sama Acedo	68
Chapter 4. 'Endured Labour' and 'Fixing Up' Money: The Economic Strategies of Roma Migrants in Slovakia and the UK Jan Grill	88
Chapter 5. 'I Go for Iron': Xoraxané Romá Collecting Scrap Metal in Rome Marco Solimene	107
Chapter 6. 'I'm Good but also Mad': The Street Economy in a Poor Neighbourhood of Bucharest Gergő Pulay	127
Chapter 7. The Mechanisms of Independence: Economic Ethics and the Domestic Mode of Production among Gabori Roma in Transylvania Martin Olivera	145
Chapter 8. Deceit and Efficacy: Fortune Telling among the Calon Gypsies in São Paulo, Brazil Florencia Ferrari	163

Chapter 9. Houses under Construction: Conspicuous Consumption
and the Values of Youth among Romanian Cortorari Gypsies 181
    Cătălina Tesăr

Chapter 10. Exchange, Shame and Strength among Calon of Bahia:
A Values-based Analysis 201
    Martin Fotta

Chapter 11. 'Give and Don't Keep Anything!' Wealth, Hierarchy
and Identity among the Gypsies of Two Small Towns
in Andalusia, Spain 221
    Nathalie Manrique

Afterword 240
    Keith Hart

Index 251

Figures

10.1	Settlement in Bomfim	202
10.2	Kinship relations between households in the Bomfim settlement	203
11.1	Inherited classification	224

Acknowledgements

This volume originated from discussions that took place during a 2012 Exploratory Workshop supported by the European Science Foundation (ESF), the Centre for Research in Anthropology (CRIA) and the Lisbon University Institute (IUL). Besides these institutions, we would like to thank all the participants of the workshop, particularly Yasar Abu Ghosh and Alessandro Simone, who do not appear as contributors to this volume. Many thanks go to the discussants – Daniel Seabra Lopes, Iulia Hasdeu, Radu Umbres and Valerio Simoni – for their input; their contributions were thoughtful and are reflected in many ideas presented in this volume. Keith Hart has been supportive of the project throughout, and we are grateful for his comments and observations at various stages; he was also kind enough to provide an afterword to this volume.

Jan Grill, Martin Olivera and Valerio Simoni read and commented on the introduction, with the latter's suggestions proving particularly instructive. We are also grateful to three anonymous reviewers for Berghahn, two of whom have since identified themselves as Judith Okely and Elisabeth Tauber. Further thanks go to David Jobanputra, whose editing was indispensable for the preparation of the individual chapters

Finally, several of the authors have become first-, second- and even third-time parents in the course of this long project. We would therefore like to dedicate this book to our splendid children.

Micol Brazzabeni, Manuela Ivone Cunha, Martin Fotta

Introduction
Gypsy Economy

MICOL BRAZZABENI, MANUELA IVONE CUNHA
AND MARTIN FOTTA

The question of Gypsy economic practices and their relation to the economies of societies in which Gypsies live lies at the heart of many anthropological descriptions of Gypsy distinctiveness, resilience and even resistance, whether these studies focus on the social organisation of economic activities, on cosmologies of wealth and prodigality or on subjective orientations. Although examining the economic practices of various Gypsy populations ethnographically can enrich our understanding of the changing interrelations between the market and the state, the contribution of this ethnography has generally only been implied and its theoretical significance rarely explored. This shortcoming is at least partially due to a lack of works that put observations about Gypsy economic strategies in comparative terms (but see Reyniers 1998).[1]

Taken together, the chapters in this volume argue that Gypsy economy is fully embedded in markets, that is, in a commercial economy mediated by money. Its existence illustrates the fact that despite modern intellectual, political and economic efforts employed to create 'the' market (e.g. Polanyi 1944; Hart 2000) and certain convergences of existing markets with the vision of 'the' market (Callon 2007: 349), the so-called market economy is best approached as a milieu of cracks, interstices and fissures on which people confer specific dimensions and characteristics through their creative actions. Ethnographies of Roma and Gypsy[2] communities are of particular heuristic significance because they describe a type of economy that is embedded in the modern economic system and created in relation to a milieu from which it cannot be dissociated, but which nevertheless cannot be fully characterised with reference to the modern economic system alone (such as being 'outside' it) without looking at the material processes that in each instance went into its fabrication. Since such an analysis might disclose worlds different from those that scholars associate with the 'economic' (Çalişkan and Callon 2009), it forces anthropologists to think through the nature of major economic processes and categories used to analyse them.

Over the past thirty or so years, anthropologists have highlighted the specificities of the economic practices of various Roma and Gypsy populations (Vlach Roma, English Gypsies, Mānuš and so on), which have given rise to some important themes and debates (discussed further below). For instance, Judith Okely (1983) and Aparna Rao (1987), among others, described Gypsies as nomadic or peripatetic service providers and entertainers who make a living by exploiting opportunities not covered by the mainstream provision of goods and services. These authors also showed how to this end Gypsies manipulate stereotypes and impressions others hold about 'Gypsies'. The Gypsy preference for autonomy and self-employment has also been noted. Leonardo Piasere (1985), for instance, stressed that the refusal to engage in wage labour underpinned processes of identity construction, implying that their full absorption into the labour market could lead to their assimilation. Qualifying this view somewhat, Michael Stewart (1997) showed that even in socialist Hungary, where Vlach Rom were employed in factories, Rom gave an ideological preference to so-called *Romani butji* (Rom work), connoting deals in the marketplace that showed one's acumen and through which men constantly recreated themselves as Rom. This focus on personhood and the creation of proper social relationships (see especially Gay y Blasco 1999) highlighted the need for researchers to pay attention not only to the description of ways in which Gypsies deal with non-Gypsies and how this becomes a source of their ethnic distinctiveness, but also to the various ways that Gypsies conceptualise articulations between gender, money, work, ethnic belonging and even their relationship to the dead, as Patrick Williams (1993) and Elisabeth Tauber (2008) have demonstrated.

These analytical developments raised two sorts of question. First, how is the social reproduction of Gypsies ensured in the face of broader socio-economic changes? Second, how does a description of economic practices recognise the position of individual Roma and Gypsy communities within societies they live in, a position that includes racism and poverty, while leaving the possibility for acknowledging a 'cosmological choice' – a choice not in the narrow sense of volition but as a self-defining capacity to determine for oneself a posture vis-à-vis the workings of states, markets, money, bureaucracies, and so on within modern societies – through which each community seeks to guarantee its continuity? As the contributors to this volume consistently attest, such characterisations should emerge from ethnography, not as a preconceived idea.

Gypsy Economy

In a variety of ways, the ethnographic studies presented in this volume try to tackle the questions raised above, building on insights gained over the past three decades.[3] The chapters not only describe different contextually specific ways of making money; they also take seriously Gypsies' frames of reference and motivations for their activities, while placing these activities firmly in the context of recent shifts in the nature of market societies – from the economic boom and expansion of third-generation welfare in Brazil, to the consequences of the economic crisis and the dismantlement of the welfare state across the Atlantic in Portugal. The concept of 'Gypsy economy', then, has to be seen in this double sense. On the one hand, it is a term that covers the economic practices and orientations of people belonging to various Roma and Gypsy populations (Gabori Roma, Brazilian Calon, Portuguese Ciganos, and so on) that for a set of reasons have been referred to and often refer to themselves as 'Gypsies'. On the other hand, it is also an interpretive lens through which to investigate how people position themselves in relation to the current economic system and to the changing nature of the roles of states, markets and finance, as well as of interrelationships between these, creating more or less viable modes of living (see Hart, this volume).

According to Keith Hart, the twentieth century saw a general experiment in impersonal society. Whether it took the guise of West European social democracies, state socialism or developmental states, Hart agues, its 'forms were anchored in national bureaucracy, in centralised states and laws carrying the threat of punishment. The dominant economic forms were also bureaucratic and closely linked to the state as the source of universal law. Conventionally these were divided according to principles of ownership into "public" and "private" sectors' (Hart 2012). Centralised bureaucracy, financial interests and (social) science, then, aligned to create a social world run according to impersonal principles (Hart 2000, 2005), sometimes referred to as the 'formal sector'.

As Hart (2006, 2012) notes, the concept of informal economy was coined to cover all economic activities that did not conform to these impersonal norms and the order they created. For those acquainted with the literature on Gypsy communities, it also is clear that many studies have described Gypsies as those who have somehow been excluded from impersonal societies' greatest achievements, including formal wage labour. Although the reasons given for this differ according to their proponents' theoretical orientations, they parallel those used to explain the existence of the 'informal economy'. For example, anthropologists have described Gypsies as those who 'did not want in' (Gmelch 1986), who refused to be proletarianised (Okely 1983), who used economic strategies developed in rural areas to adapt to a life in urban centres (Gmelch 1977), who rejected the totalisation of the modern bourgeois order (Münzel and Streck 1981), who filled in the 'spaces in between' (*Zwischenräume*), which, although found in all complex societies, were seen as more problematic within modern ones (Streck 2008). On the other side of the Iron Curtain, meanwhile, socialist planners and researchers saw in Gypsies residues of the past, but also as people who through correct approaches could be turned into modern socialist workers (see Stewart 1993).

As Hart observes, today the twentieth-century experiment in organising societies impersonally is becoming compromised. The money system has reached such proportions that no state is able to control it anymore. The world economy has become more informal, with deregulation leading to more extreme and pervasive informalisation. In different spheres, the reduction of formal regulations has expanded economic relations and social welfare based on family and community relationships as opposed to those based on contract or entitlement. In this light, social relations have come to be valued as assets, and the notion of 'social capital' as a 'resource' has made its way into the discourses of governments and agencies, which promote the increasing displacement of regulations from the legal field to the moral field of personal ties.[4] Ethnographers have provided evidence about the tensions and ambiguities that surround this 'resource' (e.g., Narotzky 2006; Cunha 2013) and how it can also compound inequality, domination and exploitation (Portes 1998; Smart 2008). These social relations are nevertheless critically important in what Loïc Wacquant (2008) calls the 'society of advanced insecurity'. The current economic crisis has increased the size of the population who are at risk of poverty, which has now reached the middle class. Shrinking job opportunities, declining state benefits, failing credit and short-term and casualised employment have also expanded uncertainty. Precarity is no longer a marginal condition, in the same way that uncertainty is no longer a particular aspect of specific ways of life (such as that of peasants); it is becoming institutionalised both as a fact and a project, a handmaiden of the entrepreneurial spirit, self-employment, flexibility. The notion of 'precariat' captures both the unstable conditions of transient labour and the states of anxiety, dislocation and risk that go with it (Standing 2011).

As far as instability, transience and elusive resources go, it can be said that this is 'the time of the Gypsies', to use the title of Michael Stewart's (1997) book. Permanent precarity – which one might associate with the current state of 'crisis' – has been a normal situation for many Roma and Gypsy communities described in this volume for decades. This raises several questions. What are the material conditions and ideational elaborations (such as with respect to notions of scarcity or abundance, value, time, insecurity) involved in their resilience? Which creative economic strategies (formal and informal) do they employ to make a living? In which aspects of existence do they invest? How do they mobilise social, cultural and economic resources in contexts of vulnerability, indebtedness and financial volatility? How do tangible and intangible assets circulate both among them and between them and non-Gypsies? And, finally, departing from approaches that reduce them to a socially excluded and marginalised population, what do they have – as opposed to what do they lack – in this respect?

Extreme caution is nevertheless necessary in order to avoid creating a Gypsy comparative bubble that neglects taking into account how various other people act in similar circumstances, or, related to this, as Keith Hart points out in his Afterword, losing sight of historical situatedness. Furthermore, it is also necessary to avoid producing a free-floating comparison dangerously near to essentialism that focuses on cultural principles and worldviews detached from historical processes or structural conditions. Living for the moment, as Day, Stewart and Papataxiarchis (1999) have rightly pointed out, may be a cosmological choice that constitutes an active response to marginalisation and social exclusion. It is also true that among various people, Gypsies and non-Gypsies alike, a total lack of resources may hinder the very possibility of projecting a future and render acts of sharing or other efforts to engage properly in social relations a more secure and reliable investment than trust in economic returns (Cunha 2002; see also de l'Estoile 2014). Indeed, rather than denote a short-term orientation, this engagement can also be as much oriented to the future as other kinds of investments. Moreover, as Elliot Liebow contended almost half a century ago, living in the present may actually express less a present-time orientation than a realistic awareness of a particular historical future – a future ridden with uncertainty or loaded with trouble: 'There is no mystically intrinsic connection between "present-time" orientation and [the poor]. Whenever people of whatever class have been uncertain, sceptical or downright pessimistic about the future this is one characteristic response' (Liebow 1967: 69). We may add that this is what Horace's famous injunction *carpe diem* actually meant: 'seize the day' – for the future cannot be trusted.

The two meanings of the term 'Gypsy economy', as we use it in this volume mirror Stewart's double sense of the expression 'time of the Gypsies'. First, Stewart used it as a shorthand for Vlach Rom practices and ideologies – for instance, swaps and loans of things that expressed equality, or communal consumption through merrymaking that recreated the brotherly ideal – through which the Rom managed to remain Rom. Second, through it Stewart tried to capture the mood characteristic of the socio-economic conditions at a particular historical juncture (see Hart, this volume): In the socialist Hungary of the 1980s, the promise of a society run on impersonal 'scientific' principles had been exhausted. Hungarians became convinced that nothing could be attained by adhering to official procedures, and that their social reproduction increasingly depended on personal ties, on dealing and hustling. They felt that theirs was 'the land of the Gypsies' (Stewart 1997: 237).[5]

Undoubtedly, the attitudes of non-Roma Hungarians in the late 1980s also conveyed a dissatisfaction with these shifts in their lifestyle, for which Gypsies served as emblematic and convenient scapegoats. Today, too, crises of bureaucratic legitimacy, especially of the European Union (EU), of political representation and of economy, which are related to shifts in state–market relations, feed particularly aggressive anti-Gypsy populism (see e.g. Stewart 2012c). It is precisely because of these ambiguities apparent in the concept of Gypsy economy that we feel that understanding Gypsy economies – that is, how individuals belonging to various communities seen as Gypsies earn a living and make sense of their activities – could shed light on the predicament and strategies of an increasing number of people in present-day economies who have experienced state withdrawal, a repersonalisation of economic practices, presentist orientations, informal employment and even life-long precarity. In what follows, therefore, we discuss the questions of niches, marginality and personhood – the three main themes that repeatedly crop up in ethnographic descriptions of economic practices found among various communities of people seen as 'Gypsies'.

Interstitial Economy

To capture the character of Gypsies as economic agents, some scholars have used categories such as 'commercial nomads' or 'service nomads' (e.g. Hayden 1979; Gmelch and Gmelch 1987; Marushiakova et al. 2005). If they found any of the existing terms too exclusive, they have resorted to more descriptive terms, such as 'artisan, trader, and entertainer minorities' (Gmelch 1986), a label that also covered forms of scavenging, such as scrap collection. All of these categories have in common a focus on the specialist role of Gypsies within the economy, and normally they appear alongside ecological concepts of 'niche' and 'adaptation'.

The concept of 'niche' highlighted Gypsy-specific insertion into the majority economy, within which they covered recognisable, albeit variously stable, economic specialisations. People were said to 'occupy' a niche, a result of their adaptation to the character of or changes in surrounding conditions (e.g. Gmelch 1977). In this usage, niche was seen as referring to 'mutable demands for goods and/or services that other communities consider inaccessible or cannot, or will not, support on a permanent basis' (Berland and Rao 2004: 4, emphasis removed). Similarly, Judith Okely (1979, 1983) understood the 'niche' of the English Gypsies to be the employment of skills to exploit a broad range of opportunities found in an environment where demand was irregular. In sum, scholars often portrayed Gypsy economic activities as occurring within pre-existent 'in-between spaces' (*Zwischenräume*) of dominant socio-economic orders (Streck 2008), with Gypsies 'adapting' to the surrounding society by finding, occupying, covering or exploiting such niches.

In the anthropological literature, such 'niche occupation' was related to the specific social organisation of Roma and Gypsy populations, as apparent, for instance, in the central position of households, the flexibility of bilateral kinship, and gender relations (Gmelch 1986). Its most systematic elaboration is found in the concept of 'a peripatetic niche', applied to non-sedentary populations of service providers (e.g. Berland and Salo 1986; Rao 1987). This term refers to a 'specialised mode of subsistence' or of 'resource exploitation', where mobile communities provide for geographically dispersed customers. In the words of Aparna Rao, 'the peripatetic strategy consists basically of combining spatial mobility and non-subsistent commercialism at the economic level with endogamy at the social level' (Rao 1987: 3).

Referring specifically to the concept of 'peripatetics', Leonardo Piasere recently observed that, like other concepts developed by social scientists to capture the character of Gypsy populations, squaring this concept with observable realities became difficult: Gypsies turned out to behave as sociological tricksters, escaping the category as soon as it was forged (Piasere 2011: 77). On the one hand, criteria used to define it (mobility, endogamy, symbiosis, marginality) had to be treated as continuums to accommodate internal variety (Rao 1987; see also Gmelch 1986). This raised questions about the usefulness of 'peripatetic' as a category. On the other hand, as Piasere argued as early as the mid 1980s, such approaches reduced Gypsy adaptation to economic and ecological determinants without exploring the meanings and social organisation that lay behind any 'peripatetic niche' (e.g. Piasere 1986).

This 1980s debate is telling, because it reveals one problem with existing approaches to understanding the specificities of Gypsy economic strategies. Terms such as 'niche' and 'adaptation' focus on the 'demand side' (that is, on consumers and gaps in the mainstream provision of goods and services). Studies starting with these conceptualisations take non-Gypsies as the point of departure, although they might document Gypsy awareness and the manipulation of stereotypes non-Gypsies might hold of Gypsies (e.g. Okely 1979). Rather than focusing on the majority 'setting' and Gypsies' adaptation to it, Piasere (1992) proposes exploring the varying conceptualisations and forms of sociality found among Roma and Gypsy communities. His work, which described, among other things, different modalities of exchange and circulation among the Slovénsko Roma in Italy, and between these Roma and the *Gaĝe*,[6] is one example of this kind of analysis (Piasere 1985). Another is Michael Stewart's ethnography of the Vlach Rom in Hungary, the most detailed analysis of Gypsy economy to date, which showed how dealing among the *Gaźos* in the marketplace was linked to the ways in which the Rom conceptualise the relationship between gender, fertility, money and work (Stewart 1997; see also Stewart 1994).

The contributors to this volume, while not ignoring the context (that is, the socio-economic conditions and ideologies of the non-Gypsies in specific countries), focus on, as it were, the 'supply' side of the niche: the conceptual apparatus and social relations behind economic practices. They try to understand economic activities in Gypsies' own terms, aware that these might be radically different from those of the non-Gypsies. Our understanding of the concept of niche economy is therefore close to Jane Guyer's elaboration of the term (Guyer 1997). Guyer sees any economic niche as a 'specialist production', with its product definitions and standardisations, expertise and replication, and as something fully grounded in a commercial economy; it is 'a recognisable social form' (Guyer 2004: 177). In fact, taken as a whole, the chapters show that if anything like a recognisable niche exists, even for a limited period of time, it has to be constantly recreated – what proponents of a performativity approach might refer to as framing and maintenance (e.g. Çalışkan and Callon 2010) – by the Gypsies.

For instance, money-making possibilities through migration often depend on the existence of specific regulations and formalities (such as EU citizenship) and do not represent simple 'arbitrage' across distances. Their specific form is therefore often temporary, but nevertheless connected with a recognisable conceptual apparatus, as Jan Grill's contribution attests. Marco Solimene's chapter shows how scrap-metal collection among

Xoraxané Romá in Rome depends on a constant circulation through the city by means of which ties with the Rome's inhabitants are maintained and differentiation from the recently arrived Roma from Romania are established. As these and other chapters show, movement and spatiality are important aspects of economic practices, albeit in more complex ways than the theory of peripatetic communities suggests. This is true even of those communities whose mode of living seems to be captured by the theory the best. Thus, drawing on her fieldwork among the Portuguese Ciganos who are known as ambulant horse traders, Sara Sama Acedo argues that it is productive to analyse Cigano economic activities as interstitial: while any Cigano interstice belongs to the socio-economic system that limits opportunities or codes territories, it emerges through concrete processes via which Ciganos confer on it specific dimensions, stability and consistency through, for instance, repetition and historical sedimentation or the naming and standardising of specific productive relations.

Marginal Economy

The authors in this volume are uneasy about describing the Roma and Gypsy populations and their economic practices as marginal in essence. While several authors describe Central European Roma living in extreme poverty in geographically peripheral communities or ghettoes, they insist on each individual situation being assessed ethnographically without foreclosing the conclusions. This is particularly true today, when changing interrelations between formality and informality, the repersonalisation of economic practices and the replacement of regular employment with precarious forms, call for a reconceptualisation of what the rule or standard of organising society is (e.g. Hart 2000).

The chapters therefore focus on forms of social action to which Gypsies subscribe. They do not limit themselves to denouncements or to appeals to state and non-state institutions, and they avoid describing the economic strategies of Gypsies as the inevitable by-products of age-old discrimination. Such denunciations, which have proliferated in recent decades, especially in the form of expert policy assessments, while laudable and important, are successful only to a limited extent. Moreover, they limit the political potential of anthropology (cf. Turner 1979). Put simply, an adequate political response to the problems that Roma and Gypsy populations face should not result in treating people as passive victims by denying them their creativity and capacity for struggle in their own terms. As a result of their primary focus on anti-Gypsyism, denunciations turn away from (functionally) positive ethnographic accounts, making anthropology itself politically irrelevant. They do not adequately reflect ethnographic research that consistently shows the range of economic strategies employed by individual communities to varying levels of success. For instance, while Hruštič's chapter describes chronic indebtedness and extreme levels of poverty among the Roma in Slovakia, who are uneasy with being categorised as 'Gypsies' by the non-Roma, Olivera's chapter suggests that Gabori in Romania are not 'poor' in locally relative terms, and that they embrace and 'reinvent' their Gypsyness.

Having made these observations, it is undeniable that the present volume comes out at a particularly difficult period for European Romanies (as well as for non-Romani Gypsies). In the last few years, Romanian Roma have been deported from both Italy and France, raising questions about the limits of the EU project, while Roma from the former Yugoslavia, who fled the region during the Yugoslav wars, have been deported from Sweden, Finland and Germany. In the past decade, Europe has seen the legitimisation of 'reasonable anti-Gypsyism' that condones policies and police practices targeting Roma (van Baar 2014) and, not unrelated to it, the rise of increasingly violent forms of anti-Gypsyist populism, which for the first time in modern history treats Gypsies as a 'fundamental source of national woe' (Stewart 2012a: xviii). As Stewart (2012b) points out, this anti-Gypsyism has to be seen in the context of the enlargement of the EU, where crises of legitimacy combine with democratic forms of engagement and identity politics.

At the same time, for most Roma, the restructuring of the economy in Central and Eastern Europe over the past two decades has meant the loss of employment, educational segregation and dependency on welfare payments. Several chapters in this volume describe the economic strategies of people living within such segregated communities and the dynamics of debt at the interface of state welfare and poverty (see Durst, Grill, Hruštič, Pulay, this volume). To be sure, the roots of the present situation, including low educational levels, have to be looked for in former socialist economies (Stewart 2002). For instance, as early as the late 1970s, Charta 77, an informal civic movement in Czechoslovakia noted that:

> in the current situation, the powers-that-be need the Romani minority to remain in a position that it is now: uneducated, without clear prospects, and ready to move from one end of the republic to the other in search of unskilled work without knowing where they are going to live ... The demand for unskilled labour will then fall, threatening the Roma with massive unemployment which will expose this ruthlessly urbanized minority

to extreme pressures, and fuse their social ostracism and material oppression with a new ethnic consciousness, all the stronger and the more cruelly it is today suppressed. (quoted in Guy 1998: 32)

When investigating the position of specific Roma and Gypsy populations, it is therefore crucial to bear in mind the historical context of each country and region (see esp. Sama Acedo, Grill, this volume). Individual communities are integrated into the majority society in different ways (see e.g. Ries 2008). Speaking about Central and Eastern Europe, Stewart observes that '[t]he diverse forms of Romany integration in different parts of Europe mean that problems arising between Roma and non-Roma vary hugely' (Stewart 2012a: xxxv). The chapters in this volume attest to such diversity, which arises from different ideas about issues such as the meaning of work, the relationship between formality and informality, the nature of race and ethnic relations, and so on (see Stewart 2001).

Besides this contextual dimension, underlying our comparative effort is the understanding that the different characters of sociality found among Gypsy populations also play a role in the style of their integration. Individual Gypsy populations interact with non-Gypsies in different ways, a feature that, as Piasere (1999) has shown, is both a mechanism of their self-fashioning and a source of differentiation between them (see also Olivera 2012; Marushiakova and Popov 2013). This influences the ways they 'assimilate the Gadje', so to say; that is, how individual communities refract socio-economic changes instigated by non-Gypsies in the midst of whom they live and to whom these communities relate in distinct ways, and how through such assimilation they remain Roma or Gypsies. In terms of anthropological politics, this means, paraphrasing Terence Turner (1979: 5), that in opposing the absolute dehumanisation of current forms of anti-Gypsyism, we find it necessary to take positive account of the humanity of the Gypsies, that is, their forms of self-ascription and the capacity for action (from economic to cultural) related to these. These may or may not be identical to the hegemonic view of what ethnic emancipation should look like (see also Stewart 2013).

Here we build on a specific strand of anthropological enquiry. Alongside Stewart's description of how Vlach Roma 'domesticated' communist factory work, we find that several other studies have also demonstrated how Gypsy refractions of any given context can vary. Leonardo Piasere (1992), for example, showed that three populations – Xoraxané Romá, Slovénsko Roma and Italian Sinti – living among the same non-Gypsies resort to three distinct modes of 'resource exploitation'. In another study he analysed how the organisation of production and provision of services can differ within a single Gypsy population residing in a single country (Piasere 1987; see also Ries and Jacobs 2009; Grill 2011). Patrick Williams, for his part, described the development of different modes of social and economic organisation within one Kalderaš Rom community network that ended up living in two cities (Paris and New York) in two different countries (Williams 1985).

As Judith Okely (1994) has maintained, if Gypsies are made into 'outsiders' at the same time as they differentiate themselves from the societies in which they live, then specificities have to be assessed ethnographically. Their perceived 'outsider' position can be seen as a limiting factor and as a result of discrimination, but it can also be embraced. Stewart (2001), for instance, has suggested that a lack of social belonging, coupled with the concomitant mistrust of authorities and of social norms, can become a source of liberty for those making a living within the informal economy, as it allows arbitrage across domains that the state, with its formal arrangements, and the majority society, with its notions of propriety, try to keep separate. Similarly, in a discussion about some of the chapters of the present volume, Radu Umbres noted that 'marginality', taken broadly as a positioning in relation to the state and 'formality', opens a space for entrepreneurship.[7]

Umbres also pointed out structural similarities between the activities of financial speculators and those of at least some Gypsies. Both groups of men (and the actors in this volume are predominantly male),[8] work in a borderland between the official and the illicit, and are generally suspicious of bureaucracy and formal propriety. Both see themselves as especially attuned to their idea of a market, which they view as uncertain and as a totality largely beyond their control, but which is also a (conceptual) space of generalised opportunities for gain. Demonstrations of one's skill in specific transactions, then, become crucial. Risk turns out to be productive at several levels: it brings rewards 'in money, status, the elaboration of the social space of markets, and the construction of a masculine self' (Zaloom 2006: 93; see also Gropper 1991; Berta 2010). It comes not as a surprise, then, that, like Stewart's Rom horse traders (Stewart 1997), the financial speculators in Chicago and London described by Zaloom are 'in it' not solely for the gain, but also for the thrill that comes with it (Zaloom 2006: 105).

Zaloom also identifies four methods that make up what she calls the 'discipline' of a commodity-futures trader: the separation of actions on the trading floor from (their lives) outside; the control of the impact of loss; the discontinuity 'between past, present and future trades by dismantling narratives of success or failure'; and maintenance of 'acute alertness in the present moment' (ibid.: 128). These parallel some of the socio-cultural mechanisms described for various Roma and Gypsy communities, mechanisms that can be seen as pointing to some common characteristics of Gypsy economies: living for the moment and being attuned to one's surroundings; separation between the 'outside', imagined as a given and dominated by non-Gypsies, which becomes a source of opportunities, and the 'inside', with morality linked to gender and sexuality; different modalities of circulation and exchange, distinct framing of actors and their relationships in transactions, and even distinct kinds of money and valuables that mark separations between one's family and immediate community, those strangers recognised as equals (and fellow Gypsies), and the non-Gypsies (e.g. Piasere 1985; Stewart 1994, 1997; Reyniers 1998; Day, Papataxiarchis and Stewart 1999; Fotta 2012; Tesăr 2012).

Of course, we do not want to overdo the comparison between Gypsies and traders in financial institutions. We would just reiterate our earlier claim that in order to understand Gypsy economy one has to pay attention to the dynamics between the state and the market, formal rules guaranteed by laws, and informal arrangements. At the same time, as in the case of the futures traders described by Zaloom, the economic activities of Gypsies are intimately linked to the creation of gendered social persons. Here, the meanings, motivations and organisation of productive activities cannot be discerned solely from the nature of the economic system, but are informed by values and meanings arising from within Gypsy sociality.

To move away from men, take the case of Sinti in South Tyrol described by Elisabeth Tauber (2006). Among these Sinti, respect (*rispetto, era*) towards the dead structures social relationships and encompasses all activities, including economic ones. Sinti women specialise in begging and selling (*manghel*), an occupation through which they provide food for their families (Tauber 2008). Although some women are proud that because they earn enough money this way their men do not have to work, *manghel* cannot be reduced to its monetary aspect. Rather, through this activity and the memories it engenders, the women forge a link between themselves and their female ancestors, and recreate their feminine respect. The centrality of respect also explains why even Sinti women who are married to non-Gypsies and who have attained a higher level of education decide to 'go *manghel*' themselves.

Tauber's analysis, which holds that 'Gypsyness' is something to be continuously performed, embodied, is consistent with the observations of several other anthropologists. As Gay y Blasco recently observed, ethnographers have 'emphasized the performative character of Gypsy/Roma identity, the fact that it is the person who, by his or her actions, enables the conceptualization of "us" as a group. Their work points, across a variety of geographic contexts, to a metonymic understanding of the relationship between the person and the community, and of the place of both in the world' (Gay y Blasco 2011: 446). In the following section, we explore how such 'metonymic understanding' underlies economic practices and their meaning.

Performative Economy

The concept of 'performance' has been employed by different scholars in the anthropology of Gypsies for different purposes. As an analytical tool and an entry point it has been used to describe and interpret a variety of phenomena, such as relations between Gypsies and non-Gypsies and the ways the former (re)present themselves to the latter, the Gypsy manner of being-in-the-world, and the way in which individuals seek to remain Gypsies and forge themselves as proper social persons. Besides the ethnographies that have focused explicitly on performance arts, such as music, song, theatre and dance (e.g. Pasqualino 1998; Van de Port 1998; Lemon 2000; Stoichiță 2008; Theodosiou 2011; Silverman 2012), they have mirrored two principal developments within social sciences: on the one hand, they have described social life as a drama whose focus is the way in which social actors enact and represent their lives; on the other, they have treated performance as an 'event' and a 'process', showing how people and cultures produce their specific and constitutive performances.

The focus on performance in the context of Gypsy economic practices can be traced to the pioneering work of Judith Okely (1979, 1983). She described techniques adopted by English Gypsies that were fundamental in allowing them to master and become successful in their economic activities, namely, 'knowing the local economy and the local people; manual dexterity; mechanical ingenuity; highly developed memory; salesmanship and bargaining skills' (Okely 1979: 23). She also highlighted Gypsy 'opportunism and ingenuity in choice of occupation, and their *flexibility in role-playing*', through which they related themselves to *Gorgios* (non-Gypsies) in the economic and political domains (ibid.: 23, emphasis added). In these economic interactions, the Gypsies variously hid or advertised their Gypsyness, and just as scholars saw Gypsies as 'adapting' themselves somewhat to pre-existing economic contexts, they also described Gypsies' skill in fitting into – and even internalising – stereotypes produced by non-Gypsies (e.g. Lemon 2000).[9] Gypsies were seen as manipulating non-Gypsy stereotypes, more or less tactically and creatively according to occasions, contexts and needs. A discontinuity is always implied between, on the one hand, Gypsies' representation of themselves to non-Gypsies through manipulating portrayals and attributes of 'ethnicity' and, on the other hand, the 'real' Roma or Gypsy way of being and living consistent with their 'ethnic identity', which differs from this presentation and impression management (e.g. Okely 1979: 33; Silverman 1982). Such a Goffmanesque perspective posits an analogy between everyday life and theatrical performance. At the same time, it is important to note that this approach makes a solid case for recognising the effects of social performances, which allow an individual to accomplish a certain task as well as to convey, manage and maintain desired impressions of the self in front of others.

A different approach to performance stresses the relational nature of the construction of personhood in an attempt to overcome the division between frontstage and backstage. It is inspired primarily by Judith Butler (1999), who analysed the construction of gender identities as embodied practices. Butler argued that the 'essence or identity that they [embodied practices] otherwise purport to express are *fabrications* manufactured and sustained through corporeal signs and other discursive means. That the gendered body is performative suggests that it has no ontological status apart from the various acts which constitute its reality' (ibid.: 173, original emphasis). Paloma Gay y Blasco explored the construction of Gypsy personhood in this manner (see also Ferrari 2010). According to her, 'Gitanos link Gypsyness to actions or performances rather than stressing essences or substances' (Gay y Blasco 1999: 14). The Gitanos of Madrid she described forged their identity around moral principles that were relational – ethnicised, gendered and aged – and their existence as a community depended on their 'ongoing enactment' by each person. Since Gitanos downplayed any disregard of the direct role of the past in the construction of identity, Gay y Blasco suggested looking at gendered identities here and now. Her aim was to describe and analyse the process of identification by which difference is generated (rather than merely expressed), a process that is inseparable from the content of Gitano values and the ways that these are objectified in the attributes of social persons (see esp. Fotta, Manrique, Olivera, Pulay, Tesăr, this volume).

Micol Brazzabeni's recent study on the shouts and calls used by Cigano traders to promote their goods in open-air markets in Lisbon points to yet another dimension of performance (Brazzabeni 2015). Through shouting, Cigano vendors 'trade [common] stereotypes' (Okely 1979) about themselves, but also about their seemingly paradoxical opposite: the traders convey the idea that they are supporters of national identity and belonging during a period of economic recession. These stereotypes, however, also 'do things'. Through such enactments, Ciganos place themselves in the world, handling a specific agency, as if this economic sector were a privileged and legitimate space within which to participate and make a statement. They act upon the world, with shouts and calls becoming 'active objects' capable of fabricating a 'reality' – in this case, a kind of 'moral economy' – about the local economic crisis, and suggest a proper response to it. Enactments, then, cannot be separated from what they do and from the environment within which they circulate (see esp. Ferrari, Solimene, this volume). In other words, for performances to have the desired effects, materialities – in the case of Brazzabeni's Cigano vendors, the organisation of the marketplace, the impact of economic recession, the predominance of Chinese goods on the market and so on – matter.

These observations bring our vision of performance close to its meaning within the performativity paradigm (e.g. Callon 1998, 2007). Identities are constructed through and in the acts of individuals and depend on the materialities within which they take place, but they are never stable, only more or less successfully maintained and repeated over time. Where does all of this leave Gypsy economy? We have argued above that any Gypsy specialisation, as a Simmelian social form, arises through the replication, standardisation or repetition of activities and through a production of conceptual apparatuses related to this specialisation that allows for the interpretation of activities or for the establishment of causal relations. Many chapters in this volume demonstrate how, for instance, different activities are defined and fabricated by Gypsies, how they are named and how they come with specific criteria of success.

Michael Stewart's well-known analysis of the Vlach Rom horse trade in socialist Hungary (Stewart 1997) is helpful for illustrating our conception of specialisation. He argued that for Rom a horse market is not a distinct sphere, but is instead subsumed under the idea of *foro* (marketplace, town) as a concept covering 'generalised possibilities' for dealing and for gain from the *Gaźos*. The Rom frame exchanges in specific ways: they treat horses as commodities, and see themselves as able through their skills of speech to convince and dominate the *Gaźos*. A deal is successful when they achieve a price that is good enough (that is, that allows them to at least buy a new horse). This success ultimately proves a Rom to be 'lucky' (*baxtale*). Stewart shows, however, that it is not possible to understand the success of the Vlach Rom in recreating themselves as 'sons of the market' with recourse solely to the criteria of neoclassical economics. Vlach Rom see their efficacy or luck (*baxt*) as depending on their righteous behaviour prior to coming to the market place. They also distinguish 'selling' to *Gaźos* from 'swapping' with other Rom that occurs after the *Gaźos* leave the market and before the police arrive; in the acts of swapping, horses are not mere commodities with a price tag, but are symbolically equated with Gypsy women. In addition, one's ease of making money is objectified in one's willingness to spend money freely with one's brothers. In other words, a Rom is 'lucky' – which is essentially a Rom criterion for success – if he constantly reformats himself as a true Gypsy. Statements to the effect that true Gypsies are 'lucky' open the ethnographic enquiry to life-worlds that should not be constrained by ideas about the nature of the market or the economy. These statements reflect the Rom view of the world and organise behaviour. The statements are 'true' within the niche of the Hungarian horse market as framed by the Rom and within which they circulate – an arrangement that Michel Callon calls a 'sociotechnical *agencement*' (Callon 2007: 319).

Stewart made it clear, however, that this niche includes social and political features beyond Rom control (but on which they might nevertheless try to impose their own meaning): for instance, the Rom prefer the trade in horses to that in other animals because of its symbolism in relation to the historically constructed inequality between Gypsies and peasants; Rom men's participation in the trade was made possible thanks to money from state-sanctioned factory work; and they had little power over the organisation of the market (such as opening hours). This prompts a fundamental question: what happens when the existing Gypsy vision of, and statements about, the world, accompanied by a specific framing of agents, goods, prices, money-making situations and so on, fails to be successful, or when material characteristics change? Chapters in this volume provide some case studies. Contrary to his expectations about the Roma in Central and Eastern Europe, Grill did not find a concept of *Romani butji* explicitly articulated in everyday discourse among the Slovak Roma (see also Olivera, Solimene, this volume). Instead, elements that characterise the concept were incorporated in certain actions and dispositions in a way that made it possible to use factory work and the Roma interaction with authorities during the socialist era as events for recreating Gypsyness. In his chapter, Fotta shows a process of negotiation of the content of core values among Calon in Bahia, which arose because today Calon money is made on 'the street' primarily through individualised moneylending and often hidden in banks from the demands of one's kin, possibilities that are ultimately linked to economic growth and to the financialisation of the hinterland of Bahia, Brazil.

Such an analysis of the economic activities of individual communities is consistent with what Leonardo Piasere called the 'circumstance approach' (*approccio della circostanza*), which characterises Gypsies as the 'people of circumstance' (*gente di circostanza*) (Piasere 1995: 22). In this sense, Gypsies could be seen as being involved in an incessant process of self-creation within the milieu they find themselves in with the 'only fixed imperative to create themselves as different' (ibid.: 22). For Piasere, this approach is best illustrated by Patrick Williams's work on the Mānuš of the Central Massif, France (Williams 1993). Williams explored Mānuš inventiveness, initiative and imagination, and the related possibility of change and innovation (see also Williams 2011). Given the position of Roma and Gypsy communities in the societies in which they live, and non-Gypsies' ignorance of the full meaning behind specific practices, the former are rarely able to impose and maintain their definition of economic interactions. Gypsy specialisations are therefore 'open', and unexpected events and situations might demand novel arrangements. This view of the forging of Gypsyness in economic performances goes some way to explaining the diversity of modes of social organisation, economic practice and related concepts found among the communities presented in the volume.

About This Book

While the importance of economic practices is well documented, works on Romani (as well as non-Romani) Gypsy groups tend to be monographs or collections of articles covering a range of topics and written by authors from diverse disciplines. To date, there has been little sustained effort to produce a comparative anthropology of Gypsy economy. Reflecting different traditions in the anthropology of Roma and Gypsies, the chapters in this volume look at the organisation of a variety of contemporary economic practices from different regions and countries.[10] They are based on intensive fieldwork conducted during the past decade; as such, beyond any 'data' they might provide, they hopefully also convey the experiential aspect of living together that characterise anthropological ethnographies in particular (see Hart, this volume). They describe forms of sociality and the meanings behind varied economic practices, as well as the ways in which they contribute to the social reproduction of specific communities.

The volume is loosely organised around four prominent themes (see Hart, this volume): monetary flows; economic strategies and market interactions; performance; and understandings of wealth and value. It opens with two chapters on usury among Roma in Central Europe, many of whom often depend on welfare payments for survival. In Chapter 1, Tomáš Hrustič contends that for many Roma living in segregated settlements in peripheral regions of east Slovakia, moneylending has become the only viable way out of poverty. Most Roma become at different times borrowers and lenders, using any cash at hand to tap into official flows of money. Lending and borrowing money, ranging from small cash loans between relatives to usury, plays a central role in personal financial life and social reproduction in these settlements, with the matrix of usury pervading the entire social system. Contrary to the non-Roma majority's moralistic representation of usury in the Romani settlements of Slovakia, Hrustič shows how, in a situation with virtually no possibilities of social mobility, usury can be advantageous for lenders as well as borrowers, although, admittedly, in the long term it opens possibilities for economic strategising and improvement only for a few, while severely limiting the financial possibilities of others.

In Chapter 2, Judit Durst deals with a challenging question: how does one explain the emergence of usurious moneylenders within a Rom community where communal life used to be based, in ideology at least, on egalitarian ethics (according to Michael Stewart), with people open to each other's demands? Her Graeberian answer is that mutual help can easily slip into hierarchy without anybody noticing it. In other words, usury in an impoverished ghetto satisfies a role of a hierarchical redistribution by means of which money that originates with the state (such as welfare) is spread out in time and made to last longer. Moneylenders are seen as part of the moral community because they 'help' when somebody is in 'need', and conflicts arise primarily when somebody tries to shun personalism and redefine usurious loans as impersonal business.

The next two chapters reflect on the historical dynamics that gave rise to specific economic activities. In Chapter 3, Sara Sama Acedo discusses how economic interstices created and maintained by travelling Portuguese Ciganos who continue to be involved in the horse trade can only be understood by taking into account the actions of the state and its ideological underpinnings, the history of interactions between various Cigano communities, and the dynamics of territorial exclusion and appropriation based on Cigano notions of relatedness. At the end of her chapter, describing the 'Nomads' Camp' in Évora, Sama Acedo shows how interactions between various pressures and interests can give rise to novel economic practices within novel geographical locations. In Chapter 4, Jan Grill also focuses on activities dependent on geographical movement, this time across state borders, describing the oscillation between 'hard work' and 'fixing up' money practised by Roma from the east Slovak village of Tarkovce who have migrated to the United Kingdom. The chapter calls attention to a fact that is often overlooked in the anthropology of Gypsies, namely, that 'hard work', such as factory labour, is not contrary to Gypsyness. The case study also shows a level of historical continuity: the Tarkovce Roma were relatively successful economically and socially during the socialist era and, in comparison with other Roma in eastern Slovakia, were also successful in navigating novel socio-economic and geo-political arrangements after its fall.

Contrary to the Tarkovce Roma, who do not foreground the concept of *Romani butji* ideologically, Xoraxané Romá, who emigrated from the former Yugoslavia to Italy in the 1970s, mobilise this concept, which allows them to bypass the current biopolitical regime that turns Gypsies into Agamben's *homo sacer*. In Chapter 5, Marco Solimene shows how 'going for iron' (that is, collecting scrap metal), as a practice encompassed by the concept of *Romani butji*, becomes a way to confirm Romá independence from the Italians and their difference from recently migrated Romanian Roma. The chapter describes how this activity, success in which is interpreted as proof of one's 'luck' and of 'divine favour', depends on the constant working of specific territories and the construction of good relations with the Italians living therein. Still focusing on the centrality of space, in Chapter 6, Gergö Pulay draws attention to how Romanian Spoitori Roma who live in the most notorious ghetto in Bucharest navigate their social world in order to avoid becoming 'dupes'. They achieve this by gaining material and symbolic value in managing 'traffic' and by becoming 'businessmen'. Pulay goes on to discuss the values that give meaning to economic practices, and focuses on two types of exchanges: what the male 'hang-out groups' call 'collaborations' and 'combinations'. Through the former they constantly recreate themselves as a community, while through the latter the rules and definitions of exchange are up for negotiation; as a result, combinations are more eventful, but also fraught with tensions.

In Chapter 7, Martin Olivera describes how the production and consumption of economic resources allows Gabori Roma in Transylvania to maintain and develop their material independence and symbolic autonomy from the non-Roma. Drawing on Sahlins's model of the domestic mode of production, Olivera foregrounds the dynamics through which Gabori society manages to establish a logic of abundance and takes possession of the world. This is achieved by conceiving of men's work as a *Romani butji*, which has consequences for Gabori conceptions of money:

unlike money from women's work, which is associated with daily subsistence, money from men's work is not treated as a means of exchange but appreciated for its use value. As such, money does not obey the logic of scarcity and becomes 'already spent' before it is actually earned.

While Olivera's chapter, like most here, focuses on men, Florencia Ferrari's contribution explores a female moneymaking activity that has fascinated non-Gypsies for centuries: palm-reading. In Chapter 8 she looks at how Calon women in the state of São Paulo, Brazil, conceive of this activity and manage interactions with their *Gaje* clients. By describing distinct levels of meaning and understanding, Ferrari unravels misapprehensions surrounding the palm-reading experience and traces assumptions rooted in different 'cosmologies'. The chapter argues that notions such as 'shame' and 'luck', or conceptions of time, are conceived differently by Calon and *Gaje*, which leads to tensions and misunderstandings about the meaning of fortune telling itself. Ironically, this turns the palm-reading event into an affectively intense encounter, affording it a potent symbolic efficacy.

The remaining three chapters connect Gypsy economic activities to their conceptions and circulation of worth and value. The Cortorari of Romania, for instance, who live scattered across several villages in Transylvania, invest in spectacularly large houses, built with money derived from economic activities facilitated by transnational mobility. In Chapter 9, Cătălina Tesăr takes up the question of the symbolism of Cortorari houses, and shows that for the outside world houses communicate Cortoraris' economic betterment and their quest for social recognition. For the inside world, however, houses participate in the symbolic construction of persons: they render their owners' achievements visible. Houses are associated with the most economically active generation – 'the youth' – and the seizing of new economic opportunities articulates with transformations of personhood across generational lines in relation to wealth.

Unlike the Central European Roma of the opening chapters for whom usurious practices are mainly internal to the communities, the Calon of Bahia, Brazil, make money primarily through lending money to non-Gypsies. Applying an anthropological theory of value, Martin Fotta shows in Chapter 10 that there are two major sources of social value that lie behind this practice. First, there is the 'shame, honour' (*vergonha*) that all Calon are supposed to have and that embodies their history as social persons. Second, there is the capability to create and control one's environment – one's 'strength'. Calon attain the attributes of social persons related to this value through creating self–other relations that are constantly traced in movements (of money, persons, households and so on); here, loaning money is the major tool. Fotta shows that despite the Calon stress on autonomy and equality, values associated with Gypsyness are unequally distributed, and there is a constant struggle over their meaning.

Continuing with the theme of internal circulation and notions of personal worth, in Chapter 11 Nathalie Manrique provides a daring reinterpretation of Gitano society as structured by the logic of the gift. For the Gitanos of southern Spain, one's propensity to share wealth determines one's place within the hierarchy of living beings. The encompassment of interactions within the idiom of giving and receiving continuously confirms the ordering of individuals and groups into hierarchical categories, which, at the same time, are conceived of as 'natural'. Givers are held to be superior to receivers, and through such relations, statuses are periodically readjusted, wealth is rebalanced and equality among peers is confirmed. At the same time, this value dynamic, which prioritises generosity, undermines any attempt at personal accumulation and the hoarding of money.

Seen as a whole, then, this book attempts to provide snapshots from different angles of various responses to the current predicament faced by a population that has always maintained its specificity while being radically open to changes in the world around it. The authors are committed to shifting attention towards a Gypsy view of economic activities and they explore how changes in the societies in which they live are refracted according to the logic internal to Gypsy socio-cosmological orders. In this specific and limited way, the authors also hope to add to the knowledge of economic processes. This hope is clearly articulated in the Afterword by Keith Hart, which closes this volume. He argues that Gypsies can become a useful lens through which to explore 'the human predicament we all share at this time'. He also cautions that this is only possible if anthropologists refrain from studying Gypsies for their own sake, and instead remain conscious of the historical situatedness of their research and of their own ethnographic methodology.

It is our conviction that at the present time, when social scientists increasingly describe and advocate conscious economic experiments in order to create a more pluralistic and human economy (e.g. Callon 2007: 349–52; Hart, Laville and Catani 2010; Gibson-Graham, Cameron and Healy 2013), the anthropology of Roma and Gypsies – people seen by others (including scholars) as characterised by their economic practices and attitudes to exchange and money – highlights the fabrication of alternative life-worlds within modern societies, alternatives that are variously stable, but that may not draw a line around the 'economic' at all.

NOTES

1. We use the terms 'Gypsy' and its variations, as in the expression 'Gypsy economy', for the tensions the term entails, and we often shift between the views of specific Romani communities described here, of non-Gypsy majorities, and of social scientists. The term also recalls some earlier theorisations on the topic that were aimed at capturing specificities of the Gypsy incorporation into national economies (e.g. Reyniers 1998; Rao 2010). Certainly, we do not suggest that the concept of 'Gypsy economy' refers to the economic practices of each and every individual who identifies themselves as a Roma, Gypsy, Traveller or as belonging to any other Romani or non-Romani community sometimes categorised as 'Gypsy'. Rather, it should be understood in a loose typological sense, as characterised by particular dynamics captured ethnographically in various ways by the chapters that follow. For the same reason, the term is used in the singular.
2. While the term 'Gypsy economy' aims to cover practices not only of the Roma, but also of Gypsies, Travellers and other populations, who often recognise that within their national settings they share similar niches and income-generating strategies (see footnote 1), all communities presented in this volume can be seen as 'Romanies' or 'Romani people' as they speak some form of Romani or Para-Romani. Currently, not all, however, identify themselves politically as Roma. While in some national contexts represented in this volume an equivalent of the English term 'Gypsy' has been rejected as derogatory (e.g. the countries of Eastern and Central Europe), in others it has been seen as less problematic and used as a term of political recognition and even of ethnic mobilisation (e.g. Brazil, Portugal and Spain). To capture this variety and to highlight that the politics of ethnicity matters on the ground, when talking about these groups collectively, we often use unwieldy 'Roma and Gypsy' communities (or populations, peoples and so on) in the plural and refer to their economic practices and strategies. The individual chapters in this volume use ethnonyms preferred by members of the communities they describe.
3. For a useful recent review, see Stewart (2013).
4. The sense of 'social capital' here follows Coleman (1988) and Putnam (2000) rather than Bourdieu (1977, 1980).
5. Similarly, Alaina Lemon (1998: 4) reports the words of a non-Gypsy Muscovite who commented about how he and his fellow intellectuals in Russia in the early 1990s – in the context of the rouble's devaluation and the anxiety about value – were forced to turn to trade in order to secure dollars. 'We are all becoming Gypsies', the man said jokingly.
6. The term used by Piasere in the cited publication. A further note on terminology is needed here. Writing about the Slovénsko Roma in Italy, Zatta and Piasere observe: 'For a Rom the Roma/*Gaǧo* distinction is the fundamental distinction; the *Gaǧe* are the "outside" by definition. For a non-Gypsy, the Gypsy is an "other" among many, a "marginal man" among many, a bit of folklore among many; in our case, a thief among many. The perceptions are asymmetrical and they reflect the way of life of the Roma in respect to the *Gaǧe*' (Zatta and

Piasere 1990: 165). Put simply, while the non-Gypsies view 'Gypsies', 'Roma', 'Gitanos', 'Cortorari' and so on as permutations on the ethnic group theme, albeit of various levels of abstractness, for individual Roma and Gypsy communities the concept of "Gadje" and its variations is a categorical division of humanity, a specific figure of thought, a non-Gypsy alterity (see also Olivera 2012: 445–67). Although commonly translated as 'a non-Gypsy' (or non-Roma), from the point of view of individual communities, Gadje and its variants do not refer to a 'group' strictly speaking. Rather, it is analytically more appropriate to speak about Gadje as the 'outside' (Zatta and Piasere 1990) or a 'given' (Ferrari 2010), with 'Gypsyness' envisaged as fabricated, through a combination of various processes and techniques, in contradistinction against it (e.g. Williams 2011). How individual communities view this 'outside' depends on historical contingencies and each community's unique socio-cosmological organisation (e.g. values and morality or the mechanisms through which the 'inside' is created). Thus, for instance, according to Stewart (1997), the *Gaźos* (his spelling) of the Vlach Rom in Hungary of the 1980s had the attributes of a Hungarian peasant from the beginning of the twentieth century; clearly for the Calon of Bahia, a region dominated by sugar plantations and of slavery up to the end of the nineteenth century, *Gaje/Gajons* will have different connotations and will be related also to mechanisms through which the 'inside', the community boundary, is maintained. Because the ways individual Roma and Gypsy communities view Gadje matters for the shape of economic practices (e.g. by guiding interactions), the individual authors gathered in this volume use terms specific to any given community. These terms are in italics and spelt according to what the authors find the most appropriate. Similarly, whenever in this introductory chapter we quote other authors, we maintain their original spelling. The non-italicised term 'Gadje', as we use later in this introduction, is our construct-concept that refers to this non-Gypsy alterity in general.
7. Radu Umbres, comments made during the European Science Foundation workshop 'The Two Sides of the Coin: Gypsy Economies Between the State and the Market', Lisbon, 20–23 September 2012.
8. This is more of a coincidence, and for each case the gender (and generation) dynamics in wealth creation, maintenance and circulation needs to be assessed ethnographically. For instance, while male economic activities are often presented by both scholars and their informants as underlying people's identity as Roma, Gypsies, Travellers or other, in other cases it is female activities that take on this role (e.g. Andersen 1981; Tauber 2008; Ferrari, this volume). Anthropologists have also documented family-based economic activities among Romani and non-Romani Gypsy communities, and the important contribution of women and children to income-generation, which becomes also crucial for maintaining flexibility and providing long-term resilience (e.g. Gmelch 1986; Piasere 1987; Helleiner 2003; Tesăr, this volume). These, however, might sometimes be ideologically downplayed (e.g. Stewart 1997; Olivera, this volume).
9. Recently, Aspasia Theodosiou criticised what she called the 'new Gypsy ethnography', that is, studies influenced by Okely's work, for implying a kind of

strategic essentialism and for 'treating the dynamics of social identification as nothing more than strategic' (Theodosiou 2010: 344). In the case of Okely, who also analysed the roles that pollution beliefs, kinship and social organisation played in Travellers' social reproduction, Theodosiou's criticism seems somewhat unwarranted. Nevertheless, her overall take on performance seems to us to point in the right direction. Treating Gypsy distinctiveness as performative should not end up reducing this distinctiveness to a mere consequence of the opposition with non-Gypsies, regardless of 'where they are' (ibid.: 329).

10. The chapters are, however, concentrated on the Central and Eastern European Roma (sometimes as migrants in Western Europe) and on the Gypsies that can be related to the Iberian world broadly speaking (Portugal, Spain and Brazil). Western and Northern Europe, North America or the Middle East are, unfortunately, not covered.

REFERENCES

Andersen, R. 1981. 'Symbolism, Symbiosis, and Survival: Roles of Young Women of the Kalderasa in Philadelphia', in M.T. Salo (ed.), *The American Kalderaš: Gypsies in the New World*. Hackettstown, NJ: Chapter, Centenary College, pp.11–28.

Berland, J.C., and A. Rao. 2004. 'Unveiling The Stranger: A New Look at Peripatetic Peoples', in J.C. Berland and A. Rao (eds), *Customary Strangers: New Perspectives on Peripatetic Peoples in the Middle East, Africa and Asia*. Westport, CT: Praeger, pp.1–29.

Berland J.C., and M.T. Salo. 1986. 'Peripathetic Communities: An Introduction', *Nomadic Peoples* 21/22: 1–6.

Berta, P. 2010. 'Economic Action in Theory and Practice: Anthropological Investigations', in D.C. Wood (ed.), *Research in Economic Anthropology*, Vol. 30. Bingley: Emerald Books, pp.277–309.

Bourdieu, P. 1977 [1972]. *Outline of a Theory of Practice*, trans. R. Nice. Cambridge: Cambridge University Press.

———. 1980. 'Le capital social. Notes provisoires', *Actes de la recherche en sciences sociales* 31(1): 2–3.

Brazzabeni, M. 2015. 'Sounds of the Markets: Portuguese Cigano Vendors in Open-air Markets in the Lisbon Metropolitan Area', in C. Evers and K. Seale (eds), *Informal Urban Street Markets: International Perspectives*. New York: Routledge, pp.51–61.

Butler, J. 1999. *Gender Trouble: Feminism and the Subversion of Identity*. New York: Routledge.

Çalışkan, K., and M. Callon. 2009. 'Economization, Part 1: Shifting Attention from the Economy Towards Processes of Economization', *Economy and Society* 38(3): 369–98.

———. 2010. Economization, Part 2: A Research Programme for the Study of Markets. *Economy and Society* 39(1): 1–32.

Callon, M. 1998. 'Introduction: The Embeddedness of Economic Markets in Economics', in M. Callon (ed.), *The Laws of the Markets*. Malden, MA: Blackwell, pp.1–57.

———. 2007. 'What Does it Mean to Say that Economics is Performative?' in D.A. MacKenzie, F. Muniesa and L. Siu (eds), *Do Economists Make Markets? On the Performativity of Economics*. Princeton: Princeton University Press, pp.311–57.
Coleman, J.S. 1988. 'Social Capital in the Creation of Human Capital', *American Journal of Sociology* 94 (supplement): 95–120.
Cunha, M.P. da. 2002. *Entre o bairro e a prisão. Tráfico e trajectos*. Lisbon: Fim de Século.
———. 2013. 'The Changing Scale of Imprisonment and the Transformation of Care: The Erosion of the "Welfare Society" by the "Penal State" in Contemporary Portugal', in M. Schlecker and F. Fleischer (eds), *Ethnographies of Social Support*. New York: Palgrave MacMillan, pp.81–101.
Day, S., E. Papataxiarchis and M. Stewart. 1999. 'Consider the Lilies of the Field', in S. Day, E. Papataxiarchis and M. Stewart (eds), *Lilies of the Field: Marginal People Who Live for the Moment*. Boulder, CO: Westview Press, pp.1–24.
de l'Estoile, B. 2014. 'Money is Good But a Friend is Better: Uncertainty, Orientation to the Future, and "the Economy"', *Current Anthropology* 55(9): 62–73.
Ferrari, F. 2010. 'O mundo passa. Uma etnografia dos Calon e suas relações com os brasileiros', Ph.D. diss. São Paulo: Universidade de São Paulo.
Fotta, M. 2012. 'The Bankers of the Backlands: Financialisation and the Calon-Gypsies in Bahia', Ph.D. diss. London: Goldsmiths College, University of London.
Gay y Blasco, P. 1999. *Gypsies in Madrid: Sex, Gender and the Performance of Identity*. Oxford: Berg Publishers.
———. 2011. 'Agata's Story: Singular Lives and the Reach of the "Gitano Law"', *Journal of the Royal Anthropological Institute* 17(3): 445–61.
Gibson-Graham, J.K., J. Cameron and S. Healy. 2013. *Take Back the Economy: An Ethical Guide for Transforming Our Communities*. Minneapolis: University of Minnesota Press.
Gmelch G. 1977. 'Economic Strategies and Migrant Adaptation: The Case of Irish Tinkers', *Ethnos* 42(1/2): 22–37.
Gmelch, G., and S.B. Gmelch. 1987. 'Commercial Nomadism: Occupation and Mobility among Travellers in England and Wales', in A. Rao (ed.), *The Other Nomads: Peripatetic Minorities in Cross-cultural Perspective*. Cologne: Böhlau Verlag, pp. 133–53.
Gmelch, S.B. 1986. 'Groups that Don't Want In: Gypsies and Other Artisan, Trader, and Entertainer Minorities', *Annual Review of Anthropology* 15: 307–30.
Grill, J. 2011. 'From Street Busking in Switzerland to Meat Factories in the UK: A Comparative Study of Two Roma Migration Networks from Slovakia', in D. Kaneff and F. Pine (eds), *Emerging Inequalities in Europe: Poverty and Transnational Migration*. London: Anthem Press, pp.78–102.
Gropper, R.C. 1991. 'Hedging the Bets: Risk Reduction among the Rom Gypsies', *Journal of the Gypsy Lore Society* 1(1): 45–59.
Guy, W. 1998. 'Ways of Looking at Roma: The Case of Czechoslovakia', in D. Tong (ed.), *Gypsies: An Interdisciplinary Reader*. New York: Garland, pp.13–68.
Guyer, J.I. 1997. *An African Niche Economy: Farming to Feed Ibadan, 1968–88*. Edinburgh: Edinburgh University Press.
———. 2004. 'Niches, Margins and Profits: Persisting with Heterogeneity', *African Economic History* 32: 173–91.

Hart K. 2000. *The Memory Bank: Money in an Unequal World*. London: Profile Books.
———. 2005. *The Hitman's Dilemma: Or, Business, Personal and Impersonal*. Chicago, IL: Prickly Paradigm.
———. 2006. 'Bureaucratic Form and the Informal Economy', in B. Guha-Khasnobis, S.M.R. Kanbur and E. Ostrom (eds), *Linking the Formal and Informal Economies: Examples from Developing Countries*. Oxford: Oxford University Press, pp.21–35.
———. 2012. 'The Informalization of the World Economy'. Paper presented at the Societa Italiana di Economia Pubblica conference 'Informal Economy, Tax Evasion and Corruption', *Pavia*, 24–25 September. Retrieved 1 April 2013 from: http://thememorybank.co.uk/2012/10/17/the-informalization-of-the-world-economy/.
Hart, K., J.-L. Laville and A.D. Cattani. 2010. *The Human Economy: A Citizen's Guide*. Cambridge: Polity Press.
Hayden, R.M. 1979. 'The Cultural Ecology of Service Nomads', *Eastern Anthropologist* 32(4): 297–309.
Helleiner, J. 2003. 'The Politics of Traveller "Child Begging" in Ireland', *Critique of Anthropology* 23(1): 17–33.
Lemon, A. 1998. '"Your Eyes Are Green Like Dollars": Counterfeit Cash, National Substance, and Currency Apartheid in 1990s Russia', *Cultural Anthropology* 13(1): 22–55.
———. 2000. *Between Two Fires: Gypsy Performance and Romani Memory from Pushkin to Postsocialism*. Durham, NC: Duke University Press.
Liebow, E. 1967, *Tally's Corner: A Study of Negro Streetcorner Men*. Boston: Little, Brown.
Marushiakova, E., U. Mischek, V. Popov and B. Streck. 2005. *Dienstleistungsnomadismus am Schwarzen Meer. Zigeunergruppen zwischen Symbiose und Dissidenz*. Halle (Saale): Orientwissenschaftliches Zentrum der Martin-Luther-Universität.
Marushiakova, E., and V. Popov. 2013. '"Gypsy" Groups in Eastern Europe: Ethnonyms vs. Professionyms', *Romani Studies* 23(1): 61–82.
Münzel, M., and B. Streck (eds). 1981. *Kumpania und Kontrolle. Moderne Behinderungen zigeunerischen Lebens*. Giessen: Focus.
Narotzky, S. 2006. 'Binding Labour and Capital: Moral Obligation and Forms of Regulation in a Regional Economy', *Etnográfica* 10(2): 337–54.
Okely, J. 1979. 'Trading Stereotypes: The Case of English Gypsies', in S. Wallman (ed.), *Ethnicity at Work*. London: MacMillan, pp.16–33.
———. 1983. *The Traveller-Gypsies*. Cambridge: Cambridge University Press.
———. 1994. 'Constructing Difference: Gypsies as "Other"', *Anthropological Journal of European Cultures* 3(2): 55–73.
Olivera, M. 2012. *La tradition de l'intégration. Une ethnologie des Roms Gabori dans les années 2000*. Paris: Éditions Pétra.
Pasqualino, C. 1998. *Dire le chant. Les Gitans flamencos d'Andalousie*. Paris: CNRS Éditions/Éditions de la Maison des Sciences de L'Homme.
Piasere, L. 1985. *Mare Roma. Catégories humaines et structure sociale. Une contribution à l'ethnologie tsigane*. Paris: Paul H. Stahl.
———. 1986. 'Review of A. Rao, Les Gorbat d'Afghanistan. Aspect économiques d'un groupe itinérant "Jat"', *Newsletter of the Gypsy Lore Society, North American Chapter* 9(3): 1–4.
———. 1987. 'In Search of New Niches: The Productive Organization of the Peripatetic Xoraxané in Italy', in A. Rao (ed.), *The Other Nomads: Peripatetic Minorities in Cross-cultural Perspective*. Cologne: Böhlau, pp.111–32.

———. 1992. 'Roma and Romá in North Italy: Two Types of Territorial Behaviour in the Same Larger Territory', in M.Casmir and A. Rao (eds), *Mobility and Territoriality: Social and Spatial Boundaries among Foragers, Fishers, Pastoralists and Peripatetics*. Oxford: Berg, pp.279–291.
———. 1995. 'Introduzione', in L. Piasere (ed.), *Comunitá girovaghe, comunitá zingare*. Naples: Liguori Editore, pp.3–38.
———. 1999. *Un mondo di mondi. Antropologia delle culture rom*. Bari: L'Ancora.
———. 2011. 'Horror Infiniti. Die Zigeuner als Europas Trickster', *Behemoth* 4(1): 57–85.
Polanyi, K. 1944. *The Great Transformation*. New York: Farrar and Rinehart.
Portes, A. 1998. 'Social Capital: Its Origins and Applications in Modern Sociology', *Annual Review of Sociology* 24: 1–24.
Putnam, R.D. 2000. *Bowling Alone: The Collapse and Revival of American Community*. New York: Columbia University Press.
Rao, A. 1987. 'The Concept of Peripatetics: An Introduction', in A. Rao (ed.), *The Other Nomads: Peripatetic Minorities in Cross-cultural Perspective*. Cologne: Böhlau Verlag, pp.1–32.
———. 2010 [1996]. 'Gypsies', in A. Barnard and J. Spencer (eds), *Encyclopedia of Social and Cultural Anthropology*. London: Routledge, pp.340–41.
Reyniers, A. 1998. 'Quelques jalons pour comprendre l'économie tsigane', *Études tsiganes* 12: 8–27.
Ries, J. 2008. 'Writing (Different) Roma/Gypsies: Romani/Gypsy Studies and the Scientific Construction of Roma/Gypsies', in F. Jacobs and J. Ries (eds), *Roma/Zigeunerkulturen in Neuen Perspektiven, Romani/Gypsy Cultures in New Perspectives*. Leipzig: Leipziger Universitätsverlag, pp.21–47.
Ries, J., and F. Jacobs. 2009. 'Roma/Zigeuner in Relationen Ethnologische Anregungen für die vergleichende Minderheitenforschung', in E. Tschernokoshewa and U. Mischek (eds), *Beziehungsgeflecht Minderheit. Zum Paradigmenwechsel in der Kulturforschung, Ethnologie Europas*. Munster: Waxman, pp.117–29.
Silverman, C. 1982. 'Everyday Drama: Impression Management of Urban Gypsies', *Urban Anthropology* 11(3/4): 377–98.
———. 2012. *Romani Routes: Cultural Politics and Balkan Music in Diaspora*. New York: Oxford University Press.
Smart, A. 2008. 'Social Capital', *Anthropologica* 50: 409–28.
Standing, G. 2011. *The Precariat: The New Dangerous Class*. London: Bloomsbury.
Stewart, M. 1993. 'Gypsies, the Work Ethic, and Hungarian Socialism', in C. Hann (ed.), *Socialism: Ideals, Ideologies, and Local Practice*. London: Routledge, pp.187–204.
———. 1994. 'La passion de l'argent. Les ambiguïtés de la circulation monétaire chez les Tsiganes hongrois', *Terrain* 23: 45–62.
———. 1997. *The Time of the Gypsies*. Boulder, CO: Westview Press.
———. 2001. 'Conclusions: Spectres of the Underclass', in R.J. Emigh and I. Szelényi (eds), *Poverty, Ethnicity, and Gender in Eastern Europe during the Market Transition*. Westport, CT: Praeger, pp.191–203.
———. 2002. 'The Impoverished Roma', *Local Government Brief*, Local Government and Public Service Reform Initiative/OSI Budapest, Summer 2002: 16–19.
———. 2012a. 'New Forms of Anti-Gypsy Politics: A Challenge for Europe', in M. Stewart (ed.), *The Gypsy 'Menace': Populism and the New Anti-Gypsy Politics*. London: Hurst, pp.viii–xxxviii.

———. 2012b. 'Populism, Roma and the European Politics of Cultural Difference', in M. Stewart (ed.), *The Gypsy 'Menace': Populism and the New Anti-Gypsy Politics*. London: Hurst, pp.3–24.

———. 2013. 'Roma and Gypsy "Ethnicity" as a Subject of Anthropological Inquiry', *Annual Review of Anthropology* 42: 415–32.

Stewart, M. (ed.) 2012c. *The Gypsy 'Menace': Populism and the New Anti-Gypsy Politics*. London: Hurst.

Stoichiţă , V.A. 2008. *Fabricants d'émotion. Musique et malice dans un village tsigane de Roumanie*. Nanterre: Société d'Ethnologie.

Streck, B. 2008. 'Kultur der Zwischenräume – Grundfragen der Tsiganologie', in F. Jacobs and J. Ries (eds), *Roma/Zigeunerkulturen in Neuen Perspektiven*. Leipzig: Leipziger Universitätsverlag, pp.21–48.

Tauber, E. 2006. *Du Wirst keinen Ehemann Nehmen! Respekt, die Bedeutung der Toten und Fluchtheirat bei den Sinti Estraixaria*. Münster: LIT Verlag.

———. 2008. '"Do You Remember the Time When We Went Begging and Selling": The Ethnography of Transformation in Female Economic Activities and Its Narrative in the Context of Memory and Respect among the Sinti in North Italy', in J. Fabian and J. Ries (eds), *Romani/Gypsy Cultures in New Perspectives*. Leipzig: Leipzieger Universitätverslag, pp.155–76.

Tesăr, C. 2012. '"Women Married off to Chalices": Gender, Kinship and Wealth among Romanian Cortorari Gypsies', Ph.D. diss. London: University College London.

Theodosiou, A. 2010. '"What Kind of People Do You Think We Are?" The Scenography of Gypsy Performances of Difference', *Identities* 17: 327–47.

———. 2011. *Authenticity, Ambiguity, Location: Gypsy Musicians on the Greek–Albanian Border*. Saarbrücken: VDM Verlag.

Turner, T. 1979. 'Anthropology and the Politics of Indigenous People's Struggles', *Cambridge Anthropology* 5(1): 1–43.

Van Baar, H. 2014. 'The Emergence of a Reasonable Anti-Gypsyism in Europe', in T. Agarin (ed.), *When Stereotype Meets Prejudice: Antiziganism in European Societies*. Stuttgart: Ibidem, pp.25–42.

Van de Port, M. 1998. *Gypsies, Wars and Other Instances of the Wild: Civilization and its Discontents in a Serbian Town*. Amsterdam: Amsterdam University Press.

Wacquant, L. 2008. *Urban Outcasts: A Comparative Sociology of Advanced Marginality*. Cambridge: Polity Press.

Williams P. 1985. 'Paris – New York. L'organisation de deux communautés tsiganes', *L'Homme* 25(95): 121–40.

———. 1993. *Nous, on n'en parle pas. Les vivants et les morts chez les Manouches*. Paris: Maison des Sciences de l'Homme.

———. 2011. 'Ethnologie der Zigeuner. Von der Begegnung zur Theoriebildung', *Behemoth* 4(1): 43–56.

Zaloom, C. 2006. *Out of the Pits: Traders and Technology from Chicago to London*. Chicago: University of Chicago Press.

Zatta, J.D., and L. Piasere. 1990. 'Stealing from the Gaĝo: Some Notes on Roma Ideology', *Études et documents balkaniques et mediterranéens* 15: 163–72.

Micol Brazzabeni received her Ph.D. from the University of Florence. Between 2008 and 2014 she was a Foundation for Science and Technology postdoctoral research fellow at Center for Research in Anthropology - University Institute of Lisbon (CRIA-IUL). She was the Portuguese unit coordinator of the Europe-wide project on housing conditions and evictions of Roma people 'We: Wor(l)ds which Exclude'. Her most recent research with Portuguese Gypsy families focuses on processes of commoditisation in Lisbon open-air markets. In addition to articles and book chapters, she is the author of *La scuola di carta* (2008), and co-editor (with Aspasia Theodosiou) of a special edition of *Etudes tsiganes* (2012) on the subject of emotion and place.

Manuela Ivone Cunha has a Ph.D. in anthropology and teaches at the University of Minho, Portugal. She is a senior research fellow at Centre for Research in Anthropology – University of Minho (CRIA – UM), Portugal. She has received the Sedas Nunes award for the Social Sciences for her research on prisons, drug markets and the penal management of social vulnerability, and has also focused on the intersection between criminalisation, gender and culture/ethnicity, and on emerging forms of vaccine refusal. She is the author and editor of several volumes, book chapters and journal articles, including an article on the ethnography of prisons and penal confinement in *Annual Review of Anthropology* (2014).

Martin Fotta received his Ph.D. from Goldsmiths, University of London, and has held a post-doctoral fellowship at the Research Training Group 'Value and Equivalence', Goethe University, Frankfurt/Main. He is currently Lecturer in Social Anthropology at the University of Kent, and his research focuses on moneylending practices of Calon Gypsies of Bahia, Brazil.

Chapter 1

 # Usury among the Slovak Roma
Notes on Relations between Lenders and Borrowers in a Segregated Taboris

TOMÁŠ HRUSTIČ

It was my second month in the field, and I had just found out that the family I used to visit for showers were usurers.[1] I was living with a family in their small house, which lacked running water and a bathroom, conducting research on religious conversion among Roma in a *taboris* near a small town in eastern Slovakia.[2] The father of the family hosting me had wealthier siblings living in town, and had arranged for me to be able to visit them in order to use their bathroom, which had running hot water. Soon, however, I realised that this family had been able to accumulate their property through usury, lending money to other Roma. In fact, they did not try to hide this from me. Moreover, they were even proud of their activity, citing it as an example that demonstrated their ability to overcome poverty through self-perceived cleverness and systematic work. According to them, their social status increased and they were able to move from the bottom of the social ladder in the Roma community to a renovated house situated in the town among the non-Roma (plural *Gadže*, singular *Gadžo*).

During the first weeks of my field research, this discovery entailed an ethical dilemma, since for me usury was morally unacceptable. Besides my moral concerns, I was afraid that visiting them might impact negatively on my relationship with poor families in the *taboris* – their clients and borrowers. I was aware, however, of my unique chance to gain insights into social and economic relations in the community. I discussed this dilemma with my friends in the *taboris*, who were clients of these moneylenders, and their replies were generally along the lines of: 'Listen, everybody knows they are usurers, but what we can do? We need to borrow cash sometimes and nobody else would lend to us. This is the reality of life in the Roma settlement'. Contrary to my expectations, moneylending was a common and accepted feature of life in the Roma settlement, at least at first sight. So I continued to visit the moneylenders, and this enabled me to gain some insights into the dynamics of usury. We had many debates about their economic situation and usurious enterprise, as well as about perceptions of money and the financial behaviour of Roma in general. I also talked about these issues with people who depended on the moneylenders' financial services. Thus, step by step, I gained a broader picture of the concepts related to usury, of the mechanisms of moneylending, and the perceptions of these practices on the part of both borrowers and moneylenders.

Debt plays a central role in the financial strategies of marginalised groups such as those in the *taboris* where I conducted fieldwork. This debt derives from the lending and borrowing of money, often involving various interest rates, ranging from relatively low to the very high rates that characterise usury. This chapter will focus on usury – the lending of money with an excessive interest rate – as a strategy advantageous to both parties involved (that is, lenders and borrowers). For usurers, lending money at a high rate of interest is a profitable investment and a way to gain social and economic power. The phenomenon of usury (in emic terms, 'lending with interest') pervades the whole system of the local *taboris* economy. Often the boundary between moneylenders and their clients is not clear, since many inhabitants of the *taboris* are at certain points borrowers and at other points lenders. This situation is similar to the one described by Deborah James of lenders and borrowers in South Africa. Here, as in the *taboris*, 'except perhaps at the extreme ends of the continuum, borrowers and lenders cannot be separated easily. Some start as one and later become the other; some are both, but at different times and in different registers' (James 2012: 26).

An Economy of Dependence

The Roma from the *taboris* belong to the group of Slovenska Roma (Slovak Roma),[3] who ceased nomadic life in the seventeenth and eighteenth centuries and speak various dialects of Carpathian Romani (Marushiakova and Popov 2001: 38). In many cases the Slovak Roma have abandoned their traditional way of life and language for various reasons; members of the middle class especially have tended to become assimilated into the Slovak majority. Many Roma in Slovakia live in rural settlements and urban ghettoes, mostly in the economically deprived eastern part of the country, and are impoverished to various degrees, characterised by generational poverty. Kinship is crucial for the Roma in segregated settlements. Nuclear families, elementary social units in these communities, are interconnected in complex families (Budilová and Jakoubek 2005; Kobes 2010). This kinship system is defined by firm bonds characterised by solidarity and sharing. Ideally, the value of solidarity is demonstrated by the sharing of food and material goods when needed and, importantly, by various egalitarian mechanisms that prevent anybody from standing out socially too much (Hübschmanová 1999: 16).

I conducted my research in a town in eastern Slovakia with a population of approximately 6,000 inhabitants, of whom about 700 were Roma. Most of them lived in a socially and territorially segregated *taboris* on the outskirts of the town, and compared to the local non-Roma population they formed a relatively homogeneous and closed group. There were also about 200 Roma who lived in the town in one of two smaller localities, or dispersed among the non-Roma majority.

Most of the activities of the Roma were focused on securing material and financial subsistence. Some 95 per cent of the adult population was unemployed and in receipt of social and various forms of welfare benefits. The social system in Slovakia provides welfare benefits to those who are unemployed, with additional benefits for people living in 'material need'. These people can apply for further welfare benefits for their families and childcare, as well as for a housing allowance. In addition, if a person is actively in liaison with the labour office and seeking employment, and is enrolled in a so-called activation programme, they receive additional money. This programme was introduced after neoliberal social welfare reform was implemented in Slovakia in 2004, when the social welfare budget was reduced dramatically. The consequences of the reform were riots among Roma and panic among the non-Roma (Marušák and Singer 2009). Due to these reforms, during the time of my research an average family with four children, with both parents unemployed, received between 6,000 and 9,000 Slovak crowns in benefits.[4] However, in most cases, people found these benefits insufficient to cover their living expenses. Most people also needed additional sources of income, and these were secured by various wage labour and informal petty services for non-Roma in the area. Another important secondary and irregular source of income consisted of collecting and selling scrap iron and seasonal fruits and herbs.

The financial possibilities available to people living in extreme poverty are different from those of people with sufficient and regular incomes. Official financial institutions do not include these people in their system; it is evident, however, that poor people need access to banking institutions and need money to ensure their financial viability. For these people, several alternative forms of credit and banking institutions exist, distinguished, for instance, by their level of formality, which individuals mobilise and combine in various ways. Official banks are used only by those who can demonstrate a regular source of income and who are employed or have pensions. Banks are wary of lending money to people from the lower classes or to those who are not able to provide proof of a regular income.

Another financial possibility for people in the *taboris* is that of various hire-purchase institutions. To obtain things by this means, a customer has to prove that they receive a regular income, confirmed by their employer, and their credit history is checked before the transaction. For this reason, this means of obtaining electronic goods, furnishings, sports equipment and the like is used mostly by middle-class employed people. However, there are increasing numbers of cases where hire-purchase institutions are also open to people on low-incomes. For example, during my research there was a boom in hire-purchase institutions selling various goods for relatively low monthly repayments. Since most Roma from the *taboris* were unemployed, they could not use the services of hire-purchase institutions, but there were some families who could arrange false documentation of employment, and were thus able to purchase furniture or electronic goods, for which they were obliged to pay small monthly instalments.

For insolvent Roma from segregated settlements – that is, the majority of inhabitants of the *taboris* – the only financial institutions accessible to them are various forms of fringe banking, such as pawnbrokers. Pawnshops directly target low-income groups and are widely used by people who do not have regular incomes. Practically every Roma family in the *taboris* possessed some objects that could be pawned, such as television sets or gold jewellery. Interestingly, many of these articles were bought in hire-purchase institutions. There were families that used pawnshops every month to obtain cash before receiving their social benefit payment. Impoverished Roma families often invested in expensive DVD players, which, besides their primary function, were used as an important commodity that could easily be taken to a pawnshop when necessary so that the family could get a small but crucial sum of cash to overcome financial hardship before receiving their welfare payment; gold served the same function. Another frequent usurious practice was for a loan shark to lend a piece of gold jewellery (a necklace or a ring, for example) to a client, who would then take it to a pawnshop. After receiving money from the pawnshop, the borrowers then had to give part of the sum obtained to the owner of the gold. For instance, if they received 1,000 crowns for a gold necklace, they would have to give 300 crowns to the usurer. The borrower would then have 700 crowns, but naturally, on the day of repayment, they would have to pay back the whole 1,000, plus administration and interest fees, at the pawnshop. Moreover, if the client was unable to repay the price of the necklace, the sum was paid by the usurer, who then added the sum to his client's account as debt with an excessive rate of interest. Thus, material commodities such as electronic goods or gold not only symbolically increased the status of their owners, but they also had an important function in being items that could be used to deal with financial hardship; in a way, they could also prevent their owners from having to borrow cash from loan sharks.

However, the most frequent way of resolving the lack of cash – especially for those families that did not possess any goods to be pawned, or in those instances when people needed larger amounts of money – was to borrow money at high interest from unofficial moneylenders. There was a significant number of people in the *taboris* who were in a continually dependent relationship with loan sharks, with practically no cash on hand during the month, because in order to repay their debt they had to give all their meagre incomes to the usurers. Thus, they became trapped in a cycle of dependence on the usurers and lived lives of constant debt. There was also a group of occasional borrowers, people who regularly received small amounts of money (from social benefits or the informal economy) and were able to be fairly economical with these. There were periods during the month, however, when they had no money and needed to borrow some cash, mainly because of unpredictable events requiring larger spending (family celebrations, house repairs and so on).

There were almost no possibilities for the Roma of the *taboris* to use official banking institutions. In the environment of a segregated settlement, the essence of the relationship between a usurer and a borrower could be defined through the concept of debt. David Graeber emphasises that in the past debt was 'the hinge that made it possible to imagine money in anything like the modern sense, and therefore, also, to produce what we like to call the market: an arena where anything can be bought and sold, because all objects are (like slaves) disembedded from their former social relations and exist only in relation to money' (Graeber 2009: 2). This is what happens in Roma settlements where dependence on debt pervades the whole social and kinship system. While in the recent past, relations within extended families or larger family-ancestral formations (*fajtas*) in segregated Roma settlements in eastern Slovakia were characterised by generalised reciprocity and mutual solidarity (Budilová and Jakoubek 2005: 13; Hübschmanová 1999: 16), today the applicability of these models needs to be reassessed, especially in cases of successful usurers in segregated rural settlements. Those individuals and their nuclear families who are able to accumulate power by lending money demonstrate this power through the act of lending itself, and, moreover, they redefine and create new hierarchical social links, which are now mediated by cash more than by generalised reciprocity. Actors on both sides – lenders and borrowers – are in the process of becoming disembedded from their old social relations, and a new set of relations is being created, associated with the possession of money through the mechanism of credit and debt. As in the South African case described by James, previously personalised forms of relationship, deeply founded on morality, tend to transform into cash-based ones (James 2012: 37).

'Only Usurers Would Lend Us Cash'

Most borrowers in the *taboris* seem to appreciate the *interešar* (usurer) for their generosity, or at least for the fact that they are willing to lend them money in situations where no official financial institution would.[5] The point is mentioned by Banerjee and Duflo, who emphasise that:

> The poor have very little by way of collateral to secure [a] loan and therefore lenders hesitate to trust them with a lot of money ... As a result, a lot of lenders are reluctant to lend to the poor. Moreover and for the same reason, informal lenders may be the only ones who are willing to lend to the poor. The trouble is that these informal lenders have to pay more for their deposits than the more formal institutions, since they are less capitalised and less regulated and do not have any government guarantees. This higher cost of deposits gets passed on to poorer borrowers. (Banerjee and Duflo 2007: 152)

Although this specific logic refers mostly to informal and predatory fringe banking companies, it also fits the case of Roma *interešars* who are the only people willing to lend money to impoverished Roma in segregated settlements. This credit is normally accompanied by high interest rates, leading the poor into dependence on their moneylender. The usurers are completely aware of the risk of lending to poor Roma, and they can perfectly articulate their arguments. In one conversation at an *interešar*'s house, I tried to challenge him over usurers' high rates of interest, arguing that they could decrease their excessive rates and still profit. In his counter-argument, he emphasised the lack of collateral and also the risk of being reported to the police:

If I take credit from a bank and I mortgage my house and I do not repay the debt, they will take my house. But if I privately lend 100,000 [crowns] to you and you will not repay the debt, what can I do? And yet, you will accuse and fink me, you will say that I [demand a] high [rate of] interest from you, and I will end up in jail. So what warranty is here in play? But if the state lends money it has a warranty.

The *interešar*'s point was that the credit operations he offers have no guarantee, unlike loans from an official bank. There is also a sharp distinction between the services of official banks and loan sharks' unofficial financial business, with its greater level of risk. As he said later in the same conversation, his services were the only option for the Roma if they wanted to borrow cash, because no official institution would lend them money.

What looks like an irrational decision to an outsider, since it leads the borrower into increased poverty, appears rational from the borrowers' perspective as a means of securing their means of existence in the short term. They are aware that the price of the loan is extremely high, but they are willing to accept it. The price is not the most important factor in the decision-making process of those caught in generational poverty. In a study based on extensive research into poor households' money management strategies, Collins et al. point out that for the poor the price of a loan is often not the most important determinant, as they take into consideration additional factors, such as the emotional cost of having to deal with unhelpful authorities, the cost of a bus ride to reach the relevant institution and so on (Collins et al. 2009: 151).

Roma from the *taboris* appreciated that usurers were willing to lend them money because nobody else would. This perspective was evident in a conversation with one of my friends from the *taboris*. He was unemployed and lived on social benefits, but was also able to earn some money by doing occasional day jobs. Moreover, he owned a car, which meant he was able to serve as a driver when other Roma needed a lift to the hospital, to official institutions in the district town, and so on. Importantly, these services were not provided for free. When his car broke down and needed a major repair, he had no choice but to borrow cash from the local usurer. In his view, this was a good investment because a functioning car was an important means of earning additional money:

> I asked for some money because I needed it. I said, 'I need money for this and this; if you lend me I would repay you some more, of course'. He said, 'My normal interest is 50 per cent. If you want 5,000, you must pay me back 7,500. So think it over'. I replied that yes, I needed money, and I had no need to think it over. So we went to the bank, he withdrew the money and lent

it to me. Tomáš, I say to you, he was stranger to me and he lent me money. My own family wouldn't lend to me! Yes, he lent with interest, but that's okay. But he was willing to lend to me!

The words of my friend reflect the typical appreciation of loan sharks by their clients. People who borrow money from usurers are well aware of the disadvantages of these transactions, but they are in a situation where, despite the disadvantages, a usurer's credit can help them to overcome complicated circumstances and hardship. Based on my research and interviews with borrowers, viewed from a short-term perspective, borrowing from a moneylender was the most suitable strategy available.

Borrowers or Lenders?

As James (2012) has pointed out, in some cases the boundary between moneylenders and borrowers is not clear at all. In the *taboris*, too, there was a significant group of Roma who were at certain times borrowers and at other times lenders. There were a few persons who had been able to make profits out of moneylending, and, obviously, on the other hand there was a large group of people who were constantly without money and were dependent on further loans from usurers. Moreover, there is also a significant group of people in every settlement who are not at the very bottom of the local social ladder but instead inhabit a 'middle' social milieu. They are able to be economical with their regular small income during the month, though occasionally they have practically no money and need cash. Sometimes they need to borrow money, like my friend who had to borrow cash to repair his car. On the other hand, sometimes they have extra cash to lend, mostly after they receive social benefits payments or after receiving irregular and unforeseen income from informal economic activities.

For example, the same person who borrowed 5,000 crowns from a local usurer to repair his car received some unexpected income four months later. He got a one-off job to drive somebody from his locality to the western part of the Czech Republic, and besides being paid for his expenses he earned an additional 1,500 crowns. Upon his return he bought a grown pig for 1,000 crowns, and lent out the remaining 500 crowns at 50 per cent interest. Moreover, after storing a portion of the pork for his family, he sold the rest of the meat to other Roma, and a significant proportion of these customers did not have cash to pay for the meat. The man and his customers struck a deal whereby the latter paid him after receiving their social benefit payments, the arrangement costing them the amount owed plus an additional 50 per cent in interest. Over one month, this person was able to make an investment of his unexpected income by buying a pig and lending out 500 crowns with a repayment price of 750 crowns. And by selling pork worth 1,000 crowns, and charging those who bought it 50 per cent interest as they could not pay for it at the time of purchase, he received back 1,500 crowns. In other words, the 1,500 crowns brought him a profit of 750 crowns (500 from meat sales plus 250 from cash loans) in addition to providing pork for his family. Importantly, this person was not an established moneylender, but he used the opportunity of a one-off job to lend money and earn some profit out of it. After all, a few months before he had himself borrowed from a local *interešar*.

I was surprised to discover that in every case, borrowing or lending money always involved interest, its magnitude dependent on the relationship between the lender and the borrower. Interest rates varied from 20 to 50 per cent per month, and in some cases were as high as 100 per cent per month. Borrowing money without interest was practically unheard of. Lending money at high interest rates was so internalised in segregated communities that people could hardly imagine a financial operation of this type without paying or demanding interest.

Moreover, if people from the *taboris* got a regular job, even if their salary was no higher than the minimum wage, they often submitted a request to a bank for a loan, and in a few cases these were granted.[6] Some people used these loans to improve and renovate their houses, but in many cases, although not recognised as established loan sharks, people tried to earn additional income by lending out cash at high rates of interest in the hope of earning sufficient money to start their own business.

This points to two facts. First, once the situation of people living in generational poverty is changed and they have the opportunity to use the services of legal financial institutions, they do so. Second, in the *taboris*, lending money at a high rate of interest is viewed as a natural and effective means of investing money and escaping poverty. Lending money at interest is a way to multiply one's income. Usury, considered a criminal activity by mainstream society and state authorities, is viewed by loan sharks as the only way to secure a decent existence in the long term. For example, when I asked local loan sharks why usury was not so frequent during socialism, the answers they gave were almost identical: 'Because then people had jobs!'

All the Roma usurers in my research setting had been poor in the past. Given this, it was clear to everybody that usury was one way to escape the vicious cycle of persistent poverty, and subsequently to make good, albeit rather risky, investments, which would allow them to keep their money safe within an insecure environment.

During one discussion with a loan shark, I asked about the possible risks of moneylending. We were talking about differences between lending to family members and lending to '*díline Roma*' ('fool Gypsies'), a term that *interešars* used for their poorest clients.[7] My host argued that lending money to a close family member, especially a brother, was even less secure because then one could not demand a high rate of interest, and there was still some family morality involved. As an example, he told me a story about how he had once lent money to his brother without charging interest:

> Did he repay me those twenty thousand crowns? No. If I had twenty thousand now, I would have invested it in a term deposit. I would have been okay and I would have been sure the money was safe. And I would have earned nice interest of 10 per cent or 12 per cent. And I wouldn't need to trouble anybody, no stress.

However, this man did not put his savings into a term deposit. His argument rests on the fact that he preferred – in his terms – to risk a life of stress, because it pays much better than a term deposit; or in other words, it is much more profitable than using the services of official banking institutions. Another important point is that lending to a close family member is usually risky, because in the event that a sibling does not repay the debt, one has limited options for reclaiming the money.

The fact that the wealthiest *interešars* moved out from the *taboris* and physically and symbolically cut some of the bonds with their complex families is significant. They are aware that expectations of mutual solidarity and demands for sharing of resources keep all family members at a comparable social and material level. As the interviewed *interešar* emphasised, it is a problem for him to lend money to his brother, which indicates that some mechanisms of identification with his complex family are still in place, although these bonds are weaker than before. Similarly, Budilová and Jakoubek describe how among members of a family-ancestral formation (*fajta*), 'money is loaned with zero interest rates (in contrast to usurious rates of 100 per cent, which are usual when money is borrowed by people from a different *fajta*)' (Budilová and Jakoubek 2005: 20), a difference that they interpret as a form of generalised reciprocity characteristic of egalitarian societies. On the contrary, however, in the *taboris* I describe here, there is always an interest rate present in any financial transaction, even one involving one's siblings. Indeed, by living outside the *taboris*, avoiding potentially problematic loans to one's brother or cousin also becomes possible.

Whenever usurers lend money to *diline Roma*, short of direct physical violence, which is nevertheless a constant latent potentiality, they utilise a variety of techniques to guarantee repayment. *Diline Roma* are in constant dependence on usurers, who use both their symbolic and their real power to secure repayment. In the past, they used to accompany their debtors to the post office on social benefit payment days, and the debtors had to give them all the cash they received. A usurer would then lend a small amount of cash to his debtor to purchase basic food supplies. In this manner, month after month, the *interešar* received practically all their debtors' money, which was justified by the claim that the virtual debt was increasing excessively and that they were just claiming their own money back.

After it became standard for some social benefits to be paid into recipients' bank accounts, the usurers were able to take possession of their debtors' ATM cards, and the situation remained similar to that involving personal withdrawals at post offices. In some instances physical violence occurred, which also had a significant performative and demonstrative function. Withholding bankcards is an example par excellence of disembedding mechanisms 'formalising' and impersonalising relationships between borrowers and lenders, and physical violence, often implemented in a performative manner, is a reaffirmation of this new form of relationship.

Usury is risky. To lend money to poor people who have limited or no income is a precarious business, and the excessive interest rate charged is meant to decrease the amount of risk. Usurers are well aware of this inverse logic. When people had jobs during the socialist era, their income was regular and they could repay their debts without any serious risk to the lender. There was no point in lending or borrowing money at a high rate of interest because people could borrow from anybody. Their financial credibility was not in question. However, after Roma lost their jobs they fell into deep poverty, and their creditworthiness became questionable. Their only chance to borrow money now is to borrow from loan sharks.

'Clever Roma' and 'Fool Gypsies'

The morality of usury in marginalised Roma communities has several dimensions. All usurers are aware that their business is illegal from the perspective of state authorities. The Roma in the *taboris* were ambivalent about usury. On the one hand, as I have argued, they appreciated the fact that loan sharks were the only people who were willing to lend them money. On the other, they felt a strong sense of injustice and held negative sentiments towards loan sharks. Usurers were also aware of these negative attitudes. In our discussions about usury, they felt a strong urge to explain their behaviour.[8] From the emic perspective of a segregated and impoverished community, they offer a substitute for those financial services that are necessary but unavailable. There were several ways in which usurers rationalised their practices. One of the most common was to denigrate their clients as fools and stupid people who were unable to secure a regular income. As one loan shark exclaimed: 'Listen! Have you ever seen a wise man earning money from another wise man? A wise man can only earn money from the foolish'.

Established loan sharks emphasised this perception of their clients as *diline Roma*, or 'foolish Gypsies', people who do not deserve better living standards because they do not know how to manage their moderate incomes, have no ability to find or keep a job, and do not know how to maintain their households.[9] They told me stories about how such-and-such a family had suddenly received a large sum of money but had wasted it in a short time, and again had to come and ask for a loan. These stories were told with disgust and served to demonstrate that these 'stupid and dirty Gypsies' did not deserve anything better. Loan sharks would always contrast their own families with those of *diline Roma*, citing examples to prove that they themselves were not fools, and that they had worked tirelessly to escape the vicious circle of poverty to secure a decent living for their families:

> The Gypsies, how do they live? At first, they throw money at slot machines. If I had this attitude my family would have nothing to eat too. I will tell you one story. We went to play football once, the whole bunch of us, and we went to a bus-station restaurant. So, what to eat? We decided on soup and bread. It was cheap. And Koro ordered schnitzel! I will always remember this. He laughed at us [and said], 'You are rich and you eat only soup and I eat schnitzel'. Okay, that was it, no problem. We went to another football tournament later and he had no money. He couldn't buy a single piece of bread and we could buy the soup again. It is a pure truth. I could have bought schnitzel if I had wanted. But he had nothing. And whose fault was it? ... I have money, I can buy schnitzel, but I will not. I am okay with a cheap sausage for 15 crowns. But I save some money for tomorrow! But they do not think this way – this is their fault. Do you remember the time when the welfare benefits were reduced by up to 50 per cent?[10] Do you know how much the Gypsies were given? From fifteen thousand [crowns] they dropped to six thousand. Had their lives improved or worsened, or was it the same? It was the same!

The usurer, using the example of buying soup instead of a schnitzel, emphasised that the *diline Roma* lack one important virtue: the ability to think ahead and to plan financially. In contrast, the usurers see themselves as having this virtue; they can be modest in their spending, can plan ahead and strategise with their investments. These distinctions are similar to those frequently verbalised by the non-Roma majority when they speak about Roma. An average Slovak thinks that the Roma live from day to day, that they cannot plan ahead and that immediately after they receive their benefits they spend them all, such that for the rest of the month they go hungry.

This dramatic disdain of *diline Roma* is typical of most loan sharks. They express disgust at the 'fool Gypsies', drawing significant distinctions between their own families and the families of their clients, who are unable plan ahead and save money, regardless of whether they receive 'six thousand crowns' or 'fifteen thousand crowns'. They use the same stereotypes when speaking about *diline Roma* that non-Roma use when speaking about the Roma in general.

The Roma who borrow money from usurers echo these arguments, stressing their self-perceived 'Gypsy identity' and its connection to attitudes towards money. During one of my discussions about the concept of *Romipen* (Roma identity) and identities in general with my friends in the *taboris*, talk turned to the differences between Roma and non-Roma. This was not a discussion with loan sharks but with people who (only occasionally) had to borrow from *interešar*s. I asked if a non-Roma (*Gadžo*) such as myself could become a Rom, or the other way around. After a series of theorisations, my two interlocutors arrived at the following conclusion:

> You will always be a *Gadžo*. You will think differently, you will live differently, you will solve your problems differently and you will never be a Gypsy. Even if you wished to be. It is not like in that film [*Gitanas*, a Mexican soap opera], that I will baptise you and you become a Gypsy. You will never become a Gypsy ... It's nature. You will never have a Gypsy nature ... You would adjust yourself to dirt, you would adjust yourself to everything, but a *Gadžo* will know how to live better than a Gypsy. I am sure, Tomáš, that you would never accept the concept of borrowing money with interest. I am sure you would never go to borrow money with interest! ... Do you understand? You have your *Gadže* dignity. You wouldn't go to humiliate yourself; you will manage your money well.

Finally, my interlocutors agreed that the ability to manage one's money well is one of the key distinctions between Roma and non-Roma identity, and that *Gadže* will always be able to manage their finances and live better lives than Roma. In this way, they linked ethnic criteria with poverty, and differentiated the middle class from those people living in generational poverty and under conditions of social segregation. Their views on poverty, access to resources and the management of money pervade their concept of *Romipen*. Other features and determinants of Roma identity, at least in this context, are downplayed. According to the inhabitants of segregated settlements, Roma live with a constant lack of resources, which in turn is one of the most important emic features of their identity. Similarly, successful loan sharks, who by lending money at high rates of interest were able to earn enough to move away from the *taboris*, adopt this paradigm when describing 'fool Gypsies' as being unable to escape the cycle of poverty. Thanks to their self-perceived virtues, they themselves were able to move upwards socially.[11] That is, they were able to enter the *Gadže* world, leaving the *taboris* both physically and symbolically, and identifying those who remained behind with the typical *Gadže* stereotypes about 'fool Gypsies'. Lending money at high rates of interest is one way (and in the most cases the only way) for Roma to free themselves from poverty.[12]

Conclusion

It is not difficult to understand that the central determinant in the relationship between lenders and borrowers is debt. Moreover, it seems that social and economic relations in segregated Roma settlements are reflected in and shaped according to people's relations with money (such as resources) and their accumulation and repaying of debt. With recent economic crises, a growing number of Roma from *taboris* seem to be caught in a cycle of economic dependence on loan sharks. The crises have mostly affected various day-labour jobs offered by local *Gadže*. More families have become dependent on the inadequate state social welfare system. The state authorities have attempted to cope with illegal usurers by using restrictive policies and legal powers, and from time to time there are legal cases in which loan sharks are convicted of usury, extortion or violence and sentenced. This does not, however, reflect a systemic change.

This chapter has argued that there are others who would willingly take up the job of those prosecuted for usury. It is not possible to draw a dividing line between lenders and borrowers. Obviously there are a few well-established and widely recognised loan sharks operating in every *taboris*, as well as many Roma who are continually dependent on these lenders. However, there is also a significant group of people who are at certain times borrowers and at other times moneylenders. In this way, the system of credit influences social relations by re-establishing a new set of relations according to who possesses money. Previously complex relationships, defined by a personalised morality in segregated settlements, are, through the disembedding process, becoming cash-based, mediated by ATM cards and the threat of violence, and despite occasional talk of morality, these relationships are reduced more or less to the dynamics of credit and debt. The new set of relations affects concepts of identity. For some people, moneylending has become the only available means to improve their economic and social situation, and though they might feel that lending to the poor at high rates of interest is immoral, their rationalisation processes neutralise these feelings. Often this rationalisation goes hand in hand with self-identifying as 'better' Roma who are able to cope with difficult situations and secure enough resources to feed their families. In their eyes, moneylenders stand in opposition to 'those dirty and foolish Gypsies who will always stay at the bottom of society'.

While the borrowers are aware of their situation, they nonetheless appreciate the fact there are some people willing to lend them cash. It is evident that unless the state employs systemic mechanisms to enable the poor to access official credit institutions – such as more numerous and more widely available micro-credit and micro-financing institutions, and more accessible hire-purchase institutions for the poor – this situation will not change.

NOTES

1. The data analysed in this chapter were collected during long-term ethnographic fieldwork in a segregated Romani settlement in eastern Slovakia in 2005/6. The primary focus of my research was not Gypsy economic strategies but rather religion and religious conversion. The finalisation of the chapter was supported by VEGA Grant No. 2/0099/15, 'Label "Roma": Its Emic and Ethic Reflections and Social Impact'.
2. I use the term *taboris* in this chapter to refer to the Roma segregated camp where I conducted my research. *Taboris* (lit. 'camp') is an emic term used by the Roma in this part of eastern Slovakia (eastern Zemplin region). Some authors writing about Roma in Slovakia also use the emic term *osada*, meaning 'Roma settlement' (Budilová and Jakoubek 2005; Nieft 2010), which is the most frequent and widely recognised name for such sites in Slovakia. I prefer the term *taboris*, however, since the term 'settlement' conceals to an extent the level of involuntariness and marginalisation involved. Moreover, I argue that successful usurers tend to move out of *taboris* into houses dispersed among the Slovak non-Roma majority, thus differentiating themselves from the 'dirty and foolish Gypsies' living in *taboris*. When referring to the general situation in Slovakia, I use the term 'Roma segregated settlements'.

3. Not to be confused with Piasere's Slovensko Roma from Slovenia (Piasere 1985). Slovak and Slovenian languages use the same adjectives to refer to their home countries.
4. The Slovak crown was Slovakia's national currency until January 2009, when it was replaced by the euro, with an exchange rate of 30.126 Slovak crowns to 1 euro.
5. In Romani, the term *interešar* (plural *interešare*) is usually used, and sometimes also the Slovak *užerník* (both mean usurer). Interestingly, the term *intereš* seems to be derived from English term 'interest'. This word entered Romani from eastern Slovak dialects that incorporated various English terms, perhaps picked up from migrants returning from the United States in the first half of the twentieth century.
6. For example, at the time of my research a few Roma were employed by the municipality as activation work coordinators. Activation work is a government programme whereby state welfare beneficiaries commit to work a certain number of hours each week in return for a small amount of money in addition to their welfare allowance. Municipalities can employ people as coordinators of this 'activation programme', who are responsible for administering a group of workers, and this coordination is recognised as a full-time job, with all the benefits such a job can offer.
7. It should be noted that when speaking Romani, usurers used the term '*dilíne Roma*', whereas when speaking Slovak they used the term *Cigáň* (Gypsy), which has strong negative connotations.
8. These rationalisations were naturally influenced by my presence, and were a common feature of informal interviews.
9. The usurers show disrespect to Roma or, in other words, their stereotypical representations of their Roma clients are identical to the representations that their non-Roma neighbours have of Roma in general (that is, that they are lazy and work-shy, that they cannot manage their money and so on). In this manner, they re-evaluate these stereotypical representations and appropriate them for themselves. This parallels the way in which Roma converts to the Watchtower Society (Jehovah's Witnesses) speak about Roma non-converts (Hrustič 2011: 29).
10. The speaker is referring to the social welfare reform of 2004, mentioned earlier. See also Marušák and Singer (2009).
11. David Scheffel (2010) uses a similar argument in his essay about Roma loan sharks from the Slovak village of Svinia. He claims, rather provocatively, that the loan sharks are slowly establishing the basis for a Roma middle class, by moving away from segregated Roma settlements.
12. In many cases usurers who were able to move from Roma settlements tend to legalise their income by establishing some form of legal entrepreneurial activity (construction, selling groceries and so on), and they gave up their moneylending business. Interestingly, there are cases of several usurers who gave up usury after converting to Pentecostal and Charismatic churches recently in Slovakia (Podolinská and Hrustič 2011: 23–25).

REFERENCES

Banerjee, A.V., and E. Duflo. 2007. 'The Economic Lives of the Poor', *Journal of Economic Perspectives* 21(1): 141–67.
Budilová, L., and M. Jakoubek. 2005. 'Ritual Impurity and Kinship in a Gypsy Osada in Eastern Slovakia', *Romani Studies* 15(1): 1–29.
Collins, D., J. Murdoch, S. Rutherford and O. Ruthven. 2009. *Portfolios of the Poor: How the World's Poor Live on $2 a Day*. Princeton: Princeton University Press.
Graeber, D. 2009. 'Debt – The First Five Thousand Years', *Eurozine*. Retrieved 25 January 2013 from: http://www.eurozine.com/articles/2009-08-20-graeber-en.html.
Hrustič, T. 2011. 'Values and Ethnicity: Religious Conversions of Roma in Eastern Slovakia to the Watchtower Society', in C. Rughiniş and A. Máté-Tóth (eds), *Spaces and Borders: Young Researchers about Religion in Central and Eastern Europe*. Berlin: de Gruyter, pp.23–32.
Hübschmanová, M. 1999. 'Několik Poznámek k Hodnotám Romů', in *Romové v České republice 1945–98*. Prague: Socioclub, pp.1–51.
James, D. 2012. 'Money-Go-Round: Personal Economies of Wealth, Aspiration and Indebtedness', *Africa* 82(1): 20–40.
Kobes, T. 2010. 'Fajta a Povaha Příbuzenství Obyvatel Východoslovenských Romských Osad', *Sociologický časopis/Czech Sociological Review* 2: 235–55.
Marušák, M., and L. Singer. 2009. 'Social Unrest in Slovakia 2004: Romani Reaction to Neoliberal Reforms', in N. Sigona and N. Trehan (eds), *Romani Politics in Contemporary Europe: Poverty, Ethnic Mobilization, and the Neoliberal Order*. London: Palgrave Macmillan, pp.186–208.
Marushiakova, E., and V. Popov. 2001. 'Historical and Ethnographic Background: Gypsies, Roma, Sinti', in W. Guy (ed.), *Between Past and Present: The Roma of Central and Eastern Europe*. Hatfield: University of Hertfordshire Press, pp.33–54.
Nieft, E. 2010. 'Všade Dobre, Doma Najlepšie? Überall schön, zu Hause am Besten? Wohnstand-ortentscheidungen, Materielle Wohnsituation und Interne Segmentierung: Einschätzung der Bewohner/innen der Ost-slowakischen Osada', Master's diss. Leipzig: Universität Leipzig.
Piasere, L. 1985. *Mare Roma. Catégories humaines et structure sociale. Une contribution à l'ethnologie tsigane*. Paris: Paul H. Stahl.
Podolinská, T., and T. Hrustič. 2011. *Religion as a Path to Change? The Possibilities of Social Inclusion of the Roma in Slovakia*. Bratislava: Friedrich Ebert Stiftung and Institute of Ethnology SAS.
Scheffel, D.Z. 2010. 'Slovenská Chudoba a Romská Lichva', *OS - Občianska spoločnosť*, special issue, 14: 47–62.

Tomáš Hrustič is a researcher at the Institute of Ethnology at the Slovak Academy of Sciences in Bratislava. He has a Ph.D. in comparative studies of religion and has carried out ethnographic research in a Roma community in eastern Slovakia. He is the co-author (with Tatiana Podolinská) of *Religion as a Path to Change? The Possibilities of Social Inclusion of the Roma in*

Slovakia (2011), and the author of several articles about Romani religiosity and religious conversions. His current research focuses on the political representation of Roma.

Chapter 2

New Redistributors in Times of Insecurity

Different Types of Informal Lending in Hungary

JUDIT DURST

It is a day at the end of January 2011, and the interim elections in Lápos, Borsod County, Hungary, are taking place. The atmosphere has been growing increasingly heated since the early afternoon. Lufi is going from house to house within the Gypsy community, and everywhere there is feverish guessing going on. Even though the ballot boxes are due to be sealed at 7 o'clock in the evening, by around 5 o'clock it has become clear that Lufi's cousin, Kópi, is winning.

Rozika is the only Gypsy chosen to sit on the electoral board, together with the few Hungarians who still remain in the village.[1] She is in a very delicate position. Her daughter married into the Balogh family – into the 'band of usurers' (*kamatolók/kamatosok bandája*), as the Gypsies of Lápos refer to them. Part of the Balogh extended family (*banda*) feels their present position is being threatened by the potential electoral triumph of Kópi. However, Rozika is supporting Kópi; she believes he will provide a better future for the village. During the election campaign, Kópi managed to win the support of the Gypsy majority by taking on some of the village men for seasonal work.

Although the official result of the election is not expected until 8 o'clock that evening, by 6 o'clock a small crowd is already gathering in front of the election office set up within the school building. By the time I join the crowd, there are around 100 Gypsies all standing in slippers and tracksuits in the slushy snow and chilly air.

The news flies fast around the crowd: Kópi promised to bring Nótári Méri, the famous Romani singer, to perform in the village if he wins the election. Several people assure me, though, that they didn't vote for Kópi because of Méri, but because of the work that he promised: 'Work is needed here, we don't want to live on benefits', they say. Kópi promised more jobs, a 'social shop' (*szociális bolt*) for those in need, and the alleviation of usury. This is why the Balogh *banda*, the settlement's informal moneylenders, cannot be seen in the festive crowd.

A few minutes before 8 o'clock, the news is announced: 'Kópi got in; we won!' For the first time in its history, the village has elected a Gypsy mayor. Yet, while the crowd celebrate in front of the school, there is another, much smaller group who keep their distance. They walk home silently after hearing the outcome. It is already clear how divided the village community really is.

Finally, Kópi's Audi rolls in at 10 o'clock, transporting the victor, his wife, his parents and his impressively muscular bodyguard, but not Méri. The crowd, by this time freezing in their tracksuits and slippers, happily make their way to the pub that has now opened for the celebration. Beer and some snacks are provided, compliments of Kópi. He starts the feast with his victory speech:

> We're gonna show [the Hungarians] that Gypsies can be up to some good, they can make something happen ... I'm just asking you to give me time; not to begin everything with you coming up to me and ripping me off, demanding I give you a grand or two. That way we won't be able to solve anything. Give me time to bring tender money to the village, so that we can create jobs to bring an end to the poverty that Gypsies here have had to suffer.

At bedtime that night, as we drift off to sleep, Szandi, one of the daughters of my Gypsy host family, says, 'I don't know how it is with you, but I didn't like it too much that Kópi came here to celebrate in his Audi and that his bodyguard was with him'. In fact, the festive atmosphere had mostly evaporated by the following day. Going hungry played a part in the cooling down of the celebratory mood, even among Kópi's supporters. 'We'll see how Kópi will manage his job' was the general public opinion of the Gypsies as early as the following morning.

Nine months later, a section of the village Gypsy community successfully conspired to send Kópi to prison. His enemies in Lápos reported him to the authorities, and their testimonies formed the basis of the charges. The testimonies were embellished, and resulted in Kópi, the not-so-long-ago celebrated Gypsy mayor, being charged with usury and abuse of power. He was accused of selling goods on credit with interest at his 'social shop' (a grocery shop where one could buy food on credit).

The old moneylenders within the Balogh *banda* were quick to capitalise on the ousting of Kópi from the village. They slowly started to regain their old clients by hanging around the shop to persuade them: 'Don't pay your debt to the shop! He is now doing time. He is in prison. Why don't you come to me? I'll give you money to buy bread for your children'.

In this chapter, by exploring the conflict between the villagers and their mayor, and by analysing the reasons for Kópi's fall, I aim to demonstrate the importance of understanding not only the economic logic but also the moral grounds of informal (unregistered) moneylending. Drawing on the work of David Graeber, among others, I will show that 'in any given situation there are several kinds of moral reasoning actors could apply' (Graeber 2010: 4). I will demonstrate that in this region people differentiate between two kinds of informal moneylending. While they approve of one type of lending, they reprove the other, and this has serious consequences for the formation of social relations between economic actors.

By interpreting local conflict in Lápos and comparing the informal lending practice of the mayor and of his rivals the Balogh *banda* (especially Zolika), my further aim is to analyse informal moneylending in its social context to show its social function. The above story prompts two main questions: First, why has the village community tolerated its local usurers, the Baloghs, for the last ten years, but ousted the new moneylender, the mayor, in a short time? Second, why does an ethnic group whose members often recognise their shared kinship ties, that emphasises the value of equality and 'brotherhood', or kinship solidarity, accept the economic activity of its moneylenders – of those who derive 'interest' (*kamat*) from the needs of their own group?

Lápos, as we will soon see, is a small, close-knit community of Gypsies related by kinship and of equal social standing. In these kinds of communities, solidarity is the 'foundation of all human sociability. It makes society possible. Everyone belonging to a group can be expected to respect this principle' (Graeber 2010: 6). Graeber goes further, claiming that in such 'personal communities the same logic extends much further: it is often difficult to refuse a request not just for tobacco, but for food' (ibid.: 6). The question arises, then, as to why, in recent times, Gypsies in Lápos have started lending not only money with interest but also food and even tobacco.

Usury: A Product of the 'Culture of Poverty'?

There is a lack of academic literature on usury in Hungary, probably due to the secrecy of informal moneylending, the practitioners of which try to hide their illegal business. The only piece of systematic research on the topic is concerned chiefly with the recently growing prevalence of informal moneylending in poor, segregated rural settlements (Béres and Lukács 2008). According to Béres and Lukács, the increasing dependency of the poor on their usurers can be attributed to two interlinked phenomena. On the one hand, for the poorest layer of Hungarian society, the social safety network (generally provided by solidarity groups, such as ethnic or kinship groups) does not exist anymore. On the other, in indebted, poor communities, 'instead of community values and social norms, anomie [has become] dominant' (ibid.: 38).

Béres and Lukács regard usury as 'the practice of moneylending related to the culture of poverty' (ibid.: 40). Accordingly, they refer to the usurer as the 'local toll-collector [exploiter] of destitution' (*nyomor vámszedője*), and they attribute the growing practice of usury to the disruption of social solidarity. The authors' use of the classical sociological concept of anomie derives from Durkheim (1897), for whom anomie is a condition where norms no longer control the activities of members of a society. Durkheim observed that social periods of disruption (such as economic depression) brought about greater anomie and higher rates of deviation from social norms. In this line of thinking, of which Béres and Lukács are advocates, usury is 'deviant' behaviour and a product of anomie.

Béres and Lukács are not the only scholars who try to interpret informal moneylending in moral terms. The figure of the demonised, 'hardhearted' usurer is a common stereotype across the world.[2] Loan sharking, as usury is called in the United States (meaning unregistered moneylending at higher rates than the legally prescribed limit), is regarded in this type of literature as 'a major source of revenue for the underworld' (Kaplan and Matties 1968: 240).

A different approach is taken by researchers (mainly anthropologists) who are rather interested in interpreting 'usury' in its social context, calling it informal moneylending, and exploring the logic and the principles that drive the actors (that is, borrowers and lenders) to take part in this economic relationship (Goddard 2005; James 2012). Related to this approach, another common method is to regard informal moneylending as a major means of acquiring autonomy and economic independence in circumstances when other income-generating opportunities are restricted or unavailable to certain groups of people (Fotta 2012).

Looking at the existing literature, however, it seems that there is a lack of investigation into the relationship between kinship and informal moneylending. The only research dealing with this topic – that is, social solidarity and lending money at interest in poor, kinship-based communities (Goddard 2005) – indicates that usury is an urban development, an appropriation of the rationale of banks' lending practices in migrant communities where a 'lack of kinship sensitivities is evident' (ibid.: 42).

This chapter is intended to contribute to our understanding of the moral grounds and economic logic of informal (money)lending in kinship-based, tight-knit, long-term poor, rural Gypsy communities in Hungary. For this purpose, I find it fruitful to view the institution of informal lending not through the lenses of 'moral decline', an 'anomic state' of economic depression and escalating poverty (Béres and Lukács 2008), but instead as embedded in the complex and constantly changing social and economic environment that has encompassed the lives of the Láposian Gypsies over the last decade.

By exploring this local social context we will also come to understand why people in Lápos do not judge informal moneylending unambiguously negatively in moral terms – except when it is not 'fairly' carried out. One of my intentions in analysing the development and subsequent outbreak of the conflict between Kópi and the Gypsy community (that is, the moneylender and his clients) is to demonstrate that social norms do play a role, even in long-term poor communities. I will show that in the event that an individual does not follow the local customary economic and social logic of informal lending that has been created through precedent, if they breach locally accepted norms, including those to do with 'helping the poor', they can be strictly sanctioned by the community in question.

Economic Life in the Village: Different Forms of Hierarchies

Lápos is a small village in Borsod, one of the most economically depressed regions in Hungary. When I started my fieldwork there in 2001, the population was around 580 people, out of which 40 per cent were Hungarian. Nowadays, it is a 'Gypsy village', as the locals call it, with 720 inhabitants including a total of three Hungarian nuclear families.

The entire Gypsy community is made up of four large extended families or 'bands' (*banda*), as they call themselves. Of these *banda*, the two most powerful are the Balogh and the Fóti. While members of the Balogh family owe their economic power to their involvement in the informal economy (mostly in terms of informal lending), the Fótis are known for their higher level of education (some of them even have vocational training, which is quite rare in the community) and their loyalty to the Hungarians – especially local state actors.

However, the vast majority of the village's Gypsy population has been struggling in a constant state of economic insecurity for the last two decades. The postsocialist transition in 1989 from a state-run economy to a market economy, which was accompanied by the closure of many state-owned factories and the entrenchment of 1.4 million wage labourers by 1994 (Kertesi 2005), was hardest on the most vulnerable members of society, namely the poorly educated and socially discriminated against Gypsies.

In Lápos, all Gypsy men of working age are long-term unemployed, most of them since the end of the 1980s. This is the kind of settlement that Wilson described as the 'ghetto of unemployed' (Wilson 1999: 6). However, this 'ghettoisation' has been a relatively recent, albeit gradual, development. Until two years ago, when the dissolution of the Gypsy settlements (an EU-funded programme) gave the final push to the out-migration of the remaining Hungarian population of Lápos (Durst 2010), Gypsies lived peacefully together with the Hungarians. The basis of their social and economic interactions was the long-established distinction between Gypsies and Hungarians, in terms of which Gypsies have an inferior status in relation to the Hungarians (see Horváth 2012). In Lápos, before state socialism, a Gypsy man could work as a day labourer for the Hungarian villagers. During the socialist era, he would be employed as an unskilled wage labourer either in the construction industry in Miskolc, the capital of the county, or in the mines. However, his wife, who stayed at home with their children, could do some occasional work such as cleaning and gardening for the Hungarians.

This system of economic relations between Gypsies and Hungarians can be best described as a form of hierarchy involving patron–client relationships. As will become clear below, I use the term 'hierarchy' in the sense in which Graeber understands it, that is, as a relation between parties where one party is considered to be 'socially superior', and that is opposed to the relations of 'communism' that are characterised by cooperation and sharing, and of 'exchange' that presume equivalence (Graeber 2010: 6).

This patron–client tie was an asymmetrical, long-term relation that comprised an element of affection as well as mutual obligations on the part of both parties. In Lápos, every single peasant (Hungarian) had their 'own Gypsy'. The client (the Gypsy) provided day labour and other small services to their patron (the Hungarian). In return, they received a small payment, either in money or in kind, which was usually well below the market price of their service. In addition to the payment, and in return for the steady availability of the client's labour, the patron also provided flexible assistance for their client whenever special needs or emergencies arose (Platteau 1995). According to the relevant literature, this rural patron–client tie was 'not limited to transactions of economic goods and services but also include[d] symbolic exchanges of personal favours and obligations' (ibid.: 767). One of these favours involved a patron lending money (without interest) to their client in situations of need.

With the out-migration of the majority of the local Hungarian population and the impoverishment of the remaining few, the long-established patron–client relation gave way to the debt relation as the dominant organising principle of local society (see also Hrustič, this volume). Not only in this village but also in other poor, segregated rural Gypsy communities in Hungary, debt relations have become the dominant type of economic connection (Béres and Lukács 2008). In Lápos, people have been living with spiralling amounts of debt in recent years. According to my last household survey in the village in 2011, 98 per cent of the Gypsy population have some kind of debt, whether to formal banks, public utility companies, pawnbrokers or local moneylenders.

Debt Relations and Other Coping Strategies

With patron–client ties and formal work relations disappearing, the Láposian Gypsies have had to look for different ways of making a living and of coping with economic uncertainty and poverty. They have only one certain and regular income source: various kinds of welfare benefits (that is, child and housing benefits, and, for the elderly, the old age pension). However, it is widely accepted that one cannot subsist on these allowances alone (Ferge 2010; Virág 2010). Hence, the Láposian Gypsies engage in different kinds of informal income-generating activities: most of them collect herbs or mushrooms from spring until autumn, some collect scrap metal, others pick through rubbish (lomizík). Some try to find occasional employment with the Hungarians in the neighbouring settlements, or, if they are lucky, the mayor will take them on for public work.

To be employed in public work is a privilege because the salary is double the amount received as welfare. Also, according to the law, one has to be employed on public works for at least one month in a year in order to remain eligible for unemployment benefit. It is the head of the local government who allocates public work. The mayor decides – generally on the basis of 'worthiness' – to whom he will bestow their favours, including the offer of a position as a public worker. 'I told them that when they come to my office shouting they appear uncivilised, blockheaded, and that until they do not cultivate their [newly acquired] garden, I will not give them employment', Kópi said to me shortly after his election. In this sense, the mayor performs the role of patron to the poor by trying to assist them (with state money), provided they learn the 'civilised', 'proper way of living' – that is, provided they fulfil the condition of becoming 'deserving poor'.

Over the last fifteen years, those few who consider themselves 'clever' enough have turned to the high-risk work of informal moneylending in order to supplement their welfare. For a group for whom access to economic success, personal wealth and social mobility by conventional means (that is, a good education and then a well-paid job) is clearly limited, the only territory for advancement is the informal economy. In this situation, informal (money) lending is one of the rare opportunities to obtain some badly needed income and gain social mobility in circumstances of chronic unemployment. It is worth noting, though, that informal lending has recently become increasingly risky, since the Hungarian government now treats usury as a criminal act punishable by up to three years in prison.[3]

However, borrowing money at interest is only the last resort for the poor in need. Before they resort to this source of 'help', they try other, cheaper loan opportunities to remedy their constant lack of cash. One widely used source of credit is the district Cooperative (*Takarékszövetkezet*). Having realised that it cannot afford to lose its best clients (the Gypsies), the Cooperative has adapted its lending practices to the changing social and economic circumstances by developing new techniques to avoid the problem of non-repayment among their occasionally employed clients (Durst 2008). The trouble with the Cooperative's loans, from the point of view of the clients, is that one can get them only once every two years, and only after having repaid the previous loan in full.

Besides the Cooperative, another formal saving and lending bank, Evidencia, has also adjusted its financial services to meet the needs of poor Gypsies. It recently found an innovative way, based not only on formal contracts but also on trust, to help those of its clients in constant financial crisis borrow and make repayments. Trust is a crucial issue in economic transactions. As Deans (2004) argues, based on the Romungro community she researched, Gypsies are more inclined to distrust 'non-brothers' ('non-*testvér*', as she calls them), including formal institutions, than extended family members. Among 'non-brothers', they only trust those with whom they have long established social or economic transactions. Among the 'non-brothers' they trust are local nurses, primarily because of the regular contact Gypsy women have with them. This is the reason why in some villages Evidencia employs the village nurse as its local lending agent. Gypsy women prefer to turn for help (*segítségért*) to her rather than to informal money-lenders, and to borrow money in a situation of financial crisis. They recognise, however, the similarities between the practices of the bank and informal moneylenders (*kamatosok*): 'She [the nurse] is just the same as the *kamatosok*', explained one of the Gypsy women, 'I ask for 50,000 forints [€200], and in the end, I have to pay back double the amount'.

Another potential source of help is the safety network of kinship – a type of social capital, a web of social favours in which members of kinship groups provide different kinds of help (access to scarce resources) to other members in need, in the expectation that these favours will be repaid sometime in the future. Following Graeber, we can refer to this safety network of kinship solidarity as 'baseline communism', a principle that covers any human relationship operating on the premise: 'from each according to their abilities, to each according to their needs' (Graeber 2010: 4). Graeber admits that instead of 'communism', he could have used a more neutral term such as 'solidarity', 'mutual aid' or even 'help'; these are the terms I will employ most often in this chapter.

Graeber's point here – that the 'the obligation to share food and other basic necessities is intrinsic to everyday morality in egalitarian societies (those not divided into fundamentally different sorts of being)' (ibid.: 6) – was held to be true in many Gypsy communities in Hungary in the recent past (Stewart 1994). Even today, the Láposian Gypsies regard themselves as members of an egalitarian society in the sense that they all have essentially the same social status: all of them are unemployed and receive roughly the same amount of welfare per head.

Recently, however, due to their extreme poverty, the pool of goods they are able to share has been shrinking. The need for and practice of sharing are still present, but to a lesser extent. The most frequently shared commodities or costs nowadays are for food, medicines and funerals. Rozika still feeds her in-laws' hungry children whenever she can 'find the means for cooking' (*kikeríti a főznivalót*). Every member of the banda still contributes, according to their financial ability, to the cost of funerals of family members. Although these circles of solidarity are generally limited to the extended family – or, with the recent rise in poverty, to close family and sometimes next-door neighbours – on the rare occasions of family tragedies they incorporate the whole village. For example, when Rozika's cousin Zsolti, a popular young man, passed away unexpectedly, leaving behind seven children, almost every Gypsy gave his widow a small amount of money on the day they received their social benefits to help cover the cost of the funeral.

These days the material resources of kinship groups have been exhausted. The only people that can provide social security and secure livelihoods in these circumstances are the local representatives of the state. However, local state actors (in particular the mayor, who is the local distributor of state provisions) provide access to economic resources (such as public work, emergency aid) only to those who are judged 'deserving' (see also Thelen, Cartwright and Sikor 2008).

For the 'undeserving' yet needy poor, there are limited options open to people for securing their livelihoods: formal lending institutions (local savings banks and pawnshops), and informal ones (moneylenders). Rozika explained why she had had to turn to the local moneylender, Zolika (one of her 'brothers'), a year ago when she was in dire need: 'You know how it works ... Earlier, I would rather have sold the TV or taken my earrings to the pawnshop so as not to go into it. I only had to go into this "money with interest" because I didn't have anywhere to turn to when I had to take Emi [her child] to hospital'.

'Doing Interest': Hierarchical Redistribution

Gypsies in both Lápos and the region as a whole have invented a specific, innovative and meaningful vocabulary regarding informal moneylending. The Hungarian term *kamatolás* (verb) or *kamatos pénz* (noun), which they use to speak of usury, can be best translated into English as 'doing interest' or 'money with interest'.

If we understand the logic of 'doing [money with] interest' (that is, informal moneylending) and the way in which borrowers and lenders construct and rationalise their behaviour as parties involved in the transaction, then we come closer to answering the main question of this chapter. Specifically, we will shed light on how it is possible that within a community such as Lápos, where people of equal social standing emphasise (ideologically, at least) the values of equality and solidarity, a few can pursue their economic self-interest by exploiting their fellows, yet still be considered a part of the moral community.

My argument here is that we need to regard informal moneylending as a hierarchical social relation, or, to be more precise, as a 'hierarchical redistribution' between parties, one of whom considers themselves socially superior.[4] What moneylenders really do is redistribute social provisions (see also James 2012). By so doing, they generate their own income from others' needs. Still, the redistributors maintain the appearance of solidarity by 'representing themselves as the protectors of the helpless' (Graeber 2010: 13).

Zolika's self-perception and rationalisation of his business is a clear example of this representation. It also indicates how important it is for him to keep up the appearance of solidarity, of helping those in need:

> I must say, those who ask for a loan from me are stupid, dumb (*buta*). They are the lowest level of the Gypsies. I can only feel sorry for them that they couldn't be born into a better family to learn to be clever (*okos*). You must be clever to find some way to keep your family. You can't live from welfare; it's not enough for anything. Those who come to me for help can't budget their money. On payday they go to Tesco and buy everything. And then on the other days they starve. At least with my help, they can eat and drink during the whole month. They can thank me that they don't starve to death.

As his remarks show, Zolika perceives himself as superior, being 'clever' enough to be able to make a living for his family, unlike the 'dumb' Gypsies in Lápos, his borrowers. At the same time, however, he also conceptualises and represents himself as a 'helper' of the poor, and in so doing he justifies his business.

In fact, Zolika's clients concur with this representation of him as their 'helper'. As Rozika said once, 'Actually, he is a good-hearted man. If the [electricity] company wants to turn off the light in your house or they want to take somebody to prison, he helps; he always pays up for them'. Of course, this is not charity; it is a loan with interest to a person in trouble.

Thanks to Zolika performing the role of 'helper', the local population more or less accepts his financial services, considering them 'fair' moneylending. The main criteria of 'fairness' (that is, where one shows solidarity with one's poor clients) seems to be universal in the region. However, in an economic sense, the fairness of the deal (that is, the rate of interest) is relative and may be different in each village. According to public opinion in Borsod, 'fair' interest is 50 per cent per item – regardless of whether the loan is paid back in a day or in a month; however, residents of different villages consider different rates acceptable or fair, depending on the local supply and the competition. While people in the neighbouring settlement of Lápos are satisfied with an interest rate of 'one-to-two' (that is, 50 per cent interest for those who are not kin, and 25 per cent for relatives), there are other places where moneylenders demand 100 per cent interest. In Lápos, where almost every Gypsy is related, the interest level is 70 per cent, even for a 'brother'. Although this meets with a great deal of disapproval among Láposians ('How stupid is it – to profiteer from a brother?!'), they still accept this rate because, as they say, 'the Gypsies here have got used to it', and because their main moneylender, Zolika, has many brothers, and therefore 'his big family would blow away all his money' if he were to make exceptions for his kin.

A 'fair' and hence successful moneylender such as Zolika knows the monthly income of all his clients off the top of his head. He knows exactly how much he can give so that they will be able to pay him back (or at least pay the interest) at the beginning of the following month. This may then lead to them asking for another loan in order to repay what they still owe, which yields yet more interest. In this way, moneylending is a regular income-earning activity for the lender, and a never-ending spiral of debt for the borrower, who may eventually lose track of how much they owe. It is almost impossible to repay the accumulated debt in one go. On the rare occasions when a borrower cannot even pay the interest, Zolika takes possession of that person's house, which he puts in the name of one of his grown-up children, while still maintaining the appearance of helping that person: instead of making the borrower's family homeless, he rents the house back to the borrower.

Although Zolika's possession of the borrower's house' may seem rapacious to many, Láposian Gypsies still place the practice in the category of 'fair lending with interest', partly because he uses his money for his own family's financial betterment. As one of his clients from his *banda* put it: 'You've got to make a living somehow. And hats off to him, he is looking after his kids with his profit'.

In contrast to the 'fair' moneylender, people from Lápos and elsewhere in Borsod decry the kind of 'vulturous' (*dögös*), rapacious lender who, as one Borsodian businessman put it, 'Only sees his own interest while exploiting the borrowers. He loans money at high interest to anybody, even to his kin. He does not invest the profit he collected, but spends it on himself'. This is the type of moneylender that the media reports on when speaking about usury.

Kópi and His Social Shop

This is the social context which frames Kópi's election as mayor. Before the election, Kópi was a Gypsy businessman with a middle-sized business, and his social network included entrepreneurs and politicians all over the county. Running his businesses was already a big achievement considering his family background. He was born into a poor family in the Gypsy settlement of a big village not far from Lápos. His level of education can be regarded as typical of his village: he had, as had many other Gypsy men, 11 years of schooling. After finishing primary school, he trained as a gas and heating maintenance service provider. However, this profession did not bring him the 'quick money' he longed for, nor did it allow him to escape the Gypsy settlement and poverty. In pursuit of financial betterment, he made his own luck by migrating to Budapest to start up informal economic activities. However, when he returned to his native village as a Gypsy with money, he found that he was still discriminated against for being a Gypsy. Gradually, he learnt how to 'sell himself' in order to be successful in every area of life.[5]

In his search for respect, he decided to try to become a local politician in order to prove to the Hungarians that a Gypsy is not their inferior, that 'a Gypsy can be up to some good, too'. He knew that he would not have a chance to become a mayor in a municipality inhabited primarily by Hungarians, however, so he had to find a Gypsy village.

For a while, Lápos seemed like a perfect choice. Although he was not socially embedded in the local community, having only two relatives there (Chita, his cousin, and Chita's sister), the local Gypsies elected him mayor. Soon he found local supporters, members of the Fóti *banda*. In return to their support, he took them on for public work after he was elected mayor.

Kópi's nine months as mayor can be summarised as follows: In his endeavour to help the village out of poverty, and to gain personally in the process (both materially and symbolically), he tried to reduce the informal lending of the Baloghs, especially Zolika. In pursuit of this, he opened his own local grocery store – what he called a 'social shop' (*szociális bolt*) – to advertise his social sensitivity towards the poor. According to his plan, he would 'help the poor Gypsies in the village to not go hungry' by letting them buy food and drink in his shop on credit. With his help, he reasoned, the Gypsies would not need to turn to Zolika in times of need.

With Kópi's arrival, the Gypsies had to adapt to a new form of 'help' from their local state representative. Up until then they had been used to a different kind of assistance from their previous (Hungarian) mayor, who had played the role of local patron during his eight years in office. He usually lent them money from his own pocket, or from the local government budget, and withdrew their debt on payday from their social benefits.

Kópi had a different idea of 'helping'. Unfortunately for him, however, he got his calculations wrong. First, he overestimated the amount he could loan out in a month. One month after the opening of his shop, his outstanding debt amounted to 5 million Hungarian forints (about €20,000). Some people even thought that the goods at the shop were 'free' because of its name. To collect his outstanding debts, he introduced a new way of lending and collecting, whereby he would lend money for the second half of the month, and then only after his borrowers had repaid their previous debt. Soon he realised that many would not pay him back of their own free will, so the only way to get his money back would be to use his power as mayor to deduct the debt from the borrower's welfare. (This was easily arranged, since in Hungary the mayor's office is responsible for distributing welfare to those on benefits.)

Thus, Kópi breached the precedent set by the old moneylender, Zolika, to which the Gypsies had grown accustomed. Such actions can be dangerous, since, as Graeber (2010) stresses, hierarchy is based on precedent. In contrast to Zolika, Kópi did not let the debts run up, but froze them for the first two weeks of the month. This caused rebellion among many of the borrowers, the reason for which was neatly explained to me by Rozika, who had previously supported the new mayor. According to her and many other Gypsies, the main problem with Kópi's new system was that he did not lend continuously, and when he froze loans for a certain period, the Gypsies went hungry:

> With Zolika it worked better. You gave in [partly repaid] your debt, but you also got back some. Let's say I owed 50 [thousand forints], but I always got back 35. Then I had the family's child benefits clear and we could keep everything going; everything was clear [tiszta, literally meaning 'fair', 'transparent'], everything was in motion, but now it is all stuck like a piece of wood.

In addition, Kópi did not take into account the tension between his two conflicting roles: that of mayor (essentially a patron) and that of businessman. The role of mayor, according to the Gypsies in Lápos, should be to pursue the 'community's interest', to provide social security and to secure local livelihoods. A shopkeeper, meanwhile, only pursues his own economic interest and does not care about the needs of his clients. Chita's mother-in-law described this tension as follows:

> He was confused. Was he a shopkeeper or a mayor? Why didn't he act like a man, like a mayor? Then we wouldn't have been troubled. He should've asked, 'How much can you give [me back]; can you clear your debt? Is that any trouble?' That's it! Not like, 'I take your social [benefits], and withdraw it, and I don't put it in your hand'.

This lack of solidarity with the poor was the final nail in Kópi's coffin. Because Kópi could not maintain the appearance of being a 'helper of the poor', as the previous mayor managed to do, and as he had also originally planned to do with the opening of his 'social shop', he failed in the sense that his enemies were successful in having him sent to prison. This was the reason why Chita (among others) felt that Kópi 'rapaciously exploits the Gypsies', and why she had therefore had enough of him. Chita finally reported him to the police with the encouragement of the district notary, Kópi's Hungarian superior. Chita explained her reasons as follows:

> Although he was of the same blood [i.e., he was a Gypsy], he couldn't think through what it was like being in need. Of course, he knew. Earlier, he had also been in a situation where he was in need. He held back 103,000 forints [€400] of mine and I was left there with 3,000 forints [€2] for the whole month. He said I must pay my debt and then he will give me [food] again from the shop. He withdrew all our money. Two days later, I went up to him and said, 'What's it going to be? I have nothing to give my children to eat'. He says, 'That's your business; work it out'. Well, I did work it out. He is now doing time; now he needs to work it out. I worked out one month; he now works out all the rest.

Conclusion: The Lessons of Kópi's Fall

This analysis of the practice of informal lending in Lápos, and especially of the conflict between villagers and their old and new moneylenders, has several theoretical implications.

First of all, it draws our attention to the real nature of informal moneylending, which is not a simple debt relation, and hence a form of unbalanced exchange (Graeber 2011), but rather a hierarchical redistribution. However, this redistribution does not seem to correct the inequalities caused by the market, as sociological theories of social inequality (Szelényi 1983) assume. To the contrary, it actually increases them, at least as far as segregated rural communities in Hungary are concerned, by producing new kinds of inequality.

The second major implication of the Láposian story is that contrary to claims in both public media and earlier studies borrowers do not necessarily condemn all kinds of usury. They differentiate between two types of informal moneylending: the 'fair' and the 'vulturous' (rapacious), as Gypsies refer to them in this region. While they approve of that which they consider 'fair', they condemn the 'vulturous' lending of money at interest, and this condemnation has serious consequences for social relations between lenders and their clients. Thanks to social norms, even in very poor communities, borrowers can sanction their debtor if they feel they rapaciously exploit them, that is, imposes debt upon them beyond locally accepted norms.

Another important lesson of the story is that informal moneylending can have positive, albeit unintended consequences for the state, the very institution that seeks to suppress it (see also Portes 2010). Informal moneylending provides a 'cushion' (ibid.: 159) or buffer between the state and impoverished, marginalised people by offering the latter cash and commodities where and when they are most needed. By providing a valuable informal financial service to a huge section of the population that has exhausted its possibilities for engaging in all formal banking and exchange systems (including the resources of kinship), it contributes to political stability and social peace. Because of this buffering function, informal moneylending survives – and even thrives in times of need – despite legal prohibition.

Last but not least, Kópi's story teaches us that the economic activity of unregistered lending has its own rules, which have to be followed if one wishes to be successful in this line of business. Above all, the moneylender must know the social norms of the community in which their economic activity is embedded. Furthermore, their rules of business conduct must be transparent (*tiszta*) and must not break the precedent established by former moneylenders to the community. On top of this, in a small-scale, tight-knit community criss-crossed by relations of kinship, in which principles of social solidarity and individual profit-maximising coexist, and whose members have become used to patron–client relations, informal moneylenders would do well to assume the role of 'helper of the poor', at least in appearance, in order to meet the expectation of social solidarity on the part of community members (his clients). The village's previous informal lender, Zolika, had been successful in this regard, whereas Kópi, his successor, had not, and this was partly the reason why this kinship-sensitive Láposian Gypsy community had tolerated its old, well-established moneylender but drove away its new one.

Nowadays, seemingly, there is peace in the village. Kópi has been released from prison and is now on probation. Having learnt his lesson, he made Zolika a 'frienemy'[6] by offering him the position of foreman on public work projects. Zolika has returned to his old business: he lends money, food, clothes (and recently even electricity) at interest to his clientele. He is once again, according to his clients, the 'helper of the poor', without whom they 'would starve to death'.

Postscript: At the time of writing this chapter, Zolika was elected deputy mayor – and Kópi got re-elected as mayor.

Acknowledgements

I am indebted to Michael Stewart and Martin Fotta for their suggestions on the first draft of this chapter. I also thank Micol Brazzabeni and Iván Szelényi for their valuable comments during the writing process.

NOTES

1. All personal names used in this chapter are pseudonyms, as is the name of the settlement. When referring to the local community, I employ the terminology used by its members. Locals refer to themselves as Gypsy (*Cigány*), and everybody else – that is, non-Gypsies (*Gadzso*) – as Hungarian (*Magyar*) or as 'peasant' (*paraszt*). The distinction between the categories 'Gypsy' and 'Hungarian/Magyar' has until now been one of the main rules governing interaction in local rural societies (Horváth 2012). My fieldwork in Lápos over the last ten years serves as the basis of my arguments here.
2. For Hungary, see Acton (2012); for a review of the 'moralising Western literature' on this topic, see Goddard (2005).
3. The newly introduced Hungarian Usury Act (2012), which represents a tightening of previous criminal law (due to the high prevalence of 'usury' in the country), declares 'zero tolerance' towards informal moneylending: even first-time offenders can face imprisonment.
4. I use the term 'redistribution' in the sense of the local discourse. In Lápos Kópi, a mayor and moneylender, is seen as the re-distributor of money that originates from social transfers, albeit this re-distribution serves as a source of his enrichment.
5. In places where nobody knew Kópi, he started to introduce himself to girls as a Greek or Italian because, as he explained, in Hungary, 'where there are (only) Gypsies and Hungarians, being a Gypsy is a shame, but being a Greek or Italian is a glory. My girlfriends used to boast about how cool it was to have an Italian boyfriend'.
6. This informal term is sometimes used in English to refer to a friend whose trustworthiness or allegiance is uncertain.

REFERENCES

Acton, T. 2012. 'The Demonization of the Gypsy Moneylender and the Social Construction of the Rom as a European Minority'. Paper delivered at the 40th World Congress of the International Institute of Sociology, New Delhi, 4 September.
Béres, T., and G. Lukács. 2008. 'Kamatos Pénz a Csereháton'. *Esély* 5: 71–97.
Deans, F.M.M. 2004. 'Culture, Community and Enterprise in a Hungarian Romany Settlement', Ph.D. diss. London: University College London.
Durkheim, É. 1897. *Le suicide*. Paris: Baillière.
Durst, J. 2008. '"Bárók", Patrónusok, Versus Komák. Eltérő Fejlődési útak az Aprófalvakban', in M. Váradi (ed.), *Aprófalusi Közelképek*. Budapest: Napvilág, pp. 137–59.

———. 2010. '"Minden évben Máshogy Fordul a Világ": A Telepfelszámolástól a Szegregált Cigány Faluig'. *Anblokk* 4: 34–38.

Ferge, Z. 2010. *Társadalmi Áramlatok és Egyéni Szerepek*. Budapest: Napvilág.

Fotta, M. 2012. 'The Bankers of the Backlands: Financialisation and the Calon-Gypsies in Bahia', Ph.D. diss. London: Goldsmiths College, University of London.

Goddard, M. 2005. 'Expressions of Interest: Informal Usury in Urban Papua New Guinea', *Pacific Studies* 28(1/2): 42–67.

Graeber, D. 2010. On the Moral Grounds of Economic Relations: A Maussian Approach. Open Anthropology Press, Working Papers Series No. 6. Retrieved 10 October 2012 from http://openanthcoop.net/press/2010/11/17/on-the-moral-grounds-of-economic-relations/.

———. 2011. *Debt: The First 5,000 Years*. New York: Melville House.

Horváth, K. 2012. 'Silencing and Naming the Difference', in M. Stewart (ed.), *The Gypsy 'Menace': Populism and the New Anti-Gypsy Politics*. London: Hurst, pp.117–35.

James, D. 2012. 'Money-Go-Round: Personal Economies of Wealth, Aspiration and Indebtedness', *Africa* 82(1): 20–40.

Kaplan, L.J., and S. Matteis. 1968. 'The Economics of Loansharking', *American Journal of Economics and Sociology* 27(3): 239–52.

Kertesi, G. 2005. *A Társadalom Peremén. Romák a Munkaerőpiacon és az Iskolában*. Budapest: Osiris.

Platteau, J. 1995. 'A Framework for the Analysis of Evolving Patron–Client Ties in Agrarian Economies', *World Development* 23(5): 767–86.

Portes, A. 2010. *Economic Sociology: A Systematic Inquiry*. Princeton: Princeton University Press.

Stewart, M.S. 1994. *Daltestvérek: az Oláhcigány Identitás és Közösség Továbbélése a Szocialista Magyarországon* (Song Brothers: Vlax Gypsy identity and the community's survival in socialist Hungary). Budapest: T-Twins Publishing/MTA Institute for Sociology/Max Weber Foundation.

Szelényi, I. 1983. *Urban Inequalities under State Socialism*. Oxford: Oxford University Press.

Thelen, T., A. Cartwright and T. Sikor. 2008. 'Local State and Social Security in Rural Communities: A New Research Agenda and the Example of Postsocialist Europe', Max Planck Institute for Social Anthropology Working Paper No.105. Halle/Saale: Max Planck Institute for Social Anthropology.

Virág, T. 2010. 'Az Átengedett Munka', in M. Feischmidt (ed.), *Különbségteremtő társadalom. Tanulmányok az etnicitás témaköréből*. Budapest: Osiris, pp.254–65.

Wilson, W.J. 1999. *When Work Disappears: The World of the New Urban Poor*. New York: Vintage Books.

Judit Durst is Honorary Research Associate in the Department of Anthropology, University College London. Her doctorate in sociology focused on social exclusion, ethnicity and reproductive decision-making among the Roma in rural 'ghetto' villages in the Borsod region, Hungary. Between 2009 and 2012 she was Bolyai Postdoctoral Research Fellow at the Institute of Sociology and Social Policy, Corvinus University, Budapest, where she is still, intermittently, a visiting lecturer. She is a member of the Scientific Committee of the European Academic Network on Romani Studies and was faculty member many times of the Central European University (CEU) Summer University on Romani Studies.

Chapter 3

 A Way of Life Flowing in the Interstices

Cigano Horse Dealers in Alentejo, Portugal

SARA SAMA ACEDO

Évora's horse market, the Feria de São João, held every June on the field of the 'Nomads' Camp', had just finished, but the members of the Riveiro family were not in a good mood. Zé and his wife condemned this Alentejo city and the Nomads' Camp, where they had been living for over a month.[1] They complained about the money 'ill spent' on two horses that they had purchased, aided by *velho* (old) Ruy. They had paid him a *cortagem* (commission) for mediating, but no one turned up at the fair to close the sale, despite *velho* Ruy's assurances. They could not ask him to return the *cortagem*. If they wished to continue living at the Nomads' Camp periodically – and, potentially, close deals further down the line – they could not jeopardise their relationship with him or with his relatives who controlled the camp.

Moreover, the Riveiros could no longer remain legally at the Nomads' Camp. The police had already ordered them to take down their tents as soon as the fair was over. They were considered 'nomads' and were treated as such. Other Ciganos living permanently in the Nomads' Camp also pressed them to leave.[2] They did not want to answer for the 'nomads' if the police returned. It was time to leave Évora and try to make up for the losses incurred there somewhere else. A multi-sided conversation ensued about the rumours heard at the fair, about who was buying and selling horses where, opportunities for fruit picking, and the pay rates that summer. Zé's brother Joaquím suggested trying their luck at the next cattle fair. He had heard about a possible buyer, and he also knew where to collect old horses for reselling to an abattoir. Either because of 'loathing' or because they did not have sure-fire contacts there, Zé left that plan to his brother, preferring to go along with his wife's proposal of returning to a small village and to its aggregation of shacks they called *a nossa casa* (our home). The place was inhabited by a part of the large group of relatives that made up Zé's and Joaquím's *raça*.³ There, they would remain until they received their next welfare payment.⁴ By clearing the weeds at the surrounding farms, they would have enough fodder for the horses, and with their family's help, they would also be able to feed their children. Zé's eldest son and his wife did not go with them, however. Recently married and without children, they wanted to 'negotiate' their own life. They decided to travel to Spain to work in the tomato harvest, as the whole family had done in previous years.

This snapshot of the life of a domestic group reveals the complexity of the socio-territorial economic dynamics of Ciganos. Among this ethnic group, only a minority are still devoted to itinerant small-scale horse trading, the main occupation of Ciganos in the region until the advent of rural mechanisation and urban development around 1950. This activity is the result of myriad interrelating practices, relationships, spatialities and temporalities, both, intra- and inter-ethnic, old and new.

The horse-trading Ciganos maintain a network of places that they have often frequented over generations. Among these, one or two stand out as places of repeated, but not continuous, residence. Deep rooting within this network, in combination with other forms of old and new territorial exclusivities, orders intra-ethnic access to material and symbolic resources. Permanence, deep rooting, territorial exclusivity and intense mobility are therefore not contradictory (cf. Piasere 1992), while the spatial and temporal dynamics of economic activities that arise from within Cigano sociality interact with, and are shaped by, official policies and regulations (cf. Okely 1983).

Central and local authorities have for decades treated poor itinerant Ciganos as 'nomads', according to two distinct 'grammars' (Bauman 2006). One links Ciganos with marginal and illegal activities, and another reflects the official identity of Ciganos as essentially 'nomadic' and 'rootless'. This official double bind often leads to a lack of coordination and interconnection in social aid programmes and policies designed to support the 'Cigano minority'. Police surveillance over their economic practices, movement and residence responds to the 'marginalist perspective', while places such as the Nomads' Camp in Évora are the spatial and practical expression of the 'nomad' as a contradictory category used to classify the poorest Ciganos. Planned as a temporary site, this was the only place in Évora where people like the Riveiros could legally camp. Over time, however, the Nomads' Camp was transformed into a place within which some Ciganos have found themselves permanently enclaved, waiting to gain access to social housing and other benefits belonging to an urban way of life. They also gradually appropriated this space through implementing new and traditional forms of intra-ethnic exclusivity and economic practices.

In this chapter, I argue that two sets of relationships must be examined in order to understand the permanence of this way of life. First, the intra-ethnic spatialities and forms of territorial exclusiveness maintained over time that regulate access to spaces of economic activities; and second, the problematic relationship between these particular Ciganos and the civil administration, which insists on classifying and keeping them as 'nomads'. By exploring the dialectics between the two, we can analyse how economic subsistence practices emerge between the urban and rural spaces, new and traditional locations for business, between fixedness and itinerancy, legal and illegal activities, and between old and new intra-ethnic power relationships. 'Interstitial' seems a fitting term to characterise this economy and the spaces in which it flows: it is part of the system at a specific moment, related to specific actions of city planners, the police, Ciganos, non-Cigano neighbours and so on, but develops according to a logic not envisioned by the authorities, between instances, gaps or cracks in a framework or structure. In the words of Pignarre and Stengers, an 'interstice is defined neither against nor in relation to the bloc to which it nevertheless belongs. It creates its own dimensions starting from concrete processes that confer on it its consistency and scope, what it concerns and who [sic] it concerns' (Pignarre and Stengers 2011: 110).

Mobility, Territories and Interstices

The theory of so-called peripatetic groups springs to mind when attempting to characterise the economic practices engaged in by horse-trading Ciganos. Authors such as Berland (1979), Hayden (1979) and Rao (1987) have attempted to theoretically capture a kind of mobility that is usually planned and systematic rather than haphazard, and linked to diffuse and fluctuating demands for goods and services, which requires active mobility in space. Their descriptions of mobility fit well with the character of mobility practised by horse-trading Ciganos. At the same time, the analysis of mobility must be completed, acknowledging the relevance of Cigano settlement practices in specific places, some of which have been frequented for generations.

One way to do this is by extending the view of these classic theorists of peripatetic groups by taking into account the contributions of authors who pointed out the relevance of territory and territoriality as a means to understand the forms of mobility and identification processes of Gypsies. For example, in the case of American Gypsy groups, Salo (1987) showed how territory was key to understanding relationships within and between the different groups within the overall Gypsy niche. Piasere (1992), while discussing the Romá and Roma in north-east Italy, similarly argued for the necessity of focusing on territoriality, not only as an adaptive strategy, which characterised the unitary theory of peripateticism, but also as a practice that responds to the history of economic and social relationships of specific groups and to their internal organisation. Recently, Theodosiou (2003), writing about the Gypsies of Parakalamos, northern Greece, analysed how the place, its location (both physical and symbolic) and history are involved in processes of otherness and identification.

In the specific case of Portugal, some anthropologists have described how the Ciganos' lived territories are traced out through administrative pressure, intra-ethnic conflicts, emotions and specificities of family histories (e.g. Castro 2004, 2007, 2010; Brazzabeni 2012a, 2012b). From a different perspective, Bastos (2007) described what he calls the 'hyperterritorialisation' of Ciganos, a dynamic of intra-ethnic status segmentation, to refer to settlement patterns in Sintra. In my own work on Ciganos from Évora, a population hierarchically stratified in terms of socio-economic status, I pointed out that neither rooting within a territory nor territoriality are opposed to mobility/settlement dynamics (Sama Acedo 2003, 2009). Besides that, I found, that rootedness in specific territories where people hold one or more places of residence is an important piece in socio-economic organisation and identification processes. Territory emerges from dynamics of specific or abstract appropriation (that is, of resources, or through representation, respectively), carried out over time. It involves some exclusivities that have their origins in the past, and as a geographical, semantic and social space, encompasses and in turn produces and reproduces the local memory of Ciganos. These exclusivities are, however, in continuous reassessment in the light of shifting inter- and intra-ethnic relationships, and are constantly updated, producing a new topography on the ground. This imbues meaning to people's present actions and projects, to the ways in which the rights to use territory are handled, and also to limitations and restrictions on the use of the territory's resources (both material and symbolic) (see García García 1976: 77; Raffestin 1981; Piasere 1987, 1992; Magnaghi 1990; Santos 2002).

Another important contribution of the classic theory of 'peripatetic groups' was the attention paid to the interrelation between the character of socio-economic 'niche' and specific economic strategies. Peripatetic groups have been seen as strategically employing a variety of flexible skills and knowledge about resources within the larger eco-cultural system in order to exploit them. In this way, people develop and maintain a 'distinct peripatetic niche', which results from satisfying 'demand for specialized goods and/or services that sedentary communities cannot, or will not support on a permanent basis' (Berland and Salo 1986: 2). These dimensions 'are subject to manipulation to some degree and it is precisely this manipulation of the social environment that is at the heart of the Gypsy adaptation' (Salo 1987: 105).

This concept of 'niche' has been borrowed from ecology and describes the process of competition between two or more groups over one or more scarce resources, as well as the concept of strategies of adaptation to a habitat (Love 1977). These processes, widely used in classic studies regarding Gypsies and their economic activities, have more recently included the complexities of intra- and inter-ethnic relationships over time and in different contexts. This is especially evident in the works of Okely (1983), Piasere (1992), San Román (1997) and Stewart (1997), as well as some authors in this volume who, from different points of view, stress the importance of focusing on the diversity and dynamism of socio-economic practices, spaces, relationships and statuses that shape the economic 'niches' of Gypsies around Europe. Not all of these reflect a search for the rational maximisation of resources or always involve a competition between majority and minority. In the case of Alentejo, for instance, there is a heterogeneity of Cigano resource exploitation within a single location, and access to resources and competition possibilities varies depending on differences in historical socio-economic statuses linked to particular places. In this sense, rather than focusing on the manipulation and management of already pre-existing resources in their environment, scholars need to recognise the diverse socio-spatial relations and instances behind and between any Gypsy niche specialisation. Concerning this, I find that 'interstice' is a concept that analytically captures this issue. It has a long tradition in anthropology (Nadel 1956; Wolf 1966; Thrasher 1967; de Certeau 1996) and has been currently revived in the discipline, as well as in human geography, to illuminate the everyday aspects of spaces, groups and activities that exist between the main economic and political institutions, between the formal and informal, the licit and illicit (e.g. Mann 1986; Holloway 2002; Galemba 2008). Within Romani studies, some scholars have also employed the term with some success (e.g. Bancroft 2005; Grygar 2006; Fotta 2012). 'Interstices' are spaces of activities that emerge and are created between instances, gaps or cracks in a framework or structure, as well as in intervals between times and places. Inasmuch as interstices arise from specific historical dynamics within a specific milieu on which they depend, but which, nevertheless, does not predetermine their nature, in what follows I address how the Nomads' Camp in Évora, an interstitial space itself, was lived in, economically appropriated and used in ways that could not have been foreseen by the authorities, and how these ephemeral interstitial activities emerged from specific historical processes and socio-logics among Ciganos themselves and between Ciganos and the non-Cigano majority.

Between the *Malta* and the 'Nomads'

Most of the poorest Ciganos of Alentejo who are still involved in small-scale horse trading are descendants of several generations of poor Ciganos left out of successive processes of settlement and incorporation into socially acknowledged employment, in which other Ciganos participated from as early as the sixteenth century (Vasconcelos 1982: 364; Coelho 1995: 213). From the second half of the nineteenth century until the period immediately prior to rural mechanisation, poor Ciganos occupied the lowest level of the regional social hierarchy, a position justified by a positive appraisal of sedentary life that enabled formal employment, and the ownership of land and working animals (Sama Acedo 2009: 83). They were part of the so-called *malta* or *maltêses* (see Ribeiro 1979: 121; Fatela 1989: 219),[5] and classified alongside unemployed seasonal farm workers, beggars and others who shared the same pitiful niche afforded by reliance on alms, petty theft and sporadic ill-paid employment. They compensated their extreme precariousness and social marginality with patronage relationships with richer settled Ciganos – unequal relationships that ended up limiting their options for taking part in urban development.

The activities of settled Ciganos were focused on raising and trading horses from at least the end of the eighteenth century, though probably earlier. Some of them were economically successful, since the region required working animals for farming, mines and the military. This Cigano elite eventually devoted itself to selling horses on a large scale, and owned or rented their own farms. Even during my fieldwork, the descendants of this elite considered themselves, and were considered by other Ciganos, as *fidalgos* (noble persons), and within the elite's oldest and most prestigious *raças*, some men were referred to as *donos* (masters). Their position was founded on the traditional relationships inherent in patronage systems within the agriculture-based Alentejo, and their power was based on their having lived in cities and their surroundings for generations, forging close links with local political, administrative and religious authorities. They maintained inter- and intra-ethnic social order, managed businesses and settlements, and distributed favours across a well-demarcated territory.

With rural mechanisation in the 1950s, the richer, urban-dwelling, horse-trading Ciganos were the first to shift to the selling of fabrics, rugs, shoes and clothing, either from door to door or in street markets. The horse-trading business itself, now less profitable, was taken up by itinerant and poorer Ciganos, who also took on small-scale agricultural work that had become available as a result of urban migration from the rural areas. These interstices depended on increased peri-urban travel between expanding urban fringes, small villages and isolated cottages.

The period of economic and political upheaval and reorganisation between 1950 and 1970 was especially difficult for the poor. Categorising them explicitly as 'nomads', the Salazar dictatorship started a major process involving the 'nationalisation and legalisation' of Ciganos, requiring them to register with the authorities and limiting their movements to the districts where they were registered. The administration also specified the exact location of Cigano camping grounds and the maximum stay allowed, and required Cigano men to perform military service. Poor Ciganos responded as was their custom: by sneaking away and turning to the *donos* to help them deal with persecution and fines. The *donos*, as part of the Cigano elite, continued to play the same double role that they had in the past, but now sought out new spaces and allies within an increasingly urban and bureaucratic society. They helped the authorities 'nationalise' poor Ciganos, paying fines for them and acting as godparents at christenings and at the registry office. However, the *donos* preferred to assist poorer members of their own *raças* who wanted to emigrate from their villages to Portugal's growing cities, rather than involving themselves in settling 'still unsettled Ciganos', which was what the authorities wanted them to do. Thus, for instance, only ten domestic groups became settled in Évora between 1960 and 1973. They belonged, or were linked through affinity, to the two longest established *raças*.

After the return of democracy in 1975, a large proportion of the poorer Ciganos started to camp around cities in Alentejo in the hope of being allocated some of the new social housing that the progressive town councils were building. There were other reasons for this migration: the gradual regularisation of horse trading, the decreasing numbers of customers in rural areas, and changes in camping sites due to the strict implementation of new property laws.[6] Cities like Évora, with weak industrialisation and a growing administrative and service sector unable to satisfy the employment demands of a low-skilled population, offered a landscape of intense informal economy and a mixture of urban and rural activities. Accordingly, poor Ciganos redirected their commercial activities within unregulated yet socially accepted interstices. In addition, the criteria for receiving new forms of welfare payment such as the *Rendimento Mínimo Garantido* (RMG), which requires the school attendance of children or a training programme for adults, could be met more easily in the cities. This payment also raised the hopes of many of buying a van and dedicating their lives to selling clothes on the street, like 'richer' urban Ciganos.

The old Cigano elite and their relatives who were already settled in urban zones, however, again delayed the arrival of poor and 'unknown' Ciganos. They refused to be identified with them, fearing to lose the status they enjoyed among non-Ciganos as *Ciganos civilizados* ('civilised Ciganos'). Nor did they want competition at a time when their own purchasing power had decreased due to the increased regularisation of self-employment, the formalisation of support for local trade, and market restrictions.[7] Although the urban Cigano elite had been losing its leverage and influence in the context of an increasingly impersonal administration based on the principle of equality, they responded by limiting their marriages to those of comparable status and by pushing others out of their residential and business spaces. They also made the most of being better positioned to access resources that the public authorities made available to citizens in need, since the bureaucratic rationale favoured settlement and employment regularisation, and the urban Cigano elite were already registered and had tax addresses.

The poorer Ciganos were once again held back from asserting their 'right to the city' (Lefebvre 1973). The alternative the authorities offered was to keep them as a 'nomadic' population. Since classifying citizens as ethnically different was against Portugal's democratic Constitution, the term 'nomads', which had been used in the past, began to be used strategically once again. The term was officially considered non-discriminatory, simply describing a way of life based on mobility.[8] However, for the poorest Ciganos, being classified as 'nomads' had important consequences. First, by associating Ciganos with nomadism and vice versa, it gave way to an administrative climate that condoned situations of poverty and exclusion, arguing that this was somehow inherent to a culturally specific minority lifestyle: as 'nomads', Ciganos were, in an essentialist manner, characterised by constant travelling, rootlessness and a lack of concern for material goods that allowed them to survive thanks to their traditional activities. Second, public safety policies viewed mobile individuals as potentially dangerous and associated them with the 'drug problem' from the moment it became institutionalised as a 'social problem', meaning that itinerant Ciganos came under constant surveillance (Costa 1995; SOS Racismo 2001).

Evidence of this situation is that only twelve Cigano families were relocated with the first allocation of social housing between 1978 and mid 2003. In the late 1980s, the shacks of nine families of poor horse-trading Ciganos were demolished. The families had been close to the new social housing developments, hoping to be relocated there as well. Instead, they were settled on a plot of land outside of the town, officially designated as the *Parque Temporário de Acampada para Populações Nómadas* (Temporary Camp for Nomadic Populations). I will discuss the character of this place later. First, I will explore how an undetermined number of poor horse dealers continue to travel across Alentejo and beyond up to the present day.

Surviving between Roots and Routes

Among people like the Riveiros, the nuclear family is the basic unit for travelling and camping. Depending on personal circumstances and economic opportunities, however, other units – such as married sons and/or daughters and their children, and/or a brother's family with their single and married sons and/or daughters – are incorporated to form larger domestic groups. Being together while simultaneously remaining independent makes it possible not only to accumulate and share, but also to diversify the labour force and resources.

A significant factor guiding the movement of these domestic groups is the calendar of horse fairs, which coincides with the local holiday. For instance, the Riveiros would 'do' the Feira de São João in Évora, and the fairs in Vidigueira, Alcaçovas and/or Estremoz, in July, then head to Ferreira and/or Cuba in September, and Feira Nova in Évora in October, returning to Évora once again in March for Os Ramos, and so on. The expression these Ciganos use for following itineraries like this is *fazer a roda* (to do the round). Many of the horse fairs are semi-legal. Officially, livestock cannot be sold outside designated areas where veterinary controls are carried out, which requires the payment of fees and, of course, transaction taxes. However, some councils, such as that of Évora, often tolerate what they describe as 'traditional' and 'quaint' practices. Ciganos can, in this semi-legal interstice, maintain the circuit of intra-ethnic exchange of horses. Simultaneously, concentrated at each fair, they present a variety of supply to the farm owners who need or wish to exchange and sell their old horses in the hope of picking up a good deal. Between fairs, they train docile horses for riding and working, maintain the breeding and rearing of active and cheap horses, and expedite the supply of older horses from rural environments to abattoirs to be turned into meat products.

The Riveiros, for instance, keep between four and eight horses throughout the year. This is the average for a domestic group. There are other richer groups who kept between twelve and fifteen horses, but I have never met a group, however large, that had more than fifteen horses at any one moment. Thus, within one year, the Riveiros bought a Lusitano mare that they sold to a Cigano elsewhere; they reared two foals and a pony, which they sold as riding horses to a rural hostel, a farm specialising in therapies for disabled children, and a private estate; they also purchased four old horses that they resold to an abattoir. However, neither the Riveiros nor any of the others repeat exactly the same process every year. It varies according to the clients and exchange networks that a group has managed to establish, and also to the state of such relationships at any given time.

In practice, though cooperation and mutual assistance are essential, harmonious reciprocity and the horizontal sharing of profitable work between members of one *raça*, or even between members of the domestic group, does not occur. During fairs, adult men leading domestic groups compete against one another to close as many deals, and as many good deals, as they can. Many *brigas* (confrontations) arise from the intensity of this competition, and from the attempt to make as many contacts as possible, and of the most profitable nature, with non-Ciganos. Other *brigas* are caused by issues surrounding the intra-group lending of money based on the sense of obligation and trust associated with 'being Ciganos' and, sometimes, 'being family'.

For itinerant horse dealers, making a living by horse trading alone is almost impossible. A good sale price could be between €500 and €1,500, but veterinary services and vaccines have to be paid for, and most of whatever is left is invested in new business. Any remainder is spent on food. As such, they complement trading with other activities, such as farm work in various regions – for instance, picking strawberries during spring, fruit and tomatoes between July and September, and olives in winter. Many have been returning to particular estates for more than a decade. The larger estates pay per kilogram harvested, each person earning about €65 to €100 per day, but given the competition from migrants (mainly Eastern European), the opportunities for local Ciganos lie with small and medium-sized farms. The owners are usually old acquaintances; although they pay smaller amounts 'under the counter', they allow Ciganos to camp and obtain fodder for their horses, and they sometimes give them clothes or food.

Begging is a last resort, whenever there is no money for food. It is not something horse-trading Ciganos brag about. Begging is mainly carried out in mid-sized to large towns, though almost never in town centres, since many are heritage sites and tourist hubs, and town councils and local retailers want these places to remain 'clean' and 'beautiful', with nothing to interfere with the architectural landscape or the experience of 'the traditional calm of the Alentejo region'. Nor can begging be carried out in neighbourhoods where richer and settled Ciganos live or sell their goods. While itinerant horse dealers are acknowledged as ethnic peers, and even qualify as the last 'authentic Ciganos' practising the 'true Cigano trades' and leading a 'traditional' lifestyle, once they cross the urban border and enter the neighbourhoods and business spaces of settled Ciganos, they are regarded with suspicion and labelled *maltêses*, 'non-civilised', 'riverside Ciganos', *peles*, *manolos* and other derogatory terms.[9] They are perceived as an element that compromises the privileged, though unstable, status and relationships of richer Ciganos with local institutions. The only spaces left for begging, therefore, are car parks and the entrances to large commercial spaces outside town centres, or the homes of old trading acquaintances.

These hand-to-mouth activities are commonly combined with RMG payments. Yet itinerant Ciganos cannot access RMG easily for reasons already mentioned. Take the Riveiros, for instance. They wanted to register in Évora because, according to them, they had enemies in Beja, where the adult learning centre and the school at which they should be officially registered were. The social worker in Évora, however, sent them back. To register with social services in Évora they would have to justify their move to a new address. Having no declared home or job there, and considered members of a 'nomadic population', they were forced to spend the autumn and winter in Évora in order to qualify. However, they never really felt at ease in the Nomads' Camp, with its more permanent inhabitants and with constant harassment from the police for camping beyond the legal time limit. This case also points to the importance of social dynamics for structuring Cigano territories, to which I turn next.

'Each Cigano on His Own Land'

The movement of Ciganos travelling across the region with their horses is linked to camping sites that form a network, thus facilitating mobility. Some of these are the camping sites made available by town councils,[10] but many others are abandoned buildings and plots of land where, in some cases, they are allowed to stay by landowners who are old business partners or have been employers for seasonal work.[11] Among such sites, individual domestic groups always have one place they refer to as *a nossa casa* (our home). Only the elderly live permanently in these settlements. Unrelated Ciganos never camp there; similarly, no one else camps in the spaces permanently occupied by other *raças*. In the case of the Riveiros, for instance, their 'home' was situated outside a small village midway between Beja and Évora, where twenty people lived in wooden shacks on a plot of land with the consent of the owner. They all belonged to the same *raça*, which also included other members in three other villages nearby.

By repeatedly returning to the same location and becoming known, Ciganos build long-lasting relationships with the *senhores* based on trust. These practices are linked to the intra-ethnic appropriation of and identification with spaces, and with maintaining order and social peace. A phrase commonly used by Ciganos to refer to this is *cada Cigano na sua terra* ('each Cigano on his own land'). Whenever Ciganos want to camp in a territory that is not considered 'their own', they have to 'get along' with the local Ciganos by asking for permission and, sometimes, if business is involved, paying the *cortagem* (a fee). As Zé Riveiro put it: 'If there are Ciganos living there, if you trade or do any sort of business, people have to ask them, and then you have to give them something, even if it's just enough to buy lunch'. In larger towns, where several domestic groups from the same *raça* live, the group of reference is the one that has been involved in horse trading for the longest time in that place.

Besides the above, people's itineraries do not cross or involve camping on land associated with those considered *contrários* (enemies), the spaces of individuals and their relatives (mainly patrilineal) with whom they have an ongoing *briga* (dispute), either of a personal nature or resulting from the actions of their relatives. These brigas are solved through the intervention of respected adult men (and sometimes women) called on to mediate and to issue the so-called *lei dos contrários* (law of the enemies), which formally separates the parties' territories so as to prevent them and their relatives from meeting until they settle their enmity. The Riveiros, for instance, could not travel or camp south and south-east of their village, since, in their own words, 'beyond Reguengos and Beja isn't ours; we have *contrários* there'.

To sum up, the territories and places of rootedness of itinerant Ciganos, and economic activities that they enable, respond to complex dynamics arising from two sets of relationships. First, there are intra-ethnic spatialities and forms of territorial exclusiveness: long-term relationships between different classes and between different *raças* of Ciganos that establish access to resources and territories; relationships between and within domestic groups that determine the state of cooperation and competition; and the family and personal trajectories that place agents in a segmented and hierarchical social space maintained over time on the basis of strict ethnic endogamy and status isogyny, as well as public assessments of compliance with certain moral conventions and rules acknowledged as pertaining to Ciganos in specific contexts. Second, there is the course of inter-ethnic relationships at different moments and in different places that establish specific forms of access to resources and their redistribution, forms of living, travelling and working and their regulation – the problematic administrative classification and keeping of some Ciganos as 'nomads'. One outcome of this classification is the Nomads' Camps planned in certain cities of Alentejo, such as the one in Évora, the character of which, however, was not fully determined by the will of the local administration.

Life In Between

The Nomads' Camps set up by some town councils are the spatial expression of socio-political and administrative attitudes towards those considered 'nomads'. They are legal spaces for the temporary settlement of Ciganos like the Riveiros, but they are also places where many become stranded indefinitely, waiting to be rehoused and to benefit from the improvements in living standards this promise brings. Such was the case of the aforementioned nine families that had been driven away from their former shacks while waiting to be rehoused in the first social housing neighbourhoods of Évora in 1987. The simultaneous fixity and ephemerousness of the camps, where everybody – the inhabitants, their neighbours and the authorities – expect them to be dismantled at any moment, open up these spaces to various economic activities and power relations, old and new.

The Nomads' Camp in Évora was an arid plain located where the city's industrial estates ended and wasteland began. An irony of urban development was that it was also located right beside the town's municipal camp site, intended for tourists. The town's visitors enjoyed shade under the trees, electricity, a swimming pool and a bar; meanwhile, infrastructure deemed adequate to meet the minimum living conditions of people classified as 'nomads' and their animals never materialised.

The authorities did not want to support projects that would give rise to public opposition. The Nomads' Camp's neighbours had expected the area to become part of the so-called strategic axes in the town's expansion, but felt this aspiration jeopardised by the existence of the camp. They pressured the council to close the camp right up to the point when the council, also fearing xenophobic violence, dismantled it in 2004. Those living near the camp justified their position by drawing on urban middle-class values, pointing to dangers to their property, an increase in crime and the accumulating rubbish at the camp. In several communications addressed to the public administration, they also argued against the core of the issue: people living in the precarious conditions of the Nomads' Camp could not be considered 'nomads'. In fact, despite being treated as such for twenty years, the camp's residents had reinforced their shacks and stopped travelling for long periods, afraid that their absence might be understood as a definitive abandoning of the camp, or as evidence of their supposed 'nomadic' lifestyle, as invented by the non-Cigano majority. Leaving would prompt the council to demolish their shacks, using their absence as proof that they had also abandoned the waiting list for council housing. Stuck in the Nomads' Camp, however, Ciganos were unable to maintain or extend their horse-trading business.

Most camp residents aspired to sell clothes at street markets, but none of them succeeded in establishing themselves in this way. Town councils, in their bid to restrict street selling, offered only a few highly expensive licences and put pressure on itinerant salespeople with continuous inspections. Even if some welfare payments could help them to get started, they also faced opposition from urban Ciganos who had been in the trade for the past forty years – these Cigano traders inherited, exchanged and purchased licences and market stalls, forming exclusive business territories.

Unable to carry out this lucrative and socially acceptable formal economic activity, they relied primarily on the welfare payments they have received since the mid 1990s, and on a host of informal economic activities. This was neither a novel development nor unique to Ciganos. Despite labour regularisation at the time, many non-skilled people in low-paying jobs combined wages with welfare payments and undeclared economic activities (such as working as cleaners and construction workers, or growing vegetables), and with forms of kinship-based reciprocity, redistribution and exchange. Some of the activities that the Nomads' Camp's residents carried out were related to opportunities created within this milieu: non-Ciganos referred to as *pategos* or *paitos* due to their low social standing and rural origins, would come to the camp to purchase construction materials and tools that Cigano children and teenagers had got their hands on; they would also buy and sell used items, especially old shotguns and old cars and spare parts. In addition, permanent residents of the camp created two profitable interstitial activities that were linked to the camp's own ambivalent nature: small-scale drug sales, acting as go-betweens for all kinds of sales and loaning money to non-resident Ciganos who periodically pitched their tents in the Camp.

Outside the town, out of sight of any neighbours, and disguised by the presence of the horse-trading business, the Nomads' Camp became a suitable site for small-scale drug sales. Even if selling drugs made it possible for many to achieve the urban lifestyle they had been otherwise unable to access, it also kept them captive in the marginal urban periphery and reinforced inter- and intra-ethnic marginalisation. After 'the drug problem' was constructed as a social issue in the 1980s (Romani 1999: 154), it became the premise used by non-Ciganos to garner support for getting the Nomads' Camp closed, and by Ciganos settled in social housing to safeguard their niche as urban middle-class travelling salespeople. The camp was turned into a symbolic space, reinforcing the stigmatising categorisation made by the non-Cigano majority: Cigano = poor = dealer = drug addict.

The other interstice that emerged within the Nomads' Camp for the permanent residents was that of intra-ethnic trade with Ciganos like the Riveiros. This was similar to the trade carried out with *pategos* (poor rural non-Ciganos) but involved cheaper products, and the possibility of purchasing on credit and repaying with favours instead of money. Also, with the arrival of welfare payments in the camp and the flow of money from selling drugs, some camp residents accumulated capital that could be loaned to poorer Ciganos to pay for a daughter's wedding, to close a good deal, to purchase a van or to cover other expenses. Traditional relationships linked to horse trading complemented these new trade relationships. Some permanent camp residents still kept a horse, or acted as middlemen in sales between itinerant horse traders and possible buyers in the area. Having been moved to the Nomads' Camp by the council afforded some residents a certain exclusiveness in relation to the territory, and some presented themselves as legitimate 'keepers of the peace' and took a small commission (*cortagem*) from every deal made within the camp. This frequently gave rise to tension and disputes which, as apparent from the start of this chapter, used to end with itinerant Ciganos being 'advised' to leave the camp and not stay beyond the time stipulated by the council.

Novel articulation between new and old relationships left permanent residents, especially the most economically successful, in a certain position of superiority over itinerant horse-dealing Ciganos. Officially unable to camp anywhere else in the area, most horse-dealing Ciganos could not avoid being reliant on the approval of the camp's permanent residents if they wanted to keep Évora as part of their 'round'. Permanent camp residents also depended on itinerant horse dealing. By dealing with the itinerants, the residents generated both social capital (relationships) and symbolic capital (prestige) in the intra-ethnic social space of the camp; these were needed because residing in the town's camp and the nature of their business could only lead to urban marginalisation. Specifically, the presence of itinerants in the camp afforded camp residents new possibilities in the marriage market, shut out as they were from matrimonial alliances with Évora's traditionally settled Ciganos and with their own close relatives. By involving people whose mobility was greater than their own, residents were also able to enlarge their own businesses. Furthermore, the presence of fairs, horses and a few tents essentially allowed the Nomads' Camp to be perceived by both non-Ciganos and urban Ciganos as a stronghold of 'true horse-trading Ciganos' in Évora – one reason why the camp had existed for so long despite the neighbours' complaints and frequent police raids.

Conclusions

Economic practices carried out by a minority of poor Ciganos who are part of the socio-economic landscape of Alentejo follow their own rationale, taking on alternative and sometimes unexpected forms, emerging from a constant rearrangement of relationships, territories, and mobility and settlement requirements. Their forms are related to the specific historical circumstances in which they belong: initially, they form part of an agricultural model based on land ownership and agricultural work, and later they are part of successive policies for regulating urban growth, trade and waged work, as well as cultural differences and lifestyles.

The economic activities of horse-trading Ciganos can best be approached as interstitial. They are based on peri-urban mobility and settlement dynamics that developed and gained meaning between old and new opportunities. They keep 'traditional' trade alive, yet respond to new economic and bureaucratic requirements regarding horse breeding and trading and the hiring of temporary agricultural labour; they continue to supply horses to old clients while gaining new ones, by juggling small and informal rural production dynamics and new forms of production geared to the city. Furthermore, they organise their activities, movements and stationary periods along two traditional intra-ethnic territorial axes. One is repeatedly enforced by domestic groups on spaces that are frequently used for activity and accommodation. Another is enforced through the hierarchical ordering of people, activities and spaces.

Economic activities and the dynamics of mobility/settlement have also developed in ways that the bureaucratic authorities did not expect in their attempts to organise and classify society. The state and the local administrations have usually approached the poorer horse-trading Ciganos, first, in an essentialist sense as a nomadic and unrooted cultural minority, and second, as a social problem bound up with poverty and marginalisation. The category 'nomads' into which these Ciganos have been slotted emerges between these two poles, as does one of the most obvious spatial and practical expressions of this – the often-named Nomads' Camps. As the particular case of the Évora camp shows, it was itself an interstice: between the permanent and temporary, between mobility and stagnation. Its enclave was also interstitial – the space between the urban and the rural, between the expectations of an expanding urban periphery and the frustrated dreams of the disadvantaged population, giving rise to particular and unforeseen interstitial economic activities. Additionally, the camp was economically interstitial between the traditional trade activities of the Cigano and non-Cigano rural environment and the small-scale trade and exchange typical of the informal, underground economy, blended with the illegal and criminal activities that cities push to their fringes.

NOTES

1. All names used are pseudonyms.
2. Cigano is the Portuguese ethnonym for Gypsies. It is both an emic and etic category.
3. Similar to Spanish Gitanos (San Román 1997: 97), for Portuguese Ciganos the *raça* is a large local and translocal group of relatives, ideally defined as patrilineal and patrilocal.
4. This payment mainly takes the form of the so-called RMG (*Rendimento Mínimo Garantido*), known as the RSI (*Rendimento Social de Inserção*) since 2003. This is a conditional cash transfer to people in severe economic hardship. Also common were widow's pensions, disability benefits and old age pensions.
5. Ciganos employ the terms *malta* or *maltêses* to design the lower socio-economic status of other Ciganos and their ancestry.
6. For instance, Decree Law 39/76-19-January, according to which neighbours could claim wasteland as private property and expel those who camped on the property without permission. This means that most camp sites are now located on newly private lands (see also Castro 2004: 64).
7. The new laws – Decree Law 340/82-25-August, Decree Law 252/86-25-August, Decree Law 340/82-14-July and Decree Law 259/95-30-September – greatly lim-

ited the products that could be sold by street vendors and at fairs, and allowed town councils to specify requirements for market and street sale permits (see Sama Acedo 2009: 200).
8. For instance, special surveillance on 'nomads' was established under Article 81 National Guard Regulations. When the Constitutional Court reviewed this article it concluded that 'nomads are not all Ciganos, nor are all Ciganos nomads: hence, there would be no discrimination based on race but a special danger strengthened by nomadism' (*Acórdão*-452/89-28- *Junho*).
9. *Peles* is a pejorative reference to the tangled hair of poor Ciganos; *manolos* is similarly pejorative, and makes reference to the appearance of Ciganos linked with dirt, outlandish clothing, and uneducated or non-urban forms of behaviour.
10. For example, the Parque Temporário de Acampada para Populações Nómadas in Évora (1987 to 2004), the Parque Nómada of Ferreira do Alentejo (1995 to 1999) and the Parque Nómada NR - Bairro das Pedreiras of Beja (2006 to 2014).
11. Decree Law 310/2002 partly regulates the settling of itinerant populations together with other activities, leaving it up to town councils to grant licences for the activities mentioned. In order to grant a camping licence, the express authorisation of the landowner, whether private or public, is required.

REFERENCES

Bancroft, A. 2005. *Roma and Gypsy in Europe: Modernity, Race, Space and Exclusion*. Andover: Ashgate.
Bastos, J.G.P. 2007. *Sintrenses ciganos. Uma abordagem estrutural – dinâmica*. Sintra: Divisão de Saúde e Acção Social, Câmara Municipal de Sintra.
Bauman, G. 2006. *Grammars of Identity/Alterity: A Structural Approach*. Oxford: Berghahn Books.
Berland, J.C. 1979. 'Peripatetic, Pastoralist and Sedentist Interaction in Complex Societies', *Nomadic Peoples* 4: 6–8.
Berland, J.C., and M.T. Salo. 1986. 'Peripathetic Comunities: An Introduction', *Nomadic Peoples* 21/22: 1–6.
Brazzabeni, M. 2012a. 'De bairro em bairro: redes sociais e circulação de uma família cigana em Villa Real de Santo António', in J.G.P. Bastos (ed.), *Ciganos e ciganofobia*. Lisbon: Edições Colibri and Centro de Estudos em Migraçoes e Minorias Étnicas, pp.267–78.
———. 2012b. 'Já abalaste? Rumor and Fama in the Organization of Lived Space', *Etudes tsiganes*, special issue, 44/45: 156–71.
Castro, A. 2004. 'Ciganos e itinerancia: realidades concelhias e formas de hospitalidade', *Cidades-comunidades e territórios* 9: 55–69.
———. 2007. 'A mobilidade, os *ciganos* e os outros: incertezas na relação com o território'. Paper presented at the First International Conference of Young Urban Researchers, Lisbon, June.
———. 2010. '*Ciganos* e a orientação explícita, mas não exclusiva das políticas sociais: a construção de um caminho em Portugal?' Paper presented at the Colóquio Dinâmicas Actuais da Pobreza e da Exclusão Social:

Conceptualizações, Politicas e Intervenções, Fundação Calouste Gulbenkian, Lisbon, 25 November.
Coelho, A. 1995 [1892]. *Os ciganos de Portugal*. Lisbon: Don Quixote.
Costa, E.M. 1995. 'Os ciganos em Portugal. Breve história de uma exclusão', in L. Cortesão and F. Pinto (eds), *O povo cigano. Cidadãos na sombra*. Porto: Ed. Afrontamento, pp.13–20.
De Certeau, M. 1996 [1979]. *La invención de lo cotidiano. El arte de hacer*, Vol. 1. Mexico City: Universidad Iberoamericana.
Fatela, J. 1989. *O sangue e a rua*. Lisbon: Don Quixote.
Fotta, M. 2012. 'The Bankers of the Backlands: Financialisation and the Calon-Gypsies in Bahia', Ph.D. diss. London: Goldsmiths College, University of London.
Galemba, R. 2008. 'Informal and Illicit Entrepreneurs: Fighting for a Place in the Neoliberal Economic Order', *Anthropology of Work Review* 29(2): 19–25.
García García, J.L. 1976. *Antropología del territorio*. Madrid: Taller de Ediciones J.B.
Grygar, J. 2006. 'Enacting Borders: Power at Interstitial Places', in J. Grygar and B. Spalová (eds), *Anthropology at Borders: Power, Culture, Memories*. Prague: Multicultural Center Prague, pp.13–25.
Hayden, R.M. 1979. 'The Cultural Ecology of Service Nomads', *Eastern Anthropologist* 32(4): 297–309.
Holloway, J. 2002. *Change the World without Taking Power*. London: Pluto Press.
Lefebvre, H. 1973. *El derecho a la ciudad*. Barcelona: Península.
Love, T.F. 1977. 'Ecological Niche Theory in Sociocultural Anthropology: A Conceptual Framework and an Application', *American Ethnologist* 4(1): 27–41.
Magnaghi, A. (ed.) 1990. *Il territorio dell'abitare*. Milano: Franco Angeli.
Mann, M. 1986. *The Sources of Social Power*, Vol. 1. Cambridge: Cambridge University Press.
Nadel, S.F. 1956. 'Understanding Primitive Peoples', *Culture* 4(2): 1–30.
Okely, J. 1983. *The Traveller-Gypsies*. Cambridge: Cambridge University Press.
Piasere, L. 1987. 'In Search of New Niches: The Productive Organization of the Peripatetic Xoraxané in Italy', in A. Rao (ed.), *The Other Nomads: Peripatetic Minorities in Cross-Cultural Perspective*. Cologne: Böhlau, pp.111–32.
———. 1992. 'Roma and Romá in North Italy: Two Types of Territorial Behaviour in the Same Larger Territory', in M. Casmir and A. Rao (eds), *Mobility and Territoriality: Social and Spatial Boundaries among Forangers, Fishers, Pastoralists and Peripatetics*. London: Berg, pp.279–91.
Pignarre, P., and I. Stengers. 2011. *Capitalist Sorcery: Breaking the Spell*. Basingstoke: Palgrave Macmillan.
Raffestin, C. 1981. *Per una geografia del potere*. Milan: Unicopli.
Rao, A. 1987. 'The Concept of Peripatetics: An Introduction', in A. Rao (ed.), *The Other Nomads: Peripatetic Minorities in Cross-Cultural Perspective*. Cologne: Böhlau Verlag, pp.1–32.
Ribero, M. 1979 [1953]. *A planice heroica*. Lisbon: Guimãraes.
Romani, O. 1999. *Las drogas. Sueños y razones*. Barcelona: Ariel.
Salo, M.T. 1987 'The Gypsy Niche in North America: Some Ecological Perspectives on the Exploitation of Social Environments', in A. Rao (ed.), *The Other Nomads: Peripatetic Minorities in Cross-Cultural Perspective*. Cologne: Böhlau Verlag, pp.90–108.

Sama Acedo, S. 2003. 'La movilidad como forma de vida en la comunidad gitana de Évora: mitos e realidades', in J.F. Branco and A.I. Afonso (eds), *Retóricas sem fronteiras*, Vol. 1: *Mobilidades*. Celta: Oeiras, pp.53–70.
———. 2009. 'Espacios vividos, espacios creados. Los "ciganos" de Évora', Ph.D. diss. Madrid: Universidad Computense de Madrid.
San Román, T. 1997. *La diferencia inquietante. Viejas y nuevas estrategias culturales de los gitanos*. Madrid: Siglo XXI.
Santos, V.R. dos. 2002. 'Espacialidade e territorialidade dos grupos ciganos na cidade de São Paulo', M.A. diss. São Paulo: Universidade de São Paulo.
SOS Racismo. 2001. *Saúde e libertade: ciganos. Números, abordagems, realidades*. Lisbon: SOS Racismo.
Stewart, M. 1997. *The Time of the Gypsies*. Boulder, CO: Westview Press.
Theodosiou, A. 2003. 'Be-longing' in a "Doubly Occupied Place": The Parakalamos Gypsy Musicians', *Romani Studies* 5(14): 25–58.
Thrasher, F. 1967 [1927]. *The Gang: A Study of 1313 Gangs of Chicago*. Chicago: University of Chicago Press.
Vasconcelos J.L. 1982 [1933]. *Etnografía portuguesa*, Bk. 2, Vol. 4: *O povo portugués*. Lisbon: Impresa Nacional-Casa da Moeda.
Wolf, E.R. 1966. 'Kinship, Friendship and Patron–client Relations in Complex Societies', in M. Banton (ed.), *The Social Anthropology of Complex Societies*. London: Tavistock, pp.1–22.

Sara Sama Acedo is a Professor of Anthropology at National Distance Learning University (UNED) in Madrid. She holds a PhD in Social and Cultural Anthropology from the Complutense University of Madrid (UCM); her dissertation titled 'Lived Spaces, Created Spaces: The 'Ciganos' (Gypsies) of Évora (Portugal)' received Doctoral Extraordinary Awards and European Mention of the Doctoral Degree from the university. Her current work is part of a collective research project Project Madrid-Cosmópolis (CSO2012-33949) that explores emerging urban practices in Spain. She has published several book chapters and journal articles on the education of ethnic minorities, the socialisation of Cigano girls and on urban spaces of mourning and dwelling. The most recent publication, on ITCs and urban public space, one outcome of her current project, will appear in *Urbanities. The Journal of the IUAES Commission on Urban Anthropology* (2015).

Chapter 4

 'Endured Labour' and 'Fixing Up' Money
The Economic Strategies of Roma Migrants in Slovakia and the UK

JAN GRILL

Almost a year has passed since Miro's last visit to Tarkovce, a Slovak village near the Ukrainian border where he grew up. He has come back for his summer holiday. We are standing outside his parents' house and catching up on news from England. With great gusto, he has been spending the money he earned during his recent migration to Britain. Earlier in the year (2007) he had bought himself a new version of the Seat Leon in shiny black. Since his arrival he has been reconstructing his house in the village centre, which he had purchased several years before from a *Gadžo* (non-Roma) family. He had already reconstructed the house once, just a couple of years ago. But, as he notes, seeing other Roma migrants investing in their houses in conspicuous ways and witnessing his own children growing up, led him to reconstruct his house again. Following the trend in the village dictated by returning Roma migrants, he had exchanged the wooden windows for new plastic ones and installed massive doors. He had hired and then closely supervised a non-Roma company to complete the construction of a new extension protruding from the back of the house and housing a new kitchen, as well as putting in rooms for the children and painting the façade a deep blue.

'All this would not be possible', he says, 'if not for England. England has saved us'. This statement was typical of remarks heard among the majority of Tarkovce Roma, or at least those who have migrated. Roma migrants from Tarkovce had left Slovakia with the hope of improving their lives. It was a hopeful move away from everyday struggles in Slovakia, characterised by formal unemployment, a shrinking and more punitive state system of support and a growing sense of the impossibility of attaining viable lives. These worsening conditions were often characterised by Roma in the oft-repeated phrase 'in Slovakia it's impossible', which was often supported by claims that 'it is not possible to live on that miserable support'. These remarks referred to a decrease in formal and informal socio-economic opportunities, paralleled by declining state support and ever-increasing living costs, leaving more families in precarious conditions of poverty.

Miro, like many other Roma, had moved to Britain following the Slovak accession to the European Union.[1] He was among the first local Roma to have left for England alongside other friends and relatives. Since then he had lived with his wife and three children in three British cities. He had done all kinds of jobs, on and off, on temporary job contracts or just working on *fušky* (one-off informal jobs paid in cash). Although he had taken up a variety of different manual jobs, formal and informal, ranging from packing newspapers to working in meat-processing factories, he knew how slowly and how relatively little one earned in these jobs.

In comparison to Slovakia, where he was struggling economically to cover his family's living expenses, England offered him the opportunity for socio-economic advancement. But, as he himself grew to realise more and more, living in England was also a hard-fought struggle of working in the type of jobs available to Central Eastern European migrants with little knowledge of English, no formal education and no other forms of capital. Miro characterised this as follows:

> With honest work (*poctivo butji*) you can't, it's impossible. Well, it is possible, but you suffer a lot for this [i.e., enduring a lot in order to earn and save up]. Look at me and Tereza [Miro's wife] – eight, twelve[-hour shifts] we were working ... And what did we earn? Nothing, just for food and flat. Nothing more. It's difficult to work like this. How many years have we been in England and only managed to save up little.

These years of working in physically demanding and poorly paid jobs in the UK, combined with frequently sharing the costs of overcrowded flats and other things with his siblings' families, had brought Miro some economic gains. These were years filled with hard physical labour (*phari butji*), which he referred to as 'honest work'.

Although he had managed to save some money from these jobs and had invested it in the moderate refurbishment of a house in Slovakia, his recent acts of more conspicuous consumption and displays of wealth, however, had come from a combination of hard labour and other economic strategies known as 'fixing up money' (*vybavinen love*). The ability to 'fix up' things (and acquire money in the process) refers to a number of ways of getting by, and in this particular case to skilful manoeuvring within different state systems and other institutions. In the context of recent waves of migration, knowing how to 'fix up' money relates to having knowledge of state systems and of how to apply for the various support schemes and benefits to which the Roma, as low-income EU migrants, are entitled. But it can also include a variety of strategies to obtain quick financial gains, which the Tarkovce Roma quickly replicated (for example, bank loans or involvement in various informal strategies). This knowledge is related not only to income-generating strategies, but also, more generally, to variously distributed degrees of social intelligence and the disposition to manoeuvre within asymmetric fields of power and interstitial spaces between different state systems. In general, 'fixing up' was often associated with the characterisation of a person 'who knows how to make money' but also how to take care of things. While mastering the skill of 'fixing up' was often contrasted with hard physical labour, there were also situations in which 'knowing how to make money' was a result of physically demanding work, or a combination of the two. More specifically in my conversation with Miro, it refers to a wide range of practices ranging from the skilful 'fixing up' of various benefits, loans and other informal practices in the grey zone between the formal and informal economy, to generating quick money and much higher financial gains rather than to long-term physical labour.

In this chapter I examine two sets of economic strategies used by networks of Slovak Roma migrants in the UK and Slovakia. Rather than ascribing greater significance to one of these, I will try to show the oscillation between these two modes that often coexist in time and space.[2] The two sets of practices are, first, tough, menial and unstable physical labour, and second, strategies based on the ability to 'fix up money' at opportune moments (which can generate much higher financial gains in a much shorter period of time). By emphasising the oscillation between and coexistence of different economic practices, my ethnographic account does not document a clear-cut division between a clearly developed concept of *Romani butji* ('Roma work') and other income-generating practices. The notion of *Romani butji* did not appear at the level of discourse and local talk, and Tarkovce Roma did not describe specific practices within this category. This ethnography of Tarkovce Roma provides a comparative case, which does not rely on the idiosyncratic relationship between independent Roma work and formations of identity. The concept of explicitly developed 'Roma work', which is central to some other ethnographic research and corresponds to particular semi-autonomous socio-economic niches (e.g. Stewart 1997; also Olivera, this volume), seems to be absent among Roma from Tarkovce. Rather than privileging one economic strategy over others, I echo some of the classical themes appearing in Roma ethnographies in relation to the capacity to snatch an opportunity 'on the wing' through skilfulness and social intelligence as a disposition. Analytically, this entails exploring social trajectories at the conjunction of particular positions and dispositions for action, of being located and moving within social fields and certain subjective capacities for action. I explore this historically acquired disposition in the particular case of Tarkovce Roma by locating their socio-economic strategies within temporal and spatial contexts.

Anthropological Approaches to Roma Economies and Work

Much of the classical anthropology of Roma groups has focused predominantly on economic strategies through which actors subvert existing hierarchies, making themselves appear superior to the dominant groups (e.g. Okely 1983; Stewart 1997, 1999). Analytically, this perspective allows anthropologists to emphasise Roma preference for autonomous work carved out within asymmetric fields of socio-economic relations intertwined with, as well as dependent on, dominant societies. Empirically, this focus privileges the Roma subversion of statecraft and resistance to dominant social and moral orders. This collective ethic often reflects a division between wage labour in the non-Roma world and Roma work, and is reflected in the collectively embraced ideology of *Romanes* (Stewart 1997), a morality inscribed by adherence to Gypsy laws (Gay y Blasco 1999), a propensity to avoid working for non-travellers for a wage (Okely 1983), or a preference for occupations based on mobility, independence and bargaining (Formoso 2000).

A particularly eloquent example is Stewart's (1997) classic ethnography of a Vlach Rom community in Harangos during the late socialist period in Hungary. Despite being employed in state socialist factories during the week, the Rom were engaged in various informal practices. In particular, Stewart highlights the symbolic significance of horse dealing for the maintenance and reinvention of distinctive identities through a socio-economic practice located outside the confines of official state-regulated work. In Stewart's account, the state ideology and practical experience of working in factories had very little impact on Rom self-understanding and 'was given little or no value in their lives' (ibid.: 241). The Rom were able to endure their work in the factory because they 'were capable of creating an alternative "economic" and social order beyond and outside the factory' (ibid.: 241). Following the disinterest of Harangos Rom in talking about their work in the factory, Stewart pays more attention to the ideology and logic of *Romani butji* as demonstrated, for example, in horse dealing at markets, through which Rom succeed in reinventing the social world and fashioning their own identities.[3] A similar distinction is evoked by Zatta and Piasere (1990) in emphasising the Roma preference for economic activities that allow maximum liberty and a tendency to avoid proletarianised jobs. They suggest that the key for Roma identities is the act of inverting the methods of production practised by non-Roma.

In studies of Roma, the field of work and labour becomes a site of struggle. Anthropologists have been quick to focus on Roma resilience and their varying degrees of involvement in, and resistance to, wage labour, which are seen as an indicator of Roma reinvention and ways of reproducing their distinctive identities in response to powerful oppressive state structures. Kata Horváth (2005) points out the recurrent tendency to emphasise the significance of the division between Roma work and paid work in the non-Roma world for reproducing Roma identity. Horváth critically reviews anthropological studies of Roma, which analytically circumscribe the striving for autonomy in income-generating strategies, and the reproduction of Roma distinctiveness amidst the adversity found among dominant societies. Rather than taking this division for granted, Horváth explores it ethnographically through her work with the Gypsies of Gömbalja in Hungary, and shows that their involvement in the wage labour of the non-Roma world does not necessarily mean some kind of loss of the 'Gypsy way of making a living' (ibid.: 40).

Following Horváth's critique, I situate Tarkovce Roma income-generating practices within ethnographic and historical contexts rather than replicating a dominant analytical perspective stemming from particular classic works on Roma. Similar to Horváth's informants, Tarkovce Roma often combine various ways of making money, which do not necessarily correspond to a greater degree of (semi-)autonomous socio-economic activity. In contrast to ethnographies documenting the existence of categories of 'Roma work' circumscribing specific practices carried out predominantly by Roma, such as horse dealing (Stewart 1997), scrap-metal collecting (Solimene, this volume), snail collecting (Horváth 2005) or blueberry picking (Abu Ghosh 2008), Tarkovce Roma do not deploy a distinctive category to speak of a specific type of work to which they would ascribe some kind of ideological significance. The contexts in which Tarkovce Roma evoke the category of 'Gypsy work' are shaped by meanings of the dominant Slovak term (*cigánska robota*) referring to poor-quality work traditionally associated with Gypsies (*Cigáni*).

Historical Continuities and Trajectories of Labour

From the beginning of my research in Tarkovce,[4] local Roma were keen to assert that 'our Roma know how to work' (*amare Roma džanen te keren*), or that they have always worked. Additionally, they proudly emphasised how, despite changing regimes and ensuing uncertainties, they were able to inventively 'think up' (*vyduminkeren*) ways of managing their livelihoods. Tarkovce Roma suggested not only that they had this creative capacity to come up with different innovative income-generating practices, but also that this predisposed them to be among the first ones to seize the opportune moment to devise and pursue certain practices. These two self-referential categorisations implied not only their skilfulness in terms of an ability to undertake skilled manual labour, but also the disposition to orient and navigate within changing socio-economic fields.

They often contrasted this positive self-representation as skilful labourers and as people actively searching out opportunities 'on the wing' with the dominant public representation of Roma as 'work-shy'. At the same time, they often deployed the same categorisation of 'lazy' or 'backward Gypsies' vis-à-vis Roma from other localities, networks and countries, or even other families from the village located in the spatial margins of what was referred to as a 'camp' (*taboris*). Additionally, some income-generating practices traditionally associated with 'Roma work', such as begging, would often be morally despised as 'being shameful' to engage in or referred to as belonging to the past, or as something Roma used to do in the 'old times' (*sar čirla*). This perspective was often displayed during encounters with Romanian Roma migrants begging or busking on the streets of British cities. When witnessing such activities, Tarkovce Roma often castigated their behaviour as morally dubious, shameful and contributing to the making of a bad name for Gypsies. While they acknowledged that in the past their ancestors used to go begging and often worked on the land of wealthier peasants in exchange for food or money, for most Tarkovce Roma such practices had been abandoned by their parents and grandparents during the socialist period.

The self-image of Tarkovce Roma as skilful and socially intelligent was often supported with reference to the socialist and postsocialist periods, in which Roma highlighted their self-ascribed primacy in seeking out, and creatively reinventing, various ways to get by. But this positive self-understanding was also evidenced by examples of their engagement with more skilled types of labour and jobs in which they would occupy more qualified posts, such as supervisory roles at their workplaces. Thus, throughout my fieldwork I was given a number of examples of Tarkovce Roma who were said to be 'masters' thanks to the quality of their work as judged by Roma and non-Roma. This practical mastery was given great recognition by Tarkovce Roma and often included social intelligence, know-how and practical skill in labour.

Becoming Socialist Labourers

As part of the socialist project aimed at transforming Roma from their lumpenproletariat condition into working-class citizens, many of the Tarkovce Roma became mobile labourers, frequently working *pro podnik* (that is, for state-owned companies). From the 1960s they were employed as bricklayers, construction workers and industrial factory workers. Additionally, some Roma men and women worked on socialist collective farms. Although most of them occupied low positions in their workplaces, many Tarkovce Roma finished their vocational training during the socialist period, and most of them were employed in state enterprises, travelling extensively for work and usually spending several weeks away from their homes in Tarkovce. This labour migration usually took place within socialist Czechoslovakia, but some Roma men also worked in various Soviet satellite states. This type of labour migration was also gendered, with men working mainly in construction while women were often employed as seamstresses. On many occasions, Tarkovce Roma men proudly proclaimed that 'we built Kosice', referring to their work on the socialist project of constructing several neighbourhoods in the regional centre of Kosice.

Among Tarkovce Roma, narratives of the socialist period in relation to work were ambiguous. On the one hand, socialist policies frequently led to their forced incorporation into a labour process in which they were located at the bottom of the working class. They were often engaged in heavy and physically demanding jobs. At the same time, the experience of working together in these workplaces and the stable income that Roma received during the socialist period often formed the basis of positive memories. This was especially true among men, for whom various work achievements, travel and associated adventures provided a springboard for public performances of the masculine self (cf. Horváth 2005: 45).[5] These stories were often recalled among men responding to each other with different variations on the same theme in search of recognition from other Roma listeners. Depending on the context and audience, these stories ranged from recalling hardships and productive achievements at work to jokes and anecdotes about adventures they had had outside work. Importantly, these stories were reinforced by the fact that they were referring to events experienced alongside other Tarkovce Roma inside as well as outside their workplaces. This was often the case despite the fact that, at least in theory, policymakers orchestrating the socialist ideology in relation to the 'Gypsy question' emphasised that Roma workers should be dispersed among their work brigades. The Roma were to be put to work alongside qualified non-Roma workers to enhance their skills and imbue them with a new work ethic. However, in the everyday realities of socialist Czechoslovakia, many Tarkovce Roma ended up working in the same work groups (Davidová 1965: 77–78; cf. Jurová 1993). They frequently declared that they worked with a 'good crowd' that was constitutive of good 'companionship' (*partija*).[6] To have good *partija* at one's workplace has continued to play an important role in Roma experiences of labour in the postsocialist period. Ranging from highway construction and working on the railways in the Czech Republic to their labour in food-production factories in the UK, Tarkovce Roma, and men in particular, generally preferred to work alongside their relatives and friends than to work alone.

In addition to Roma compulsory enrolment in the production processes, the socialist state launched various efforts to address the issue of Roma housing. In particular, this meant efforts to liquidate Roma settlements, seen as survivals of a 'backward' way of life (see Jurová 1993; Donert 2008). In Tarkovce, the socialist task of dismantling the old Gypsy settlement, which was spatially removed from the village centre, entailed a differentiation between families who moved out in order to construct their own houses and those who stayed in the old settlement until they were forced to move. The state provided a system of incentives to help poor Roma move and construct their own houses inside, or at least closer to, the village, which was inhabited predominantly by non-Roma up until the 1960s. Thus, a number of Tarkovce Roma managed to 'fix up' money from various state loans, to secure materials and to construct brick houses in close proximity to the village centre.

House construction was seen by the state as an indicator of the advances of the socialist project, but from the perspective of these families it was a sign of successful 'fixing up' and social mobility. They echoed this success by stating that 'even during socialism we knew how to live' and that 'we had a [good] level [of living standards]'. This proclaimed 'level' was evidenced by different ways of combining income-generating activities, but also by managing to skilfully manoeuvre within the socialist system by getting various loans or taking extra jobs to secure a higher income. Many Tarkovce Roma proudly stated that they managed to build their houses themselves using various state loans, the use of state materials and resources and the material and physical help of their extended families (a situation that is not dissimilar to non-Roma residents of Tarkovce). Even the building of houses was an index of their practical skill as labourers and their social intelligence in exploiting state support to their advantage and betterment. Additionally, many Roma families would engage in cultivating and selling their own vegetables to other Roma, as well as other forms of exchange in the socialist informal economy. Some asserted that their parents and grandparents had 'learnt how to *gazdovat* from the peasants'. The notion of *gazdovat* referred both to ways of farming and cultivating vegetables and fruit in their own gardens, and to ways of running the household and managing money. More generally, it also implied 'knowing how to live', which was contrasted with the behaviour of other Gypsies who were seen as socially marginal, symbolically lower and backward people (*degeši*) located at the opposite pole of the Roma spatial and symbolic continuum – such as Roma from other villages or Roma residing in the more poverty-stricken areas of Tarkovce, such as the camp (*taboris*).

The Unequal Road to Postsocialism

During the postsocialist period, most Roma continued to work informally in various precarious jobs, despite becoming formally unemployed. Opportunities in the formal job market in the region became scarce, more temporary and less secure. The resurgence of ethno-racial discrimination prevented Roma from accessing most of these jobs unless they already possessed sufficient social connections with potential employees. Consequently, more and more Roma became officially categorised as long-term unemployed, which led them to combine state benefits with various informal income-generating strategies (*fušky*). While women became more immobile and tended to stay in Tarkovce with some occasional seasonal work, many men entered labour-migration networks as construction workers or as ancillary workers on construction sites. During the 1990s, many of the men started to work with two local Roma businessmen in the Czech Republic on railway and highway construction projects. Periods of labour migration would range from several weeks to months of work in the Czech Republic, after which Roma labourers would return to Tarkovce (Grill 2009).

Some better-off Roma families were involved in selling cigarettes, alcohol, sweets and clothes smuggled from the Ukraine. These families would have a sufficient number of social connections with the smugglers in borderland villages, as well as the requisite economic capital, to enable them to purchase large amounts of smuggled goods at relatively low prices and then sell them in Tarkovce at higher prices. They would often own a car or could afford to pay someone to drive them to acquire the goods that they later sold. Additionally, some of these families were often engaged in lending money for what they called 'giving money on *kejčen*' (lending at high rates of interest). These types of moneylending and new forms of indebtedness contributed to the redrawing of nested hierarchies, forms of interdependency and moral ties in Tarkovce from the 1990s to the present day (cf. Hrustič, this volume). I also heard stories of several families who travelled to Turkey during the early 1990s to purchase clothes, which they later sold in Slovakia.

These various practices can be more broadly seen as attempts at 'fixing up' money. These practices were re-adjustments to previous types of hustling and inventive responses to the changing socio-economic context. What these efforts have in common is their spatio-temporal dimension, which is characterised by a snatching of opportunities 'on the wing' against the backdrop of changing socio-economic conditions. Few Tarkovce Roma have hesitated to travel or to try out previously untried strategies, seeking out different social fields and economic niches, in the hope of benefiting from these possibilities at opportune moments.

Additionally, several poorer Roma found temporary seasonal jobs in agriculture with local private farmers (for instance, harvesting tobacco). Some women also searched in the fields to collect gleanings (corn, herbs or chestnuts), which they then sold. Although similar to examples of 'Roma work' (cf. Horváth 2005), I have never heard people refer to these pursuits as *Romani butji*. In all these activities, most Tarkovce Roma oscillated between physically demanding labour in exploitative conditions, such as construction work in the Czech Republic and attempts to think up different income-generating strategies that would bring them more money within a shorter period of time.

From Asylum Seeking to 'Endured' Labour Migration

In addition to labour migration to the Czech Republic throughout the 1990s, another avenue of socio-economic mobility for Tarkovce Roma appeared in international migration, becoming one of the most explored. With the worsening socio-economic conditions and growing ethno-racial discrimination in Slovakia, many sought asylum in various Western European countries in the late 1990s and early 2000s. These asylum-seeking migrants managed to save up money obtained from the receiving host states' support provided while they waited for a decision on their asylum application, and from informal jobs carried out during that period. Following Slovakia's accession to the EU in 2004, many of these Roma started to travel to Britain as labour migrants. Suddenly, Roma migrants became classified as Slovak citizens and members of the European Union, with official rights to reside and work in Britain. Tarkovce Roma have been among the first Slovak migrants to British cities.[7]

Most of these Roma migrants were employed as temporary workers, finding work through job agencies. This usually meant earning the minimum wage (though deductions made by job agencies often meant that they earned even less) or working without a legal job contract. The jobs provided through agencies were also highly unstable and dependent on work performance and social connections. To be registered with a job agency involved 'flexible' workers being told not to come when it is 'not busy' (*nane busy*). In practice, this often meant alternating between periods of working for twelve hours at a time, such as in the run-up to Christmas when there is high demand for food, and periods of staying at home without being called on for several weeks. For example, Miro was employed for a long time packing newspapers. Although keen to work and to get paid overtime, he often had to wait several days before he was called. The regularity of work often depended on one's relationship with a line manager, the job agency, a friend or broker, one's performances on the job and, not infrequently, bribing one of the agency's employees.

While most Tarkovce Roma stayed in rather marginal and unstable positions as part of the temporary labour force, a smaller number managed to get more long-term jobs. These individuals often gained recognition from others for being employed directly through a *podnik* (company), in contrast to the majority of Roma, who found work via job agencies. Additionally, any progress within workplace hierarchies was praised by Roma as reflecting one's skill and intelligence combined with a good command of English. For example, I often heard of relatives who were praised for 'already having a yellow hat', reflecting an upward mobility on the ladder of workplace hierarchies. Some of these Tarkovce Roma who came to occupy relatively high positions in the production process were said to be working as 'supervisors' or 'managers'. These achievements were seen as resulting from an individual's intelligence (*godi*) connected with a proven record of being a skilful and diligent labourer (*baro robotníkos*) who has good connections with their superiors. This combination also echoes the notion of 'masterly work' (*majstrovska butji*), which was often used to describe the work of a skilled and experienced labourer recognised for the quality of their work. This combination also means that one's social intelligence, as an attribute of being Roma and a yardstick for gauging one's success at navigating within income-generating opportunities, does not necessarily have to stand in opposition to wage labour and can be employed within the social field of the paid workplace. Its skilful deployment can bring better contracts, greater flexibility at work or less physically demanding job positions.

Many Roma also found a relatively regular yet unstable income through various daily *fušky* (informal one-off works) for (frequently 'Pakistani') 'bosses'.[8] These jobs would vary from cleaning and renovating flats to delivering vegetables for grocery shops and cash-and-carry businesses. In all these jobs, ranging from informal one-off roles to more stable positions for various entrepreneurs, Tarkovce Roma tended to prefer working alongside their relatives or friends. While daily commutes to relatively distant factories were not a big problem if going together with Roma friends and family, jobs requiring travelling alone and working individually tended to be relatively rarely chosen.

These jobs exemplify a common trajectory for Tarkovce migrants, who were predominantly employed as low-skilled temporary manual labourers, often taking the positions most peripheral to the production process in the UK labour market, and usually facilitated by a job agency or by informal mediators. These brokers were usually other Roma with an accumulated volume of social capital who helped others obtain work, at times for free as a favour to friends and family and at other times involving a charge for their services. These jobs are often characterised by migrants as the 'dirtiest' and 'smelliest', such as working at 'car wash', sorting out refuse at rubbish dumps or working alongside co-workers considered 'dirty and stinking' (i.e other 'Gypsy' migrants, non-Roma 'Polish' or 'Slovaks'). Migrants often worked in 'cold' conditions, such with frozen meat or chicken. Due to physically demanding labour and long shifts, migrants often described these as 'heavy' (see Grill 2011).

Working in the UK has often been described by Roma as 'hard' (*phares*) and as involving 'big suffering for the money' and 'hard labour' (*phari butji*).[9] The term *phares* refers not only to the physical demands of these types of job but also to the 'heaviness' induced by the related conditions and circumstances structuring the everyday rhythm and pace of life. One must have the capacity and acquired disposition 'to endure' (*birinel*) demanding working conditions, as well as the strength 'to endure' (*likerel*) and to cope with the disrupted intensity of social ties with their closest. For example, when Tarkovce Roma referred to 'endured' labour, they often related it to the fact that these jobs made it difficult for them to spend more time with their children, or that they entailed separating members of extended families for long periods of time. While they would characterise their efforts and persistence in these jobs as a sacrifice for their children and as a general striving for a better life, they also reflected upon the physical consequences of such jobs.

Despite the physical hardship, the low salaries and the mostly temporary nature of the work, these jobs were often seen relationally as allowing the Roma to earn more money than they would get in Slovakia. Many Tarkovce Roma reiterated that the 'great poverty' of the past had been replaced by the relative wealth of the present thanks to migration. The fact that many of these migrants succeeded in their new lives in Britain was given as an example of their skilfulness and willingness to work despite the difficulty of the hard labour conditions and exploitative regimes of work they experienced. The poorly paid jobs they took and endured were risky, frequently dangerous, and part of the low-wage economy. There was a certain contradiction and ambiguity about the 'heaviness' of the opportunity in Britain, such as that between statements to the effect that 'I suffered a lot to (earn) this money', accompanied by frequent citations of the injuries and health problems suffered because of these types of job, and claims that in England 'We have a chance to earn'. It was through this type of long-term work and accumulated saving that Tarkovce Roma eventually managed to set aside some money.

At the same time, many Tarkovce Roma were simultaneously exploring other possibilities to 'fix up money'. And while the story of exemplary workers and tough labourers was the one told to most outsiders (such as journalists), a closer look shows a combination of 'endured labour' and other practices through which some Tarkovce Roma tried to improve their financial position. It was through a mixture of skill and social intelligence, of 'luck' (*bacht*) and of 'God's help', that some Tarkovce Roma managed to seize opportunities to make more money. It was this combination of and shifting between hard toil and other ways of 'fixing up' money that enabled some Tarkovce Roma to purchase big cars and houses, and make conspicuous displays of wealth and power.

Ways of 'Fixing Up' Money

As the case of Miro in the introduction makes clear, Tarkovce Roma were well aware of how hard they had to toil in order to earn money in Britain. They had to work and 'endure' physical labour. During the early years of migration, most Roma worked long hours and were poorly paid. It was then that some Tarkovce Roma started to explore other ways of generating money without having to endure so much physical labour and 'suffering'. These ways of 'fixing up' money were often said to be characteristic of the Tarkovce Roma capacity to inventively 'think up' ways of managing their livelihoods. But it was not enough to be able to identify these ways. Crucially, the level of one's practical skill and disposition was judged by the extent to which Roma managed to put these methods into practice.

Although these ways of 'fixing up' money were praised as reflecting the inventive qualities of Tarkovce Roma, most of them were based on knowledge acquired through various encounters during the settlement process in their new niches (in Britain but also in other places they inhabited on their previous migratory journeys). While some actions were informed by a readjustment of dispositions acquired in their previous social fields to the new conditions in Britain, a lot was learnt from other groupings occupying similar niches in their new destinations. The process of learning how to 'fix up money' was often situated at this particular conjuncture between prior dispositions and readjustments to new conditions. These groupings were represented in essentialising terms that ascribed certain characteristics and economic practices to particular categories (e.g. 'Pakistanis' or 'Russians'). In this process, Tarkovce Roma would often learn about various opportunities from other Roma, such as 'Roma from [a neighbouring] town [in Slovakia]' who had migrated earlier and already had the necessary knowledge and connections, or from other networks. Some of the Roma, for example, suggested that they had learnt from 'Pakistanis' how to manoeuvre within the British state system in order to receive higher amounts of money from social benefits (to which they were mostly legally entitled due to their low income and EU citizenship). Some families made some readjustments to certain details of their personal circumstances in order to be granted higher benefits or to be eligible for other forms of support. The ability to do so required a social connection to someone knowledgeable person who was willing to help for payment or as a favour. The Roma who gained these types of knowledge quickest were then in an advantageous position in terms of knowing how to 'fix up' money. So when new migrants arrived, more experienced migrants were often contacted to help out with filling in applications, finding work or registering at job agencies. These forms of help were sometimes provided for free to friends or family members, but more frequently a payment of some sort was required.

The Roma used migration for skilful manoeuvring of formalised practices to create various ways to 'fix up' money. Halfway through my fieldwork, for instance, several Tarkovce families brought news of potential ways of making 'big money'. This involved doing business with several men whom everyone referred to simply as 'the Russians'. Although no one really knew who these men were or where they had come from, everyone knew of several families who had made deals with them. Using Roma people's bank cards, the 'Russians' promised to perform a trick that allowed them to withdraw many times more than the card's limit. The sum acquired was then divided between the Russians and the Roma. However, although promising the possibility of significant monetary gain, the activity was a highly risky enterprise and its success was far from guaranteed. While some families were said to profit from this, many other families suggested that it did not work and only 'ruined' one's bank account. Success and failure were explained with reference to luck, timing and the skill of the Russians. At times, failure was said to be due to trickery or a lack of skill on the part of the Russians. Alternatively, both the Roma and the Russians evoked 'bad luck' in terms of the timing of the trick, which was said to be crucial for succeeding in the action. Many other Roma were wary of these types of schemes and criticised them.

This type of risky deal demonstrates several important aspects of strategies to 'fix up money'. It illustrates how some Roma families explored the window of opportunity open to them within the initial years following Slovakia's admission to the EU. Due to the experiences of asylum-seeking migration in the UK, many Tarkovce Roma possessed sufficient amounts of social and symbolic capital to enable them not only to be among the first Slovak migrants to Britain, but also, crucially, to act quickly within the interstitial spaces of various systems opened up and facilitated by the Slovak entry to the EU. These pathways were often temporary and quickly closed off. For example, some of the Tarkovce Roma's knowledge of English and the system afforded them an advantage over less experienced migrants to whom they offered help in exchange for varying fees. The Roma were aware of the limited duration of these efforts, and knew that the key to success was not only to understand certain techniques or mechanisms but also to explore these at a particular moment.

Many of the 'fixing up' strategies disappeared within a couple of months or years following wider socio-economic changes and the influx of new migrants. This coincided with increasing supervision of and restrictions placed on new EU migrants by state institutions, growing negative perceptions leading to greater scrutiny and suspicion, and the over-exploitation of these economic niches and avenues by other migrants. The temporal dimension of these practices also highlights the pace of gossip and the transmission of knowledge about different ways of making quick money. These opportunities arising 'on the wing' would often appear and disappear quickly, and migrants' efforts at exploring them would end up with mixed results.

Concluding Remarks

This chapter has explored the economic strategies of Tarkovce Roma, which have historically oscillated between paid physical labour and various ways of 'fixing up' money through skilful manoeuvring within different state systems. I have used 'oscillation' as a term that, complementing prior ethnographic studies focusing on the resistance and reinvention of Romani identities within specific socio-economic niches, as well as analysing state violence and oppressive disciplinary efforts, allows us to simultaneously consider engagements with different state systems and types of wage labour. Rather than seeing niches of wage labour and of Roma work as opaque, or as located in opposition to each other ideologically or spatio-temporally, one can argue for viewing these practices as coexisting. Their successful combination and practical mastery have helped Tarkovce Roma to continuously manage their livelihood during turbulent times of socio-economic discord. In contrast to the clearly delineated ideological resistance to wage labour described in various anthropological studies, the Tarkovce Roma incorporated some elements of socialist ideology and of *Gadžo* social order while rejecting other aspects of these in order to skilfully manoeuvre within the confines of the state system. This process of incorporation was selective, conflicting and contradictory. Their engagement in arduous work in factories and on construction sites during the socialist era, or in food production factories in Britain, did not necessarily conflict with Roma modes of self-understanding. Lacking elaborated discourses pivoting on the notion of *Romani butji*, Tarkovce Roma did not maintain any clear ideological distinction between wage labour for non-Roma and more autonomous economic niches, which were crucial to the reinvention of their Roma identity. I suggest that this lack does not necessarily have to be interpreted as an indicator of Tarkovce Roma assimilation during socialism or as a loss of 'traditional' cultural forms and autonomy; rather, it can be seen a matter of blurring boundaries, selective acquisition and transformation in which they incorporated some elements while resisting others. In other words, their wage labour within the socialist economy and their contextual and selective use of elements of socialist ideology translated into the desired attainment of the notion of 'progress', which did not necessarily conflict with their sense and performance of being Roma. Becoming a diligent labourer, regardless of whether this was claimed only at a discursive level or whether it was also put into practice in the eyes of their co-workers and superiors, was not necessarily mutually exclusive to a constant readiness to exploit state systems to their own advantage.

Through this historically informed account I have outlined several continuities in the social trajectories of Tarkovce Roma. I have shown how Roma incorporation into various types of wage labour in the non-Roma world from the socialist period to the present day, coupled with various ways of 'fixing up' within interstitial spaces of the state and changing social fields, contributed to them acquiring certain dispositions that enabled them to skilfully navigate within the grey zones emerging from larger geo-political transformations. It was not necessarily the type of work that mattered to Tarkovce Roma, but rather the way in which one managed to succeed in generating income, guided by skilful manoeuvring and social intelligence. One might locate this process within a shifting continuum of constant adaptation and active responses to larger socio-political changes, rather than as adherence to more clearly delineated, rigorously maintained ideological boundaries.

NOTES

1. All names in this chapter have been changed by the author.
2. The notion of oscillation can be compared to discussions of 'fuzzy' logics (Piasere 1998) and on 'separation/amalgamation' (Williams 2011).
3. Olivera's (2012) work on Gabor Roma also emphasises the centrality of 'Roma work' in the process of identity construction. See also the chapters by Olivera and Solimene (this volume).
4. I carried out participant observation among Roma in Tarkovce and in selected migration destinations in Britain between 2006 and 2008. I have conducted a number of research revisits since 2008.
5. Due to space limitations, it is beyond the scope of this chapter to address the gendered differences between Roma men and women in the workplace.
6. The same term *partija* was used when referring to the act of 'making a good crowd' of men who would get together to drink or go on adventures.
7. These forms of migration are not specific to Roma and must be situated within wider patterns of labour migration from Central Eastern Europe (see e.g. Berger and Mohr 1975; Eade, Drinkwater and Garapich 2006; Ryan et al. 2008, 2009; Favell and Nebe 2009; Burikova and Miller 2010; Ryan 2010; Kaneff and Pine 2011; Parutis 2011; Morosanu 2013; Marushiakova 2014). Tarkovce Roma occupy similar structural positions to other migrants from the region, and frequently work alongside each other in low-skilled jobs within the UK labour market. However, more recently, Roma migrants have encountered

new forms of stigmatisation in Britain leading them to occupy some of the lowest positions within workplace ethnic hierarchies (see e.g. Fox, Morosanu and Szilassi 2012; Grill 2012; Morosanu and Fox 2013).
8. These casual jobs (*fušky*) usually consisted of cleaning, bricklaying, gardening and painting, and payment was in cash (£20 to £35 per one-off job or per day).
9. This juxtaposition echoes the opposition between 'working for a wage as *pares*: heavy' and the 'Gypsy work; ... "light" and "easy"', described by Stewart (1997: 25). However, this division was much more blurred among Tarkovce Roma.

REFERENCES

Abu Ghosh, Y. 2008. 'Escaping Gypsyness: Work, Power and Identity in the Marginalization of Roma', Ph.D. diss. Prague: Charles University.
Berger, J., and J. Mohr. 1975. *A Seventh Man: The Story of the Migrant Worker in Europe*. Harmondsworth: Penguin Books.
Buriková, Z., and D. Miller. 2010. *Au Pair*. London: Polity Press.
Davidová, E. 1965. *Bez Kolíb a šiatrov*. Kosice: Východoslovenské vydavateľstvo.
Donert, C. 2008. '"Citizens of Gypsy Origins": The Roma in the Reconstruction of Czechoslovakia, 1948–1989', Ph.D. diss. Florence: European University Institute.
Eade, J., S. Drinkwater and M. Garapich. 2006. *Class and Ethnicity: Polish Migrants in London*. London: Centre for Research on Nationalism, Ethnicity and Multiculturalism, University of Roehampton.
Favell, A., and T.M. Nebe. 2009. 'Internal and External Movers: East–West Migration and the Impact of EU Enlargement', in E. Recchi and A. Favell (eds), *Pioneers of European Integration: Citizenship and Mobility in the EU*. Cheltenham: Edward Elgar, pp.205–23.
Formoso, B. 2000. 'Economic Habitus and Management of Needs: The Example of Gypsies', *Diogenes* 48(2): 58–73.
Fox J.E., L. Morosanu and E. Szilassy. 2012. 'The Racialization of the New European Migration to the UK', *Sociology* 46(4): 680–95.
Gay y Blasco, P. 1999. *Gypsies in Madrid: Sex, Gender and the Performance of Identity*. Oxford: Berg Publishers.
Grill, J. 2009. '"Mange mište pro Čechy": Slovenští Romové na Českých Stavbách', Czech Made. Retrieved 10 March 2013 from: http://migraceonline.cz/cz/e-knihovna/mange-miste-pro-cechy-mne-je-v-cechach-dobre-slovensti-romove-na-ceskych-stavbach.
———. 2011. 'From Street Busking in Switzerland to Meat Factories in the UK: A Comparative Study of Two Roma Migration Networks from Slovakia', in D. Kaneff and F. Pine (eds), *Global Connections and Emerging Inequalities in Europe: Perspectives on Poverty and Transnational Migration*. London: Anthem Press, pp.78–102.
———. 2012. '"It's Building Up to Something and It Won't Be Nice When It Erupts": Making of Roma Migrants in Post-industrial Scotland', *Focaal* 62: 42–54.
Horváth, K. 2005. 'Gypsy Work – Gadjo Work', *Romani Studies* 15(1): 31–49.
Jurová, A. 1993. *Vývoj Rómskej Problematiky na Slovensku po Roku 1945*. Bratislava: Goldpress Publishers.

Kaneff, D., and F. Pine (eds). 2011. *Global Connections and Emerging Inequalities in Europe: Perspectives on Poverty and Transnational Migration*. London: Anthem Press.

Marushiakova, E. 2014. 'Roma from Southeastern Europe: Living and Working in Migration', Working Paper. Berlin: IGK Work and Human Lifecycle in Global History.

Morosanu, L. 2013. 'Between Fragmented Ties and "Soul Friendship": The Cross-border Social Connections of Young Romanians in London', *Journal of Ethnic and Migration Studies* 39(3): 353–72.

Morosanu, L., and J.E. Fox. 2013. '"No Smoke Without Fire": Strategies of Coping with Stigmatised Migrant Identities', *Ethnicities* 13(4): 438–56.

Okely, J. 1983. *The Traveller-Gypsies*. Cambridge: Cambridge University Press.

Olivera, M. 2012. *La tradition de l'intégration. Une ethnologie des Roms Gabori dans les années 2000*. Paris: Éditions Pétra.

Parutis V. 2011. '"Economic Migrants" or "Middling Transnationals"? East European Migrants' Experiences of Work in the UK', *International Migration* 52(1): 36–55.

Piasere, L. 1998. 'Le culture della parentela. Un approccio cognitivo fuzzy', in L. Piasere and P.G. Solinas (eds), *Le Culture della parentela e l'esogamia perfetta*. Roma: Centro Informazione Stampa Universitaria, pp.1–202.

Ryan, L. 2010. 'Becoming Polish in London: Negotiating Ethnicity Through Migration', *Social Identities* 16(3): 359–76.

Ryan, L., R. Sales, M. Tilki and B. Siara. 2008. 'Social Networks, Social Support and Social Capital: The Experiences of Recent Polish Migrants in London', *Sociology* 42(4): 672–90.

———. 2009. 'Family Strategies and Transnational Migration: Recent Polish Migrants in London', *Journal of Ethnic and Migration Studies* 35(1): 61–77.

Stewart, M. 1997. *The Time of the Gypsies*. Boulder, CO: Westview Press.

———. 1999. '"Brothers" and "Orphans" Images of Equality among Hungarian Rom', in S. Day, E. Papataxiachis and M. Stewart (eds), *Lilies of the Field: Marginal People Who Live For the Moment*. Boulder, CO: Westview Press, pp.27–44.

Williams, P. 2011. 'Ethnologie der Zigeuner: Von der Begegnung zur Theoriebildung', *Behemoth* 4(1): 43–56.

Zatta, J.D., and Piasere, L. 1990. 'Stealing from the Gago: Some Notes on Roma Ideology', *Études et documents balkaniques et mediterranéens* 15: 163–72.

Jan Grill is Simon Research Fellow at the Department of Social Anthropology, University of Manchester. He joined the University of Manchester in 2012 after completing his Ph.D. in social anthropology at the University of St Andrews. He has carried out ethnographic research with Roma groups, exploring issues related to different forms of migration from Central Eastern Europe. He previously worked as a temporary lecturer at the University of Manchester and held a Re:Work Fellowship with IGK Work and Human Life Cycle in Global History at Humboldt University, Berlin, and an ERSTE Foundation Fellowship for Social Research.

Chapter 5

'I Go for Iron'

Xoraxané Romá Collecting Scrap Metal in Rome

MARCO SOLIMENE

The Roma in Italy are faced with a blend of indifference and discrimination intrinsic to the legal order and its representatives, as well as to the media and contemporary political discourses (Brunello 1996; ERRC 2000; Sigona 2002, 2005; Clough Marinaro 2003, 2009; Simoni 2005, 2008; Piasere 2006b, 2012; Petronio 2008; Tosi Cambini 2011).[1] Italian authorities seldom concern themselves with the Roma, and when they do their intervention consists almost uniquely of policies of exclusion and repression. Projects of integration are few, are designed in a top-down manner and often confuse integration with assimilation (Sigona and Monasta 2006). The policy of the so-called 'nomad camps' (*campi nomadi*) is a paradigmatic expression of Italy's attitude towards the Roma (ERRC 2000; Sigona 2002, 2005). As Saletti-Salza (2003: 49–54) argues, camps find their *raison d'être* in a political category, that of the nomad, which in turn finds tautological proof of its existence in the existence of the nomad camps. Illegal camps are precarious encampments in parklands, abandoned buildings and deserted parking lots; their inhabitants are exposed to harsh weather, a lack of basic facilities and the constant threat of eviction by police. Legal camps – far less numerous than illegal ones – are shanties situated on the outskirts of Italian cities, and have proven to be devices for the confinement, control and discipline of the bodies, minds and ultimately the lives of their inhabitants (Brunello 1996; Todesco 2004: 103; Piasere 2006b; Clough Marinaro 2009; Daniele 2011, 2013).

The Roma, therefore, are treated as what Bauman calls 'exceeding humanity' (Bauman 2004: 34–58), cumbersome social waste to be disposed of in camps that express and produce a relation of non-belonging to majority society (Piasere 2006b). This situation has brought some scholars (Todesco 2004: 103–4; Piasere 2006b; Clough Marinaro 2009; Solimene

2012, 2013) to compare the figure of the Gypsy in contemporary Italy to Agamben's *homo sacer*, the banned man exposed to the biopolitical violence of the exception (Agamben 1998, 2005). This comparison has proved particularly apt for describing the harshness faced by the Roma in recent years. Indeed, the influx of migration from Romania following the EU's enlargement in January 2007 provoked panicked reactions in Italian society. Authorities responded by framing the presence of the Roma as a national 'security emergency' (*emergenza sicurezza*) and by enforcing exceptional measures, which subjected the Roma to systematic evictions, increased surveillance and confinement, continual police raids, harassments and expulsion (Sigona 2008, 2010; Clough Marinaro 2009; Costi 2010; Clough Marinaro and Sigona 2011; Solimene 2011a).

Scholars have often noted the role played by economic activities in the negotiation of power relations between Roma communities and non-Roma (see e.g. Okely 1979, 1983: 49–65; Kaprow 1984; Piasere 2000; Golino 2004; Engebrigsten 2007). In their studies of, respectively, the Hungarian Vlach Rom and the Romanian Gabori, Stewart (1997, 1999) and Olivera (2012; also this volume) have provided powerful ethnographic descriptions of the strict interconnection between Romani occupations (*Romani butji*) and the process of identity construction. *Romani butji*, described as a matter of savoir-faire and a way of doing things, is embedded in an ethos opposed to that which pervades the mode of production of non-Roma societies. As such, it represents an important marker of distinction with the non-Roma, reinforces the Rom and Gabori vision of themselves as cunning and lucky (*baxtalé*) – in the Gabori case, also blessed with divine favour – and thereby confirms (at least ideologically) the independence of the Rom and Gabori from the strictures and dictates imposed by non-Roma society.

The present article builds on this body of work. Its aim is to present a case study that explores practical and symbolic implications of scrap-metal collection carried out by some Bosnian Xoraxané (Muslim) Romá families living in the Rome metropolitan area.[2] Drawing on an ethnographic case from my research, I will discuss the practices of collection, separation and sale of the metal before turning to the spatial strategies adopted by the Romá and the relations they establish with their working territories. My aim is to show how 'going for iron' (*te ǧa pala sastri*), as the Romá call this activity, contributes to the negotiation of group identity in relation to both the *Rumuni* (the Romá term for the Romanian Roma, many of whom collect scrap metal too) and the non-Roma, and to demonstrate how this activity responds perfectly to the ambiguities and contradictions of the Italian socio-economic system, ultimately triggering mechanisms of mutual appropriation between individual Romá and specific working territories. I will also argue that 'going for iron' is encompassed in the symbolic system of Romani life, and allows the Romá to bend the biopolitical figure of the Gypsy/*homo sacer* to the Romani agenda. This activity thus turns into an occasion for the Romá to assert and produce their independence from the biopolitics pervading Italian discourses about the Gypsies/Roma.

The Everyday Practice of 'Going for Iron'

The subjects of this chapter are several families of Bosnian Xoraxané Romá living in the south-western periphery of Rome. These Romá migrated to Italy between the 1960s and the 1990s; today, many are present illegally within Italy's borders, and some (particularly among the younger generations) lack official documents attesting to their identity. This situation exposes them to the measures that turn immigrants (especially irregular ones) into non-persons in juridical and social terms (Dal Lago 2004). Given their borderline legal condition and the impediments the Roma in general encounter in the Italian labour market (CGIL et al. 2009), the Romá rely heavily on the informal economy, their repertoire ranging from begging, scavenging and collecting scrap metal to selling counterfeit merchandise and second-hand vehicles.[3]

Some of the families I discuss here dwell in an authorised nomad camp situated in a marginal area of the Magliana district. This settlement is an expanse of containers and caravans, encircled by a metal fence and kept under surveillance by private security hired by the municipality. To maintain a place in the camp, the Romá must have a visa, pay a monthly fee and observe a code of conduct that regulates behaviour and practices within the settlement.[4] Other families dwell instead in illegal nomad camps, that is, precarious clusters of tents, shacks and/or caravans distributed in parklands and interstitial spaces of the Magliana district and faced with the constant threat of eviction.

I have known these Romá since 1999 and still visit them during my regular sojourns in Rome. A number of families were involved in the ethnographic fieldwork I conducted between April 2007 and May 2008. During my immersion in the daily lives of the Romá, I had the opportunity to observe and participate in scrap-metal collection. In Rome, this activity is colloquially called *ferrivecchi* (old iron), a term that applies also to the object of collection and to the collectors themselves.[5] Once a typical occupation of the Roman underclass, over the last three decades scrap-metal collection has gradually been abandoned by the non-Roma and taken over by the Roma, who nowadays embody the new figure of the *ferrivecchi* in Rome. For the Romá, 'going for iron' means collecting metal objects from dustbins and skips, the roadside and wasteland, or directly from people who want to get rid of old metal; after collection, the metals are extracted, sorted, and eventually sold to Italian metal dealers.

The Romá combine collection, separation and sale in varied ways. Some perform these activities in the same day; more often, however, the Romá dedicate a specific working day to the separation process and the sale of valuable metals (such as copper, brass, steel, aluminium), maintaining a regular income by selling cheap but cumbersome iron on a daily basis. There is usually no day of rest, though work is less intense on weekends, when metal dealers are closed (or open only in the morning) and Italians are not at home (or just do not want to deal with Gypsy *ferrivecchi*). In order to collect and transport metal, the Romá use lorries. Men work usually with brothers and/or older sons – though sometimes they are accompanied by wives or daughters. Those needing additional labour (especially families that can afford more than one lorry) hire day-workers, predominantly *Rumuni*, who are assigned to heavy manual duties (loading, unloading and sometimes separating metals). The daily wage of these workers is between €25 and €35, plus food and cigarettes. Cases of long-lasting work relations are not rare; nonetheless, most *Rumuni* see working for the Romá as temporary, something that they seek out only occasionally.[6]

A typical working day starts around 7 o'clock in the morning. Coffee and cigarettes accompany the wait for the arrival of workers, who usually live in neighbouring settlements; the lorries leave as early as possible in order to avoid the morning traffic congestion. Each Rom working with scrap metal has areas of collection that he habitually visits – generally peripheries, conurbations and small towns surrounding the metropolitan area – and in a working day he usually crosses two or three adjacent ones. Routes follow roughly outlined itineraries adjusted according to time, loading capacity, traffic and appointments with customers. Movements between areas are quick, and secondary roads known to locals are preferred to major arteries, which are congested and more rigorously controlled by the police.

Once inside an area of collection, the lorry slows down. Megaphones are turned on to broadcast a formulaic message announcing the arrival of 'your *ferrivecchi*!' and specifying the services provided: 'We collect iron, metal, old cookers, fridges, washing machines, stoves, gates, bathtubs!' 'We clean gardens and basements!' Sometimes, to focus on the search and spare the voice, the Romá use pre-recorded tapes (which every Rom records for himself as a sort of personal signature). The area is meticulously canvassed, street by street, in search of scrap or somebody responding to the broadcast announcement. The Romá specifically stop at building sites, smiths, farms and houses where renovations are taking place; there, they check 'whether there is *ferrovecchio* and help is needed to get rid of it'. The Romá also pay a visit to their regular customers, who often tip them off about working opportunities in the neighbourhood. Most of the metal is collected directly from people who stop the *ferrivecchi* to give away old scrap. Sometimes metal objects are found near gates or entrances to dwellings. In this case, the Romá make sure to get permission to take them; if they find no interlocutor, they leave the objects there, considering their monetary value insignificant in comparison to the possible repercussions of being suspected of theft in a neighbourhood. In most cases the scrap material is loaded immediately; when this in not feasible (such as when it is too cumbersome or is not yet ready for removal), the Romá make an appointment to pick it up later (obtaining the promise that it will not be given to the competition). Systematically, the Romá leave their phone numbers 'in case of future need'.

Two or three times a day there are pauses for coffee and food, usually in bars situated on habitual routes and/or at the borders of collection areas. In these bars, the Romá maintain friendly relations with landlords, employees and customers, who may provide tips about traffic and working opportunities and information about neighbourhood gossip. Conversations are comprised of jokes and of small-talk about the two main topics in Italian bars (football and politics), everyday life experiences and even relatively personal issues about health and family; thus, interactions in bars also prove precious occasions to construct and maintain familiarity with a territory.

Collection usually continues until afternoon or until the lorry is full; then the Romá return to their settlement, unload the lorry and sort the metal out. The removal of non-metal elements and the separation of different metals are loud and messy operations. Hammers, axes and grinders are employed to dismantle the objects collected. Fire can be used to soften the plastic cover of electrical wire (and thus facilitate the extraction of copper); sometimes the Romá let the plastic melt completely, with the consequent rise of black columns of acrid smoke. Usually the work of separating materials involves different family members: women help by tending the fire and moving light loads; children sometimes contribute by tearing the plastic insulation from electric cables; adult men carry out the tiring and dangerous use of tools.

The final phase consists of selling the collected materials to Italian private companies dealing in scrap metal. Here, the valuable metals are first unloaded and weighed separately by an operator. The lorry, now loaded only with iron, is then driven onto a weighing scale and subsequently unloaded in an open space. The bulldozers regularly clearing this space sometimes speed up the unloading operation by hauling the scrap from open lorries with a giant vice; their operators use this opportunity to ensure that no other materials (such as stone or concrete) is concealed in the load to increase the weight. Once emptied, the lorry is weighed again and the amount of iron unloaded can be calculated. Finally, the Romá enter the dealer's office and get paid.

Since the scales are rarely precise, and both parties have a repertoire of techniques for cheating,[7] arguments between Romá and metal dealers are not uncommon. Most frequent disagreements concern the quality, price and weight of the metals. The Romá try to raise the weight and value of their scrap by questioning the precision of the scale or the dealer's ability – or reliability – to read instruments and recognise metals. Also, the Romá make claims about other dealers offering better prices, emphasise that loyal customers such as themselves deserve better treatment, and complain that given the lack of work the cost of fuel will 'eat' the day's income. The dealers in turn point out the potential losses in being too accommodating with the requests of every *ferrivecchi*, complain about the expenses of being in the business, question the ability – or reliability – of the Romá to recognise metals and read the scale, and underline that the same drama is staged every single day. The reciprocal controls, bargains and arguments characterising the whole transaction signal a certain level of discretion and flexibility in the business, but they also indicate that relations between Romá and metal dealers are characterised by mutual distrust. Nonetheless, every Rom eventually chooses a dealer to do business with; usually, the choice falls on one who is situated in close proximity to their settlement, but who also offers better prices and is reputed to be more reliable than others, easier to outwit, and/or more accommodating.

While selling to the dealers, the Romá use the opportunity to chat with other *ferrivecchi* (mostly Romá, but also other Roma and Italians) about the day's luck, the rumours in the business and the latest vicissitudes in the Romani world. The moments spent at metal dealers, therefore, are also important social occasions: a Rom gains new insights and information about the business of the *ferrivecchi*, but also maintains and develops sociability in the Romani world, especially with Romá living outside their settlement.

The everyday practices connected to 'going for iron' described here cannot be isolated from a process of constant appropriation of space. This argument echoes that proposed by Tauber (2008: 162–63), who noted that Sinti women begging in northern Italy appropriated a working territory by constructing a number of good relations with locals, and by producing mental maps functioning as mnemonic tools for remembering routes, persons and places to frequent (and those to avoid). By analysing the spatial strategies of the Romá and their relations with customers, the local population and authorities, I will thus show that 'going for iron' is embedded in a meticulous labour process directed at gaining and maintaining familiarity with working territories and acceptance by those living therein.

Spatial Strategies and Mutual Appropriations

The collection of scrap metal practised by the Romá is concentrated around Rome's conurbations and its neighbouring coastal towns. These localities (conglomerations of industrial areas, districts with a great deal of construction in progress, and rural zones) are easy to reach, rich in raw materials and subject to relatively low surveillance by the authorities. Movement occasionally extends beyond the 100 kilometre range from the settlement; in farther and less accessible areas competition is lower, and privileged relations with the local population may provide good loads that counterbalance the expense of time and fuel.

In order to optimise the collection process and maintain the pressure of the Gypsy *ferrivecchi* within a territory's threshold of tolerance, the Romá follow two guidelines: first, a system of rotation grants a territory some resting days before being worked again by the same Rom; second, a partition system accords the right of usufruct of a territory to the first collector who enters it – until his departure.[8] The partition system, which is the outcome of a tacit agreement between collectors who regularly work the same area, is a general principle rather than a mandatory rule; its stringency fades with social distance between collectors or in moments of high competition. Besides, the Romá working an area for many years somehow consider all the other collectors intruders – especially if they belong to other Roma groups – and thus may deliberately contravene the partition system to assert their prerogative on a territory they reckon as properly theirs. Therefore, open quarrels and arguments between *ferrivecchi* are not rare. Indirect confrontations, however, are far more common: behind a facade of non-belligerence, competitors curse each other, try shortcuts and other manoeuvres to cut their rivals out of a collection area, and bad-mouth each other to their own customers.

What certifies a neighbourhood as a Rom's working territory is the establishment of good and durable relations with the local population and authorities. In their area, the Romá have their habitual clients, who do not turn to the competition to get rid of scrap, who spare them a fruitless search for metals by informing them if other *ferrivecchi* have already passed by, and who call if there is work to be done, tip them off about anyone who is clearing a basement, or introduce them to neighbours. Even relations with the police are relatively good (or at least non-conflictive) in the habitual working territories. This ensures that one can work and not be subject to repeated spot checks or suspected of stealing from building sites. Also, just like any other citizen, police officers may become clients of the Romá after being introduced to the *ferrivecchi* by a neighbour or taking a Rom's phone number right after a random check in the street – Boban, one of my Romá interlocutors, still boasts about the several lorries he loaded when clearing the cellar of a police station.

It may be asserted that the Romá select their territory just like a territory chooses its Gypsy *ferrivecchi*. In this sort of mutual appropriation, the Romá eventually turn into normal elements of the local landscape, and the topographic and human landscape of a working territory becomes familiar to the Romá. While wandering with Nasser (a good friend of mine among the Romá) around a coastal neighbourhood in search of scrap metal, for example, I realised that this Rom was a well-known face at the newspaper stand and the local supermarket, a regular customer of the local tobacconist and the petrol station. Some clients treated him as an old acquaintance, and his lorry was immediately recognised by locals as that of a familiar *ferrivecchi* whose service was available to everybody. Nasser in turn disclosed to me rhythms and vicissitudes of the lives unfolding on the streets and behind the gates we were driving by: the man living in the red house was a retired surgeon and his sons were living in Rome; the woman Nasser had previously greeted along the main road was divorced, and her daughter was often in hospital with liver problems (and she was throwing a bathtub away, but that was not worth the trouble of reaching her); the guy we had been chatting with at the bar was a carpenter and a good client, while his brother was scum and in jail (Nasser had once refused to buy a car from him, as he mistrusted the *Gağó*).[9]

Therefore, access to an area of collection and the abundance of what is collected mainly depend on what Piasere calls the '*Gağikanó* capital' (Piasere 1999: 98), that is, a Rom's network of long-lasting relations among the *Gağé* and their ability to gain the latter's appreciation and respect.[10]

Gağikanó capital is the key to the best source of metal and information about it, and is also the instrument that breaks the invisible barrier of diffidence towards the Gypsies, allowing the Romá to eventually gain acceptance in a working territory. Furthermore, relational networks and a good reputation may lead to other economic transactions, open up the possibility of legal employment (required in order to request a visa) or simply provide new insights into the *Gağikanó* world. The importance of *Gağikanó* capital in a working territory can be observed in the efforts the Romá devote to cultivating it, such as by showing availability, producing narratives of symbiotic relations with their customers, displaying cultural similarity with the Italians and remarking on the history of relatively peaceful coexistence between the 'Bosnian Gypsies' – *Zingari Bosniaci*, as the Romá define themselves to the Italians – and Italian society.

This effort to maintain good relations with a working territory has become crucial in recent years, as the influx of migrants from Romania has had serious repercussions on the scrap-metal business. Once many newly arrived *Rumuni* began collecting scrap metal, competition increased drastically; it also grew harsher because, the Romá lament, the *Rumuni* (as EU citizens) have relatively easy access to documents and make arrangements with non-Roma Romanians working on building sites. But the major impact of the recent migration of the *Rumuni* originates in the fact that the anti-Gypsy sentiment pervading Italian society has been exacerbated by the proliferation of Gypsies roaming the city in search of scrap and the increased frequency of theft from building sites and railways, which Italian media and the Romá attribute mainly to Romanian Gypsies (Solimene 2011b: 642-44).

In other words, the recent deterioration in relations between Rome and its Romani population affected the reputation of the Gypsy *ferrivecchi* in general, also jeopardising the good relations the Romá had established with their working territories. In the last few years, therefore, the Romá have worked hard to convince the Italians of the difference between Bosnian and Romanian 'Gypsies'. Distinctions are made explicit by describing the 'Bosnian Gypsies' as hardworking providers of a useful service and by patiently explaining to the Italians that – using the words of the Romá – 'the Bosnian Gypsies have been living in Italy for decades without hurting anybody ... At most our women steal wallets, but with sleight of hand and only from tourists', and that the 'Romanian Gypsies – instead – are nasty and violent', they 'do not respect Italians nor other Gypsies', they are arrogant 'because their stay in Italy is only temporary', they 'drive too fast and use megaphones too loudly, ask fees for their services and take scrap without permission'. Difference between Bosnian and Romanian 'Gypsies' is also demonstrated to customers by the separation of roles between the technical tasks performed by the Romá and the simple manual tasks reserved for their *Rumuni* workers, or by the embarrassment exhibited by the Romá in conversations with customers and Gağé acquaintances about the rude behaviour of their workers.

In their interactions with the *Gağé*, therefore, the Romá distance themselves from the *Rumuni* by portraying the latter as arrogant, boisterous, rough and uncivilised – an inverted version of the self-image the Romá present to Italians. By proposing an idealised convergence of moralities and a commonality of interests with the Italians, and opposing these to the antagonistic morality and interests of the Romanian 'Gypsies', the Romá attempt to restore a delicate balance with their working territories, cut out the competition and thus maintain their place in an increasingly competitive field of business.

Baxt, Šoró and Divine Favour: The Symbolic Implications of 'Going for Iron'

The collection of scrap metal has no place of honour in the economic eclecticism of the Romá. Unlike activities such as begging (*te ğa te mang-*) and pick-pocketing (*te ğa te čhor-*) – which the Romá somehow consider traditional occupations of Slavic Romá women[11] – 'going for iron' is just 'work' (*radí*), the same practised by the *Gağé* poor; and like other manual occupations of the *Gağé*, it is dirty and physically exhausting. Besides, increased competition and the exacerbation of anti-Gypsy discourses within Italian society are making the activity of the Gypsy *ferrivecchi* more difficult, riskier and less remunerative.

Nonetheless, in many families, scrap-metal collection remains an important source of regular income. This may be partially explained by the relative tolerance this activity encounters in Italian society. Indeed, because collecting scrap metal is a traditional occupation of the Roman underclass, Romans consider it a proper job that, unlike other Gypsy activities such as begging and stealing, requires effort and provides a useful service to citizens and society. This accommodating attitude is also recognisable among the authorities: despite the recent rise of media attention to thefts of copper from factories and railways, and despite the multiplication of legal restrictions posed by local authorities (ReteOnu 2012; Stasolla 2012), police officers tolerate the presence of the Gypsy *ferrivecchi* as long as it does not provoke malcontent in the local population or lead to blatant or serious illegal acts.

Yet 'going for iron' is not just an adaptive response. As a form of entrepreneurship that entails considerable independence in the organisation of everyday life, it is met with praise by the Romá. In addition, this activity is embedded in the Romá's wider efforts in their daily lives to cultivate and confirm their ultimate independence from the strictures and impositions of the *Gağikanó* world. In order to understand this latter point, it is necessary to examine the association between 'going for iron' and Romani *baxt*, divine favour and *šoró*. The issue is complex, but I will hazard a concise synthesis.

In the Romani perspective, *baxt*, divine favour and *šoró* constitute the connective fabric of success in life. *Baxt* is a complex concept that might be approximated to the *Gağikaní* idea of 'luck' or 'chance', though it does not coincide with this. Indeed, like the Vlach Rom described by Stewart or the Gabori portrayed by Olivera, the Romá conceive baxt as a combination of luck, efficacy, prosperity and happiness. *Baxt* also expresses and nourishes the distinction between the Romá and the non-Roma by unifying the former around a specific (Romani) socio-moral comportment opposed to that of the *Gağé*. God, 'who', the Romá assert, 'sees everything', appears as the most powerful deliverer of *baxt*, as He dispenses favours and punishments according to the judgement connatural to divine gaze.[12] In other words, fortunate (*baxtalé*) events can be interpreted as the outcome and the expression of the personal and typically Romani ability to foster, recognise and activate *baxt* and the divine favour that procures it. The importance of proper conduct in the achievement of success in life highlights the role played by *šoró*. Literally meaning 'head', *šoró* is the combination of cunning, knowledge, wisdom, determination, sense of justice and respectability characterising the Romá and above all the important and prestigious ones – the so-called *baré* (big) Romá. *Šoró* is the expression of *baxt* and divine favour bestowed on a person; in turn, by conferring the sense of right and wrong, proper and improper, the *šoró* procures divine favour and *baxt*.

Viewed in this light, 'going for iron' gives the *ferrivecchi* the opportunity to gain a reputation among the Romá by cultivating and confirming personal success. Choosing the right itineraries, procuring a good customer, finding a massive load of copper, getting through a police check despite minor irregularities, negotiating successfully with the metal dealer, cutting an intruder out of a collection area with a skilful manoeuvre, avoiding a car accident or injuries at work – all these circumstances reflect and corroborate a Rom's *baxt*, *šoró* and privileged relation with God. No less importantly, this fact has implications for group identity: as Gay y Blasco argues in her discussion of Gypsy/Roma 'metonymical strategies', the individual 'by her/his actions enables a conceptualization of "us, as a group"' (Gay y Blasco 2011: 445). In other words, personal success in 'going for iron' confirms the idea that the lives of the Romá as a group are consistently characterised by the presence of *baxt*, divine favour and *šoró*.

A series of reflections follow these considerations. First, 'going for iron' contributes to negotiating and establishing group specificity within the Romani world. Here I specifically refer to the relations between the Romá and their *Rumuni* workers. At first sight, Romá and *Rumuni* appear to have rather tense relationships. The Romá treat the *Rumuni* rudely, shouting curt orders and harshly reproaching behaviour that seem lazy or unresponsive. The *Rumuni* respond to their 'boss' – as they call their Romá employers – with equal rudeness, and though they eventually obey, they often do it slowly, listlessly and with grumbling.[13] The Romá often complain that the *Rumuni* 'cannot be left alone, because they don't want to work', that they 'listen only if you scream at them', that they 'smoke too much, and always expensive cigarettes' and that they 'do not know how to behave properly with customers'. The *Rumuni* in turn grumble about the hardship of their work and the low and sometimes irregular wages (especially compared to the allegedly high incomes of their tight-fisted and lazy bosses).

It may be argued that these apparently tense forms of interaction in fact conceal relaxed and egalitarian working relations; indeed, despite appearances, Romá and *Rumuni* joke and tease each other in a friendly way. Yet it should not be forgotten that jokes and teasing construct identities and negotiate the relations of power between them (Radcliffe-Brown 1940; Sarnelli 2003; Aime 2004: 125–30). Thus, although more relaxed and less hierarchical than the relations Okely (1979: 21) observed between English Gypsies collecting scrap and their non-Gypsy workers, the relations between the Romá and their *Rumuni* workers are characterised by some asymmetries. Indeed, the role separation and the fixed wage of the *Rumuni* suggest that the latter have nothing to do with the entrepreneurship of their employers; the *Rumuni* ideally remain employees hired and paid on a daily basis independent of the day's luck, which also means that they are restrained from investing with the Romá in Romani *baxt*, divine favour and *šoró*.

A second set of reflections concerns the role 'going for iron' plays in delineating the opposition between Romani and *Gağikaní* identities. Dealing with scrap metal, the Romá find value in things and objects collected from the *Gağikanó* world; but this value passes unnoticed by the *Gağé*. The latter's waste (such as stereos, bicycles, work tools, building materials) may be kept within the Romani world and reused; more often, they are sold back to the *Gağé* at street markets (though this activity is marginal among the Romá) and to metal dealers. Thus, waste is returned to the *Gağikanó* world, which is willing to buy what it previously declared useless and worthless by giving it away as scrap. The point is that the magic touch or the keen eye of the Romá may reveal a value in things that the narrow-minded and dumb *Gağé*, who are evidently lacking in *šoró*, fail to notice. To use Stewart's apt characterisation, this allows the Romá to produce themselves as 'the ultimate *bricoleurs*, able to turn whatever is at hand ... to some good use' (Stewart 1997: 20).

Thirdly, 'going for iron' contributes to re-elaborating power relations with the *Gağé* authorities. I recently argued that what is at stake in the relations between the Romá and Italian authorities is the definition of the life of both parties (see Solimene 2013). Through apparently irrelevant gestures and comments, the Romá undermine the sovereign (and arbitrary) power of Italian state officers by revealing the latter's true identity: state officers are just ordinary *Gağé*, hidden behind a state garb but actually at the mercy of the cunning and tactics of the skilful Romá. I showed that by resignifying biopolitical categories such as 'Gypsies' and 'nomads', and by leveraging them to manipulate state officers, the Romá renovate the thin but crucial distinction between themselves and the *homo sacer* they supposedly embody. In other words, 'Gypsy' and 'nomad', allegedly non-Romani instruments for the subjection of the Romá, are turned into Romani tools of emancipation. This allows the Romá to assert that what determines success and failure in life (for both Romá and *Gağé*) are not the powers of the *Gağé* (with their laws, strictures, concessions and labels), but rather *baxt*, divine favour and *šoró* – three crucial things on which the lucky, smart and righteous Romá plainly have a better grip than the *Gağé*.

This interpretative framework may help to clarify the implications of 'going for iron'. Like the case of the English Gypsies described by Okely (1979, 1983: 58), success in scrap-metal collection depends on a Rom's interactional skills and capacity to tactically perform stereotypes. Collecting scrap metal, the Romá introduce themselves as *ferrivecchi*. This ethnically neutral category places interactions outside the potentially conflictive frame characterising Italians' general attitude toward Gypsies, but it also implies the silent admission of the Gypsy identity of the *ferrivecchi*. Therefore, this tactical self-representation is framed within a productive misunderstanding (cf. La Cecla 2002: 23–24) that enables the Romá to bypass the initial resistance of their interlocutors and eventually present themselves through stereotypical images of the Gypsy that foster empathy, such as that of the pre-modern 'Gypsy' striving to keep up with modernity, the honest and hardworking 'nomad' confined in a camp yet trying to live as a decent person, and the exotic 'nomad' who is nonetheless integrated into Italian society (thanks to the support of good-hearted Italians) and who, like many Italians, despises most Gypsies.

When tactically playing with stereotypical images of the 'Gypsy' or 'nomad' in interactions with customers, police officers, metal dealers and acquaintances, the Romá demonstrate their ability to manipulate the *Gağé* by playing with the latter's collective imagery, the same imagery that portrays the Romá as inferior, dirty and uncivilised, and which nourishes and legitimises the biopolitical discourses targeting the Roma in Italy. Thus, using Agamben's terminology, it can be asserted that when 'going for iron' the Romá bend the biopolitical figure of *homo sacer* to the Romani agenda, thereby asserting their emancipation from the law that defines them as Gypsies.

Scrap-metal collection is thus an entrepreneurial activity that involves practices such as turning waste into valuables, circumventing bureaucratic strictures and legal impediments, shunning the diffuse anti-Gypsy sentiments but still using them to cut out the competition of the *Rumuni*, and realising an (albeit fragile) integration that authorities' discourses deny and hamper. Success and failure in these practices are associated with a Rom's *baxt*, *šoró* and relation with God. In other words, 'going for iron' is an opportunity for the Romá to express and nourish, once more, the undeniable (at least in the Romani perspective) fact that what ultimately stands behind life's vicissitudes are *baxt*, *šoró* and divine favour – three features of Romani life – and that the lives of the Romá are thus far from being determined by the biopolitical powers of the non-Roma.

Conclusions

This chapter has explored the activity of scrap-metal collection carried out by some families of Bosnian Xoraxané Romá in the Rome metropolitan area. After describing the collection, separation and sale of the metals, I turned to explore the spatial strategies adopted by the Romá, their relations with customers, metal dealers and the authorities, and the delicate but resilient bond they have with their working territories. Finally, by highlighting the connection between 'going for iron' and *baxt*, divine favour and *šoró*, I have demonstrated that the collection of scrap metal is embedded in the negotiation of relations with both the *Rumuni* and the non-Roma.

The hostility displayed by the Romá towards the *Rumuni*, evident in the 'othering' narratives that appear to bring the Romá closer to their

Italian associates, cannot be reduced to a process of deceiving the *Gaǧé*; the Romá really do consider the *Rumuni* different, dirty, uncivilised and noxious – judgements often reciprocated by the *Rumuni* (Solimene 2011a: 142–50). Yet in actual fact, Romá and *Rumuni* share an existence in Italian nomad camps, their identity as Roma in its opposition to the *Gaǧé*, and everyday gestures connected to their work as Gypsy *ferrivecchi*. This proximity eventually blurs the separation of roles between bosses and workers: the Romá participate in manual labour while the *Rumuni* are sometimes appointed to technical tasks, and even the daily wage of the *Rumuni*, supposedly fixed, is subject to small variations according to the luck of the day (a fruitful day usually means a bonus). In other words, entrepreneurship and investment in *baxt*, divine favour and *šoró* – in theory, limited to the Romá – are ultimately shared (to some extent) with the *Rumuni* workers. Besides, working relations sometimes evolve into friendship, cooperation, mutual help and even familial linkages. This proximity blurs distinctions between groups, yet it does not disrupt the ideological assumptions generating these distinctions (Solimene 2011b: 645–49).

A similar ambivalence – which, borrowing Herzfeld's terminology, follows the logic of 'social usages' rather than that of 'strict definitions' (Herzfeld 1987: 123–85) – pervades the *Gaǧikanó* world and its relation with the Gypsy *ferrivecchi*. The *Gaǧé*, indeed, distrust and despise the Gypsies, complain about the continual passage of their lorries full of scrap and about the acrid black fumes caused by burning plastic insulation, produce bureaucratic obstacles and legal impediments to scrap-metal collection, and carry on the formal repression of informal economy. But it is also true that there are gaps and inconsistencies in the policies of control and repression, that the formal obstruction of scrap-metal collection is accompanied by diffuse tolerance towards the activity, that the informal economy flourishes as the structural counterpart of the Italian formal economy (ISTAT 2005), and that Italian collective imagery about the Gypsies includes sentiments of compassion and fascination, and a belief in the possibility of the individual redemption of the Gypsies (Todesco 2004; Piasere 2006a).

A series of works suggest that the economic activities of Roma, Travellers and Gitano communities are not passive adaptations but rather active responses to the wider socio-economic systems within which they are embedded, and to which they contribute – albeit partially and/or intermittently (see Beynon 1936; Okely 1979, 1983: 49–65; Kaprow 1984; Salo 1986; Piasere 1987, 2000; Silverman 1991: 113–20; Nagel Lauwagie 1995; Golino 2004; Engebrigsten 2007). As a source of regular income for the Romá, 'going for iron' may be seen as a case of adaptation. The work of the *ferrivecchi* is an activity that few Italians are still willing to carry out, yet it is part of the economy of the majority society: it represents the first link in a chain that involves local metal dealers, national reclamation companies and sectors of the global market.[14] Furthermore, 'going for iron' fits the Italian social, political, economic and cultural landscape, which is characterised by the blurring and intertwining of acceptance and rejection, formality and informality, legality and illegality.

Yet 'going for iron' is not a mere adaptation to the opportunities offered by the wider socio-economic context: it nourishes the roots of the Italian economy and contributes to the perpetuation and enrichment of Italian society, including the (previously mentioned) contradictions and ambiguities that characterise it. Besides, 'going for iron' is also a refraction of a Romani ideology, and herein lies its crucial importance. By including their work as *ferrivecchi* in the cosmological construction gravitating around *baxt*, divine favour and *šoró*, the Romá make this activity an everyday practice in de Certeau's (1984) sense, confirming the independence of Romani life from the constraints and exclusionary forces of Italian society.

In the present climate of heightened anti-Gypsy sentiment in Italy, with nomad camps increasingly serving as zones of exclusion and with society and the state treating the Roma as Agamben's 'bare life', the Romá manage to appropriate and be appropriated by specific neighbourhoods, and to challenge their association with the biopolitical figure of the Gypsy and *homo sacer*. Scrap-metal collection plays a definite role in this process of emancipation, and this provides further evidence that economic practices and the ideological elaborations surrounding them may prove powerful tools of resistance to domination, and thus that they represent, as Day, Stewart and Papataxiarchis assert, an 'active response to … conditions of marginalization and social exclusion … that at times may constitute a cultural and political critique' (Day, Stewart and Papataxiarchis 1999: 7).

NOTES

1. In this chapter I will refer to 'Gypsies' and 'Roma' as two semantically different terms. 'Gypsies' will reflect the perspective of those who consider themselves as non-Gypsies and attach this label to a non-well-defined group of persons; 'Roma' will instead refer to the actual group of persons who identify themselves as Romani and are often categorized as 'Gypsies'. The reader should nonetheless keep in mind the complexity and ambiguities, highlighted by the current debate in the so-called Romani studies, inherent to both the construction of the Roma as a distinct group and the deployment of different terms to name it.

2. The term 'Romá' (sing. Rom) will be used exclusively in reference to my interlocutors, in order to distinguish them from other Roma communities living in Italy.
3. Any list of the working activities of the Romá would be partial and incomplete, as every family adopts specific economic strategies that vary according to the ever-changing opportunities offered by the wider socio-economic context.
4. For example, the camp must be kept clean and tidy, fires are not permitted and movement in and out of the settlement is restricted at night-time.
5. *Ferrivecchi* is plural; *ferrovecchio* is its singular form, but this is used only in reference to the material collected (the single collector is just called a *ferrivecchi*).
6. Many Romanian Roma use this opportunity to make a small amount of money, learn a job and shortly after start working on their own.
7. Romani tricks to increase the weight include 'forgetting' to remove non-metallic parts or rinsing copper wire with water. Metal dealers, in turn, allegedly rig the scales and cheat on calculations.
8. Piasere (1987) reported a similar system among Xoraxané Romá from Kosovo begging in the Verona area in 1970s. I observed the same principle being adopted by Romá women begging in the city centre of Rome (Solimene 2014).
9. *Gağó* means a non-Roma man (plural *Gağé*).
10. *Gağikanó* (fem. *Gağikaní*) is the adjectival form of *Gağó*.
11. Note that, although considered part of 'tradition' (*tradicjia*), the majority of Romá women practise these activities only occasionally.
12. Note that, though not subordinated to *baxt*, God does not produce or control it.
13. Interactions are carried out in Romanés, but sometimes Italian is used as a bridge language.
14. Some of the scrap metal collected in Rome is brought to international harbours such as Gioia Tauro and shipped to China and India.

REFERENCES

Agamben, G. 1998. *Homo Sacer: Sovereign Power and Bare Life*. Stanford: Stanford University Press.

———. 2005. *State of Exception*. Chicago: University of Chicago Press.

Aime, M. 2004. *Eccessi di culture*. Torino: Einaudi Editore.

Bauman, Z. 2004. *Wasted Lives: Modernity and its Outcasts*. Oxford: Blackwell.

Beynon, E.D. 1936. 'The Gypsy in a Non-Gypsy Economy', *American Journal of Sociology* 42(3): 358–70.

Brunello, P. (ed.). 1996. *L'urbanistica del disprezzo: campi Rom e societá italiana*. Rome: Manifesto Libri.

CGIL, CISL and UIL. 2009. Rapporto OIL situazione dei migranti e popolazione Rom e Sinti in Italia, in relazione alla Convenzione ILO n. 143 del 1975 e del Decreto Legislativo n. 215 del 2003. Retrieved 21 January 2013 from: http://www.uil.it/immigrazione/Rapporto-OIL09.pdf.

Clough Marinaro, I. 2003. 'Integration or Marginalization? The Failures of Social Policies for the Roma in Rome', *Modern Italy* 8(2): 203–18.

———. 2009. 'Between Surveillance and Exile: Biopolitics of the Roma in Italy', *Bulletin of Italian Politics* 1(2): 265–87.
Clough Marinaro I., and N. Sigona (eds). 2011. 'Roma and Sinti in Contemporary Italy', *Modern Italy*, special issue, 16(5): 583–666.
Costi, N. 2010. 'The Spectre that Haunts Italy: The Systematic Criminalisation of the Roma and the Fears of the Heartland', *Romani Studies* 20(2): 105–36.
Dal Lago, A. 2004. *Non-persone: L'esclusione dei migranti in una societá globale*. Milan: Feltrinelli.
Daniele, U. 2011. *Sono del campo e vengo dall'India: Etnografia di una collettivitá Rom dislocata*. Rome: Meti.
———. 2013. *Questo campo fa schifo: Etnografia dell'adolescenza Rom tra periferie e scenari globali*. Rome: Meti.
Day, S., E. Papataxiarchis and M. Stewart. 1999. 'Consider the Lilies of the Field', in S. Day, E. Papataxiarchis and M. Stewart (eds), *Lilies of the Field: Marginal People who Live for the Moment*. Boulder, CO: Westview Press, pp.1–24.
de Certeau, M. 1984. *The Practice of Everyday Life*, trans. S.F. Rendall. Berkeley: University of California Press.
Engebrigsten, A.I. 2007. *Exploring Gypsiness: Power, Exchange and Interdependence in a Transylvanian Village*. Oxford: Berghahn Books.
ERRC. 2000. *Il paese dei campi: La segregazione razziale dei Rom in Italia*. Rome: Manifesto Libri.
Gay y Blasco, P. 2011. 'Agata's Story: Singular Lives and the Reach of the "Gitano Law"', *Journal of the Royal Anthropological Institute* 17(3): 445–61.
Golino, S. 2004. 'La teoria economica di fronte ai Romá: Elementi per la definizione di un'economia romaní', in L. Piasere and C. Saletti-Salza (eds), *Italia romaní IV*. Rome: Centro d'Informazione e Stampa Universitaria, pp.185–210.
Herzfeld, M. 1987. *Anthropology Through the Looking Glass: Critical Ethnography in the Margins of Europe*. Cambridge: Cambridge University Press.
ISTAT. 2005. *La misura dell'economia sommersa secondo le statistiche ufficiali: Anno 2003*. Rome: Conti Nazionali.
Kaprow, M.L. 1984. 'The Ultimate Anarchists', *The Sciences* 24(4): 38–41.
La Cecla, F. 2002. *Il malinteso*. Rome: Editori Laterza.
Nagel Lauwagie, B. 1985. 'Explaining Gypsy Presence: A Comparison of the Reactive Ethnicity and the Ecological Competition Perspectives', in J. Grumet (ed.), *Papers from the Fourth and Fifth Annual Meeting of the Gypsy Lore Society, North American Chapter*. New York: Gypsy Lore Society, pp.129–48.
Okely, J. 1979. 'Trading Stereotypes: The Case of English Gypsies', in S. Wallman (ed.), *Ethnicity at Work*. London: MacMillan, pp.16–33.
———. 1983. *The Traveller-Gypsies*. Cambridge: Cambridge University Press.
Olivera, M. 2012. *La tradition de l'intégration: une ethnologie des Roms Gabori dans les années 2000*. Paris: Éditions Pétra.
Petronio, A. 2008. 'La questione Rom e la soluzione del non-modello', *Studi Zancan* 3: 35–46.
Piasere, L. 1987. 'In Search of New Niches: The Productive Organization of the Peripatetic Xoraxané in Italy', in A. Rao (ed.), *The Other Nomads: Peripatetic Minorities in Cross-Cultural Perspective*. Cologne: Böhlau, pp.111–32.
———. 1999. *Un mondo di mondi: Antropologia delle culture Rom*. Bari: L'Ancora.

———. 2000. 'Antropologia sociale e storia della mendicitá zingara', *Polis* 14(3): 409–28.
———. 2006a. *Buoni da ridere, gli Zingari*. Rome: Centro d'Informazione Stampa Universitaria.
———. 2006b. 'Che cos'é un campo nomadi', *Achab* 8: 8–16.
———. 2012. *Scenari dell'antiziganismo: Tra Europa e Italia, tra antropologia e politica*. Florence: Seid Editori.
Radcliffe-Brown, A.R. 1940. 'On Joking Relationships', *Africa* 13(3): 195–210.
ReteOnu. 2012. Rovistatori: Non serve reprimere ma valorizzare le competenze. Retrieved 26 December 2012 from: http://www.reteonu.it/index.php?option=com_contentandview=articleandid=71:rovistatori-non-serve-reprimere-ma-valorizzarne-le-competenze-andcatid=3:generalandItemid=9.
Saletti-Salza, C. 2003. *Bambini del campo nomadi: Romá bosniaci a Torino*. Rome: Centro d'Informazione Stampa Universitaria.
Salo, M.T. 1986. 'Peripatetic Adaptation in Historical Perspective', *Nomadic Peoples*, special issue, 21/22: 7–36.
Sarnelli, E. 2003. 'Relazioni scherzose: Senegalesi e autoctoni in un mercato di Napoli', in C. Gallini (ed.), *Patrie elettive*. Torino: Bollati Boringhieri, pp.25–60.
Sigona, N. 2002. *Figli del ghetto: Gli italiani, i campi nomadi e l'invenzione degli Zingari*. Civezzano: Nonluoghi.
———. 2005. 'Locating the "Gypsy Problem". The Roma in Italy: Stereotyping, Labelling and "Nomad Camps"', *Journal of Ethnic and Migration Studies* 31(4): 741–56.
———. (ed.) 2008. 'The Latest Public Enemy: The Case of the Romanian Roma in Italy'. Retrieved 30 March 2011 from: http://osservazionbe.org/documenti/OSCEpublicenemy.pdf.
———. 2010. '"Via gli Zingari dall'Italia [Gypsies Out of Italy]!" Social Exclusion and Racial Discrimination of Roma and Sinti in Italy', in A. Mammone and G. Veltri (eds), *Italy Today: The Sick Man of Europe*. London: Routledge, pp.143–57.
Sigona, N., and L. Monasta (eds). 2006. *Cittadinzanze imperfette: Rapporto sulla discriminazione razziale di Rom e Sinti in Italia*. Naples: Edizioni Spartaco.
Silverman, C. 1991. 'Strategies of Ethnic Adaptation: The Case of Gypsies in the United States', in S. Stern and J.A. Cicala (eds), *Creative Ethnicity: Symbols and Strategies of Contemporary Ethnic Life*. Logan: Utah State University Press, pp.107–21.
Simoni, A. (ed.) 2005. *Stato di diritto e identitá Rom*. Turin: L'Harmattan Italia.
———. 2008. 'I decreti "Emergenza nomadi": Il nuovo volto per un vecchio problema', *Diritto Immigrazione e Cittadinanza* 10(3/4): 44–56.
Solimene, M. 2011a. 'Romá bosniaci a Roma: Negoziazioni spaziali e identitarie', in M. Bressan and S. Tosi Cambini (eds), *Zone di transizione, spazi pubblici e diversitá culturale: Studi etnografici in quattro cittá italiane*. Bologna: Il Mulino, pp.113–66.
———. 2011b. '"These Romanians Have Ruined Italy". Xoraxané Romá, Romanian Roma and Rome', *Journal of Modern Italian Studies* 16(5): 637–51.
———. 2012. 'Death and Places: Emotional Intersections among Xoraxané Romá in Rome', *Études tsiganes* 44/45: 232–49.
———. 2013. 'Undressing the Gağe Dressed in State Garb: Bosnian Xoraxané Romá Face to Face with the Italian Authorities', *Romani Studies* 23(2): 23–48.
———. 2014. "The Rootedness of a Community of Xoraxané Romá", in I. Clough Marinaro and B. Thomassen (eds), *Global Rome: Changing Faces of the Eternal City*. Bloomington: Indiana University Press, pp.129–42.

Stasolla, C. 2012. *Sulla pelle dei Rom: Il piano nomadi della giunta Alemanno*. Rome: Alegre.
Stewart, M. 1997. *The Time of the Gypsies*. Boulder, CO: Westview Press.
———. 1999. '"Brothers" and "Orphans": Images of Equality among Hungarian Rom', in S. Day, E. Papataxiarchis and M. Stewart (eds), *Lilies of the Field: Marginal People Who Live For the Moment*. Boulder, CO: Westview Press, pp.27–44.
Tauber, E. 2008. '"Do You Remember the Time When We Went Begging and Selling": The Ethnography of Transformation in Female Economic Activities and its Narrative in the Context of Memory and Respect among the Sinti in North Italy', in J. Fabian and J. Ries (eds), *Romani/Gypsy Cultures in New Perspectives*. Leipzig: Leipzieger Universitätverslag, pp.155–76.
Todesco, D. 2004. *Le maschere dei pregiudizi. L'innocenza perduta dei pregiudizi positivi: Una categoria esemplare: Gli Zingari*. Rome: Quaderni di 'Servizio Migrantes'.
Tosi Cambini, S. 2011. '"The Social Dangerousness of the Defendant is at One with Her Own Condition of Being Nomadic": Roma and Sinti in Italian Courts of Law', *Modern Italy* 16(5): 652–66.

Marco Solimene is a post-doctoral researcher in the Department of Anthropology, University of Iceland. He is a member of the Permanent Seminar of Romani Studies at the Centro di Ricerche Etnografiche ed Antropologia applicata Francesca Cappelletto, University of Verona, of the Roma Discussion Group, London's King's College, and of the European Academic Network on Romani Studies. He holds a master's degree in sociology from the University of Rome La Sapienza, Italy, and a Ph.D. in social anthropology from the University of Iceland. His research focuses on anti-Gypsyism and Romani resistance, as well as Romani movements and transnational practices. He has published several articles, most recently in *Études tsiganes* (2012) and *Romani Studies* (2013).

Chapter 6

'I'm Good but also Mad'
The Street Economy in a Poor Neighbourhood of Bucharest

GERGŐ PULAY

Mahala and Gypsyland, since I entered you,
There is no meat left on my bones; there is no meat left on my bones,
The little that is left, oh, ah, all is burnt and all is roasted.
If I try to weight it; I don't even find a little bit,
Not a little bit, not one gram; because enemies ate it up.
— Popular Romanian Gypsy song

The above lines are taken from an old gem of Romanian urban Gypsy folksong, or alternatively the music of the *mahala*, the neighbourhood or the slum, as it is sometimes translated.[1] The song depicts these legendary spaces of melodramatic social imaginary and their unfavourable, destructive conditions and adversarial social relations, which made them capable of absorbing anyone who entered them and lived there. Although its name does not appear in this song, it is hard to imagine a neighbourhood in Bucharest that is more exposed to such infernal myths than Ferentari, an ultimate 'Gypsy area' (*Țigănie*) in town, a projected container of urban ills like poverty, crime and drug abuse that threaten better parts of the city with invasion in the eyes of respectable citizens, a dangerous place and a ghetto, or else an internal Orient in continuous need of development and taming by the forces of civilisation.

Such images can easily be contrasted with observations that would show a rural–urban buffer-zone instead of a ghetto, or a mixed area of Roma and non-Roma Romanian inhabitants instead of a fully enclosed Gypsy settlement. When writing about such places, the simple critique of misleading appearances, unjustified urban legends or actors who reinforce stereotypes runs the risk of relegating the whole analysis to the realm of representations or mere fiction, much like walls that need to be demolished so that one can see what lurks behind them. However, we should also keep in mind that such powerful myths of a place are far from being simple fictions that emerge from the outside, since they provide the very raw material to work with, not in the least for residents, whenever they wish to talk about themselves and their fate in connection with their habitat.

Historically, the southern peripheries of Bucharest have been associated with the prevalence of lower classes, especially Sector 5, where the neighbourhood of Ferentari is located. During the period of socialist industrialisation, poor-quality blocks of flats and workers' dormitories were erected here in response to housing shortages and the migration of workers into the city, but generally the local landscape is dominated by sub-standard rural-type housing to this day (Marcińczak et al. 2014). Throughout the first decade of the postsocialist transition, this became one of the neighbourhoods with the highest concentration of unskilled and (officially) unemployed workers in the city (ibid.: 11). Moreover, this period brought to the neighbourhood new waves of settlers who had lost their homes in other areas of the city due to demolitions, property restitution or overall impoverishment.

Being aware that they live in the 'most infamous' (*cel mai rău famat*) neighbourhood in town, the inhabitants of Ferentari that I came to know are striving to manage their disadvantageous situation. Some of the available assets for this pursuit are the proofs of personal worth or the quality of the immediate spaces – such as the household or the street corner – that they strive to control. These are crucial resources for getting by in an environment where, due to the malfunctions of the local state, the structural problems of the wider society turn into personal problems to be faced on a daily basis; furthermore, these problems often give rise to widespread suspicion concerning the unreliability of others. In order to avoid the unsettling prospect of getting absorbed by this space and hence becoming a 'fool' or a 'dupe' (*fraier*), many people strive to create value both in material and non-material terms as entrepreneurs or 'businessmen' (*bișnițari*) in the midst of an unpredictable and constantly changing environment that seems to offer little but deprivation (when considered from a systemic point of view). Their creation of value defines an 'interstitial domain' with a moral framework that helps to distinguish activities that are not strictly legal but nonetheless socially acceptable from obviously criminal and illegitimate ones (Pardo 1996). This domain allows for a constant balancing between formal (or licit) and informal (or illicit) activities: people potentially rely on the resources of both, whilst trying not to fall into the traps of either of them.

The main protagonists of this account belong to an extended family of Spoitori Gypsies.[2] Several members of this family partly work as street vendors around some open-air markets close to the neighbourhood, selling goods such as melons, potatoes and flip-flops during the summer, and clothes and hats (purchased from a Chinese wholesale market) in winter. Without renting an official stall, they can constantly keep their prices below the ones available in the marketplace. Apart from this business, and the occasional trips of the men to Spain as street musicians with their accordions, the family established an officially registered scrap-collecting site in the neighbourhood. Here they buy scrap metal and plastic from collectors who work at the street level, which they later sell in larger quantities and for a higher price to firms that handle scrap metal at industrial level, and that organise its transportation to a port where it is sold to foreign agents.

Since the main purpose of this chapter is to present some of the norms and principles behind these activities – which are significant aspects of the livelihood strategies of many other inhabitants I got to know in the streets of the neighbourhood (Roma and non-Roma Romanians alike) – I also include several other actors in my account. These identify the street, sometimes being represented as a space of Gypsy dominance, with the notion of the 'school of life' (școala vieții) and its lessons of getting by, as opposed to the realm of formal education. Nevertheless, this does not imply the exclusivity of Gypsies amongst those who regularly hang out and make deals in the street. The street economy of this mixed urban neighbourhood in Bucharest represents the intermingling two senses of the Gypsy economy in practice (see Introduction, this volume). The ethnographic material in this chapter largely concerns the everyday management of this ambiguity. In order to highlight this process, my analysis starts from some of the elementary forms of exchange that are part of the street economy, especially amongst the younger male inhabitants of the neighbourhood.

Spaces of Trust, Spaces of Fear

Whatever I said to my acquaintances in the neighbourhood to justify my sustained presence, they kept on searching for their own explanations as to why I had moved to the area as a foreign student writing about Romania or Bucharest. As Lucian, a talented Spoitor Gypsy trader, told me sometimes, 'You are here because this is the neighbourhood where the greatest traffic is going on!' This notion alluded to the manifold relations of exchange, trade and barter between inhabitants in the neighbourhood's public spaces and with outsiders at the nearby marketplaces. The topic of traffic could arise with reference to the exchange of mobile phones in the street or to the trading of votes during elections, arranged by a network of vote traffickers (*traficanți de voturi*), or to the activities of the area's drug dealers (*traficanți de droguri*). Apart from these cases, traffic could be also going on with second-hand cars from Bulgaria, contraband cigarettes from Moldova or driving licences that could be purchased without an exam more easily from Hungary than elsewhere. Apart from the trafficking of commodities or 'merchandise' (*marfă*), many of my acquaintances had an extensive record of trips abroad to countries such as Turkey, Spain and Italy. In the early stages of my fieldwork I could make my acquaintances laugh at my naivety, when I sadly noted during a farewell celebration that a person's decision to migrate might mean that we would not see each other for quite some time. But in fact, these people could return to the neighbourhood almost as quickly as the preparations were made for their departure. Contrary to the image of a 'hidden', peripheral zone populated by victims of social exclusion in need of salvation – as it is promoted in the discourse of NGOs and certain sociologists of the underclass – these forms of trafficking suggested that the neighbourhood can be understood as an extremely busy intersection between diverse local and transnational networks. As with other actors in these networks, the traders in the neighbourhood seem to rely more on the freedoms and liberties of local life – in other words, the malfunctions of the local state – than the residents of other parts of town.

The vivid scenes of street economies as well as the entrepreneurial activities enacted by the inhabitants of peripheral zones have been haunting the imagination of scholars and the broader public for many years. Some authors tend to attribute a relative autonomy to these places or discover a certain 'magnetic attraction' in their everyday life, where the reliance on informal livelihood strategies or their combination with formal employment can have empowering and also redistributive effects; for others, this freedom of engaging in informal labour translates to increasingly exploitative relations, traversing the boundaries of the domestic realm, family and neighbourhood (Mollona 2005). The family and the household (Smith and Stenning 2006), as well as marginal and stigmatised urban territories (Wacquant 2008), have been prominent locations where researchers and policy experts alike have sought instances of such self-organised economic activities. At the same time, ideas of unregulated trade as boundary crossing or as a form of profiteering that violates the sense of order among ordinary citizens, where traders appear as small-scale followers of state officials who paved the way with their 'gigantic rip-offs', have been widely discussed in connection to the postsocialist world (Humphrey 2002; Konstantinov 1996).

The contribution of economic anthropologists to these debates seeks to reconcile contradictions between accumulation and social equity or production and circulation (Hart 2000: 99–103). Understanding everyday economic engagements in local settings requires consideration of the moral frameworks in which the pursuit of material and non-material goals and the creation of value and virtue interact with one another (Lambek 2008). In other words, I suggest a view of entrepreneurialism and trading activities as acts that create social persons and relationships in which the issues of trust and distrust play a crucial role. It is precisely in these acts that we can identify the creation of value as it 'emerges in action' or as a process in which the capacity of persons to act 'is transformed into concrete, perceptible forms' (Graeber 2001: 45). This account is dedicated to understanding this process through a focus on economic action amongst the inhabitants of the streets of a poor neighbourhood in Bucharest.

The concept of the street is essential here, as it sets the scene for most of the male-dominated activities I discuss in the chapter. As we learn from accounts about the US inner city at the end of the twentieth century (e.g. Wacquant 2004), spaces of 'protected sociability' as islands of stability and order form a binary opposition to the street with its 'predatory economy' and unpredictable forms of physical violence. At first sight it is appealing to rely on similar assumptions in the case of this Bucharest neighbourhood, where inhabitants also associate the street[3] with the interpersonal risks and challenges that make everyday life in the neighbourhood 'wild' (*sălbatic*) in some respects. In the case of the stray dogs gathering and barking in the street or the largely homeless drug users lying around on street corners, the strategy of the authorities seemed to follow the logic of leaving urban ills to accumulate in such a marginal zone, where they were to be dealt with mostly by the locals themselves. It is precisely their continuous engagement with the street and their social environment that renders the dichotomies such as that between a 'protected sociability' and a 'predatory economy' rather simplistic. While oppositions between the street and the household are indeed central to the way inhabitants talk about their everyday lives, these can obscure rather than reveal the interstitial domain where the protagonists of this account manage their livelihoods and strive to obtain value in material as well as non-material terms.

Madness and Silent Armament

During one of my returns to the neighbourhood, my wallet disappeared on a bus. I had no idea how it happened exactly; all I could see was that my bag was open at the station where I got off. Such incidents can provoke long and heated discussions amongst the inhabitants of the neighbourhood, in which everyone feels obliged to take a stance on whether or not they witnessed anything or were involved in any way.

'God may help you!' said the lady sitting in the ticket booth at the bus station, where I returned in the hope that maybe I had left my wallet there. 'Beware!' she continued. 'This is a neighbourhood of thieves, junkies and criminals!' Although it contained only a small amount of money, the loss of my wallet also provoked passionate reactions among members of the extended family of Spoitori Gypsies with whom I had the closest relation in the neighbourhood. After similar calls for God's help and subtle references to my own inattention, one of their first comments was that the thief who took my wallet must have been an ethnic Romanian. As they said, the Gypsies who have done such things left the neighbourhood a long time ago and went abroad or to prison, and the ones who remained are 'civilised' – in other words, the latter no longer engage in such minor affairs but have more serious businesses, such as the one with scrap metal. In order to show his solidarity and willingness to help me in my plight, Vasile, the head of the extended family, went to his house and then came back to the street with a gun that he concealed under his shirt. 'Tell me, who was it? We'll find the guy and get back your wallet with even more money than you've lost!'

However small and haphazard, such an incident can evoke the whole territorial stigma that is imposed on the neighbourhood (as a place of 'thieves, junkies and criminals') and potentially threatens all inhabitants with the possibility of being part of the same dishonoured categories, which requires immediate acts of separation (Wacquant 2008). All of this happens in a zone characterised by the weakness of the local state, whose main agents – the police – are seen by inhabitants as either corrupt and practically absent or as simply inefficient players. In the winter of 2010, an empty house along the main road of the neighbourhood began to burn after a group of homeless people made a fire inside. Inhabitants gathered in the street to follow the fire fighting and to discuss the event. They blamed it all on the policemen who would only have inspected such buildings if they had received bribes. On the other hand, during their hasty patrols when they were looking for drugs and drug dealers in the neighbourhood, policemen regularly stopped people in the streets and carried out identity checks on those who had nothing to do with drug trafficking. Such unpleasant incidents of unwarranted police suspicion were part of the context in which inhabitants expressed their everyday indignation towards the police and the state.

Moreover, the possession of a gun suggests a sense of alertness in terms of being ready to resolve everyday troubles by personal means. Some of my acquaintances in the neighbourhood liked to boast to each other about the weapons or other violent assets they owned. These objects were part of the constant flux of commodities that were sold and bought on the street. Their possessors sometimes depicted themselves as collectors of and great experts on these items in ways similar to those with a reputation as collectors of and great experts on porn videos. However, it is important to add that this was a silent armament and that I have never seen these assets being used in accordance with their intended purpose. As a matter of fact, the primary function of these assets was to mock others, or else to test someone's interactive skills and proper reactions in the seemingly ambiguous situations when they are openly displayed. Even among the members of male-dominated groups, the actual proof of power and control over the immediate environment was the absence of violence or physical force. This non-violence could be possible, for example, because of the reputation of having an extended network of kin and 'brothers' (*fraţi*) as a backup (the latter term of course not implying actual blood relations in any sense). One might argue that within this field of relationships an act such as showing up with a gun is in itself a symbol of trust, based on the mutually shared assumption that ultimately no one will pull the trigger.

To quote a common phrase with which men like to present themselves in the neighbourhood, 'I'm good but also mad' (*sunt bun dar şi nebun*). As is usually the case with some of the most powerful phrases we learn during fieldwork, this laconicism is hard to translate, since it is inscribed with many of the mores and practices associated with street life.[4] First of all, it suggests that the speaker is endowed with values that are generally associated with goodness among ordinary Romanians, such as that of being 'nice' (*cuminte*) or, perhaps more importantly, of being 'civilised' (*civilizat*). In fact, I never met anyone in the neighbourhood who did not claim these respectable titles in one way or another, or who did not attribute the opposite to others. Beyond this, as the second part of the saying continues, such qualities of goodness are not enough for the successful management of the self and of one's livelihood: a certain element of 'madness' is necessary to gain the reputation associated with fully valuable personhood.

Madness in itself represents the direct opposite of all those values that 'civilisation' or 'obedience' stand for, and from this point of view it belongs to those unwanted others who can be held responsible for the bad reputation of the neighbourhood. In this sense, madness is a prerequisite for persons who are unreliable and unpredictable, which is why it is located outside the realm of social relations that can be governed by the principles of trust, equality and collaboration.

The main exponents of this kind of madness in the neighbourhood are the 'junkies' (*drogați*) and especially the 'homeless' (*boschetari* or *vagabonzi*), the lowest of the low in the local hierarchy of social value. As a matter of fact, those who are labelled with such a dishonourable title do not have to be homeless in a literal sense, nor do they have to be inclined towards violence. The actual threat posed by these unwanted others has more to do with their unpredictability as well as their mastery of mimicry, which they use to conceal their predatory intentions. Bogdan, a middle-aged non-Roma Romanian chauffeur who grew up in the area, introduced 'savages' (*sălbatici*) to me in this way:

> There are no friends here – just forget this idea. They are hanging out only to make some profit. You have to be afraid here. You think they are your friends, but once you let them into your house, they'll rush you (*tăbărî*) and you won't get rid of them; they'll take all your stuff, and only your bare ass will remain.

A former local Roma politician expressed similar views concerning street life:

> You never know who is with whom. You are talking to someone one moment and you don't know whom you are talking to, because you don't know what games they play behind your back. You are with X, and you talk to Y, or you fight against Y and maybe X and Y are friends and they collaborate. It's hard.

I kept hearing these anxious comments about distrust throughout my fieldwork, regardless of the amount of time I spent in the neighbourhood or the number of people I became familiar with. It would be logical to conclude that if there is a society in which each member claims the status of the 'civilised' for himself and considers most others to be lacking this value, then antitheses to being civilised, such as being mad or a vagabond, must be ascribed strictly to these others, who must be kept at a safe distance from the self with its secure spaces and relationships. However, this is not the case. Madness was apparently not the exclusive domain of those who do not share the respectability that comes with having a home or a household. No matter how much a man liked to insist on my good luck in coming into contact with him instead of with the wrong ones in the neighbourhood, I hardly knew anyone who could not recall certain periods of 'madness' or 'vagabondage' (*vagabonzeală*) in his own past. Note how the initial distinction between 'us' and 'others' vanishes in the following recollection of Radu, a Gypsy man in his mid thirties who was married and had a daughter. Radu worked as a courier but was also one of the regulars on the street corner:

> Let me tell you something: you found us, the good boys, the nice ones, but if you had met others [laughs] ... you don't want to see that other nature! May my family die [if I lie to you], but if you came some years ago, when we all gathered here, you would have run away! [Laughs] It was big-time vagabondage; it drove us crazy. Drinks, shouting, roaring music non-stop from the morning until the evening, with just the brothers. We also did a few wrong things, as kids do.

Indeed, the division between the obedient and civilised self of the present and the madness of the past is a common way of assuming both as part of the same personality. Moreover, this temporal division at the level of the person corresponds to a common view about changes over time in the neighbourhood. As my acquaintances often pointed out, those times when the neighbourhood was a truly dangerous place, with 'fights all over the place', are long gone; now, it's only 'the name' – in other words, the bad reputation of the area – that persists.[5]

Nevertheless, such a distinction between the past and the present is not the only way in which the different 'natures' of madness and obedience are incorporated by the same person. While the opposites of what is understood as a civilised status – such as unpredictability, the inclination to violence or disrespect towards the primacy of the family and the household in terms of one's expenditure of time and money – might have been dominant only in a person's past or previously in the neighbourhood, these customs and inclinations have never fully disappeared, and neither does it seem desirable to lose them completely. In order to obtain the material and personal properties that are joined together in the idea of owning 'value' (*valoare*) and gaining recognition in the context of street life, men have had to preserve at least some parts of their madness as qualities that they keep under control but that can potentially burst out if the circumstances or other parties demand it. After all, this is similar to the idea that the name and reputation of the neighbourhood is still in circulation in spite of the fact that it is a 'quiet' (*liniștit*) place at present. During the evenings we spent on the street corner, Lucian, the Spoitor

Gypsy trader, liked to recall the times when he established his fame as 'the greatest devil of this zone', thanks to his reprisals against those who wanted to outwit him. He saw this as the source of the respect that he still enjoyed from many of his neighbours, even though he had stayed clear of trouble since having children.

The division of the different sides of a person's reputation was most clearly articulated in those highly ritualised moments when men accepted each other as friends or bestowed the title of 'brother' on each other. Shortly after making his cautionary comments about the prevalence of predatory 'wilds' in the neighbourhood, Bogdan stated the following:

> If you are my friend, we remain like that until we die. I do for you whatever you want. For me friendship matters the most. But if someone upsets me – it can be an outsider – then I don't care about anything anymore (*nu țin cont*). If he picks a quarrel with you and I see it, I go and kick his ass (*îi dau în cap*). You might think I'm mad, but I'm not. We are friends until you put your knife to my throat, then I go out of my mind, and I will kill you before you kill me.

Self-affirmations of this kind may recall observations of Bourgois and his colleagues about the moral economy of violence that is 'based on a disposition to sociality and generosity' but 'requires a facility for rage and an anxiety over insult that exacerbates community insecurity' (Kadandinos et al. 2014: 10). Nevertheless, in our setting it is crucial to see how such ostentatious acts can verge on the domain of joking relations, re-creating the everyday terms of conviviality rather than pushing for further violence. The threat of violence may be present even in those situations that mark the beginning of (or later, the reinforcement of) an existing collaboration between peers.

Collaboration and Combination

Like others, Bogdan could prove his value by showing that he could keep his 'madness' under control, as a potency that he retained in practice and maintained as part of his reputation, which allowed him to remain in control of his social environment and hence avoid becoming a 'fool'. As a practice and a potency, madness was most commonly identified as 'not caring' (*nu ține cont*), or in terms of generosity and other forms of temporary excess. One's 'madness' and one's ambition to become a great man were nearly impossible to distinguish, which explains why occasional personal and financial losses were inherent to this pursuit. As my acquaintances sometimes put it when recalling their previous losses from either gambling or some other unsuccessful investment, 'I know I have lost a lot, because I have my ambitions and my madness, as any man has some kind of a madness.' In relation to these losses, the role of the wives of these men was to defend the priorities of the household. This was the case during men's prolonged cycles of 'honouring' each other through mutual calls for drinks in the street near to a grocery store. In some of these cases a woman's silent protest strategy was to go to the place of 'honouring' together with her children to parade them in front of her husband in order to remind him of his domestic obligations.

From the men's perspective, however, these acts of honouring provided the significant moments when they established the kind of long-term cooperation they defined as 'collaboration', governed by the principles of equality and mutual benefits.[6] As they said about such relations, 'We help each other reciprocally. If you don't have [something], I give you; if I don't have, you give to me. This is real friendship'. The group of peers in 'collaboration' constituted the basic unit of social life in the streets; they were the medium between the family and the household on the one hand, and the potentially wild outside world on the other. The intimate relation between peers was marked by acts such as frequent and playful sham battles, mocked vituperations, or the fact that they were allowed to dig in each other's pockets without recrimination. All the peer groups of this kind with which I became acquainted during my fieldwork had both Roma and non-Roma Romanian members. 'Collaboration' relied on the triple mechanism of mutual defence, control and support, and they assured one another that if one of them were under attack, all the others would take it as a personal offence and act accordingly. In sum, 'collaboration' was the result of exchange as an uncertain, highly tactical activity aimed at extending a sense of community (Gudeman 2009).

At least as an ideal type, 'collaboration' can be distinguished from another form of economic transaction commonly known in the street as 'combination' (*combinație*), the latter depicting short-term or occasional forms of exchange in which the rules, the value of the transferred objects and the personal worth of the participants were all open to negotiation and bargaining, implying a series of risks but also unforeseen possibilities to be realised in such a deal. Though 'collaboration' and 'combination' differed in time scale, they were nevertheless interlinked in various ways. First of all, every 'combination' included the promise of developing 'collaboration' between peers, even if it was actually not achieved in the end. In this respect, 'combination' was similar to the type of informal exchange described by Stan (2012) in her ethnography on bribing practices in the postsocialist Romanian healthcare system, where the status of the bribe as gift or commodity can be defined only in retrospect in relation to the very act of exchange. It follows from this that 'combination' can also signify those rich moments of social creativity when new information, possibilities and resources are discovered and a new idea of order is introduced. In such moments, the kind of social learning that is commonly associated with the street reached some of its highest peaks. Accordingly, engagement in 'combination' was desirable for anyone who wished to develop their skills in bargaining and business in general, or to avoid the misfortunes associated with the situation of 'fools' (*proști*) who subject themselves to boredom and are doomed to remain impoverished by accepting even the smallest gain in their specific field of occupation.

Given that the purpose of these acts was to gain material and non-material values, as well as some sort of control over the social environment, simple rational calculation is far from being the only, or even the most important, skill that neighbourhood entrepreneurs like Lucian were striving to acquire. 'Counting' (*socoteală*) was an indispensable skill for them, one that they cultivated perpetually during their deals or while banishing occasional boredom by playing the popular card game *remi*. Still, apart from this and the social control they could exert through the fear and respect encoded in their local reputation, these businessmen also put a huge emphasis on what they called 'observing the motions rapidly' or having an 'electronic head' or mindset in order to succeed at social navigation (Vigh 2009). To put it another way, in a social and economic environment of uncertainty, and faced with an ensuing need for alertness, it was not simply luck that traders needed, but more specifically the gift of being able to figure out other people's intentions or inner thoughts, even if the respective person intended to hide them from others. Altogether these much-desired personal qualities of traders helped them circumscribe a realm that we might consider non-rational and, in this sense, external to well-executed calculations. However, this is definitely not the way the traders themselves would perceive it. As Lucian once told me:

> I'm not a fool (*prost*), I just look at a person and I already know all his thoughts, what's in his head and what's not, if he is my enemy or someone close to me, if he wants to tell me something or if he wants to hide it. I feel all this. May my son and daughter die [if I lie to you], but I can even feel when the police are behind me. As it was last time [around the market], I felt that there might be something, I said "let's put things in order quickly," and they were there already. I'm a kind of person who quickly perceives anything. Maybe it's three at night, and I'm sleeping, and I'm just like now,

feeling bad, almost dying of exhaustion – but still, if I hear the smallest noise, I jump up immediately, while others just keep on sleeping.

If 'collaboration' signifies those relationships in which partners mutually accept the rules of reciprocity in the long run, then 'combination' marks the very margins of this sociality. This is where 'rip-offs' can take place, since the rules of exchange are open to negotiation, and formerly unimaginable profits can be realised, together with the possibility of outwitting others or being outwitted by them. Consequently, it is during these affairs that traders can continue experimenting with crucial assets – such as the power of their reputation, counting, and 'understanding the moves rapidly' – and potentially extend the realm of 'collaboration' and interests. However, as I show in the next section, this is far from being a one-way process.

The Interstitial and the Illicit

During their spontaneous celebrations after successful business deals – for instance, buying a new plot of land in the neighbourhood or finding a particularly gainful load (*încărcare*) of scrap metal – Spoitori Gypsy traders liked to praise themselves as bandits or *mafioți* in an obviously positive light, even if they were outsiders to domains where the area's notorious *mafioți* pursued their illicit activities, such as moneylending or dealing in prostitutes and drugs.[7] The direct and indirect outcomes of these illicit activities were omnipresent in the life of the neighbourhood. Still, it was not only the moral or ethical imperatives of these people that kept them at a safe distance from direct involvement in the circles and activities of those they identified as *mafioți* 'for real', without positive camouflage or irony. The story of Claudiu and one of his mates is a powerful example of the quickly emerging distance between peers due to one's involvement in the underworld. The two men developed this distance by emphasising their status in the dual sense of the material value they could exhibit and the personal worth they claimed in relation to one another.

Claudiu was a Gypsy man in his twenties who made a living out of performing small services at a nearby cemetery before opting for a much more lucrative job as a pimp. This switch was marked by a whole set of conspicuous changes in his appearance, beginning with an intense regime of bodybuilding, wearing Ray-Ban sunglasses and driving a new BMW; he also acquired a whole new set of clothes with particular items such as a spectacular set of tee-shirts in the colours of the Italian flag.

The evaluation of his turn towards the underworld was a complex matter for peers, not in the least because someone's move towards a domain of illicit activities could offer access to resources and opportunities to others outside that domain. Accordingly, whatever they thought of Claudiu's new business in moral terms, when peers could afford it, they could still enjoy his assistance in making prostitutes available for them at reasonable prices in Bucharest's city centre, an area that they rarely visited otherwise, let alone for the purposes of pure pleasure. Still, in many respects it became impossible for them to accommodate Claudiu's changed status. To begin with, he stopped hanging out with the others in the street. Then, in the summer of 2012, he was invited to a wedding celebration by a family of Gypsies on one of the streets not far from the house where he lived. Following the usual custom in the neighbourhood, after the church service the celebration continued in a courtyard where family members and invitees gathered to eat, drink and enjoy the live music. The gates of the courtyard were left wide open to allow a whole audience of uninvited people (*neinvitați*) from the area to stare at the merrymaking from outside, though of course the limits between the zone of invitees and the uninvited were unequivocal for all.[8] Claudiu got an invitation to the wedding from the men of the host family. However, he used the occasion to demonstrate his changed status. Although he came to the celebration accompanied by some of his brothers and wearing his tee-shirt with the Italian tricolour, he remained out in the street among the uninvited, drinking his own wine and soda and requesting a few songs from the musicians from that distance. Claudiu's companions among the hosts perceived this as a great offence, but they decided to downplay it so that the flow of the celebration remained uninterrupted. It was this seeming disinterest – letting the annoying gestures go unnoticed – that proved in the end that Claudiu and his current position belonged to a domain that the others could hardly affect and might not even want to get involved in.

A few weeks later there was a further incident involving Claudiu, this time with Remus, a young and chubby non-Roma Romanian man who liked to hang out with the others from the area, at least when he was not at work. Like many other young males from the neighbourhood, Remus had professional training as a waiter, although he pursued this profession only occasionally after he was fired from a restaurant. Instead, he made his living through temporary jobs such as selling firewood or riding his scooter as a delivery boy for a local pizzeria. On a summer day, Claudiu was around the corner in the company of 'his sly ones' (*șmecherii lui*), as the others said, when Remus passed by on his scooter. Claudiu looked at him and asked off-hand if he was 'still running around only with that scooter'. As Remus told me later, 'he took me for a fool' (*fraier*), and as he continued, 'I said, "What the fuck do you want?" I'm not as slick as you are, get the fuck out, I piss on you!⁹ And then I left'. The next day Claudiu messaged him through others, saying that he should calm down and not revile him anymore in front of others, or else he might be beaten. 'This is what he said', Remus summarised, 'words of a fool!'

Although the management of this affair still fits the usual framework where partners resolve their interpersonal conflicts largely by verbal rather than physical means – for example, by discrediting the other as a sucker or a fool – the message containing Claudiu's threat was the last exchange I heard about between the onetime peers. Later, as we were discussing the events, Remus asked rhetorical questions while recalling the times when principles of mutuality and equality guided their relationship. 'When he was in trouble, who was standing next to him? Wasn't it me? Didn't I take him into my house, take responsibility for him and all that? I helped the man as I could'. In retrospect, he could take a moral stance by enumerating his gestures according to former 'collaboration'; but he could hardly exert any control, let alone obligation, towards his former peer. At the same time, such a disruption in personal relationships clearly shows the boundary between the interstitial and the illicit economies of the area, together with the dramatic change of status that was induced by someone's turn towards the latter. Several months later, Lucian and his brother from the family of Spoitori Gypsies told me that Remus had taken to selling drugs. And, as they feared that his involvement in the drug trade could bring unnecessary police scrutiny onto their own business with scrap metal, they had stopped all contact with him.

Conclusions

The inhabitants of the 'most infamous' neighbourhood and the ultimate 'Gypsy area' of Bucharest do not tackle their disadvantageous situation in a way that would decidedly make them into 'fools'. Rather than dwelling on this status, the people I have presented in this account are taking advantage of the multiple resources and opportunities offered by the street, whereby they are striving to become entrepreneurs or 'businessmen' in an uncertain and constantly changing economic environment. It is in this context that exchange practices and forms of economic or entrepreneurial action unfold and – at least ideally – end up in the creation and achievement of material value and personal worth that is not available to 'fools' who are known to accept exploitation without restraint at their workplace or in the street. The personalised nature of these transactions and the significance of developing trust and reliable personal relations are essential to these activities.

Because these resources are scarce and limited, the processes of making and breaking these relations are highly ritualised. If one way of exercising control is through the fear or respect generated by the display of violence (even if it is not deployed in the end) and 'madness', another way is through the losses a man is willing to incur for the sake of his peers. Exchanges of this kind are grounded in the ideals of equality and the mutual will to avoid predatory or exploitative ways of profiting from one another. At the same time, the margins of this sociality are marked by 'combinations', which are also the testing ground of entrepreneurial skills. Accordingly, the forms of exchange and the business-making ventures that these people pursue at once create and maintain a livelihood, as they aim to take a stand that allows for some control over the flow of objects, information and people in the streets. These acts are crucial in both gaining and losing the social value attributed to a person, which is particularly apparent at those points where the interstitial and the illicit economies of the area coincide with each other.

NOTES

1. In Romanian, the lyrics are: *Mahala si țiganie, de când am intrat in tine, / N-a ramas carne pe mine, n-a ramas carne pe mine, / Puținica ce-a ramas, of, of, tot s-a fript si tot s-a ars. / Dacă stau s-o cântăresc, nici o litră nu găsesc / Nicio litră, niciun gram, că-i mâncată de dușmani.* Among the many existing versions of the song, I quote here the one by the late Florică Roșioru. Source: Florică Roșioru, Mahala și țiganie, *Cintece lăutărești*. Eurostar 2007.
2. Gypsy (*Țigan*) is a widely accepted denomination both among Roma and non-Roma Romanian inhabitants in this neighbourhood. At the time of my fieldwork, whenever the denomination 'Roma' was used there by someone in everyday Romanian speech, it was almost invariably a person with some relationship to NGOs. Spoitori (Spoitor in singular) is the denomination for a group of Roma in Romania who traditionally worked as coppersmiths and animal traders, living predominantly in the south of the country. The people I have been working with no longer practise these occupations. The Spoitori Gypsies themselves used the denomination of Rom or Roma only when they spoke Romani language, as native speakers. I gave pseudonyms to all the protagonists of this chapter.
3. Notably, the imaginary of 'the street', as used in English in such contexts, does not overlap entirely with the Romanian usage of the word *stradă* in the situations I describe here. Instead, several other expressions are used, such as 'outside' (*afară*) or 'around the corner' (*la colț*).

4. To complicate things further, the term *nebun* can have another sense when used in a different context, meaning literally 'not good'. In this instance, *ne-* (not-) is a prefix negating *bun* (good).
5. My acquaintances in the neighbourhood liked to emphasise that the whole venture of moving there would have been impossible for me in the past, in the 1990s or just 'some years ago' because of the probability of assaults and petty theft that were then customary, especially against outsiders.
6. For a classical account of such brotherly relations, see Stewart (1997). In my account, however, the group of 'brothers' is not ethnically homogeneous.
7. Similar to the ironic tone with which my acquaintances referred to themselves as *mafioți* in this case, the severity of the area's actual mafioți is also questionable. For example, a local Roma politician made a comparison based on his own experiences between the actors of the underworld in Romania and those from Moldova. As he said, the ones from Romania are all talk and no action: 'they are like people with water pistols' compared to the ones in Moldova. If in the aforementioned case the Gypsy traders glorified themselves as *mafioți* by means of irony, in this case the actual mafioți were disparaged in a similar manner.
8. When the zone of invitees had to stretch out in front of the house, the organisers usually put rugs on those parts of the street, thereby preserving the limits between the invitees and uninvited visitors.
9. Swearing that one is going to 'piss on' someone (*mă piș pe el*) is one of the stronger ways to express disregard or dishonour among men in the neighbourhood.

REFERENCES

Graeber, D. 2001. *Toward an Anthropological Theory of Value: The False Coin of Our Own Dreams*. New York: Palgrave Macmillan.

Gudeman, S. 2009. 'Necessity or Contingency: Mutuality and Market', in C. Hann and K. Hart (eds), *Market and Society: 'The Great Transformation' Today*. Cambridge: Cambridge University Press, pp.17–37.

Hart, K. 2000. *The Memory Bank: Money in an Unequal World*. London: Profile Books.

Humphrey, C. 2002. *The Unmaking of Soviet Life: Everyday Economies after Socialism*. Ithaca, NY: Cornel University Press.

Kadandinos, G., L. K. Hart, F. M. Castrillo and P. Bourgois. 2014. 'The Moral Economy of Violence in the US Inner City', *Current Anthropology* 55(1): 1–22.

Konstantinov, Y. 1996. 'Patterns of Reinterpretation: Trader-Tourism in the Balkans (Bulgaria) as a Picaresque Metaphorical Enactment of Post-Totalitarianism', *American Ethnologist* 23(4): 762–82.

Lambek, M. 2008. 'Value and Virtue', *Anthropological Theory* 8(2): 133–57.

Marcińczak, S., M. Gentile, S. Rufat and L. Chelcea. 2014. 'Urban Geographies of Hesitant Transition: Tracing Socioeconomic Segregation in Post-Ceaușescu Bucharest', *International Journal of Urban and Regional Research* 38(4): 1399–417.

Mollona, M. 2005. 'Factory, Family and Neighborhood: The Political Economy of Informal Labour in Sheffield', *Journal of the Royal Anthropological Institute* 11(3): 527–48.

Pardo, I. 1996. *Managing Existence in Naples: Morality, Action and Structure*. Cambridge: Cambridge University Press.
Smith, A., and A. Stenning. 2006. 'Beyond Household Economies: Articulations and Spaces of Economic Practice in Postsocialism', *Progress in Human Geography* 30(2): 190–213.
Stan, S. 2012. 'Neither Commodities nor Gifts: Post-socialist Informal Exchanges in the Romanian Healthcare System', *Journal of the Royal Anthropological Institute* 18(1): 65–82.
Stewart, M. 1997. *The Time of the Gypsies*. Boulder, CO: Westview Press.
Vigh, H. 2009. 'Motion Squared: A Second Look at the Concept of Social Navigation', *Anthropological Theory* 9(4): 419–38.
Wacquant, L. 2004. *Body and Soul: Notebooks of an Apprentice Boxer*. Oxford: Oxford University Press.
———. 2008. *Urban Outcasts: A Comparative Sociology of Advanced Marginality*. Cambridge: Polity Press.

Gergő Pulay is a doctoral candidate at the Central European University, Budapest. Previously he was an international fellow at the New Europe College in Bucharest, and a doctoral fellow of the Marie Curie SocAnth International PhD Programme Promoting Anthropology in Central and Eastern Europe. His dissertation discusses regimes of value and practices of exchange in a territorially stigmatised, mixed Roma and non-Roma Romanian neighbourhood in Bucharest.

Chapter 7

 The Mechanisms of Independence

Economic Ethics and the Domestic Mode of Production among Gabori Roma in Transylvania

MARTIN OLIVERA

It is mid October; winter is coming. Bobi has been waiting for months for *the* job of the season. He would like to marry before the end of the year but must first 'make money'. He wants to throw a beautiful *biav* (wedding), which would show his parents, uncles, aunts and cousins that he is not just anyone, or at least that he is not one of those who marry quickly around a lean chicken dish and a few beers. He could have had a respectable wedding last year while he was working for 'his' boss in a nearby village, where he worked several months on the rooftop of a factory that produced motorcycle helmets. But at the time, Bobi did not feel 'ready' for marriage. And, of course, all the money earned a year ago is a distant memory.

If Bobi does nothing serious before the snow and ice arrive, the prospect of marriage will be delayed for at least six months. The young man knows that his parents care for him, his aunts looking at him askance: 'This boy doesn't seem to want to marry' (*Kodo baro șavoro inka ci kamel te lel Romni*). In this context, everything worries and annoys him. And his mood darkens as the days shorten. But one morning, while he is preparing for another day of inactivity, Ianos, a former neighbour, enters Bobi's house: one of his distant cousins needs gutters for her new home.

The next Sunday, I accompany Bobi when he goes looking for Ianos and his mother, so she can show us the road and, more importantly, introduce us to her niece. We arrive there an hour later, shake hands and let the *Gaži*[1] do the presentations. The niece promptly takes us to see the house. 'My husband is in Italy for work', she explains. 'We have just completed the construction of the house. We want to install the gutters before winter'. Then, she asks, 'Well, how much will you take for the job [gutters and drainpipes]?' Bobi adopts a highly professional reflective air before delivering his answer:

> Hmm, I don't know. It must be measured. You know, I work by the metre. A metre of gutter is 80,000 lei.[2] A metre of pipe is 130,000. And then there are the hooks [which support the gutter]. For you, I'll do them for 40,000 instead of 50,000. Well, that's all. You know, I'm not one of those Gypsies who tell you one price and then charge you double at the end. I tell you, you only pay for what you need. This is why I cannot tell you the exact price right now. Because if I say something and at the end there are four or five metres more or less, you'll tell me that this is not what we had agreed on. I cannot tell you 'It's 8 million' or 'It's 11 million', because if ultimately it is 10 million, that is not correct.

Given all these figures the *Gaži* worries, and inquires, 'It will be 10 million?' At this point, Bobi has not yet measured precisely, but the price range previously given was already high. The woman, who obviously needs a total price, adds, 'Because 10 million is possible'. The young Rom can only be satisfied. The *Gaži* herself proposes a good price, very good even. Bobi doesn't say 'yes' or 'no' but 'probably', adding that he works 'by the metre', and begins a tour of the house with his tools. 'You know, the [galvanised] sheets are expensive today', Bobi continues. 'That's why it may seem a little expensive, but I am not one of those who will use 0.3 millimetre sheets, because in this case, you would come to me in six months asking me to pick up the pieces. I work so that everyone is satisfied: me and you'. The *Gaži*, who is now convinced, asks when he will come to do the work and what she should prepare. Bobi leaves his phone number and tells her to call as soon as she has collected the money, then they will begin the work.

After a quick estimate, it turns out the material needed to complete the project should cost around 2.5 million lei. With the help of his brother and a brother-in-law, Bobi hopes he can do the work in two (long) days, with a further two days of homework to prepare the elements (gutters, pipes, angles and brackets). The profit should be at least 7.5 million lei for four days of actual work, at a time where the average monthly wage in Romania is around 3 million lei. The house looks as if it will be a great opportunity, 'a good job' (*jek lasi butji*). Bobi also wants the *Gaži*'s neighbours to notice the beautiful gutters and to ask about him. If he can get a second project of this kind soon, he may be able to plan the wedding that he aspires to. And this should be soon, because otherwise the money for the first job will already have been squandered by the time the money for the second one appears.

Kana naj love, naj patjiv ('No money, no respect'). This sentence in Romani, frequently heard among Roma, can be understood in two ways: you need money to respect your fellows, and you need money to be respectable. The two meanings embody the idea that collective belonging is not a given and abstract fact but a dynamic and active practice. To be a Rom among the Roma, to live *Romanes* (in the Rom way), you have to hold your place in exchange circuits that bind individuals and families together: you must take your place and you must keep it. And for this, you need money. From this perspective, Rom economic practices can be regarded as a 'total social fact' (Mauss 1925), intimately embedded in all other aspects of social life. In other words, the economy is not simply a part of the reproduction of social order but is actively involved in the production of society. This may seem paradoxical, since it is common to see Gypsy societies as precarious, and indeed, although there are rich Gypsies, the vast majority of them can be seen as facing economic insecurity. Their livelihood does not seem assured in any sustainable manner. And when some generations manage to get out of this 'insecurity', this 'success' doesn't seem to be transmitted: the livelihood of rich Gypsies somehow often remains 'precarious'.

I propose here to discuss how the economy produces Roma's society – the *Romanes* (the way the Roma are among themselves but also in relation to the *Gaže*) – while ensuring a complete symbolic independence of Roma society.[3] To do so, we have to look at the economy not only as a production process but also as a form of ethics, and to consider how Roma produce resources as well as how they spend them. The analysis will allow us to understand how a society that is scattered and drowned in otherness, and that is usually seen as socio-economically marginal and politically dominated, manages to establish a logic of abundance and to take possession of the world, including that of the *Gaže*.

The Domestic Mode of Production and Gabori Practices

From his fieldwork among Hungarian Gypsies in the 1980s, Michael Stewart writes about Roma who feel like they are 'living lightly and easily in an uninterrupted free lunch' (Stewart 1997: 26). The phrase echoes Marshall Sahlins's famous formula in its study of 'primitive' economics, where he speaks of an 'original affluent society' and a 'logic of abundance' (Sahlins 1972). And as we will see, both expressions are in some sense applicable to the Gabori, even though the majority of them live in a somewhat precarious material situation according to Western standards of 'development'.

In various ways, anthropologists studying semi-nomadic Gypsy groups, mainly in Western Europe, have drawn comparisons with hunter-gatherers and/or peripatetic populations in order to analyse their socio-economic dynamics (e.g. Okely 1983; Rao 1985; Formoso 1986; Gmelch 1986; Reyniers 1998; see also Stewart 2013: 417 for a general overview). Concerning the Gabori, the comparison between hunter-gatherer/peripatetic communities and Roma is not necessarily relevant: kinship organisation and dynamics, residential logics as well as forms of sociability and local integration are in many ways comparable to peasant realities rather than to a former 'nomadic lifestyle' (Olivera 2012: 273–310). Focusing on the domestic mode of production (DMP) as theorised by Sahlins will be helpful for overcoming the natural tendency to oppose Gypsies and sedentary peasants – who are presented as being obviously and definitely different (e.g. Formoso 1986) – and, doing so, will contribute to 'de-Gypsify' our perception of Rom economy. Indeed, Sahlins's work on the DMP allows us to place ethnographic data and interpretations in a broader framework. Although the example of hunter-gatherers is famous, Sahlins makes it clear that the DMP can also be characteristic of some peasant economies (Sahlins 1972: 88), making particular reference to the work of Chayanov (1986) on Russian peasant households.

Sahlins defines the DMP as being based on a sexual division of labour, direct access to resources, simple technology and authority vested in age. If the DMP structures an economy centred on and limited to production for consumption, by no means does it correspond to self-sufficient societies. Commercial exchange takes place, but money is valued according to its use value rather than its exchange value (Sahlins 1972: 82–85). According to Sahlins, these economies are structurally under-productive, with limited production targets. And as we will see, this perspective is particularly useful for understanding Roma's economic practices beyond the rhetoric of marginality or the 'culture of poverty' (Lewis 1959).

The incomes of Gabori households are of two kinds: money earned while carrying out 'Rom work' (*Romani butji*) and money earned from other sources. For many Roma, 'Rom work' nowadays consists in working with sheet metal (guttering, roofing), though it is not limited to this. It is an exclusively male activity in which the Roma show their 'know-how'. Ideally, men spare their talent for *Romani butji*, leaving their wives with the burden of the household's daily subsistence. Sometimes, Rom women lead commercial activities; they 'make markets', selling various seasonal items, but although this activity is based on trade it is not considered 'Rom work'. The low sums women gain in this way are added to the money or to the donations in kind that are brought in by family members who occasionally work for their neighbours (for example, in agriculture), or else they are added to the modest child benefits and to the money that is regularly borrowed from the same neighbours. Indeed, all Gabori families that I know of have debts (*kamimo*), which they repay as regularly as they take on new ones, mostly from the *Gaže*. Mothers are responsible for these frequent small loans which are interest-free: this money helps to buy food at the market, to pay for medicines, to purchase a canister of gas or to pay off an electricity bill.[4]

The two types of income (feminine and masculine) as well as expenses are, ideally, maintained in two distinct and independent spheres. Of course, sometimes the product of *Romani butji* sustains the daily life of the home, and conversely the money made by women can be used for 'unnecessary expenses' (such as a visit to relatives or buying nice clothes). This is not the official rule, and when it happens, the money is transferred in full (from the man to the woman or vice versa). Thereby, the sexual division is maintained, disregarding necessary adjustments: women (helped by their children and their daughters-in-law) take care of the subsistence of the household using modest amounts of daily income, while men (helped by their elder boys and possibly other visiting relatives) save their time for the prestige of money earned and spent *Romanes*. Women practise a centripetal economy (grabbing), men a centrifugal one (dilapidation) (see also Stewart 1994: 57). The two logics sometimes clash, which can lead to stormy marital disputes, but everybody knows by experience that the two movements support each other, both being centred on the domestic group.

Rom women produce no surplus; everything is consumed. Encouraging and seeking donations or in-kind exchanges, the economy of domestic subsistence remains as much as possible outside the market economy. This is not to deny the importance of commercial exchanges as such: Rom families trade with their neighbours on a daily basis (purchases, loans, barter, services) and they buy at the market. As Sahlins notes, 'subsistence production' does not imply 'self-sufficiency' (Sahlins 1972: 83). Exchanges take place, but aim to 'meet the immediate needs of the living, not a profit ... Like peasants, primitive people remain constant in their pursuit of use values, related always to exchange with an interest for consumption, so to production with an interest for provisioning. And in this respect, the historical antithesis of *both* is the bourgeois entrepreneur with an interest in exchange value' (ibid.: 83). At this point, it becomes readily apparent that the economy of domestic subsistence, headed by Rom women, corresponds particularly well with the DMP as theorised by Sahlins.

The case of 'Rom work' seems more problematic: it is located outside of the sphere of domestic subsistence, it involves trading with the *Gaže* and, in theory, it produces superfluous income, which might seem to contradict the DMP on all counts. Yet we will see how the only goal of 'Rom work' is to ensure the subsistence of the domestic group, even though this might appear to be already assured. This paradox can be resolved by looking at 'Rom work' not simply as a 'labour process' characterised by rigid criteria, but as the expression of a kind of 'know-how', embodying qualities and tending to verify them. In a word: as ethics.

Romani Butji: Roma 'Know-how'

The 'traditional craft' of the Gabori, as generally recognised in Romania today, is putting up gutters and, more broadly, tinsmithing (Romanian *tinichigerie*). They do not have a monopoly on this craft, either in Transylvania or elsewhere, but they are commonly called *Țigani cu burlane* ('Gypsies with pipes') or, by some, *ciotârnari* ('gutterers'). However, only fifty years ago the Roma did not make gutters. Some elders were tinkers, boilermakers, tinsmiths or blacksmiths, but most of them lived off farming, supplementing their income with occupations such as stonemasonry, brick making, trade and the recovery and sale of glass or animal skins. Guttering only developed after the 1960s (coinciding with the time when families began to be scattered throughout the country under communism), becoming a widely practised activity among Gabori during the 1970s and 1980s.

The hammer (*ciokano*) is now, for Roma as for *Gaže*, a symbol of Gabori 'authenticity' or 'traditionalism' (Houliat 1999), but 'Rom work' cannot be reduced to the handling of this single tool. And it is not because they do the same job that the Gabori form a community of peers; rather, it is because they are peers that many of them have adopted this profession over the last few decades.

Moreover, tinsmithing is not inherently more prestigious than another activity. It just so happens that many Roma are tinsmiths today, and this is how they show their quality. Many men unanimously perceived as 'successful' did not build their prosperity by working metal. Some are market traders (of clothes, shoes, for example), while others, in recent years, have worked as junk dealers: they roam the villages in search of antiques to sell to Western clients or other non-Gabori Roma (see Berta 2009). There are also manufacturers of wooden furniture for export, car sellers and car-body repairers. Some Roma practise or have practised many of these activities, alternately or simultaneously. And although none of these trades involves a hammer, in the eyes of the Roma they all express Rom 'know-how'.

The Romanian term that corresponds to the English 'trade' or 'craft' is *meserie*. Roma often use the word when speaking *Gažikanes* (Romanian or Hungarian), but they have no equivalent in Romanes. The word *butji* means 'work', understood as paid work, and not 'trade' or 'craft'; *Romani butji* is thus the 'Rom way of making money'. Instead, they use the term *meștero* (which is close to the Hungarian word *mester*, meaning 'master', 'craftsman') to denote the artisan, the 'professional', the 'master'. One can (or should) be a *meștero* as a tinsmith, but also as a shoe seller. But not all male activities that generate an income are *Romani butji* (for example, wage labour is not), and *Romani butji* is not a specific trade. It is therefore crucial to identify how 'Rom work' can be characterised. And by approaching 'Rom work' as 'know-how', we can emphasise the decisive importance of the context in which the action is executed, and out of which success cannot be measured. From this point of view, 'know-how' may be related to the Greek *Metis*, the cunning intelligence highlighted by Detienne and Vernant (1993). It seems to meet here a conception of professional and, more generally, individual success based on the notion of 'effective intelligence' also found in other Roma communities (Stoichița 2008).

Ideally, the Roma do not solicit their clients. Of course, during difficult periods they sometimes do, travelling to neighbouring villages to offer their services where they have spotted new or renovated houses. But Roma prefer to be asked by the *Gažo*. The same logic seems to be at work in their business practices. Șamu, for example, spends eight months of the year in Hungary, where he sells shoes. For years, he has been setting up his stand at the same markets in the same cities. Talking about his job, he explains why he appreciates it so much:

> It's easy, not tiring. You just have to know the people, to talk to them. The *Gažo* arrives, you watch how he is dressed and then take out the pair of shoes that suits him well. Then, he comes back, next month, next year. Or he sends his children, his friends. That's good, you earn well. But you must not pray or beg, like a Gypsy. This is not good; they don't like it.

The good trader is therefore not a haggler enticing random passers-by. Instead, he is the one who manages to draw his *Gaže* to him, to make them ask for him.

Thus, mobility is not a characteristic of *Romani butji* but a consequence of its practice, when Roma develop what they call their *prinženimo* far from their place of residence. The *prinženimo* (lit. the 'known people') can be translated as 'relational capital', and is materialised in the small notebook containing names and phone numbers of *Gaže* that every Rom carries in his pocket, next to a comb. Pişta, for example, lives for five months a year 150 kilometres from his home, where he stays in the house of his *Gažo* 'boss', who provides him with work for much of the season. Roma use the term *patrono* (boss) to describe these 'important' *Gaže* who regularly provide them with work. They are essential elements of the '*Gažikano* capital' (Piasere 1985: 144). The Roma speak of a 'boss' not so much because he has some control over them, but because of the authority he has over other *Gaže*; thus, the *patrono* is an 'important man' whom the Roma consider they can deal with on an equal footing. When saying 'my boss' (*moro patrono*), a Rom does not subordinate himself but literally appropriates the *Gažo* and his influence, at least rhetorically.

A Good Job and a Good Price

When a Rom installs gutters, sells jeans at the market or goes through villages in search of old objects, he instigates direct relationships with *Gaže* clients, which grants a total (technical and moral) independence of the *meştero*. Ideally, the Rom owes nothing to anyone, not even to his client. We now have to understand how these characteristics create a feeling of high profitability.

The 'Gypsy economy' has often been perceived as favouring what Sahlins called 'negative reciprocity' (Sahlins 1972: 195; see also e.g. Piasere 1985; Formoso 1986), but it seems that Gabori economic practices do not fit with this idea.[5] The Roma do not idealise either theft or bargaining. All these are worthy of *Řumunguri* (who are, according to Gabor ideology and which joins here the *Gaže* stereotypes about the *Ţigani*, those 'depraved Gypsies' with no culture nor morality), or of some *Gaže*, but not of 'our Roma', the 'noble and respectable Roma' (*patjivale the rajkane Roma*). It is not so much a moral judgment that makes these acts senseless, but rather reasons more deeply rooted in the experience that Roma have of the world and the way they access its wealth. Indeed, the idea of fraud implies selling something at a price that does not match its 'true' value. Therefore, rogue and buyer must agree on the value of a good or service. For their part, Roma do not attach any inherent value to any objects, neither for 10 nor 100 metres of guttering.

Although there is theoretically a price limit under which it is mathematically no longer profitable to install gutters, in practice this is quickly overlooked. The price per metre is always far higher than the cost of the raw material, to the point that ultimately they are no longer directly correlated. This is possible through the wholly manual nature of the work: all you need are hands and time, neither of which are scarce resources among Roma. The workforce is not lacking, a Rom is still supported by his sons and often helped by a nephew or a stepson. All males of working age within the household contribute, to some extent, to the labour process. On the other hand, the goal of the *meștero* is not to accumulate jobs in order to realise an overall profit. It is not the overall volume of work that determines the profitability of *Romani butji*, but rather the conditions of execution and remuneration of each specific *butji*.

Trading antiquities seems to fit particularly well with this concept of profitability, which is mostly dependent on the talent and luck (*baxt*) of a *meștero*. In this activity, the value of objects is in no way related to any labour process, but only to the knowledge and relationships of the Rom. Even the market value fluctuates. The 'invisible hand of the market' acts quite randomly here. There is no predetermined and 'reasonable' profit to be made from a sewing machine or an old cast-iron skillet, given that prices may sometimes vary fivefold. Then, as traders or tinsmiths, Roma can give the impression of considering only the possible 'profit margins', disconnected from investment and the labour process.

The 'good price' (*lașo prețo*) is the one that corresponds to a specific situation, to one *Gažo* and his characteristics; it all depends on the size of the house, on the relationship with the client or with those who referred him to the Rom and, of course, on the *Gažo* himself, his resources and the face he presents. In the situation described above, Bobi is lucky three times: the house is tall and angular, the *Gaži* does not discuss prices herself, and the amount offered is generous. The first, and decisive, part of the work that leads to a contract is greatly simplified. Indeed, work does not start until both parties have agreed on a price. Roma distrust the *Gaže* and know they will always try to pay as little as possible (and as late as possible), or even avoid paying altogether. The first challenge is therefore to achieve a 'good price'. But this is not, from the Roma's point of view, the product of an agreement or a compromise between the client and themselves, since no limits are posed a priori to their profit.

Ideally, the Rom is alone to establish, thanks to his talent, a 'good price', even if the customer formulates it themselves. The Rom must assess and judge his *Gažo*, talking to him properly in order to make him understand how much they have to pay. Therefore, like Bobi in the example above, Roma avoid giving a price too quickly. They prefer to let the clients talk about themselves and their family, explaining their situation and expectations. In doing so, Roma do not bargain with the Gaže and 'don't Gypsify together' (*nu na țiganim așa*). This way of doing things, though it allows the Roma to impose their conditions (or at least gives them this impression), is often relevant for the client too, who feels at ease dealing with a calm and serious 'professional'.

If the *Gažo* intends to haggle over prices, it often happens that the Rom categorically refuses. The latter can, in a princely manner, decide himself to grant a 'discount', anticipating the possible reluctance of the client, but he will not yield to direct demands. I have often been taken aback by the attitude of my companions who refused to pursue further discussion from the moment the *Gažo* began, according to them, to bargain too hard. Whereas in my opinion, the work would have easily been obtained with a little negotiation, the Roma shook the recalcitrant *Gažo*'s hands, wished them good health and left, while I remained a few seconds on the spot, incredulous. It was not a bluff to force the stubborn negotiator to change their offer: the *Gažo* did not run after them and the Roma were genuinely happy not to have to work for such a 'peasant' (*țăran*), even though they had no money in their pocket. Had they not said just a few minutes earlier that they absolutely needed to make some money to pay off a specific debt? Perhaps. But what I had not understood is that Rom money is not made at any price.

In any case, when they try to achieve a 'good price', Roma do not mean to cheat on their clients. When they come back from 'good work' (*lasi butji*), they do not boast of having tricked a 'fool'; instead, they take pride in having such a 'good *Gažo*'. And a 'good *Gažo*' is not a 'moron' who is ready to pay millions for something that is not worth anything. No – a 'good *Gažo*' is someone intelligent (*vokoșo*) and respectable (*patjivalo*), someone who trusts the Roma and seeks their skills and services not by default, error or misunderstanding, but because they are 'worth it'. Conversely, these *Gaže* deserve the Rom, they are good payers, do not discuss the price, are good advertisers among their fellows, and so on. And they will give some food to the working Roma, and a few drinks to toast the work. They chat from time to time but do not stay the whole day watching how it goes. As I always observed, Roma cannot stand it when a customer tries to check their work constantly. On several occasions, my companions threatened in such circumstances to stop working and leave everything behind (with the old gutters and tiles removed). No one ever executed their threat, but the displeasure was real: their anger was more directed towards themselves than towards the *Gažo*, who ultimately behaved as an ordinary 'peasant' (suspicious, vicious, miserly, for example)

– the antithesis of a 'good *Gažo*'. And a real *meştero* should have been able to recognise this at first glance, before he agreed on the job.

Therefore, a 'good job', which can be discussed at length among Roma, is one that is done with a 'good *Gažo*' in good conditions and for a 'good price'. This is the right way to 'make money', easily and honourably. And this is how the *meştero* is not just an artisan employed by a client, but also, somehow, a helpful friend, as well as a Roma who knows their trade.

A positive personal relationship, total independence, profitability: such are the qualities of *Romani butji*, more than mere formal characteristics. We understand now how the first two dimensions are structurally related, and we begin to see how profitability can be evaluated (or devalued). In classical economics, profitability is defined as the ratio between a result and the capital needed to achieve it. Concerning the Roma, it is not the financial aspects, the physical effort and/or the time invested that mainly determines the profitability of *Romani butji*, but the relational capital. Building up such capital and finding ways to value it in order to make money depends exclusively on the Rom – on his own value and his 'know-how'. But if the Roma practise these 'profitable' activities, why are they rarely rich and, when they are, why is this wealth always perceived as transitory? To answer this question, we must return to the Rom economic mode of production, placing it in relation to its goal: spending or, more broadly, Gabor sociability.

The Ethics of *Bare Roma*: The 'Great Men'

A utilitarian perspective would show us how this *Romani butji*, which only serves to generate superfluous income that is meant to be squandered, is totally unnecessary. This would actually be in line with what the Roma think: it is precisely because it is not 'necessary' or 'required' that their work is 'beautiful', 'free' or, in a word, Romani. However, the 'beauty' of male action is made possible by discrete and regular female tasks, which the Roma do not deny: *Mori Řomniasa, ci ala te merav bokhatar!* ('With my wife I won't die of hunger!'). Yet both sexes work for the subsistence of the household, not only because the income from 'Rom work' regularly disappears, discreetly, in the female pocket, but because the domestic group (*gazda*) is the focal point of Roma society: following Gabori ideology, women's work ensures its continuity (people have enough to eat and do not die of cold), while male labour maintains the place of the household in society: it motivates and develops relationships with other domestic groups.[6]

Kana naj love, naj patjiv: you need money to respect your fellows; you need money to be respectable. Indeed, it takes money to dress properly, to visit kin and allies and to offer them coffee and drinks in town when meeting, to buy a pig for the holidays, to organise a beautiful baptism or to repaint the main room nicely, to marry a son or a daughter, to put fuel in the car or to pay a driver to visit in-laws (*xanamica*) 200 kilometres away.[7] To live *Romanes*, respectful and respectable, is expensive. The *Gaže* are regularly surprised by this, and stare wide-eyed at their Gabori neighbours when they explain how much they spent over the weekend by visiting a parent, which might be the equivalent of a month's salary. Romanian and Hungarian neighbours can only note that, despite the good relationships they have, these Gypsies are definitely not like them: they live in a house without modern conveniences (such as modern bathrooms or toilets), they regularly need to borrow money to purchases essential medicines or pay a bill, yet they do not hesitate spending large sums on foolish stuff.

Somehow, the *Gaže* attach too much value to money in order to squander it. The Roma see only a use value, essential but always relative. Money, in this sense, is the fuel for the engine of Rom sociability. The latter does not have to run continuously (which might lead to dangerous overheating, since the vast majority of Roma cannot indulge in continuous 'good spending'), but a 'respectable Rom' must turn it on from time to time, depending on their capabilities.

Roma society is a society of domestic groups, which ideally are free and equal. But although all Roma are 'noble and respectable', some are more equal (and noble) than others. One particularly 'important' man is a *Rom baro*, literally a 'big man'. He is someone who can afford to run the engine of Rom sociability more often. More often because, ideally, every Rom must tend to behave like a 'big man', with a duty to spread his wealth and spend it (Godelier 1982: 254).

Thus, the Roma do not work to occupy their hands or to amass money, but always in order to meet specific needs. In the case of Bobi, the need in question was his wedding, but it could equally be renovating a room in one's house, buying a car, visiting distant relatives or paying particular debts (money borrowed to renovate a room, to buy a car, to visit relatives, etc.). The money earned through *Romani butji* is somehow already spent before being earned. Therefore, a profitable job is one that allows one to complete the projects or desires of the moment under good conditions. It is for this reason that installing a fixed length of guttering for exactly the same amount but at two different times and for two different *Gaže* may be a failure in one case and a success in the other.

Trade practices seem to follow the same logic: Roma who leave for several months to sell shoes in Hungary put aside the money they make during their stay not in order to accumulate capital 'just in case' but in order to spend it 'at home' (*khere*) in a way they had already planned (more or less precisely) before they left. *Avav parpale kana sima destul love* ('I'll come back when I have enough money') is a common saying. 'Enough money' in this context means enough to enlarge one's house, enough to change one's car, and so on. Thus, the fruits of their labour are almost squandered a few days after their return, and they are forced to leave once again, having considered other ways to spend money they do not yet have.

Rich (*barvale*) Roma flaunt their wealth: they have nice clothes, a nice car, a nice house (at least a beautiful main room), beautiful children, good *Gaže*, and so on, but they may have no money in their pocket for several days or weeks at a time. This is a not a huge concern, because when they need money, they will do what it takes, even borrowing from a 'good *Gažo*' in an emergency. To be 'rich' is therefore not to have well-stocked bank accounts and full pockets. This is not because the accumulation of 'exchange value' is morally 'bad' or 'anti-social' in itself (and conversely, that 'generosity' is necessarily 'good'), but, more fundamentally, because it does not make sense. Why accumulate what abounds? The expression 'to make money' (*te kerav varăso love*) is explicit: money is not a scarce resource that is 'earned' but a potential, and potentially abundant, profit to be revealed. This is the task of the Roma, their vocation. And the *Gaže's* economy never stops producing exchange value – it is its foundation (Weber 1930; Marx 2013).

Therefore, Rom ethics is not a philosophy of renunciation, as Stewart suggests in a certain way when he writes that Vlach Rom he described delude themselves by renouncing what they cannot have (Stewart 1994: 61). This interpretation appeals to our own conception of money and wealth, where accumulation and sharing are contradictory. This is true in the context of economic thinking based on the notion of scarcity. However, Gabori economic practices do not match this ideology, as we saw through the prism of the DMP. Yet in their own way, Roma fully participate in the market society. But, although 'Rom work' is based on trade and they never stop buying goods, their business practices, including their conceptions of 'good price' and profitability, proceed from a different logic than that of classical economics. The men's prodigality, fruit as well as motivation of *Romani butji* helps the Roma access the global economy while, paradoxically, strengthening the DMP: in the hands of Roma, money is never anything else but a use value.

Roma families who break with the DMP, living solely from income earned from wage labour undertaken by the household head (or from state benefits, which is quite impossible in the Romanian context) may eventually 'leave' the *Romanes*, the Roma's sociability. This is not because wage labour is in itself irreconcilable with Rom ethics, but because its exclusive practice is actually not compatible with the DMP: fixed incomes no longer meet specific needs, but only correspond to the time accumulated or spent. Whatever the wages, money becomes scarce.

This is the situation of Ianko, a fifty-year-old Rom employed for decades in a large state enterprise. Although Ianko earns a decent wage (higher than the national average), his relations with other Roma are minimal. Since he does not do any 'Rom work', he has no way of making a place for himself in Roma's society. The man is held by a chain that contradicts all the qualities of *Romani butji*: he has no productive relationships with 'his' *Gaže*, and so has no anecdotes and 'know-how' to show; he doesn't have any control over his time and therefore cannot decide how to spend his income. By placing him in a world of scarce resources, Ianko's economic practice belies the *Romanes*. Thus, while he probably earns more money than the majority of his fellows, he and his family are forced to stay away from Rom sociability and may end up joining the world of the *Gaže* (after being 'Řumungurised'). The distinction between Roma and *Gaže* will no longer carry any meaning or utility for them. Indeed, the *Gaže* are not just 'those who are not Roma' for moral reasons (such as being 'greedy', 'selfish', 'hardworking' and so on). They are the 'other' whose economy is not based on the DMP; those, rich or poor, for whom money and wealth are a scarce resource.

The Irruption of Chance (*baxt*): A Distinction

The whole Rom economy seems to be driven by one aspiration: expanding the domestic economy and its principle of abundance to the whole of society, to the whole world. To achieve this, the Roma must exclude from the social field those for whom money is a scarce resource in order to overcome the constraints of reciprocity towards them (Sahlins 1972: 191–200).

Since their economic practices are so radically different from those of the mainstream economy, Roma are bound to see an ontological disjunction between themselves 'as a group' and the 'other', while necessarily developing individual relationships with 'their *Gaže*'. Indeed, it is not 'against' the *Gaže* that Roma erect their society, but they are both economically tied to and symbolically separate from them. The existence of the *Gaže* as an objective category that is naturally separate from Roma society may appear as a necessary condition for the reproduction of the DMP in the socio-historical context of European modernity and its economic forms. From this point of view, the *Gažo* would not be a testimony of an exotic classification adapted to the European context, but a product of (and witness to) the integration of Roma in their local environment.

The perspective of the DMP does not explain why Roma society exists, but helps us to understand how social relations are produced among peers and also with the 'other'. One question remains unresolved, however. According to Sahlins: 'the DMP anticipates no social or material relations between households except that they are alike. It offers society only a constituted disorganization, a mechanical solidarity set across the grain of segmentary decomposition' (Sahlins 1972: 95). Thus, there must be something 'extra', a pulse or 'grand forces of integration', in the words of Sahlins (ibid.: 95), leading units to intensify production and to collaborate a priori. In our case, it must be a basis for the distinction between Roma and *Gaže*, which can explain Roma successes and failures beyond the specific context and thus make this 'know-how' a collective quality, motivating cycles of reciprocity between Gabori individuals and households (including matrimonial reciprocity). This 'something' is what, in other contexts, Mauss found in the Maori *hau* and *mana*. Sahlins, when discussing Mauss, conceptualises the *hau* as a 'principle of fertility', and emphasises the fact that it enables 'things' that are already here, already known to produce 'new significations' (new knowledge-objects-relations) while revalidating productive categories (ibid.: 149–84). In the Polynesian context, *hau* and *mana* create social relations in a concrete sense, as they motivate the opening of reciprocity cycles. They 'do' the peers by founding 'productive' relationships through which reciprocity, ideally, can never end.

Returning to the Gabori economy, what is this 'surplus of meaning' through which Roma's society tends to become a space of generalised reciprocity? What is the principle of 'fertility' from which abundance is derived? That 'something' over which *Gaže* have no power and that the Roma are presumed to control is *baxt* (luck, fortune). It is this 'supplementary ration' – the 'floating signifier' – that introduces discontinuity, forges new links, establishes productive oppositions and gives rise to knowledge and resources 'inside a totality which is closed and complementary to itself' (Lévi-Strauss 1950: xlix). Luck explains why Roma ultimately 'know how to do' (*ženen te keren*); it is the collective result of their individual successes, transcending particular cases to become an expression of their collective condition. 'Gypsies are quick to suggest that the dice are stacked in their favour', writes Stewart (1994: 53). The idea of *baxtale Roma* (fortunate/lucky Roma) is not, however, a fiction, nor an illusion. It corresponds to reality, the reality according to which Roma act, and following which they consider the actions of each other.[8]

Through *baxt*, Roma are finally freed from the concept of 'scarce wealth'. Money has only a use value, it abounds, you just have to know 'how to do' – even if it is not always easy. But because they are *baxtale* (fortunate), Roma know how to do, and this talent in turn allows them to check and nurture their luck. *Baxt* is the only 'capital' to be accumulated and is not a finite quantity. The 'spirit' of the Rom economy is definitely not that of bourgeois capitalism captured by Weber (1930): the Roma's *beruf*, vocation or 'task of existence', is to be wealthy, not by capital but by luck. Thus, unlike *Homo economicus*, they do not, so to speak, 'stumble constantly on the finished Creation', or rather, for them Creation is never ended, thanks to *baxt*.

NOTES

1. *Gaži*: a non-Gypsy woman (masc. *Gažo*; plur. *Gaže*).
2. At that time during my fieldwork (2002), €1 equalled 32,000 lei.
3. The data and analysis presented here are based on a broad ethnographic study conducted over 30 months between 1999 and 2007 among Gabori families, mainly in areas between Deva and Târgu-Mureș in Transylvania, Romania. In this article, the word 'Roma' refers only to Gabori and '*Romanes*' to their own way of being Roma.
4. Sometimes men can also borrow money, from other Roma (non-Gabori) in most cases, to finance more important and prestigious spendings. These loans come with interest (often over 20 per cent).
5. 'Negative reciprocity is the attempt to get something for nothing with impunity ... Indicative ethnographic terms include "haggling" or "barter", "gambling", "chicanery", "theft" and other varieties of seizures' (Sahlins 1972: 195).
6. Of course, this is not to say that women have no social role outside the household: they hold in particular a decisive place in matrimonial strategies and politics, and usually have a broader perspective on kinship organisation than their husbands (who often tend to take their official agnatic rhetoric as reality).
7. Romani *xanamic* is equivalent to Romanian *cuscru* ('father-in-law', i.e. the father of one's son- or daughter-in-law). More broadly, the term embodies the relationship between people whose children marry each other.
8. *Baxt* is not only a concept that shapes the way Roma interpret personal or collective events; it is also an individual and biological quality marking their intimate physicality. For more details, see Olivera (2008).

REFERENCES

Berta, P. 2009. 'Materialising Ethnicity: Commodity Fetishism and Symbolic Re-creation of Objects among the Gabor Roma (Romania)', *Social Anthropology* 17(2): 184–97.
Chayanov, A. 1986 [1925]. *The Theory of Peasant Economy*. Madison: University of Wisconsin Press.
Detienne, M., and J.P. Vernant. 1993. *Les ruses de l'intelligence. La métis des Grecs*. Paris: Flammarion.
Formoso, B. 1986. *Tsiganes et sédentaires. La reproduction culturelle d'une société*. Paris: L'Harmattan.
Gmelch S.B. 1986. 'Groups that Don't Want In: Gypsies and Other Artisan, Trader, and Entertainer Minorities', *Annual Review of Anthropology* 15: 307–30.
Godelier, M. 1982. *La production des grands hommes, Pouvoir et domination masculine chez les Baruya de Nouvelle-Guinée*. Paris: Fayard.
Houliat, B. 1999. *Tsiganes en Roumanie*. Rodez: Éditions du Rouergue.
Lévi-Strauss, C. 1950. 'Introduction à l'œuvre de Marcel Mauss', in M. Mauss, *Sociologie et anthropologie*. Paris: Presses Universitaires de France, pp.ix–lii.
Lewis, O. 1975. *Five Families: Mexican Case Studies in the Culture of Poverty*. New York: Basic Books.
Marx, K. 2013 (1867, 1885). *Capital*, Vols. 1 and 2. Ware: Wordsworth Editions
Mauss, M. 1925. 'Essai sur le don: forme et raison de l'échange dans les sociétés archaïques', *L'année sociologique* 1: 30–186.
Okely, J. 1983. *The Traveller-Gypsies*. Cambridge: Cambridge University Press.
Olivera, M. 2008. 'Éthique et gestes de la chance: la baxt des Gabori de Transylvanie', *Études tsiganes* 30: 142–59.
———. 2012. *La tradition de l'intégration. Une ethnologie des Roms Gabori dans les années 2000*. Paris: Éditions Pétra.
Piasere, L. 1985. *Mare Roma. Catégories humaines et structure sociale. Une contribution à l'ethnologie tsigane*. Paris: Paul H. Stahl.
Rao, A. 1985. 'Des nomades méconnus: pour une typologie des communautés péripatétiques', *L'Homme* 25(3): 97–120.
Reyniers, A. 1998. 'Quelques jalons pour comprendre l'économie tsigane', *Études tsiganes* 12: 8–27.
Sahlins, M.D. 1972. *Stone Age Economics*. Chicago: Aldine-Atherton.
Stewart, M. 1994. 'La passion de l'argent: les ambiguïtés de la circulation monétaire chez les Tsiganes hongrois', *Terrain* 23: 45–62.
———. 1997. *The Time of the Gypsies*. Boulder, CO: Westview Press.
———. 2013. 'Roma and Gypsy "Ethnicity" as a Subject of Anthropological Inquiry', *Annual Review of Anthropology* 42: 415–32.
Stoichiță, V.A. 2008. *Fabricants d'émotion. Musique et malice dans un village tsigane de Roumanie*. Nanterre: Société d'Ethnologie.
Weber, M. 1930. *The Protestant Ethic and the Spirit of Capitalism*, trans. T. Parsons. London: Allen and Unwin.

Martin Olivera is a lecturer in Social Anthropology at Université Paris 8, Centre National de la Recherche Scientifique UMR 7218, and a member of the steering committee of the Urba-Rom European Academic Network. After an extended fieldwork among Gabori Roma in Romania, his current work focuses on migrant Roma living in precarious settlements in France. He is editor of a special issue *Etudes tsiganes* (2010) and author of *Roms en (bidon)villes* (2011) and *La tradition de l'intégration: une ethnologie des Roms Gabori dans les années 2000* (2012).

Chapter 8

 Deceit and Efficacy
Fortune Telling among the Calon Gypsies in São Paulo, Brazil

FLORENCIA FERRARI

One of the ideas the Calon hold about the *Gajons* (non-Gypsies) is that the latter are fools and easy to 'take advantage of'. 'We have no study, but we are cleverer than the *Gajons*', as one Calon explained to me. 'On the street', the relation with the *Gajon*, with whom business is done or whose palm is read, is imagined as asymmetrical, and advantage can be taken of it. Palm reading, which is my focus here, is largely a female activity, and the main way Calins make money 'on the street'. This chapter, then, neither explores how palmistry relates to Calon sociality nor compares the present case with other examples of similar activities elsewhere. Rather, it concentrates on ethnographically showing the relation between a *Cigana* and a *Brasileiro* (a non-Gypsy Brazilian) in the street, paying attention to how meaning is constructed in this interaction, which is replete with tensions, expectations and suspicion.[1]

A Cigana Day

I arrive early one morning at the Calon camp on the outskirts of São Paulo which I have recently started to visit. I barely open the car door when I hear one Calin shout, 'Come in, come into my tent'. Other Calon gather around; they bring a chair and make me sit, as one calls out to another, 'Give her coffee'. They fill a cup from a thermos flask. The children arrive; other women approach and observe with reserve. One of them asks me if I am going to the city with them to read palms, and if I have brought along the Calin dress, covered in lace and ribbons, that they had sold me the day before. 'Come here, Florencia, I'll teach you how to read palms',

Vanessa calls to me from inside her tent. When I join her, she grasps my hand and begins to explain:

> You take the person's hand like this, you look her in the eye and look at the palm of the hand, and say thus: 'Bless you, there is a man who likes you ... is he blond or is he brown-haired?' Then, you wait for her to answer, and you continue as follows: 'You like him, but he is drifting away; a woman likes him'. Then you call me to bless her. If you take [money] off her, we share it fifty-fifty.

Next, an elderly Calin issues me with a warning: 'Don't say a word to the others. We are telling only you. Do you come reading palms with us?' Calins say that the places where they read palms, as they say, where they 'give luck' (*dinhá bahje* in Chibi), must be negotiated with the police, because if not one 'gets a 171'. In the Brazilian criminal code, Article 171 stipulates that a fraud means 'to obtain, for oneself or for another, illicit advantage, to another person's loss, inducing into or keeping somebody in error, by means of artifice, scheme, or any another fraudulent means'. Fortune telling is thus classed as fraud both by the Calin and the state.

The elderly Calin's plea for me 'not to tell the others' would normally raise an ethical problem, since a 'secret' is usually disclosed to a researcher thanks to a relation of complicity and intimacy created in the course of fieldwork, during which both sides build up trust, expecting loyalty and respect. But the context in which this 'secret' was disclosed to me was not a relation of this type. In fact, these women had 'confessed' to me the artifice of their palm reading a few days after meeting me. And, furthermore, even at a point in my fieldwork when they still used invented names – names used only in interactions with the *Gajons* – in my presence, that is, when they clearly treated me as an 'unknown' *Gajin* with whom one has no complicity and to whom information is not absolutely trusted. The fact that they presented themselves to me as 'deceivers' of the *Gajons* was far from telling me a secret; rather, it was more akin to a 'Gypsy performance'. This paradoxical situation led me to suspect that there was something beyond this 'deceit' in palm reading.

When analysing the practices of fortune telling among English Gypsies, Judith Okely (1996) arrived at a similar interpretation, namely, a suspicion of the current equation of fortune telling with 'deception'.[2] Seeking to problematise Western notions of rationality, she shows that 'magical and exotic beliefs', such as those in foretelling, are widespread in Western metropolises and suburbs. Okely argues convincingly that, although fortune telling is enunciated by Gypsies as a trick and considered fake, a sentiment echoed in countless newspaper articles, its effectiveness 'cannot be explained simply as skilful deception' (ibid.: 101). The practice enjoys credibility due to its effects. Drawing a parallel with the shaman and the psychoanalyst, Okely discloses the 'Gypsies'' special function and her 'esoteric/exotic' knowledge within a (our) society guided by values such as planning, predictability and control.

As I have shown elsewhere (Ferrari 2002: 216–18), the Gypsy is identified in the Western imaginary with the trickster, a figure of ambiguous and equivocal character, mediating between the worlds of the living and of the dead, between present existence and future knowledge. In this position, Gypsies, seen as exotic, marginal figures who simultaneously fascinate and frighten, adjust well to the role of fortune tellers, providing an alternative experience to the one lived in ordinary life, characterised by rational dimensions ordering *Gajon* society. According to Okely: 'dominant society bestow that [supernatural] power upon Gypsies because they associate them with the non-rational. The Gypsies then rationally explore *Gorgio* [non-Gypsies] non-rationality' (Okely 1996: 94). Okely's analysis frames the supernatural in terms of what the *Gorgios* view as irrational belief, engaging with Evans-Pritchard's (1937) well-known argument about the Azande: 'My analysis of fortune-telling reveals how "non-rational" beliefs on a par with those of the Azande are pervasive among a whole cross-section of individuals in Britain, despite their acquaintance with at least the elementary principles of Western science' (Okely 1996: 5). She perceptively questions the stereotype of Gypsy irrationality in palm reading, seeking to understand it as a relation with the *Gorgios*. By inverting the signs in the relationship with the rational, whereby Gypsy behaviour is posited as rational and that of *Gorgios* as irrational, however, she nevertheless revalidates the categorical opposition and thus remains inside its logics.

The context I am describing here led me in a different direction, not only because it is not England, but mainly because of a different agenda. This agenda is informed by the so-called 'ontological turn' in anthropology (see e.g. Paleček and Risjord 2013), and my aim is to explore Calon conceptions of the palm-reading encounter between Calin and *Gajon*. Here, the Western opposition between rational and irrational gives little account of the problems that emerged in my experience among the Calon. If the deceit is not deceit alone, it is appropriate to investigate it ethnographically. It will be necessary to describe what takes place in the relation between the '*Cigana*' and the *Gajon* to understand what the deceit effectively operates.

The Reading Frame

We finally leave for the city. The women crowd into my car: Tereza, her children Vanessa and Juliana, her daughter-in-law Leia, plus two other girls. We stop in a car park a block away from the central square in a town near São Paulo. We step out of the car dressed up as *'Ciganas'*, myself included. The sight of a group of *Ciganas* walking by causes a stir: people stare at us, talk and point at us. We arrive at the square. 'We stay here; *julinaro* [police] let us', says Juliana. *Garrons* in the stores, snack bars and game shops in the area already know my companions. Vanessa crouches; Tereza soon gives me orders: 'Call, call the *Garrins* for us'. As I observe the passers-by, the women begin their patter: 'Hey, hey, come read the palm'; 'Let me read your fortune'; 'No need to pay for talking'; 'Let me see your hand, come over here'; 'Give us a word'; 'One minute of your attention'. They make a typical gesture – the outstretched arm with the palm turned down while opening and closing – prompting the passers-by to halt. Beyond 'calling' *Garrons* with words and gestures, a more incisive approach – making use of the body – also finds its place. Most of the passers-by turn away, try to release the hand, saying 'Leave me!', 'No!', 'I do not believe in this', 'I am evangelical', 'Let me go!'. They retrieve their hand, pull an angry face, walk straight on without stopping by, curse the women. I look at Tereza and she says, 'A *Cigana*'s life is tough!' But many people do slow down or stop by when they hear 'Come here to have your fortune told'. The scene is repeated many times. There are waves of success: when there are two women reading palms, it is easier to persuade a third person. 'Here everybody can have their palm read – lady, gentleman, girl – just take a look', says Tereza as she points to the other people who are letting the Calins read their palms. When business is slow (*parado*, lit. 'still'), the Calins talk and gossip, using Chibi words. I closely followed several readings, and in what follows I reproduce an imaginary dialogue with typical expressions and intentionalities.

The *'Cigana'* takes the hand of the passer-by and points to the lines on the palm. As the passer-by looks at their own palm, the *'Cigana'* scrutinises the customer's face:

CALIN: I'll speak to you of a person who likes you. Is he blond- or brown-haired?
GAJIN: You are the one to tell me.
CALIN: He likes you, but he is drifting away. A dark lady is doing you harm.
GAJIN: Dark hair?
CALIN: Yes, a lady with dark hair wishes you ill. If I tell you her name, do you give the Cigana a token?
GAJIN: I will.

CALIN: Place it here in my hand. [*The person places R$1–2.*]³ The name of the lady is Rose. Do you know a person called Rose? [*The Gajin's expression turns thoughtful, assenting head, an air of concern.*] So, she is the woman who is doing you harm. If the Cigana goes to the crossroads and casts a spell for you to keep the man you like, would you give money for the candles and flowers?

GAJIN: I don't have any more money.

CALIN: You have money there for another commitment, to pay bills.

GAJIN: But this I cannot spend.

CALIN: Nothing works out for you. Every man who you like, it never works out. This woman cast a spell (*Macumba*) on you. When you need something, you don't give [money to Ciganas]? You have to give the Cigana money to undo the evil. Give me the money.

[*The woman opens her purse, retrieves her wallet and gives the Calin some money.*]

CALIN: God bless you, you'll see, we'll go there on Friday to cast a spell for you. Come here, she will bless you.

[*She calls another Calin.*]

CALIN: If you give 50 reais more, I bless you, so you go with God and no further evil will happen to you.

[*In some cases this is successful. The Calin then makes a prayer.*]

There is a relationship between the time spent in a palm reading and the amount of money obtained. If a reading is sustained for up to thirty minutes, the attempt is successful. The themes that emerge keep repeating – troubles with love, money and health – and form the field of 'misfortune' explored by '*Ciganas*'. The reading expands in stages. The Calin starts asking for 'a little money for the *Cigana* to speak of someone you like'. Most people who allow the reading do not go past this first phase. When the Calin realises that the interlocutor is not yielding any more money, she says 'God bless you' and lets them go. Such readings last a few minutes and yields R$2.

There are occasions when the person finds themselves taken by the Gypsy word. The vocabulary used by the Calin harks to a 'supernatural' universe in continuity with Brazilian religious syncretism, which includes references to Umbanda, such as *Macumba* (a pejorative slang term for black or luck-related magic), *Caboclo* (one of the spirit entities of Umbanda), 'to tie up', and at the same time to popular Catholicism, like doing the sign of the cross, blessings, pleading with God for a blessing and praying to Our Lady (*Nossa Senhora*). This syncretism takes place not only as 'Gypsy-like performance' in the street. Rather, the Calon's daily life is impregnated by elements of popular Catholicism. The image of Our Lady was present in all of the tents that I saw. Many families travelled to Aparecida – a popular pilgrimage site. Beyond the popular Catholic register, the Calon will equally seek blessings from Afro-Brazilian cult ministers (*pais e mães de santo*). The Calins are therefore acquainted with, and share, the elements of the *Gajons*' religions.

The Calin's first step in fortune telling is to tune into the afflictions of the *Gajon*. The situation demands that she employ a great perceptive capacity to read the customer's face and bodily expressions. It is from this that she will be able to create a picture of financial dire straits or perhaps a negative love scenario in the customer's life, solutions to which will demand prayers and candles, and ultimately an additional payment. At this moment, the fortune teller calls another Calin to bless the customer and requests that the customer place the money 'in the *Cigana*'s hands'. 'It is not for me', she explains. 'I will only bless it, and you take the blessed money away'. Once the money is in her hand, the Calin builds a fresh negative situation, saying, 'If you don't leave the money with the *Cigana*, no good will come to your life'. The person thus sees themselves as responsible for their own fate: either the money is given and one rests assured that the future will be as the *Cigana* vows, or it is not and one has to accept living with the '*Cigana*'s curse'. This interactive picture is laden with an affective load that circulates between the Calin and the *Gajon* and vice-versa. The initial 'catch' will only be efficient if the Calin is able to affect the other emotionally. She employs her body, her voice and her gaze in order to create the necessary connection that will frame the reading.

Bateson's concepts of 'frame' and 'metacommunication' (Bateson 1972: 177–93) throw light on this interaction. Bateson defines metacommunication as a level of abstraction in verbal communication where the conversation's subject is the relation between the two speakers. In the case of fortune telling, the 'frame' – a set of messages exchanged between two individuals over a certain period of time, establishing a border with what is outside – is metacommunicative, as the message that defines the frame implicitly or explicitly instructs or contributes to the understanding of the messages enclosed within. The Calin begins by seeking to affect the *Gajon*. The notion of deceit haunts the beginning of the relationship. The *Gajon* questions the knowledge of the '*Cigana*'. Contrary to expectations, the reading is not a monologue but a dialogue or, to continue with Bateson, a metalogue, which is built from the substance supplied by the *Gajon* and instigated by the '*Cigana*'. The '*Cigana*' retrieves the *Gajon* from the midst of passers-by and creates a secluded space, a 'frame', and soon develops a dialogue of affection and images. The notion of deceit is outside the frame (in the analogous manner that a 'lie' or 'nonsense' is outside the 'frame' of dreams). When she says that 'somebody is doing you harm' and names the person, or that money evades the individual because somebody has cast a spell, the *'Cigana'* sets in motion a series of emotions that envelop the *Gajon* into the parallel reality created by the reading's frame. From then on, the idea of deceit loses its meaning, because the 'future truth', something 'to be foretold', starts to depend on the action of the customer themselves.

Similar to the situation described by Holbraad (2004, 2012) in the context of Cuban Ifá divination, in order to understand the 'truth of the *Cigana*', it is necessary to imagine an alternative concept of truth: our terms must be shaped in such a way that they behave according to the use of native concepts. The 'truth' of the Ifá is not defined by an extant correspondence with something already in existence, but instead is understood as a 'modifier', both of the subject and of reality. Likewise, the *Cigana*'s speech must not be evaluated within a regime of truth where 'truth' and 'lie' (or 'deceit') are verifiable verdicts, in a relationship that opposes speech and something 'real', pre-existing; instead, it must be taken as a generator of relations in the present. The *Cigana* commands an extensive repertoire in order to lead this metalogue – she has ways of avoiding situations leading to exposure, wielding 'joker' formulations of open interpretation. The reading is directed so that it is now about the relation between the *'Cigana'* and the *Gajon*, and fortune is defined within this interactive picture as a product of the relation between the interlocutors. The *'Cigana*'s speech does not anticipate a future that is 'there', on the palm of the hand; instead, the reading acts in the present, urging the customer to act in it too. The divination of the future gives way to the production of the future, and this depends on actions in the present, involving the *Gajon*'s money and the consequent action by the *'Cigana'*.

There is no way to leave the 'frame': any movement will suffer the implications defined by the instructions given in the messages that circulate within it. If the *Gajon* tries 'to escape' the frame, leaving the 'reading', the *'Cigana'* informs them that the consequences of such an action are defined by the frame, that is, that 'all evil that may befall you' will be linked to the relation established inside the frame. The truth of fortune telling is the truth built inside this picture by means of the exchange of knowledge and affection.

Fortune and Future

The gap between two conceptions of time becomes evident in fortune telling. On the one hand that of the *Gajon*, who wishes to anticipate, to plan and to control what we call the 'future'; and on the other, that of the Calon, who shifts the focus of the action into what we call the 'present'. In fact, several aspects of the Calon ethnography point to an 'emphasis on the present', a feature shared with Gypsies in other parts of the world. Michael Stewart describes Hungarian Vlach Rom as people who show 'little thought for the future and little interest in the past' (Day, Papataxiarchis and Stewart 1999: 2), associating this orientation with a mode of social organisation based on freedom and autonomy, in opposition to the institutionalised and hierarchical character of society at large. 'To live for the present' might be seen as an active response by these people against the mainstream, which victimises them. More than a 'reply' or a 'response', I understand this orientation towards the present in 'Calon thought' as part of social intentionality, unveiled in daily practices.

The Calon do not speak of their ancestors, they do not tell myths, they do not exercise their individual memory making it part of a collective memory. If one asks an elderly Calon how their grandparents lived, they will likely reply, 'I do not remember; people do not keep this', that is, they do not maintain this knowledge. What was lived by previous generations does not constitute a definite repertoire, such as 'history' or 'memory', to be passed on to younger generations (even though one could trace the origin of countless habits that have endured throughout the centuries). Thus, each person lives inside the temporal framing of the duration of one's own life. The Calon 'past' is a time relative to the subject who speaks, but never prior to the time of one's own life as a transcendental duration. This dealing with what has already 'passed' figures more sharply in Calon eschatology, which operates to eradicate the deceased from the world of the living (cf. Williams 1993). Calon grieving demands various practices: belongings must be burnt; photographs must not be kept; the deceased's name must not be pronounced, lest the spirit should return to haunt the living; colourful skirts and tent decoration must be replaced by old or pale-coloured clothes, and nothing 'happy' should be displayed; Brazilian country music (*sertaneja*), which is routinely played in Calon' daily life, must be silenced. The place where the deceased lived must be abandoned: nobody 'can bear' the memories that it yields. Calon undertake laborious work (*trabalho*) – as they call grieving – in the form of the deletion of traces, a kind of machine for the suppression of the past.

The negation of a transcendental past on behalf of an immanent present is expressed in Calon eschatology and in diverse dimensions of social life. Calon are known by the nicknames they are given in the course of their lives, and they reserve their first and family names to the scope of relations with the *Gajon*. Chibi is conceived not as a mother tongue 'given' by the parents but as knowledge to be acquired in the interaction with other Calon in the course of one's life. The ideas around food consumption play a similar role. The Calon eat only what has been cooked that day. Leftover food is either thrown away or given to their animals. They do not cultivate the land because, I was told, 'there is no point in planting and then leaving it behind'. The image of working in the present to enjoy future incomes is seen with disdain by the Calon. This logic is valid only for lending money at interest, precisely when the Calon do not work and earn an income at the expense of the *Gajons*.

Many of the Calon men whom I met loaned money to *Brasileiros* (non-Gypsy Brazilians). My research, which was carried almost exclusively among women, lacks detail concerning such operations. However, Fotta's (2012) ethnography of the Calon of Bahian Recôncavo, which is entirely dedicated to exploring the Calon economy and especially its financial logic, renders explicit a native conception of future (*futuro*) that corroborates my suggestions. He follows Calon credit networks and flows involving Calon men and the *Gajons*. The possibility of 'making future' (*fazer futuro*) is central to the decision of where a family settles and does businesses; to 'make future' means to take advantage of opportunities. Fotta calls attention to the fact that the word *futuro* is taken from Brazilian Portuguese speech, but that it gains a specific meaning among the Calon, and one not shared by *Brasileiros*. 'There is no future here' is how a family defines a place where it is no longer possible to live. A dowry is given to a fiancé so that he can 'make future'. Especially in the masculine context 'on the street', the idea of 'making future' relates to Calon ideas of proper morality and behaviour: the Calon often criticise each other for being 'without future', as they refer to a person who is deemed lazy, addicted to gambling or of a passive nature, that is, unable to act as a man. The success of a man's action depends on how he relates to others in the present. Events and decisions are thought about in the present and subject to the unexpected, a *modus operandi* that is opposed to a deliberate construction of the world in view of a medium-term temporality.

'Making future' therefore implies taking advantage of opportunities in the present. A person 'without future' is someone who is not willing to do what is expected in the present. The time that is beyond the present is not subject to capture. Any attempt to make an appointment or to arrange an activity with a Calon is a difficult task for a *Gajon* who relies on a diary and a watch. The dates and times of medical appointments, bill payments or even baptisms are very often missed due to the scant attention that the Calon devote to the calendar and to the very idea of 'commitment'. Therefore, there is no conception of anticipation and planning for the future. Calon daily life is characterised by improvisation, that is, the innovative creation of a present from the chances offered at each moment.

This notion of 'future' linked to an action geared towards the present helps us to unravel aspects of the misunderstanding (*pace* Wagner 1981) around the idea of 'fortune' or 'future luck'. The task of understanding the notion of 'luck' remains unfulfilled. Michael Stewart calls attention to the shift in the meaning of 'luck' (*baxt* in Romani) in the context of the horse trade among the Vlach Rom of Hungary. The latter's concept of luck, he argues, is different from 'ours'; *baxt* encompasses luck, efficacy, prosperity and happiness, and is 'one of the constitutive qualities of the Gypsies … [I]t was the very nature of the Gypsies to be lucky' (Stewart 1997: 165). In contrast to our conception, *baxt* does not differentiate a person from another, and only partially covers the notion of chance. Stewart observes that '[w]e associate luck with coincidence … but for the Rom luck was the consequence of righteous behaviour' (ibid.: 165). A 'correct' attitude, then, is associated with ideals of 'purity', and '[t]he Rom became lucky only by maintaining proper relations with their wives and thereby keeping themselves pure' (ibid.: 166).

The reading of people's fortune is less a vision of a future world made up of coincidences subject to anticipation by Gypsy foretelling capabilities, and more a world built by one's actions. From the *Cigana* point of view, 'luck' and the 'future' depend on the action of the customer in the present. This explains why the Calins attribute the lack of potential luck to the customer's current tightfistedness. The inscription of fortune telling in Calon 'cosmology' clarifies some fundamental aspects implied in the position of the Calin, but it does not encompass all that takes place in the palm-reading interaction. Likewise, one cannot reduce the analysis of the reading to the *Gajon*'s need to deal with their 'non-rational' issues. Fortune telling includes these two sides and, moreover, encompasses the relation between them.

Equivocation and Effectiveness

The intersubjective picture of 'divination' involves a relation in which a series of perceptions, expectations and affections are exchanged. A Calin sees a non-Calon as a *Gajon*, a Brazilian – 'foolish', 'dirty', 'shameless' and 'solitary'. A non-Calon sees the Calin as a 'Cigana', an ambiguous character who is alluring and yet causes fear.

The Calin imagines that the non-Calon has an image of her and thus refers to herself as *Cigana*, as if subscribing to the stereotypes allocated to her in order to manipulate this fact in her favour. In the street, the Calon play up to the *Cigana* image that they assume the Brazilians have of them. And, it must be noted, they are careful not to carry out this *Cigano* performance with known *Gajons* such as myself. If by chance we met a group of Calins unknown to me who were reading palms, it was enough for my Calin friend to say I was *conhecida* (known) for them to give up trying to read my palm.

The concepts of the *Cigana* and the Brazilians do not go hand in hand, as they are informed by each side's 'cosmologies' about the 'other'. Roy Wagner formulates cross-cultural meeting as a mutual misunderstanding, informed by the premises and conceptions of each side. Wagner pays particular attention to the encounter between the anthropologist and the native individual: 'Their misunderstanding of me was not the same as my misunderstanding of them' (Wagner 1981: 20). His analysis renders explicit that all cultures have non-negotiable assumptions (such as the notion of 'Nature' for 'us, Westerners') through which it gives meaning to the world. The anthropology that seeks to understand the meanings that other peoples give to the world must be aware that it is mediated by assumptions of their cultures. All description of another culture, observes Wagner, is necessarily filtered by our own terms, and therefore must be considered relative, as its content is the result of a relation and never an objective apprehension of what 'it is out there' ('society', 'social group', 'culture').

Eduardo Viveiros de Castro (2004) develops this idea of the meeting as equivocation in his discussion of Amerindian perspectivism. He defines perspectivist anthropology as a method of 'controlled equivocation', that is, of anthropological translation able to give an account of the misunderstanding intrinsic to perspectivism, typically an inter-specific (between humans and non-humans) meeting where the definition of the terms is relational and situational: 'Blood is for humans the same as cassava beer is for the jaguars, exactly in the same sense that a sister for me is a woman for my brother-in-law' (ibid.: 9). Viveiros de Castro warns that an equivocation is not an error, a mistake or a deception:

> Deceptions and errors suppose premises that are already constituted – and constituted as homogeneous – while an equivocation not only supposes the

heterogeneity of the premises at stake, it poses them as heterogenic and presupposes them as premises. An equivocation determines the premises rather than being determined by them ... The equivocation itself is what determines the premises more than it is determined by them ... The equivocation is not that which impedes the relation, but that which founds and impels it: a difference in perspective. (ibid.: 8–10)

Viveiros de Castro's proposal considers a difference between the equivocation characteristic of every cultural encounter and the specific equivocation of the meeting between anthropological knowledge and native knowledge, which ideally must be 'controlled' in order that the result of the anthropologist's work does not refer to their own worldview only. Like Wagner, Viveiros de Castro sees becoming aware of the assumptions of one's own culture as a precondition for describing the life of people in other cultures.

But is 'controlled equivocation' exclusive to the domain of anthropological knowledge production, or is it possible to recognise it in other modalities? It seems to me that in the Calon case we are facing a situation of this type, since we have observed a dimension of 'control' in the equivocation particular to the meeting between *'Ciganos'* and Brazilians. Let us examine which perspectives are at play and what the equivocation is about.

The speech of the *'Ciganas'* and of their interlocutor complete one another, building a continuous discursive field. The *Cigana* takes up the role of the one who tells the fortune, and the *Gajon* legitimises it; it is the intersubjective relation that establishes such positions. One is built by the other. The centrality of the *Gajon* interlocutor to the 'reading' of their own fate is such that in the end one no longer knows what was 'divined' by the *'Cigana'* and what was said by the *Gajons* themselves. However, we know that the Calin leads the process; she 'controls' the frame. The *Cigana* is skilful in the manipulation of what her intuition says is valuable for the other. In this sense, she explores and takes advantage of the 'equivocation', rendering the relation asymmetrical. Such asymmetry is not exclusive to the palm-reading situation; rather, it is strategically explored by the Calon in distinct situations with the *Gajons*. It takes place whenever a word at once carries a shared Brazilian Portuguese meaning and a non-shared Calon meaning – as it does with the notions of 'luck' and 'future'.

Another significant example is the misunderstanding caused by the ambiguous use of the word *vergonha* (shame). During my fieldwork, an elderly Calin was once explaining to a Brazilian woman that her family could not throw a previously arranged party because her brother had died and the family was 'ashamed' to do it. Not comprehending the logic of the use of the word 'shame' in this context, the *Gajin* said, 'Shame is to steal and kill, there is no need to feel shame'. The old woman, already knowledgeable about the layers of meaning that this word involves and the equivocation it produces, replied, 'We feel *vergonha* throwing a party but not being able to offer food and music'. The solution found by the old lady satisfied the *Gajin* while remaining loyal to the Calon meaning underlining the prescription of a specific behaviour towards the deceased and what is expected from the hosts of a reception (that is, abundance and festivity). For the Calon, *vergonha* is more than a powerful emotion. When they speak of *vergonha Cigana* or 'our shame' (*vergonha nossa*), they deploy a linguistic use followed by a possessive pronoun whose sense is not found in Portuguese language dictionaries and that seems to be exclusive and specific to Calon. *Vergonha* is the word that they offer as a translation for the Chibi term *laje*, which is also associated with the notion of *marimé* (dirty, unclean) in ethnographies of the Roma in Europe. Among the Calon, *vergonha* is conceived as a 'good' that one can 'have' or not and whose ownership generates value. But this good must not be confused with 'property', or substance. The 'production' of *vergonha* depends on actions in the present. This notion of *vergonha* motivates a series of practices that are linked to the construction of Calon personhood and differentiates them from the *Gajons*, who remain ignorant of such Calon meanings.

Returning to the reading, equivocation control consists in deploying the image in which the person's tightfistedness and fate become connected (when, for instance, the Calin says 'If you find yourself in need and you give nothing [to the *Cigana*], nothing will go right for you'). Captured within the frame, the customer will thus be responsible for their own fate, and this depends on them being generous, that is, giving money for the prayer of the '*Cigana*'. The imaginary of the '*Cigana*'s curse' takes advantage of this empty meaning: each person will fill in the malediction with one's own problems and ghosts, conferring power on the speech of the '*Cigana*'.

If fortune telling among these Calins is not based on an esoteric knowledge regarding the lines of the hand, it certainly does depend on an art of performance that implies listening and perceiving, and which takes time for one to master. The repertoire of solutions for each situation is accumulated over time. Tereza, the old woman, is the most successful reader and therefore earns more money – perhaps for cutting a more sombre and disturbing figure than the others, and consequently being feared the most.

On another occasion, I went to a police station with a young Calon and his cousin, Cilene, to help solve a problem regarding an impounded car. At a certain point, a police officer called Cilene over and asked if she could read his palm. She agreed and entered his office. A little later, she came out and said: 'He actually enjoyed it. He wants a woman. He is single; he wants children. I told him there was a surprise in store for him'. 'Surprise' is another example of a term empty of meaning, open to whatever the *Gajon* attributes it. In terms of 'social function', the '*Cigana*' could well be placed between a priest and a psychoanalyst.

Effects and Sorcery

But this is not all, and we will see why Okely's analysis is limited with regard to understanding Calon ethnography. After another day in the streets, Tereza shows the other Calins a photo of a man and a middle-aged woman and states: 'Poor woman, she cried so much. She asked me to get the man back to her, and said that if the "Gypsy woman's" prayer works out, she would return to give me more money. I'll take it to the centre'. Tereza, out of mercy or out of a sense of chance, covets the success of her customer. Then, exceptionally, she seeks to 'outsource' the magic by taking the plea to an Afro-Brazilian (Umbanda) religious centre she attends. Now, if the *Cigana* confesses her lack of 'supernatural' powers in palm reading, she simultaneously reaffirms the existence of such powers elsewhere, in this case, in the hands of Umbanda ministers, with the Calin taking up the role of mediator between the street and the sacred house. But there is more. There is actually a widespread practice of 'sorcery' among the Calon. In Itapecerica, the women light candles 'in the bush'. Tereza attributed her weakness to witchcraft presumably used against her by her sister-in-law. In another camp the rumour went around that one Calin separated from her husband because of a spell: a young woman's skirt full of knots was found in the rubbish.

If palm reading is not itself understood as bearing any 'supernatural' powers, these are certainly part of Calon sociality in the form of spells, and can therefore be transposed to the relation between Calon and *Gajons*. Significantly, the Calon do not read each other's palms, which confirms the meaning of deceit in palm reading, but they do cast spells on each other, and no one doubts their efficacy. If we return to the idea that fortune telling is constituted within a metacommunicative frame, we recall that the '*Cigana*' presents herself initially as someone who reads the future, involving and isolating the client within the frame, while actually speaking of the present, quickly taking up the place of someone who is able to affect and transform the future (such as with a 'curse' or the promise of a spell). This manoeuvre effects a transition from the initial equivocation to the next phase, in which the power to cast a spell, attributed by the Calin, becomes important. At this moment, the expectations of the '*Cigana*' and of the client meet. In a cul-de-sac for the Gajon, both understand the effects of the threat posed by the '*Cigana*'s curse', and the initial deceit seems to give way to a hinge where the meanings of one and the other partially coincide.

Of course, such dissolution of deceit requires the client themselves to participate in the efficacy of the '*Cigana*'s' sorcery. The kind of relation that is built in the 'street' is better understood if we consider an imaginary shared by Calon and *Gajons*, linked to the religious syncretism democratically disseminated among all echelons of Brazilian society, which includes so-called Gypsy spirits (Thiele 2006; Vos 2007). Calon have assimilated the Brazilian religious universe, which articulates popular Catholicism along Afro-Brazilian matrices, at the same time as they use it to render it different – to render it *Cigano*. The Calins attend Afro-Brazilian rituals and seek blessings, yet they also have their children blessed and get married in Catholic churches. In the reading of palms, they mix prayers to Afro-Brazilian deities and healers with blessings, holy cards and the sign of the cross. This shared 'mixed' imaginary is what bestows meaning on prayers and sorcery both for the '*Cigana*' and for the *Gajon*, rendering the reading effective.

Deceit and Contradictions

The dissolution of a dimension of the equivocation within the frame of fortune telling poses a further question. If indeed the Calins can 'do sorcery' or make a 'plea' to the Afro-Brazilian minister, that is, if indeed they find ways of manipulating 'powers' in order to change people's fate, why do they deliberately speak of fortune telling as deceit, as they did to me on the occasion described at the beginning of this chapter?

This is something I wish to keep open, but it I would venture to suggest that talk of 'deception' is a Calon mode of speaking about differentiation.[4] The shared universe between the Calon and the *Gajons* is peopled by affections (sorcery), miracles and entities wielding powers; nevertheless, the *Cigana* produces herself as different, creating an asymmetry in the face of the *Gajon*. From the point of view of the Calin, the asymmetry is produced not so much by means of the sorcery (to which both Gypsies and *Gajons* are subject), but instead by means of deceit, for she makes a point of showing that she does not read anything at all from the palm of the hand. This deceit could be thought of as a differentiation metaphor that produces 'Calonness'. But here is the 'controlled equivocation': this deceit ends up producing effects over those *Gajon* who believe in the reading, sometimes transforming 'foretelling the future' into agency, thus liberating the *Gajon* to act according to the fortune told.

The descriptions above leave us facing a set of contradictions. On the one hand, the whole affair takes place as if the *Gajons* were aware that the Gypsy women deceive (after all, the criminal code defines palmistry as fraud), yet they nonetheless take up the risk and let themselves be captured within the 'frame' of fortune telling. On the other hand, the Calins openly treat palm reading as 'fraud' at the same time as they consider 'luck' a consequence of the appropriate action by each individual in the present, and they manipulate 'supernatural' powers and seek to attain efficacy by means of sorcery, candles and prayer requests to Afro-Brazilian religious ministers. It is clear that the simplification that reduces this interaction to 'deceit' is insufficient for understanding the phenomenon. Instead of offering a reductive solution, I would rather multiply the description of what is taking place. The *'Cigana'*, with her visual, gestural and linguistic repertoire, produces an exchange of affections with the *Gajon*. Her efficacy can only be measured as performance by means of its capacity to engage the *Gajon* in a relationship that produces effects.

Translated from the Portuguese by Gavin Adams.

NOTES

1. A note on terms is in order here. Calin and *Gajin* are the feminine forms of Calon and *Gajon*. Calon use a variety of terms to refer to *Gajons*, including *Garrons* and *Rarlons*. I will use these according to how they appear in context. Meanwhile, the Portuguese term Cigana means both 'Gypsy woman' (noun) and 'Gypsy' (feminine adjective); the final 's' marks the plural. I employ the word Cigano/Cigana in two ways: *Cigana* (italics) is an ethnographic category used by the Calon; 'Cigana' (in quotation marks) is a category used by the Gajons and the state, a term loaded with stereotypes regarding Gypsies (Ferrari 2002, 2006). I deliberately employ *'Cigana'* (italics and quotation marks) to indicate moments when there is an overlapping of the *Gajon*'s perception of the 'Cigana' and the Calins' self-denomination *Cigana* built into the palm-reading interaction. Finally, Calon refer to their lexical repertoire as Chibi, from the word *chib*, meaning "language" in Romani.

2. For alternative interpretations of fortune telling, see Leland (1892) and Andersen (1987).
3. The Brazilian currency is the reais (R$). At the time of my filedwork, €1 was worth about R$2.60.
4. In this sense, palmistry could be related to the Sinti ideas of *manghel* (to beg), described by Elisabeth Tauber. She notes that '[a] woman confirms her Sinta-ness through *manghel*, her ability to control the Gage [non-Gyspsies], and her capacity to be different to the Gage' (Tauber 2008: 166), and that '[t]o *manghel* is to demonstrate, among other practices of Sinti life, the concept of being Sinti in relation to or in the presence of the Gage' (ibid.: 173).

REFERENCES

Andersen, R. 1987. 'A Subtle Craft in Several Worlds: Performance and Participation in Romani Fortune-telling', Ph.D. diss. Philadelphia: University of Pennsylvania.
Bateson, G. 1972. *Steps to an Ecology of Mind*. New York: Ballantine Books.
Day, S., E. Papataxiarchis and M. Stewart. 1999. 'Consider the Lilies of the Field', in S. Day, E. Papataxiarchis and M. Stewart (eds), *Lilies of the Field: Marginal People who Live for the Moment*. Boulder, CO: Westview Press, pp.1–24.
Evans-Pritchard, E.E. 1937. *Witchcraft, Oracles, and Magic among the Azande*. Oxford: Clarendon Press.
Ferrari, F. 2002. 'Um olhar oblíquo. Contribuições para o imaginário ocidental sobre o Cigano', Master's diss. São Paulo: Universidade de São Paulo.
———. 2006. 'Ciganos nacionais', *Acta literaria* 32: 79–96.
Fotta, M. 2012. 'The Bankers of the Backlands: Financialisation and the Calon-Gypsies in Bahia', Ph.D. diss. London: Goldsmiths College, University of London.
Holbraad, M. 2004. Defining Anthropological Truth. Paper delivered at the 'Truth Conference', Cambridge, 24 September 2004. Retrieved 1 May 2013 from: http://nansi.abaetenet.net/abaetextos/defining-anthropological-truth.
———. 2012. 'Truth Beyond Doubt: Ifá Oracles in Havana', *HAU: Journal of Ethnographic Theory* 2(1): 81–109.
Leland, C. 1892. *Gypsy Sorcery and Fortune Telling*. London: Fisher Unwin.
Okely, J. 1996. *Own or Other Culture*. London: Routledge.
Paleček, M., and M. Risjord. 2013. 'Relativism and the Ontological Turn within Anthropology', *Philosophy of the Social Sciences* 43(1): 3–23.
Stewart, M. 1997. *The Time of the Gypsies*. Boulder, CO: Westview Press.
Tauber, E. 2008. '"Do You Remember the Time When We Went Begging and Selling?" The Ethnography of Transformation in Female Economic Activities and Its Narrative in the Context of Memory and Respect among the Sinti in North Italy', in J. Fabian and J. Ries (eds), *Romani/Gypsy Cultures in New Perspectives*. Leipzig: Leipzieger Universitätverslag, pp.155–76.
Thiele, M.E. 2006. *Trickster, Transvestiten und Ciganas: Pombagira und die Erotik in den afrobrasilianischen Religionen*. Leipzig: Leipziger Universitaetsverlag.

Viveiros de Castro, E. 2004. 'Perspectival Anthropology and the Method of Controlled Equivocation', *Tipití: Journal of the Society for the Anthropology of Lowland South America* 2(1): 3–22.

Vos, D. 2007. 'Ori o povo cigano! De Opkomst van de Zigeunergeesten in Umbanda', Master's diss. Leiden: Universiteit Leiden.

Wagner, R. 1981. *The Invention of Culture*. Chicago: University of Chicago Press.

Williams, P. 1993. *Nous, on n'en parle pas. Les vivants et les morts chez les Manouches.* Paris: Maison des Sciences de l'Homme.

Florencia Ferrari holds a doctorate in social anthropology from the Department of Social Anthropology, University of São Paulo. Her research among Calon Gypsies has resulted in several articles in academic journals, and in the book *Palavra Cigana: Seis contos nômades* (2005). Since 2002, she has been the editor of the anthropology series at the Brazilian publishing house Cosac Naify, publishing the works of Claude Lévi-Strauss, Pierre Clastres, Roy Wagner and Eduardo Viveiros de Castro. Since 2012, she has been an editorial director at Cosac Naify.

Chapter 9

Houses under Construction
Conspicuous Consumption and the Values of Youth among Romanian Cortorari Gypsies

CĂTĂLINA TESĂR

Over the last ten years, I have had the chance to watch the shifts in both the architecture and the interior decorations and furnishings of a particular house. In 2003, Luca owned the highest and most spectacular brick house in the Cortorari neighbourhood. It had the advantage of being located at the top of the steep track that leads up to the Gypsy settlement. Anyone taking that track would marvel at the unusually glittery metal turrets and large ionic columns of the front porches of Luca's house. Luca and his large family (his wife, his unmarried daughter, Luca's married son and his family) lived in an adobe hut adjacent to this imposing mansion. I can only imagine the kind of life they had, sharing a few square metres for all their eating and sleeping needs. Luca has never invited me inside his shabby hut. However, he seized every opportunity to give me a guided tour of the mansion, which had been under construction for a while. He would show me every room while reiterating names of the various construction materials used, the quantities used and their costs. The pleasure he took in recounting the sums of money he had spent on the building and the sincere admiration he showed for the materiality of the concrete that made the mansion grow left me speechless every time. Luca was presenting himself as 'the biggest *rom* [Cortorari man]', and his self-appreciation appeared to me incongruous when seen against the conditions under which he lived his day-to-day life.

To my surprise, at a time when the mansion seemed to be close to completion, I saw Luca having it knocked down. His neighbours' conjecture was that other houses in the neighbourhood had already surpassed Luca's in height, its turrets no longer visible to someone climbing the track up to the settlement. However, Luca explained to me that he wanted to change the design and construction materials in accordance with the new trends he had seen during his travels. In 2008, Luca had his house rebuilt, this time taller and larger. Cortorari houses follow the train-car style seen throughout the region, with a front room facing the street and the rest of the built space stretching out behind it. Luca's mansion now filled not only the whole plot attached to the hut – initially allotted to a stable and a vegetable garden – but also part of the ditch that stretched between the row of houses and the road that crosses the neighbourhood. In the economy of the village, the ditch is assigned a precise infrastructural role: it collects rainwater, thus preventing the flooding of houses. When Luca's son, Emil, bought the first and, to my knowledge, still the only Mitsubishi car in the settlement (a much sought-after make of car), he realised that there was no space available to park it either in their courtyard or in front of their house. The mansion took up all the space. Therefore, Emil had to ask a neighbour for permission to park the car in his courtyard.

Because of diabetes, Luca had one leg amputated. From his wheelchair parked in the shade of his manor-like house, he would shout orders at the painters decorating the interior of the house or to the workers unloading construction materials in front of it. Ongoing building work requires money, and I was interested to learn about the deals that kept the money flowing into Luca's pockets. He boasted about having managed to get welfare payments from the Italian state on account of his health problems and about his success in begging abroad, which he attributed to his physical disability. However, his neighbours explained that Luca's son, Emil, had taken over the business of making money and, together with it, the stewardship of the building work. In 2010, Emil embarked on the enterprise of building a clone of his father's mansion – a 'twin house', in his words.

His whim to build a replica of his father's house makes Emil an exceptional character among Cortorari. Normally, the extended family is accommodated in s single house. Yet the fanciful 'twin-house' design is not unheard of in Romania. Journals, web sites, tourist blogs and architectural design web pages, as well as anonymous YouTube posts abound with photos and videos of twin mansions owned by rich Romanian Gypsies. Emil and other Cortorari surf the web in search of the latest trends in housing styles. Wherever they go in Romania or abroad, they keep their eyes peeled for novel structures, colours and styles of house decoration. They all want to emulate the most magnificent buildings they encounter. Although, to my knowledge, Emil's project of building a 'twin house' is still unique in the Cortorari settlement, the ongoing nature of building work, which I described for Luca's house, is a general state of affairs here. I have been visiting the Cortorari neighbourhood for a dozen years now, and during this time it has expanded both in width and in length. New houses for young couples are still being built, crammed into the narrow space between two existing houses. People have even started building their houses on land located on the outskirts of the settlement, which only a few years ago looked like barren fields. Buildings have mushroomed, taking over all of the empty plots that in the past served as borders between the Cortorari neighbourhood and the nearest village. In fact, the new Cortorari houses are built beyond the official boundary of the village. Nobody has bothered to move the village's name plate to reflect the neighbourhood's expansion. Prosperity might be the word that best describes Cortorari acts of extravagant consumption, which are visible both in men's prominent bellies and in ongoing projects of house construction.

I have never ceased to be struck by the contradiction between ubiquitous affluence and the incompleteness of houses, a contradiction that forms the core concern of this chapter. In the early 2000s, I concluded that the unfinished character of these houses was due to their owners' (limited) economic means at a time when Romania's transition to a market economy was breeding uncertainty. Yet the principle, according to which the completion of a house depends solely upon possession and wise management of financial resources, cannot account for Luca's action of tearing down what appeared to me to be an almost finished mansion. To add to my consternation, the wealthier that Cortorari became, the more prevalent was the incompleteness of their houses.

The building of imposing brick houses is closely linked to the new economic possibilities brought about by transnational mobility, a daring journey that Cortorari have been undertaking for almost two decades now. The intersecting paths of transnational migration and building houses in migrants' homelands are acknowledged worldwide. Few ethnographies, however, have emphasised the 'perpetually ongoing projects' (Dalakoglou 2010: 763) of migrant house construction. Houses in Albania stand as proxies for absent migrants in processes of creating transnational relatedness (ibid.: 761–66). In Peru, the open and changing nature of houses is interpreted as a reflection of 'their owners' constant and pressing desire for betterment' (Leinaweaver 2009: 785) coupled with 'the local political economy of insecurity' (Lobo 1982: 39, cited in Leinaweaver 2009: 785). In both of these cases, houses are active agents in the production of relatedness (Carsten and Hugh-Jones 1995) in contexts in which people involved in labour migration are largely absent from their homelands. In contradistinction to Peruvian and Albanian migrants, who sponsor building work by sending remittances back home, Cortorari do not settle in the countries to which they migrate. Rather, they incessantly and irregularly go back and forth, making money and investing it in houses permanently under construction. How are we then to understand the interrelatedness of people and houses, and what are the ways in which ongoing building work is linked to the production and reproduction of social relationships among Cortorari?

This chapter discusses the meanings and representations of consumption behaviour among Cortorari in postsocialist Romania in light of local conceptions of reproduction and relatedness. Transformations of the state after the collapse of communism, especially the liberalisation of borders brought about by the process of joining the European Union, forged new economic practices among Cortorari, who turned to Western Europe as an El Dorado of available resources. This was the case with other Gypsies from Central and Eastern Europe, some of whom, such as former Yugoslavians (see Piasere 1987), reached the West before the fall of the Iron Curtain. Unlike the chapters of Grill and Solimene (this volume), which provide detailed descriptions of the economic strategies of Gypsies in migration contexts, I focus here on forms of investment in the home country. Why Cortorari have chosen the house as the ultimate vehicle of their consumption behaviour and why they are so reluctant to finish their houses will become apparent through consideration of both the internal dynamics of relatedness and the Cortorari representation of their positioning vis-à-vis neighbouring Romanian peasants.

I begin by sketching out the social history of Cortorari, focusing on their transition from tents to houses and the accompanying shift in economic practices that this entailed, which intertwines with changes in their perceived position within the broader village context. Then I move on and discuss the idiom of visibility – as manifested in, among other things, houses – in which Cortorari couch their desire and readiness to incorporate broader socio-economic changes. The visibility of houses is opposed to the invisibility of certain material items that Cortorari inherited from their ancestors, namely, chalices. Possession of these objects is constitutive of conceptions of personhood and relatedness as they are articulated in the realm of long-term reproduction, which assumes both a future and presentist orientation of developmental cycles in the domestic group (Goody 1971). The flow of chalices in marriage and inheritance transactions alludes to the rebirth of kinship and makes room for the mundane consumption behaviour objectified in spectacular houses. Cortorari consider their houses to be a sign of their civility, all the more so as houses have traditionally been a central idiom of peasant sociality. I conclude the chapter by arguing that the ongoing construction of houses is intimately related to the presentist and future orientation of Cortorari life-cycles.

Cortorari Livelihoods: Past and Present

There are just a few villages in Transylvania, central Romania, where you can find Cortorari and their homes. Over the last twenty years, Cortorari and their families have been living scattered all over Central and Western Europe. Even though many spend as much if not more time abroad than in Romania, Cortorari do not make efforts to build homes for themselves in the countries they migrate to. Instead, they sleep in the open, in parks and underneath bridges. The idea of renting or buying a temporary dwelling place abroad has hardly ever crossed a Cortorari's mind. Cortorari consider their home (kher-al) to be where their houses (kher-a) are. The Cortorari term kher-al defines the place in which their domestic affections are centred as it translates both as 'home country' and as 'one's home' (that is, the physical construction of one's house and the affects embedded in the kin relations that the house accommodates). Houses, as physical, social and symbolic forms, are placed at the core of the phenomenon of mobility.

No longer than half a century ago, Cortorari resided exclusively in tents. The name Cortorari derives from the Romanian *cort* (tent), and *cortorari* literally means 'tent-dwellers'. Cortorari do not have a word in their language equivalent to the Romanian Cortorari. Like other Romani-speaking populations – such as the Gabor studied by Olivera (2012) – they speak of themselves as belonging to a kind of people whom they refer to as *ame Roma* (we, the Roma), and from which non-Cortorari Roma and *Gaže* alike are excluded. Cortorari possess some of the attributes that the *Gaže* assign to 'exotic' Gypsies – the mythical and historical image of the Gypsy, as it were – such as the wearing of colourful skirts by women and the skilful working with copper by men. Well aware of the romantic stereotyping of unsettled Gypsies, Cortorari take delight in recalling their former nomadic life, which would singularise them as more 'real' and 'authentic' than other Gypsies. In contradistinction with the discourse of elders, which portrays life in tents as healthier and happier than their current life in houses, Cortorari have been more than successful in appropriating the house and making of it a matter of cultural elaboration.[1]

For Cortorari, the process of sedentarisation started in the 1950s, when the communists came to power in Romania. In an attempt to improve the welfare of Gypsies, the new regime forced them to buy houses and to take care of their personal hygiene. Old people remember how men had their hair and beards trimmed and how children were dragged to schools. At that time, some Cortorari had just returned from the deportation camps in Transnistria where they had been taken during the Second World War. Cortorari embraced forced sedentarisation both because, as some survivors confessed, it gave them the chance to 'be more like the rest of the world', and because it could prevent potential further incarceration in concentration camps. During the communist period, Cortorari engaged in various livelihood activities strictly divided by gender. Men traded in horses and were involved in the manufacture of copper utensils needed in peasant households, such as stills. Women, meanwhile, ran the house and went from door to door offering services such as palmistry and card reading to peasant women. Additionally, they engaged in the hard work of pig husbandry, for which they scavenged the neighbouring towns and carried home loads of discarded foodstuff on their backs.

If we give credence to elders' stories, Romanian peasants and Cortorari have generally lived in harmony. Old Cortorari used to put up their tents on the outskirts of the villages where they were later forcibly sedentarised. This also happened in Băleni, the village where I carried out fieldwork between 2008 and 2010. Romanians' narratives described their relationship with Cortorari in the distant and more recent past in tones infused with amity and benevolence. These feelings were bred by the acknowledged difference in the economic and social standing of the two populations. At the time when Cortorari led a nomadic life, Romanians were better off, respectable householders (*gospodar*) who looked down on Cortorari with pity. The latter were unkempt and ragged; without estates of their own, they 'only owned the sky above their heads', as people say in an attempt to convey the idea of a life that juggles freedom with risk, contingency and chance. Nowadays, such a clear-cut hierarchy is disputable, given that Cortorari have proven shockingly economically successful of late. Their economic betterment is most visible in their housing. Although Romanians concede that Cortorari would never be able to master the skills and care a household requires, they are nonetheless jealous of the latter's affluence.

Cortorari gain the bulk of their money from informal economic activities, especially begging (*manglimos*), carried out in Western European countries. Elsewhere, I have shown that Cortorari conceive of begging as work (*munca*), which allows for the accumulation of wealth, in contrast to manual labour (*kerel buti*), such as coppersmithing by males and pig husbandry by females, which is carried out within the confines of the household and whose yields are redistributed among relatives (see Tesăr 2011).

Besides the different management of expenditure when begging abroad and performing manual labour at home respectively, the gender configuration of labour is particularly noteworthy. While at home, economic activities are clearly divided by gender, but abroad, begging is practised by both males and females. The playing down of the importance of gender together with the underscoring of the idiom of age in begging activities is of paramount importance to understanding the meaning attached to ongoing building work on Cortorari houses, as will become clear below.

A Politics of Visibility

The way they dress and the way they build their houses makes Cortorari strikingly visible in the landscape they inhabit. The Transylvanian built environment is, for the most part, a homogeneous grey. Here, people wear dark outfits even during the hottest days of summer. They make their presence unobtrusive by spending the time working in far-removed fields or behind the high fences of their households. Against this background, Cortorari people appear as a splash of colour. Women with long, bright red skirts and men with pinkish shirts and black lofty hats fill the streets from sunrise till late at night. They are everywhere – coming and going at the bus station and in front of the doctor's surgery, getting off trains, crowding the shops, selling trinkets and copper artefacts along the highway, or queuing in front of the village hall or post office – and they wave at everybody, even anonymous drivers who happen to drive by. They always have something to sell or some news to communicate very loudly.

In Băleni, Cortorari houses, erected in the eastern part of the village, quite a few along the highway, dominate the whole village and are surpassed in grandeur only by a medieval fortified church. Made from durable brick, their glittering turrets point towards the sky. I suggest that Cortorari endeavours to make themselves visible is a political statement about their participation in the broader world by sharing the resources and knowledge on which the very reproduction of their society depends. Political philosophy regards attempts to make oneself visible as efforts to be recognised within an intersubjective field of action, whereby processes of inclusion and exclusion of the 'other' underscore the politics of identity and/or inequality (Dixon and Peachey 2012: 1). This leads me to argue that the Cortorari quest for recognition equates with their partaking in history and social change.

I return to Luca to substantiate my claim. Luca's house is located on the main track along which Cortorari houses are clustered. With the exception of its turrets, the Cortorari neighbourhood is not visible either from the village centre or from the highway that goes through it. Luca's nephew, Banu, lives in a house bordering the highway. He is quite a regular presence in Luca's house, his visits being either disguised as a request to borrow a tool or simply overtly performed for no other reason than chatting or even partaking in a general silence. On a hot summer's day, Banu, Luca, Luca's wife and I were sitting under a tree at the side of the ditch in front of Luca's house. We were all eating sunflower seeds, spitting out the shells, deep in our own thoughts. Banu broke the silence by addressing Luca:

> Hey, uncle (*kako*), I don't know how you don't get bored. I couldn't live in your house. You cannot see anybody if you sit here on the side of the ditch, outside your house. Me, I spend my days sitting or standing on the side of the highway. You can't even imagine how many cars pass by. I wave at them and they [i.e. the drivers] wave back. Some people stop and chat to me ... And that's how I learn what's new in the world.

Banu was not inferring that Luca sees nobody. On the contrary, Luca has a good view over the whole Cortorari neighbourhood, and he can keep an eye on most of the Cortorari who walk up and down the road. What Banu was inferring is that Luca does not see and subsequently is not seen by the broader world, by the non-Cortorari with whom, by way of consequence, he does not communicate. In contrast, Banu, who trades in copper artefacts on the side of the highway, engages not merely in economic exchanges with his customers but also in exchanges of information. One thing that kept surprising me was the knowledge of global political and economic issues that Cortorari hold. The conversion rate of the euro, new state regulations regarding the flow of immigration, discrimination policies against Roma in Italy and France, changes in welfare policies both at the national and European level – all this news Cortorari learnt before I did. It took me a while to understand how it was that Cortorari – illiterate people who do not read newspapers and most of the time misunderstand the elitist language of media newscasts – nonetheless held extensive knowledge of contemporary economic and political circumstances. I propose that for the Cortorari, visibility and the desire to be visible to the outside world, as manifested in either the size of their houses or their colourful outfits, equate with participation in broader socio-economic changes.

Invisible Chalices and Cortorari Reproduction

Cortorari consider themselves descendants of a common group of ancestors, and they intermarry. Marriages are central rituals that reflect the organisation of gender differences, the allocation of property and the mastery of political relations. Cortorari consider their wealth (*averea*) to reside in the possession of a limited number of material items, namely chalices (*taxtaja*), which have been passed down from their ancestors and have a pre-eminent role in practices of filiation and marriage.[2] Chalices are made of gilded silver and were manufactured by craft guilds from Transylvania in the seventeenth and eighteenth centuries. Chalices are the dominant metaphor of value and a point of reference in Cortorari understandings of relatedness and personhood.

Cortorari have a strong androcentric ideology: women are attributed less symbolic value than men and are excluded from the inheritance of ceremonial wealth. Maleness and femaleness are achieved through procreation within wedlock. Marriages are processual; they are repeatedly concluded and broken off. Their endurance is contingent on the production of children, that endurance being normally guaranteed by the birth of a male offspring to a new couple. This is so because male offspring are seen as the essence of the reproduction of a family. The transmission of a chalice from a father to his son is secured only when a man has male offspring. Under such conditions, the nurturing of children necessarily involves a long-term future-oriented dimension. Parents pool their energy and efforts in order to deliver to the world culturally competent actors: daughters (*šeja*) and sons (*šave*) who are bodily capable of becoming *romni*, a married Cortorari mother, and *rom*, a married Cortorari father (see Tesăr 2012: 130–31). The successful realisation of parenthood coincides with the transition from being parents to being grandparents. Because the latter control the flow of chalices, they assume the role of arranging the marriages of their grandsons. The old people (*al phure*) are thus symbolically associated with chalices.

Although these material objects circulate vertically as heirlooms, in marriage transactions, rights (*dreptul*) in the objects are surrendered to wife-givers in exchange for cash dowries (*zestrea*).[3] The chalice does not change hands at any time. As a matter of fact, in spite of the rhetoric of flow and movement in which Cortorari couch the social life of chalices, these material items have a static nature: they are permanently kept tucked away in the houses and granaries of non-Roma Romanian peasants. It is nonetheless the multifarious social entitlements in a chalice which are circulated among people and which connect a person to numerous others. When I explicitly asked Cortorari what a chalice was good for, they said that it 'brings a daughter-in-law' and 'binds co-parents-in-law'. The youngest son is normally the heir of a family's chalice. As heir, the youngest son attracts a cash dowry whose value is calculated proportionally to the value attached to his chalice at his marriage. He is expected to give money to his brothers as compensation for their shares (*partea*) in the inherited chalice; this money usually comes from the marriage payment that he receives from his wife-givers. In exchange for the cash dowry, wife-givers gain entitlements to arrange further (cousin) marriages between female descendants on the bride's side and male descendants on the heir's side in the future. Meanwhile, the heir's brothers use their cash share of the dowry received by the heir to build houses for their new families.[4] With the influx of capital coming from transnational mobility, the value of the cash dowry has increased and houses have become larger. People say that it is advisable to conclude alliances in order to keep inherited wealth (chalices) in the family; in other words, the male descendants of heirs should marry female descendants of non-inheriting brothers, alliances that are normally accompanied by the writing off of the marriage payment. Yet the heir is happy to receive a large dowry from outsiders (that is, families who do not possess a chalice). By the same token, non-inheriting brothers prove eager to receive larger compensation shares with which to build bigger houses.

Despite marriages with outsiders being morally condemned, they nonetheless occur frequently, giving everybody an incentive to multiply economic gains. Those without a chalice need large sums of money to pay the dowries needed to marry off their daughters. An heir's brothers endeavour to procure resources for building their own houses, which otherwise would be financed from the compensation received from shares in a chalice. In so doing, they secure themselves the chance to marry their daughters to the sons of their brother, the heir to the chalice, thus concluding alliances that prevent their wealth being surrendered to strangers.

It becomes apparent that chalices – 'sacred objects' (Godelier 1996) that act as gifts and are withheld from being exchanged outside the local marriage market – are mobilised in consumption practices that are bound to the liberalisation of the flow of people and goods in present-day Romania. Cortorari prosperity – as objectified not only in houses, which form the core concern of this chapter, but also in lavish wedding ceremonies, or in the enormous quantities of meat and expensive bottles of alcohol that tower on tables laid at kinship gatherings – is intimately related to the circulation of chalices. Transactions which are being concluded around these cherished material items work as a catalyst for the flow of money embedded in dowries, compensation shares and houses. Moreover, the supreme motivation behind the movement of money goes beyond an individual human life and touches upon the reproduction of generational cycles, a long-term realm dominated by the chalice. The successful replacement of a generation by another and the flow of chalices – as entanglements of both heirlooms and marital endowments – are closely entwined. Cortorari say of chalices that 'they are our life'; they thus attribute their own fertility and vitality to these objects.

Though chalices are pre-eminent in Cortorari talk and in their social reproduction, they are kept hidden (*garade*) in the custody of ethnic Romanian peasants. Like other groups of Gypsies, such as the Mānuš (Williams 1993) and the Sinti (Tauber 2006), who developed models of reproduction based on practices (such as the relationship with the dead) that are invisible to outsiders, Cortorari sociality is constructed and revolves around chalices, objects that remain invisible in everyday life. The chalices are vectors in creating extensive webs of relatedness: transactions in compensation shares, dowries, debts and promises to pay circulate intergenerationally, linking a person to numerous others.

I hold that chalices and the significance with which they are imbued have a central role not only in Cortorari social reproduction (that is, the replacement of people and things in time, and thus their endurance) but also in the incorporation of modernity into people's life. In other words, the chalices are active agents both of the growth of kinship as an invisible realm and in the growth of people as a visible realm objectified in their magnificent houses. Cortorari assign a permanent quality to chalices and discursively oppose them to the transience of houses. Yet seemingly contrary to what they are saying, Cortorari endeavour constantly to build larger and more solid houses. It is to the meanings attached to houses in relation to both the majority society and internal sociality that I dedicate the remainder of this chapter.

'We've Become Civilised': From Tent to Palace

Cortorari consider their mansions the expressive form of their betterment, understood both as economic advancement and especially as enlightenment and social development. They are adamant in their stories that they exchanged the tent for the villa-type house and that, by so doing, they went from 'savagery' straight to 'civilisation'. They associate their tent life with backwardness and the current turn in their life's trajectories with upward mobility.

When I first set foot in the Cortorari neighbourhood in 2001, it looked like a huge building site, since the residents had just started working on new imposing houses next to their original shabby huts. The people themselves were caught up in the process of constructing new livelihoods and reshaping their lifestyles. One could smell the prosperity of the market economy in the dust rising from the unpaved road and from the brick masonry of the new houses. Back then, there were no fences to demarcate households. People wandered about from one house to another, handing out bowls of food to neighbours, which made it difficult for me to associate people with their dwellings. Some Cortorari did not wait for their new houses to be finished before moving in their personal belongings and the furniture in which they were trading without worrying about the missing doors or windows.[5] Nobody bothered about taking the main track to reach the homes of their relatives when they could freely cut a new shortcut through someone's back garden. Gradually, as the number of newly built houses increased and the buildings themselves grew taller and taller, the more they resembled, in the ways they policed physical barriers and apertures, folk representations of private estates. In 2008, all the back gardens were closed off and the front yards fenced. People's movements were now shaped by the materiality of barriers coupled with the presence of fierce dogs in almost all households. Some of the houses looked like finished buildings dyed in bright greens, oranges, pinks or reds. However, piles of bricks were still lying on the sides of the unpaved road that crosses the neighbourhood. Lorries with construction business logos on them were continuously rolling by, stopping here and there to offload building materials such as tiles, lime or timber.

Not long ago, people were preoccupied exclusively with the size of their house the exterior walls of which were left unplastered – and paid little or no attention to aesthetics. Gradually, however, not only did Cortorari start painting the exterior their houses, but they also started decorating the interiors, with the style of decoration and materials used changing over time. The interiors of their houses shifted in style from what people termed *țărănește* (peasant-like) to *rajkane* ('modern', lit. gentleman-like). Houses in the former style were richly adorned, with floral patterned walls on which colourful rugs were hung, with embroidered curtains, and hand-woven wool blankets covering the beds. Houses in the latter style are more austere, with walls in plain colours and no hanging rugs; the old thick blankets have been replaced with thin synthetic Turkish throws in lively colours, while the candelabra have been replaced by spotlights. Cortorari speak of the changes in their domestic architecture and tastes in interior decor in terms of progress and evolution. To their mind, the new fences, the new interiors and the overall transformation of houses testify to the fact that Cortorari have become gentlemen-like (*rajsalen*). This expression is derived from the noun *raj*, which is attributed with different meanings depending on the context. A *raj* can equally be a Gypsy who leads a luxurious life, or a non-Gypsy who has an office job and a secure income; one who has overcome an alleged stage of backwardness (*înapoime*) and is highly civilised, but also any person who lives in prodigal extravagance, be it a king, a nobleman or a Cortorari.

This opposition, between *țărănește* and *rajkane*, connotes a process of refinement or civilisation that Cortorari envisage as moving them nearer to the living standards of ethnic Romanian peasants. Cortorari believe that it is *rajkane* to attend to the interior of one's house. Mastery of ownership and care of the house is a central moral value among Romanian peasants (Nicolescu 2011); it is thus the utmost *Gaže* characteristic. When they smoke indoors, Cortorari do not use ashtrays, objects that, to their minds, are specific to *raj-a* (gentlemen); instead, they simply discard their ash and butts on the floor, which the women are expected to clean continuously. One should not imagine that Cortorari do not have ashtrays in their homes. On the contrary, they display ashtrays in glass cases for non-Cortorari visitors to see. Likewise, Cortorari know that good manners stipulate the use of cutlery at mealtimes. They do keep cutlery in their homes, yet they usually make no use of it, given that 'only the good mannered/civilised eat with forks'. Among Cortorari, the moral evaluation of *rajsalen* is not at all clear and straightforward. There is no easy way out of the riddle. Some say with envy that those who excel in *rajsalen* (such as people who have built an indoor toilet) have 'brought shame' on themselves by disrespecting the Cortorari moral code.[6] Yet the envious ones also dream of building an indoor toilet as soon as they can afford it. Regardless of the moral overtones it carries, the concept of *rajsalen* is thought of as a processual undertaking intimately linked to consumption behaviour.

Miller characterises consumption as empowering and ultimately egalitarian, an act that allows consumers 'to employ their resources for the self-construction of their individual and social identity' (Miller 1995: 38). In light of this argument, one can conclude that consumption is about the politics of identity. Yet consumption is also about the politics of inequality: when the lower strata and the disadvantaged, who have historically been denied access to the forms of consumption of the upper strata, grasp new economic possibilities, they cling to consumption as a means of contesting, if not reversing, old hierarchies (Thomas 1998: 434; Osella and Osella 1999: 1004). By the same token, practices of consumption destabilise the distinction between centre and periphery (Howes 1996). From this perspective, the fact that Cortorari choose the mansion as the ultimate form of consumption should not appear surprising, given that the house(hold) has customarily been the paramount idiom of Romanian peasants' sociality, in which both social recognition and the objectification of success were couched. Moreover, within the configuration of the multi-ethnic village, the house has long been acknowledged by villagers as a marker of distinction between peasants and *Ţigani* (Gypsies), instantiating long-standing social hierarchies. Cortorari engage in the process of *rajsalen* not merely as a quest for redefining Cortorariness, but also with thoughts of redefining their social position as perceived by the 'other'. Cortorari consumption behaviour complies with the model of conspicuous consumption developed by Veblen (1899): it articulates both status competition inside the notional community and emulation in relation to the outside.

Houses under Construction and Processual Marriages

Cortorari mansions are not only signs of upward mobility and of a project of *Gaže*-oriented civility; they are also family-oriented consumer goods, and the meanings attached to ongoing building work are revealed in the light of the replacement and reproduction of domestic groups. Consumption behaviour as expressed in housing assumes a long-term dimension, oriented towards present and future, which characterises Cortorari understandings of the person and relatedness. Cortorari all vie to pass on to their offspring the biggest, most beautiful and spectacular houses, and the motivations that underlay their economic behaviour are related to the prosperity and well-being of the forthcoming generation. In the present, houses objectify the economic success of the generation that is the most active in begging activities abroad. In this respect, consumption also assumes a presentist orientation.

Money derived from begging is invested in houses. As mentioned previously, begging abroad is performed by both men and women. Age and kinship status, as well as notions of personhood, are nonetheless major consideration in the social organisation of the work of begging, which is family centred. The extended family, which normally comprises three generations with their accretions, shares a house and constitutes the atom of Cortorari sociality: it should pursue common interests and pool resources. It is the middle generation – parents of marriageable and newly-wed children – that is the most economically productive. Because begging takes place far from the security and comfort of the domestic unit, it is not suitable for unmarried persons. Women are expected not only to be virgins but also to be in good health at marriage. This ideal can only be attained through the close surveillance of girls, who are kept in the confines of the household before marriage. Boys of their age should also receive proper nurture at home (that is, prevented from getting engaged in excessive physical work while being fed on meat-based meals) in order to attain suitable maturation. Successful realisation of maleness and femaleness, which coincides with the transformation of children into parents, is contingent on the nurture the former receive from their own parents. Young couples should tend to their offspring and, only when the latter approach marriageable age, are they to start making begging expeditions abroad, leaving children in the care of their grandparents.

In the economy of the domestic unit, the old (*al phure*) exercise control over the flow of chalices with which they are associated. The middle generation – the youth (*al terne*) – are in charge of earning the money to invest in housing. They are thus symbolically associated with the aesthetics and the comfort of houses. Cortorari houses are recent phenomena, and some of them have not yet witnessed the death of one generation. Unlike European peasant houses, which are symbols of permanence and fixity associated with the *longue durée* of intergenerational inheritance (see Pine 1996), Cortorari houses are as transient and dynamic as their marriages, with which they are intimately connected.

In marriages, people are assigned to houses, and the latter, as containers of both people and objects, publicise the successful realisation and endurance of an alliance. When a bride comes to live in her spouse's parental house, the new couple is allocated a separate room that contains only the necessities of life. This room will be furnished and decorated with items of the trousseau tendered when the production of children occurs, thus securing the continuation of marriage. The domestication of the living place is an intricate process congruent with biological reproduction. The new couple has an uneasy and in-between status: seen as an accretion of the groom's parents and grandparents' household, it is nonetheless excluded from decision making inside the household and is economically dependent on the adults.[7] The liminal condition of the new couple surfaces clearly in the position of the daughter-in-law (*bori*), who does not participate in the household's communal meals and is expected to complete all the domestic chores by herself. The *bori* puts all her labour to the service of her parents-in-law and her economic activities are confined to the household. She usually helps her mother with pig husbandry yet she has no control over the gains derived from it. Her husband attends to his father's coppersmithing without laying any claims to the yields of his work. Only later in life, when their own son approaches a marriageable age and consequently a new daughter-in-law is expected to arrive in the household, will this couple gain autonomy in economic activities and control over their own money. They start engaging in begging and invest the gains in changing the design of the house and its interior decorations.

Despite the ongoing nature of house building, Cortorari hold that it is not advisable for one to bring a daughter-in-law into one's house unless the house is finished, or that it is bad (for wife-givers) to have the ritual that communicates the severance of a daughter from her parental family held in an unfurnished room. These sayings suggest that every house is expected to reach its completion stage, which is associated with the conclusion of an alliance. The ritual that publicises the severance of a daughter is held in the 'best room', which is the most public space in a house. It is the centre stage of life-cycle rituals (marriages and funerals). The room contains the most valuable objects, including the best bedding and carpets, and the glass cases where the packaging of consumer goods brought from abroad is displayed. Each generation of parents of marriageable daughters is expected to customise this room in accordance with the latest fashion in house interiors. Parents of male offspring are equally expected to provide the wherewithal for the latest in home improvements, which currently include parquet flooring, double-glazed windows and metal doors.

The accomplishment of a domestic cycle is thus publicised through the completion of a house. Marriages endure only through procreation, and sometimes they are broken for trivial reasons, such as a bride's failure to adjust to the demands of her parents-in-law or a small quarrel over the marriage payment. Until their youngest male offspring's marriage is secured – ideally by the birth of a son – parents are expected to work on their house continuously, making changes to it so that it reaches the 'completed' stage on the occasion of the youngest son's marriage which, itself, can be one in a series of marriages (and hence of completed houses). Given that generations follow one another at great speed (marriages occur in a person's early teens), and that marriages are concluded and broken off equally rapidly, it is not surprising that Cortorari houses are permanently under construction, despite the ideal of their being completed on the occasion of a marriage.

The fact that Luca's son, Emil, embarked on the troublesome enterprise of building a new house should be understood in light of the argument currently being advanced: located within developmental cycles of the domestic group and individuals' economic projects, consumption assumes a long-term dimension, oriented towards future and present. Let us conclude by discussing these two attitudes towards time enmeshed in consumption behaviour. Firstly, Emil had a son whose marriage was expected to be arranged in about two years' time, when Emil would have already 'completed' a house suitable for a daughter-in-law. The construction of the house is thus constituent of the process of the replacement of generations. Secondly, Emil's motivations for building a replica of the house built by his own father articulate the idea that houses objectify the work performed by the youth in the present. Owning two houses is a sign of this extended family's prosperity. Its visibility substantiates their access to pockets of knowledge about the flow of money both along state welfare chains and within intersubjective donor–beggar exchanges.

Cortorari have incorporated consumption practices into both local cultural reproduction and wider transnational mobility projects. Their economic affluence is intrinsically linked to notions of reproduction and relatedness: the visibility of their houses and the invisibility of their chalices are two sides of the same coin, that is of the creativity that permeates both the long-term realm of the replacement of domestic cycles and the presentist orientation of individuals' economic ventures. Over time, Cortorari have continued to be Cortorari in spite of changing state regimes, lifestyles and economic practices, and they have done so precisely by integrating wider social-economic transformations into their sociality. The transition from tent to house has not made Cortorari less Cortorari. On the contrary, the house, perceived as a sign of civility that brings Cortorari closer to their Romanian neighbours, is subject to internal cultural elaboration; its perpetual incompleteness, materialised as changes in aesthetic tastes and ideas of comfort, speaks of enduring values attached to chalices and ensuing notions of personhood and kinship.

Acknowledgements

The research for this article was made possible with the support of a Wadsworth International Fellowship offered by the Wenner-Gren Foundation and held at University College London between 2007 and 2012. I want to thank the editors of this book for their valuable comments on earlier drafts, and especially Martin Fotta, for our continuous conversations regarding my work. I am also grateful to the Cortorari who unconditionally and affectionately welcomed me into their homes and families, and led me by the hand into the intricacies of their culture.

NOTES

1. For the idea of Gypsies appropriating things from the *Gaže* and endowing them with their own meanings, see Williams (1993), Stewart (1997) and Okely (2011).
2. For a detailed description of chalices among Romanian Gabor Roma, see Berta (2007, 2009, 2010). Berta translates the vernacular term *taxtaja* as 'beakers', though I find the word 'chalice' to be a more appropriate translation. According to my own estimate, about thirty such chalices are in possession of Cortorari in the village of Băleni. The community comprises approximately 700 inhabitants and 80 households.
3. Cortorari dowry consists both of cash, which flows from wife-givers to wife-takers, and of a trousseau which is passed from a mother to her daughter. Both the cash dowry and the trousseau are tendered in instalments at significant moments such as the production of children.
4. Residence is (patri)virilocal: the youngest son lives with his parents and inherits their house, while his brothers, if there are any, are expected to build their own houses in which to live with their wives; daughters, meanwhile, move into their husbands' houses. As will become clear in this chapter, parents are in charge of the management of the resources for building a house.
5. In the early 2000s, a common economic strategy was trading in antique furniture collected from villages across Romania.
6. Because of their pollution beliefs, which prescribe that faeces should be kept at a distance, Cortorari privies are normally located at the far end of their back gardens.
7. The bride's parents bear her living expenses.

REFERENCES

Berta, P. 2007. 'Ethnicisation of Value – the Value of Ethnicity: The Prestige-item Economy as a Performance of Ethnic Identity among the Gabors of Transylvania (Rumania)', *Romani Studies* 17(1): 31–65.

———. 2009. 'Materialising Ethnicity: Commodity Fetishism and Symbolic Re-creation of Objects among the Gabor Roma (Romania)', *Social Anthropology* 17(2): 184–97.

———. 2010. 'Economic Action in Theory and Practice: Anthropological Investigations', in D.C. Wood (ed.), *Research in Economic Anthropology*, Vol. 30. Bingley: Emerald Books, pp.277–309.

Carsten, J., and S. Hugh-Jones. 1995. 'Introduction', in J. Carsten and S. Hugh-Jones (eds), *About the House: Lévi-Strauss and Beyond*. Cambridge: Cambridge University Press, pp.1–47.

Dalakoglou, D. 2010. 'Migrating – Remitting – "Building" – Dwelling: House-making as "Proxy" Presence in Postsocialist Albania', *Journal of the Royal Anthropological Institute* 16(4): 761–77.
Dixon, L., and J. Peachey. 2012. 'The Paradox of Representation and the Problem with Recognition: What Does it Mean to be Visible?', *Anthropology Matters Journal* 14(1): 1–6.
Godelier, M. 1996. *L'énigme du don*. Paris: Fayard.
Goody, J. (ed.) 1971. *The Developmental Cycles in Domestic Groups*. Cambridge: Cambridge University Press.
Howes, D. (ed.) 1996. *Cross-cultural Consumption: Global Markets, Local Realities*. London: Routledge.
Leinaweaver, J.B. 2009. 'Raising the Roof in the Transnational Andes: Building Houses, Forging Kinship', *Journal of the Royal Anthropological Institute* 15(4): 777–96.
Lobo, S. 1982. *A House of My Own: Social Organization in the Squatter Settlements of Lima, Peru*. Tucson: University of Arizona Press.
Miller, D. 1995. 'Consumption as the Vanguard of History. A Polemic by Way of Introduction', in D. Miller (ed.), *Acknowledging Consumption. A Review of New Studies*. London: Routledge, pp.1–53.
Nicolescu, R. 2011. 'Solid Houses and Distant Homes. The Morality of Domestic Space in Southeast Romania', *Martor* 16: 69–81.
Okely, J. 2011. 'Constructing Culture through Shared Location, Bricolage and Exchange: The Case of Gypsies and Roma', in M. Stewart and M. Rövid (eds), *Multi-disciplinary Approaches to Romany Studies*. Budapest: Central European University Press, pp.35–55.
Olivera, M. 2012. *La tradition de l'intégration. Une ethnologie des Roms Gabori dans les années 2000*. Paris: Éditions Pétra.
Osella, F., and C. Osella. 1999. 'From Transience to Immanence: Consumption, Life-cycle and Social Mobility in Kerala, South India', *Modern Asian Studies* 33(4): 989–1020.
Piasere, L. 1987. 'In Search of New Niches: The Productive Organization of the Peripatetic Xoraxané in Italy', in A. Rao (ed.), *The Other Nomads: Peripatetic Minorities in Cross-cultural Perspective*. Kohl: Böhlau, pp.111–32.
Pine, F. 1996. 'Naming the House and Naming the Land: Kinship and Social Groups in Highland Poland', *Journal of the Royal Anthropological Institute* 2(3): 443–59.
Stewart, M. 1997. *The Time of the Gypsies*. Boulder, CO: Westview Press.
Tauber, E. 2006. *Du Wirst keinen Ehemann Nehmen! Respekt, die Bedeutung der Toten und Fluchtheirat bei den Sinti Estraixaria*. Münster: LIT Verlag.
Tesăr, C. 2011. 'Tigan bun traditional in Romania, cersetor de-etnicizat in strainatate: Politici ale re-prezentarii publice si etica muncii la romii Cortorari', in S. Toma and L. Fosztó (eds), *Spectrum: Cercetari Sociale Despre Romi*. Cluj Napoca: ISPMN – Kriterion, pp.281–312.
———. 2012. 'Becoming Rom (Male), Becoming Romni (Female) among Romanian Cortorari Roma: On Body and Gender', *Romani Studies* 22(2): 113–40.
Thomas, P. 1998. 'Conspicuous Construction: Houses, Consumption and "Relocalization" in Manambondro, Southeast Madagascar', *Journal of the Royal Anthropological Institute* 4(3): 425–46.

Veblen, T. 1899. *The Theory of the Leisure Class: An Economic Study of Institutions*. New York: Macmillan.

Williams, P. 1993. *Nous, on n'en parle pas. Les vivants et les morts chez les Manouches*. Paris: Maison des Sciences de l'Homme.

Cătălina Tesăr holds a doctorate in social anthropology from University College London, based on research on the sexual, economic and political dimensions of early-age marriages among a Romanian Romani-speaking population. She is currently a postdoctoral fellow at the Romanian Institute for Research on National Minorities Cluj, Romania, as part of the research project 'The Immigration of Romanian Roma to Western Europe: Causes, Effects and Future Engagement Strategies', funded by the European Union under the 7th Framework Programme 'Dealing with Diversity and Cohesion: The Case of the Roma in the European Union' (GA319901). She is also a researcher at the Museum of the Romanian Peasant, Bucharest.

Chapter 10

 # Exchange, Shame and Strength among Calon of Bahia
A Values-based Analysis

MARTIN FOTTA

This chapter is an attempt to apply aspects of an anthropological theory of value to the socio-cultural organisation of Calon of Bahia, Brazil. I examine the actions of Calon men and the meanings of these actions, and explore how values arise from social relations and contribute to social reproduction. A theory of value seems particularly appropriate because, rather than focusing on fixed social forms, it looks at the processes of their generation. Calon society is 'amorphous': there are no transcendental institutional frameworks or defined social groups; Calon insist on personal autonomy and equality between men, and violence stymies the codification of power; individual households change settlements easily, and a settlement is abandoned following a death of any important male (and sometimes also female) inhabitant; there is no generational inheritance of objects and no recognisable collective rituals. Calon are explicit about the importance of their actions and continually submit each other's acts to a series of questions about their meaning and truthfulness; what community does exist consists of social persons who are subject to this ethical reasoning (Ferrari 2010).

This chapter describes how, within such system of social organisation, people attain different value levels objectified in the attributes of social persons and encoded in space. Following David Graeber (2001), I take value to be a process in which meaning is turned into desire and action: value is how people represent the importance of their actions to themselves. Using the ethnographic example of a small Calon community in Bahia, I argue that there are two major sources of value among Calon: *vergonha* (honour, shame) and *força* (strength). Although Calon expect these qualities to be harmoniously united within the character of social persons, they are often contradictory and contested. The tension between values has become salient in recent years due to the fact that the attributes of *força* increasingly depend on monetary exchanges. Here, value and influence stemming from money hidden 'on the street' pose challenges to the maintenance of the attributes of honourable behaviour.

A Settlement in Bomfim

In September 2012, Eduardo's household moved to Bomfim. Besides the large plot on which their house stood, they also owned a sizeable plot of land across a dirt road. Gradually, Eduardo's relatives moved onto this plot, arriving from all over the region. Kiko, Eduardo's oldest son, came first. Eduardo's brother-in-law, Eduardo's brother and the brother's son came next. With them, Eduardo's sister's son, who had already lived elsewhere in Bomfim, moved his tent onto Eduardo's plot. In turn, a few affines of Eduardo's kin built their tents just behind a fence surrounding the plot. In this manner, within a few months a new settlement emerged on and around the plot owned by Eduardo. Although Eduardo's presence and his land entitlement made it possible for the settlement to emerge, he kept his distance from others. Not only did he live on the plot separated by the dirt road from the area where his relatives lived in tents, but he usually sat in front of his house and kept out of the daily affairs of his relatives across the road.

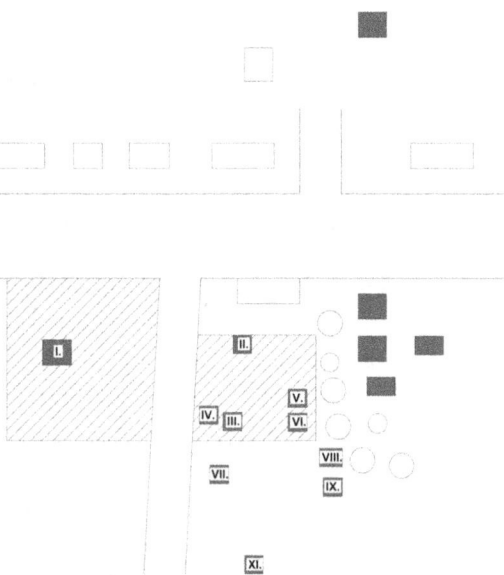

Figure 10.1: Settlement in Bomfim. Calon tents are in grey; Eduardo's house is marked 'I'.

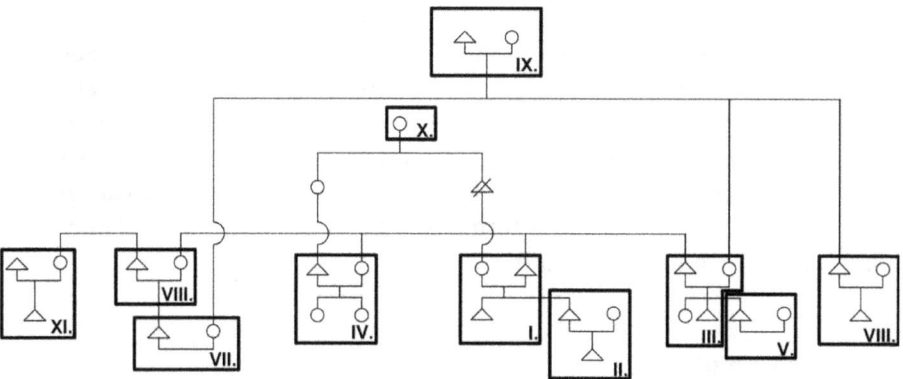

Figure 10.2: Kinship relations between households in the Bomfim settlement. Numbers refer to the households in Figure 10.1.

Eduardo's older son Kiko commented to me bitterly: 'Look at Eduardo. He could be a boss (*chefe*) of everybody here. But he doesn't want to'. He went on to explain how his father could achieve this: 'You know, not giving them [people in the settlement] money, but lending them money. But he is *descarado*'.

Becoming a *chefe* and behaving in a *descarado* manner – that is, disgracefully or shamelessly – lie on a single continuum, as they both reflect one's reputation among Calon. This reputation is constructed through the circulation of money, objects and people against the background of transactions between Calon and *Brasileiros*, the non-Gypsies.[1] Eduardo 'could' become a *chefe* because he is a successful moneylender, one of the most dominant Calon men within the circle of towns around Bomfim. The reverse is true, though, and his son Kiko criticises him for being unresponsive to the needs of his relatives and refusing to convert his wealth 'on the street' (*na rua*) – primarily imagined as money in a form of predatory loans extended to *Brasileiros* – into deferred exchanges with people living around him that are imagined as exchanges between equals from which both parties benefit. Through such transformations, Eduardo would come to be seen as a *chefe*, capable of mobilising others living around him. This would empower others to act too, since the manipulation of deferred exchanges between Calon become active interventions in the unfolding of the future and opens up spaces for further opportunities. In fact, the potential for improving their positionality through their relationships with rich and influential Calon is one reason why Calon decide to change settlements.

But Eduardo hesitates to 'convert value forms' by blocking the flow of money, or rather by not creating novel flows (e.g. Fajans 1993: 9). Such blocking (diverting or concealing) has become easy in present-day Bahia. Today, Calon rely less on their relatives for physical support, and money is no longer made through trading animals across large distances. Loans to *Brasileiros* (against cheques, bank cards and conditional cash transfer cards with PINs) that tap into formalised flows of money are relatively safe and easily hidden from others.

Vergonha and *Força*

There is pressure on rich men like Eduardo to make their wealth circulate in loans to relatives, and Calon constantly negotiate between autonomy and relatedness, concealment and circulation – topics explored by Michael Stewart in his ethnography of Hungarian Rom (Stewart 1997). For Calon, however, underlying these tensions and their resolution is not a striving for unity and harmony 'among brothers' – an ideal that the Rom see as constantly undermined by household and kinship interests. Instead, in a manner similar to Spanish Gitanos (Gay y Blasco 2004: 163–65), Calon of Bahia consider latent enmity among *Ciganos* (Gypsies) and the privileging of one's family and personal gain as legitimate, and men need to constantly demonstrate their complete presence and control.

Both Bahian Calon and Hungarian Rom create a Gypsy world in the midst of non-Gypsies through various kinds of transactions. In exchanges with non-Gypsies – the 'outside' – both groups value their skills and even applaud predation, but the difference in ideology underlying transactions constituting the 'inside' is telling: while the Roms' preference is for communal merrymaking (*mulatsago*) and self-representation as open to the needs of others, emphasising equality and generosity (Stewart 1997), Calon insist on treating transactions among themselves, even those framed as 'help' (*ajuda*) from a father to a son, as exchanges from which each actor profits, in which negotiation always takes place, and which always lead to deferred payments; in the case of monetary loans, these deferred payments always involve interest.

Such deferred exchanges foreground not only people's autonomy and self-interest but also their trust in the future acts of another, their agency in potential. By 'producing exchange' (cf. Fajans 1993), people create themselves as social persons in relations with others and gain social attributes associated with Calon values. A successful moneylender may become a *chefe*, or he may be seen as *descarado*. Although Calon envision the capability to make 'money on the street' as constitutive of the ability to strengthen the agency of others through deferred exchanges, the values that give meaning to Calon actions can lead to opposing tendencies.

Among Calon there are two broad sources of social value. First, there is *vergonha*, or *laje* in Calon Romani, which can be roughly translated as shame or honour. Second, there is one's ability to create one's environment. This environment is constructed by extending one's space-time through the creation of self–other relations (cf. Munn 1992), and is traced in the circulation of people and objects. This capability for creating movement and thus gaining control over one's environment is considered a characteristically masculine value. Stationary life is seen as moribund, and men who are incapable of finding opportunities or are addicted to gambling are described as being 'without a future' (*sem futuro*), or 'dead' (*morto* in Portuguese, *mulon* in Romani). Unlike *vergonha*, this value does not have an explicit name, but is a composite of various attributes associated with masculinity. I will refer to it as *força* (strength). The mechanism generated by *força* and *vergonha* that I describe in this chapter lends credence to Graeber's observation that in various social milieus there often exist paired sets of key values – one stated, encompassing and integrative, the other implicit and connected to individual assertion (Graeber 2001: 74).

In some ways, my argument about the articulation between the two value templates echoes Teresa San Román's (1975) discussion of 'honour', 'shame' and 'prestige' among Gitanos in Spain, which she connects to the concept of *lache*, which connotes being in a position of discredit or timidity. In a style of Mediterranean anthropology characteristic of the period, San Román argues that 'shame' relates to transgressions of sexual norms by women, while 'honour' becomes most visible through men's reactions to offences. 'Prestige', like my concept *força*, is gained primarily through the circulation of money, control over one's environment, hosting and so on. Drawing on the work of Florencia Ferrari (2010), however, I conceptualise *vergonha* in a different way. Although preoccupation with the female body might be at the core of this value sentiment, it is seen in acts of both men and women. At the same time, it is not only a means of mediating and controlling transgressions, but also a generative and functional complex motivating people's actions and beliefs. *Vergonha* is a mode through which 'Calonness' as a socio-cultural realm is created through a novel patterning of relationships from the indistinct *Gaje* world (Ferrari 2010; cf. Fajans 1983).

Vergonha is recognised by Calon as 'our value' (Ferrari 2010: 83). All Calon *qua* Calon are supposed to have *vergonha*, since this is what distinguishes them from *Gaje*. But it has to be made explicit and manifested – in Calon terms, it has to '[be made to] appear' (*aparecer*) (Ferrari 2010: 119–22, 2011: 735). Ferrari sees *vergonha* as a structural transformation of pollution taboos found among other Gypsy populations. Like these taboos, *vergonha* becomes objectified in concrete media – appearances and things such as dresses, ways of cleaning, or interactions between men and women – which must then be witnessed by others.

Besides these instantiations, Calon men foreground other acts – such as exchange negotiations, violent postures or the quick turnover of money in card games – in which they demonstrate their worth and which give rise to a morally meaningful order. Calon see their environment as potentially dangerous and unstable, but also a source of income, where opportunities can be created and seized. A man stabilises his environment and creates opportunities for gain in three basic ways. The first is by building up relationships with *Brasileiros* with the aim of finding several large clients who will take out serial loans. His capability to make money 'on the street', to create opportunities and to find new clients is sometimes glossed over as 'making the future' (*fazer futuro*). Second, he also has to show willingness to enforce his words and deeds (such as loans) with violence if necessary. All Calon men are expected to be *valente* (bold or brave). Lastly, increasing control over his surroundings objectifies his level of strength (*força*). Such strength is gained over time and is something that is attributed to older, but active, men who live surrounded by others, especially their adult sons. *Força* comes closest to the composite masculine value I referred to above and that I named after it: when a man makes money easily on the street because he has a good reputation among non-Gypsies, it proves him to be a man of *força*; when he can count on others, especially his sons, to back up his claims or to avenge him, it is because he has *força*.

Força is sometimes referred to as one's 'name' (*nome*), and for Calon, towns and regions often become associated with specific family names. In other words, a man's level of *força* reflects his reputation in the eyes of other Calon, including their knowledge (however imprecise) of the amount of money he has 'on the street' in the form of loans to *Brasileiros* and deferred payments from other Calon. His ability to borrow from other Calon becomes a confirmation of his autonomy and of his trustworthiness, and reflects not only his past actions but also their hopes about his future behaviour.

My understanding of the ability to create and control one's environment as a Calon value is inspired by Nancy Munn's analysis of value in Gawa, a Massim island in Melanesia. According to Munn, the source of value for Gawans lies in control over what she calls an 'intersubjective spacetime', 'a spacetime of self-other relationships formed in and through acts and practices' (Munn 1992: 9). Through a series of transformative acts, such as hospitality, travel and exchange of *kula* valuables, Gawans constitute their space-time as well as themselves. Acts that seem unimpressive, such as hospitality, are preconditions of reaching a more expansive value level. Value, in other words, is visible through the significance of people's acts in the eyes of others (such as in one's fame circulating with *kula* valuables).

Just like Gawans, Calon create value and gain the attributes of social persons associated with it through spatiotemporal transformations that translate people's acts into a social order. In the process, a Calon society is produced, which, through a feedback loop, motivates people's future acts (cf. Graeber 2001). Munn (1977) shows that there are successive forms of transformations in which Gawans can achieve increasingly powerful control over their space-time. Similarly, among Calon there exist different modalities of space-time control: violence is a mechanism demarcating one's space and exchange partners (Fotta n.d.), while fabrication of one's *vergonha*, its 'making apparent' in concrete circulating media, is a way in which the *Gaje* world is successively 'encompassed' within vergonha's domain (Ferrari 2010).

Nevertheless, for both Gawans and Calon, exchanges play a crucial role in such space-time expansion, of which they also become an idiom. Calon value becomes objectified in the patterning of space, but this spatial order is fragile. There is nothing akin to a communal 'fame of Gawa' reaching over to other islands, or to kula valuables and canoes to which one's name could be attached. Rather, the effects of exchanges have to be constantly enacted since they are short-lived and threatened by violence or defaults on payments.

The Encompassment of Money by *Vergonha*

For Calon, monetary transactions serve as repeated recognitions of their shared agency and equality among Calon, and of the difference between Calon and *Gaje*. Calon of Bahia make a living primarily through lending money at interest to non-Gypsies, a niche specialisation that has emerged within the context of the financialisation of daily life in small-town Bahia.

Over the past decades, financial institutions and services have become increasingly dominant in people's lives, while stabilisation of the value of currency, the expansion of the welfare state and economic growth, among other things, have increased the amount of cash in circulation (Fotta 2012). Deferred payments among Calon do not engender a sense of hierarchy between men, but are signs of autonomy. All transactions (*rolos*) among Calon – whether swaps, purchases or loans – lead to deferred payments at stipulated dates. These are valued not as promises to repay but as events highlighting acts of repayment, renegotiation and the enchainment of future behaviour (cf. Muldrew 1998). In Graeber's (2010) terminology, Calon men constantly reframe transactions among themselves as 'exchanges' between equals, whereby both parties are seen to profit from recombinations of time and money that open spaces for further negotiations. In treating these exchanges as singularised acts (exchanges) they dodge the potential for 'hierarchy' that could arise if they were framed as promises (debts).

There are various techniques to distinguish two kinds of transaction. Unlike loans to *Brasileiros*, in deferred payments among Calon there is no transfer of collateral even when large sums are involved. Calon are expected to return money without much ceremony, although they let everybody know that they have arrived to pay their debt. In contrast, they go first thing in the morning to collect money from *Gaje* clients before the debtors can leave their houses; between two Calon such behaviour would be seen as a loss of face and possibly a sign of mistrust or dependence. When a *Jurón* (a non-Gypsy individual) does not pay on time, a Calon demands a payment of at least one month's interest, with the principal plus interest to be paid the following month. Among Calon, interest does not accumulate over time, or a new deal is negotiated – there is no rate as such. In fact, Calon try to turn *Juróns* into long-term clients by convincing them to keep the principal and to pay only the interest for as long as possible. This option is not viable with other Calon – this would be living off another's money.

Although money is made 'on the street' among *Brasileiros*, the capability to 'make the future', to back transactions up when necessary and to establish long-lasting relationships with *Brasileiros*, is valued only when it circulates as aspects of social persons among Calon. In this way, a man's relationships with *Brasileiros* become part of his status. His reliability and skill are continuously assessed and become sources of his reputation, of his *crédito* (credit) or *nome* (name). Evaluation is recursive, and a failure or inability to honour deferred payments to other Calon or to establish stable clientele among *Brasileiros* influence his capacity to borrow; in other words, although Calon may portray each additional failure as a temporary shortcoming, it takes an increasingly longer time to overcome.

To be able to evaluate successfully, people try to get an idea of how much money a man has 'on the street'. Names of strongmen often reach beyond their home ranges, but any approximation depends on social distance – sons have more precise information on their fathers' deals than unrelated Calon living in distant settlements. Especially when surrounded by their relatives, people mention how much money they have *em giro* (in circulation), in the bank or in loans 'on the street'. Thus, Eduardo's relatives said that he had inherited at least R$300,000 from his childless uncle, and once he exclaimed that he had R$130,000 'on the street'.[2] It is in this manner that we should understand Kiko's demands regarding his father: Eduardo could become a strongman by lending money to other Calon around him because he was rich (*rico*). But there is no conversion of money from one value register to another; instead of becoming a medium of *vergonha*, it remains concealed in banks and loans. I should stress here that such invisibility is only partial. Another's 'money on the street' (*dinheiro na rua*) is seen as portrayable in theory, although this knowledge remains incomplete and uncertain.

Picturing people's 'money on the street' brings about the possibility of money's modal 'encompassment' by *vergonha*, whereby the character of money as a tool of abstraction (that is, as a transcendent entity) is suppressed through immanence of expenditure. Drawing on Martin Holbraad's (2005) analysis of money in Cuban Ifá cults as a 'purely multiple' object, I want to suggest that for Calon, this quality of quantity makes money a double medium. On the one hand, money is a medium of exchange and a tool of forging relationships, such as when a man strikes a deal with another. On the other, money as the total sum any man has 'on the street' – an aggregate of the payments he expects to receive in the future from *Gaje* and Calon debtors – serves as a medium within which that man's behaviour towards others can be evaluated. Put simply, the totality of 'money on the street' serves as a ground for the displacement of movement. It is not only a whole from which a part can be taken and used for another transaction, but also, as a totality, an environment that makes it possible to picture any expenditure as displacement.

This quality of multiplicity inherent in the money that one has 'on the street' becomes a ground against which *vergonha* can be made to 'appear'; it is thus also a mechanism for change in value register. For example, when a man 'spends' a large sum trying to save his dying relative despite his financial difficulties (known to others), he simultaneously highlights the impossibility of thinking of his money as a future potential, a transcendent abstraction. He cannot, for instance, ponder splitting that sum into one or more interest-bearing loans to *Brasileiros*, since in this moment of expenditure-as-displacement, calculation and commensurability between domains are obviated. Conversely, Eduardo's attempt to negate the encompassment of his money by *vergonha* – his refusal to refuse to calculate – led in specific moments to conflicts with his relatives.

Through the constant making of deals, then, each man creates his own environment, his 'morally informed spaces of interaction' characterised by certain forms of relationship (McCallum 2003: 71): settlements crisscrossed with small subsistence loans denoting mutuality; personal home ranges replete with card games and agonistic deals with other Calon highlighting autonomy and equality; predatory relationships with non-Gypsy clients marking moral differences between *Ciganos* and *Gaje*; and areas associated with enemies and unknown Gypsies with whom deals are never struck. Time is constantly 'punctuated' (Guyer 2006) by dates of repayment and negotiation among Calon, by collection dates from *Brasileiros* and so on. Among Calon, debts never clear up totally, and when a man dies his obligations are forgotten, whereas *Gaje* debts as well as any money owed to the dead man by other Calon (but not other way around) are inherited by his sons. Money is 'generic', in Graeber's (1996: 6) terms, and through exchanges every Calon creates himself and his world (cf. Hart 2009). Multiple deals create the totality of a man's 'money on the street', which others try to assess. In the unstable Calon world, this totality-as-environment becomes a source of stability.

In more general terms, Calon 'society' is at least temporarily created through the existence of an audience that evaluates one's actions and whose opinion matters to one (Graeber 2001). Exchanges with *Brasileiros* and the gains they bring are encompassed by *vergonha*, and although Calon present their actions 'on the street' and their exchanges as a sort of male game freed of women (cf. Stewart 1997), most of the day-to-day 'work' of moral assessment – gossip and arguments – is done by women.

Equality and Hierarchy

Some men are better than others at being Gypsies and at gaining attributes associated with Gypsyness. Take the Gitanos of Madrid described by Paloma Gay y Blasco (1999), for whom the notion of respect (*respeto*) represents the central virtue that guides interactions between people. Although in general terms, men are on a higher plane of virtue, as it were, than women, and older men are similarly higher than younger men, some men are better at behaving according to this notion. This leads to hierarchy and power: 'it is the extent to which their behaviour approaches the ideal of the "man of respect" that determines the extent to which other people, within and outside their families, willingly submit to their influence' (ibid.: 158). In their daily lives, men attempt to behave and to be seen as behaving as 'men of respect', especially through displays of *conocimiento* (knowledge) and *formalidad* (decorum). According to Gay y Blasco, '[i]t is in so doing, and in managing to have their behaviour acknowledged along these lines, that they place themselves in hierarchical positions vis-à-vis others – and it should be remembered that, in the Gitano context, hierarchy generates inequality, that is, unequal access to the deference and obedience of others' (ibid.: 160). Men who have demonstrated consistency in their behaviour throughout their lives may become 'mediators' in their old age – arbiters embodying 'Gitano way of being' recognised across patrilines, which normally split Gitanos into so-called *razas* (ibid.: 161).

Calon of Bahia lack Gitanos' formalised segmentary organisation, formalised feuding (and its resolution), the institution of 'mediators' and, in fact, any concept akin to 'Gypsy law' (*ley Gitana*). Nevertheless, some men are more successful that others in gaining attributes and objects associated with Gypsyness, which in turn determines their ability to influence others. Terence Turner's analysis is useful for understanding the dynamic relationship between Calon insistence on men's equality and autonomy on the one hand, and continuous processes of hierarchisation on the other (e.g. Turner 1979, 2003, 2006, 2009).

Drawing on his fieldwork among the Kayapo, an indigenous Amazonian society of central Brazil, Turner argues that in non-commodity-producing societies, the production of social persons and kinship is the main locus of value relation, since this production encompasses the production of internal subsistence. The key to understanding political and social hierarchy, then, 'is to understand how forms of social value are produced in the process of producing social persons' (Turner 2003: 11). As a result of this social production, values – realised in objects and the attributes of persons associated with them – become unequally distributed, since 'surplus product *in forms of value* is appropriated from direct producers of social persons by indirect producers who control the essential means of this production' (ibid.: 12, original emphasis).

Among Calon, there is nothing comparable to the elaborated Kayapo cosmological and ceremonial system, complex communal institutions or the shared self-image of their society as a whole. Nevertheless, values associated with Calonness, which are considered integral aspects of social persons, are unequally distributed, because relations of production through which Calon produce themselves and their world enable the appropriation of surplus product by 'indirect producers who control the essential means' of production (ibid.). Among Calon, these relations of production rest on control over marriageable daughters, dowry money and even relations with *Brasileiros*. These are crucial for a Calon man to establish his spatio-temporal control and to gain the attributes of social person.

Put simply, a man's status is established on the basis of his capability to be attuned to his surroundings, which are viewed as unstable and potentially dangerous, and in this way to create his own environment. Institutions such as *Gaje* debts, weddings, dowries, feuding and mourning, which create alliances, mark out enemy spaces and show people's commitment to the ethics of *vergonha*, serve to navigate this uncertainty. Attributes of Calon social persons as objectifications of value depend on people's social identities and relationships, and are thus connected to individuals' life cycles.

Life Cycle and Recursive Hierarchisation

A dowry brought by a woman to her new household consists of two parts: the interior furnishings associated with her and her household, and the money given explicitly to the groom to 'make the future' 'on the street'. From that point on, a man's actions are evaluated on the basis of how he can 'bring meat' (that is, make money) for his household. Using the monetary part of the dowry, and with the help of his father, the newly married man intensifies his deals with Calon and *Brasileiros*. He aims to 'establish' (*estabelecer*) himself among *Brasileiros* by opening one-way monetary flows that 'bring meat', allowing him to host other Calon and to strike further deals. The meaning and truthfulness of his actions are constantly discussed by other Calon. Through monetary transactions a man makes a living, builds relationships with others, forges himself as a Calon man (*homem*) and, simultaneously, creates an environment for further evaluation.

Normally, in the early stages of a marriage, a couple lives alongside the groom's family, but they are free to move to other settlements. Throughout their lives, households change settlements frequently, with men building up and losing their *Gaje* clientele and their reputation among Calon along the way. Settlements emerge around strongmen, that is, around men who have a good position among non-Gypsies, are respected by other Calon in the area and live surrounded by their married sons and other relatives.

Associating with strongmen allows others to navigate their surroundings better – to 'make' their own futures and to profit from the strongman's name in the area or from his protection. But unlike the Gitanos of Madrid discussed by Gay y Blasco, Calon social organisation lacks objectified attributes of social persons (see also Ferrari 2011: 728–32). There is no concept akin to 'men of respect' that would code a man's position, no objects such as walking sticks that would serve as symbols of his authority, no *razas* that he would transcend by his very being (Gay y Blasco 1999: 135–37, 157–61; also Manrique, this volume). Therefore, besides a man's power to influence others on the basis of his unique personal history, Calon use money to expand their sphere of action. As Turner points out, the medium in which value is realised influences what people think value is (Graeber 2001: 78, 2009: 108). The use of money, then, is not without consequences: value is ephemeral, immanent and tied closely to one's person, because it is realised in performance through a generic but fungible medium that all Calon men constantly talk about: money.

Gaining control over one's surrounding through spatiotemporal acts requires continuous effort. Status takes (social) time to gain; put simply, no young unmarried man can become a strongman. Given the organisation of the social production of personhood among Calon of Bahia, values associated with masculinity are unequally distributed. As I show below, households are prerequisites for transformative acts to take place, but the essential means for creating new households (that is, brides, dowry money, relationships with important *Gaje*) are controlled by older men. Despite Calon emphasis on equality, it helps when a man has parents to arrange his wedding, a rich and strong father, and sons or brothers willing to stand up for him.

Hierarchy among Calon is an outcome of the production and distribution of social values and depends on an individual's life cycle. In an environment that is seen-cum-created as unstable, where people can lose attributes of both *vergonha* and *força*, hierarchy is 'recursive'. One's position depends on the constant evaluation of one's behaviour by others, and successive failures to behave accordingly take progressively longer to overcome. Thus, some Calon were unwilling to lend to the still-wealthy Calon I knew because they were convinced that he was going broke with unexpected expenditures. On a different occasion, people criticised a man for apparently being unwilling to spend money to get his son out of prison, accusing the old man of scheming too much and refusing not to treat money as a way to calculate alternatives. In other words, the relation between the two value templates – *vergonha* and *força* – is contested.

Values and Influence

David Graeber (1996) has suggested that there are two modalities of power: a power to act directly on others and a power to move others to action. The first is invisible, a hidden potential to act on the world in the future, while the second is visible, based on the histories of objects and persons, and therefore on acts performed in the past. Graeber construes these as pure forms, the extent and interrelationships of which vary between cultures.

Graeber's insights underlie much of my analysis here. I have argued that *vergonha*, which must be made to 'appear' and which embodies one's personal history and relationships, is a source of a 'specific' form of power. Eduardo, for instance, is deemed *descarado*, a quality also described as *sem-vergonha* (shameless). He is not a *chefe*, and others do not treat him as one, despite his objective wealth and his being at the centre of the settlement in Bomfim. Eduardo's case also points to the shift in the modality of influence – with the rise of moneylending, having and moving money has become the prime component of one's *força*. Money, which as Graeber shows is associated with a person's hidden, generic powers to act, invites hoarding and invisibility, a tendency that is challenged by others.

A pivot between the two sources of influence, an idiom of transformation of value form, is the sharing of food. Whenever a Calon visits another to strike a deal, before they get to business, the former is first repeatedly offered food to eat. A failure to offer food to one's visitors is considered shameless, and people complain about such behaviour to others. Besides being a way to influence other people's opinion of oneself, and thus of increasing the chances of striking a deal (Munn 1992), offering food is also a demonstration of concern for others and a confirmation of equality. People eat quickly, and nobody offers thanks, while the hostess downplays the meal she has prepared, saying, for instance, that 'the meal is no good' or that 'it's the only thing we have in the house'. The message is that this is not hosting, but something that Calon do. It is a baseline 'communism' that is not shared with *Gaje* but on which equality in 'exchange' between Calon is grounded (Graeber 2010). It is 'a demand, an imperative, not an invitation' (Tauber 2006: 127).

This basic schema extends to other relationships. Not eating is a tool for the contraction of social interaction – for instance, in mourning. Similarly, a man can refuse to eat at a home of a Calon who repeatedly fails to live up to expectations, a process that can ultimately lead to 'not speaking with each other' (*não se falar*) (cf. ibid.: 131). The debtor is said to 'eat' the creditor's money, denying the creditor's agency and blocking his capability to 'make a future' (*fazer futuro*) – to 'bring meat' home, give food to visitors or to engage in other transformative acts.

One's tent or house, as a nexus of marital relationship and a place into which food is brought and from which it is offered, as well as its size, cleanliness, location and position vis-à-vis other tents or houses, 'semiotically embodies the series of transformations in personal identity and family structure that constitutes the process of production of the person and family' (Turner 2006). The creation of new households is indexical: through this act the increment in people's values becomes objectified. The household is the major component of a production process whose ultimate product is a social person: women and men begin to be judged more systematically in relation to *vergonha* after they get married; with the household in mind and the dowry money in hand, a man is expected to intensify his exchanges 'on the street', to demonstrate acumen and to increase his control over the environment through various transformative acts. The household of a strongman, as an objectification of his status, is the biggest and most central in any settlement. The space in front of it becomes a sort of central plaza of the settlement that visitors cannot avoid, and where values – objectified in loans and discussion of people's *vergonha* or valour – circulate. The end of the household is accompanied by a de-objectification of these personal attributes (cf. Turner 2006): on a man's death, his tent and furnishings are destroyed or sold, and the surrounding settlement, the objectification of the unique assemblage of relationships that the man co-created, is abandoned. The value attached to the social person gained through the man's transformative acts is not inherited by his sons; only the money, 'a frictionless surface to history' (Graeber 1996: 6), is (see also Robbins and Akin 1999: 18–19).

But this is hardly a stable order. Although ideally united in the attributes of strongmen, the value templates of *vergonha* and *força* may pull in diverse, even contradictory, directions. Take Beiju, for instance, who had been arrested for the illegal possession of firearms. One evening shortly after his release, he told a group of male relatives that he used to have R$15,000 'on the street' prior to his arrest, but that he spent R$10,000 on bail. Of the remaining money, Beiju explained, 'two thousand is not mine, it is Hugo's [a Calon living in a settlement nearby]'. The men present could envision the dent in the totality of Beiju's 'money on the street', and were aware that his options were limited; they realised that Beiju, a feared and bold man, was 'dead' and incapable of creating further movement. But nobody doubted Beiju's *vergonha*, or that he would actually pay Hugo. The huge dent in the totality of his 'money on the street' showed

Beiju to be something of 'an honourable loser'. On the opposite pole, there are 'shameless rich men' accused of behaviour akin to Eduardo's, who deny having money despite the hardships of their relatives (see also San Román 1975: 193).

Refusing to Become a *Chefe*

Eduardo repeatedly refused to use his skills and wealth to become a *chefe*. He kept his distance from others and was too sly to let them know much about his deals. The only exception during the six years I have known him was when, after he had fled Santaluz, he had to rely on his family due to concerns for his personal safety. He bought a plot in São Gabriel and invited some of his relatives to join him; they agreed, because, among other reasons, their own settlement had fallen apart after its strongman had died.

Returning to the story with which I began: When I visited Eduardo and his relatives one weekend while they were living in Bomfim, Kiko described his father as *descarado*, and complained that although he had stood up for him recently in a serious conflict, his father 'never helped him anymore' and 'never even bought nappies or milk for his grandson [Kiko's son]'. 'He [Eduardo] also sees that his relatives do not have money, but he does not lend them any', Kiko continued.

Several people lacked money. There was an argument between a blind father and his married son, whose tents were behind the fence encircling Eduardo's plot, after the son had sold the father's gas canister in order to buy groceries. It also seemed that Eduardo's brother, Renato, would not have enough money to buy food that weekend, but Eduardo had refused to lend him R$100, claiming he did not have anything to spare. They left it at that.

This angered Kiko. 'Yesterday I brought him 2,000 [reais] from Muritiba', he pointed out to me. Nevertheless, he did not tell his uncle Renato about this money – men keep out of the deals of others, and, moreover, Eduardo was his father; rather, more privately, he complained to me about his father being *descarado*. But Kiko avoided telling Renato where he himself had got groceries on credit, although he let everybody know that he had managed to do so. Like most men, Kiko was proud of his relationship with *Brasileiros*, and he did not want his gambling uncle to misuse his name and thus harm his position.

While we were eating lunch in Kiko's tent, Renato hung around purposelessly nearby. 'He is walking inside and out of his tent hungry', commented Kiko's wife, and they called him to join. Renato ate quickly and pushed his plate aside abruptly, as if he was doing Kiko and his wife a favour, had to force himself to eat and was slightly disgusted by the food. 'That's enough', he exclaimed, and stood up and left.

Over the days to come, Kiko repeatedly related his grudges about his father to relatives who visited Bomfim. He was planning to leave his father's settlement and return to Muritiba, where, during the year that he had lived there, he had built up a stable clientele. In contrast, his move to his father's plot in Bomfim proved to be a bad one: he had gained less than he had anticipated, while his relationship with his father had deteriorated. It was also clear that Eduardo was unwilling to adopt the role expected of him and to act as 'a *chefe* of everybody here'. In fact, Eduardo was planning to move elsewhere and to leave his relatives behind.

Conclusions

Reflecting on her fieldwork among Gitanos in Saragosa in the 1970s, Miriam Kaprow recalls, 'I could not locate anything among the Gypsies I had come to study resembling a genuine group' and could not pinpoint 'a whole culture with its internally coherent systems of religion and symbols' (Kaprow 1992: 218). The social organisation of Calon presents similar challenges. Calon lack, and constantly undermine the emergence of, the fixed social forms that anthropologists have normally analysed as kinds of hypostatised mechanisms of social reproduction. Taking my cue from an anthropological theory of value, rather than exploring social forms, I have discussed the process of generation that lends stability and resilience to Calon social life over time. I have argued that Calon are busy producing exchanges, and in the process they produce themselves: they gain attributes of social persons relating to values of *vergonha* (shame or honour) and of *força* (strength or a capability to manage an unstable environment). Through these acts people also construct specific dimensions of their world – their relationships with *Brasileiros* and especially with other Calon. One's social status is unstable, and hierarchy, as objectified spatially in a settlement's composition, is temporary. Indeed, none of the settlements I lived in exist anymore.

By reinterpreting the specific content of their key values, Calon are able, more or less successfully, to assimilate and refract broader socio-economic changes while remaining Calon. To postulate the existence of such socio-cosmological continuity, however, does not mean that the refraction of any particular historical situation does not cause changes in the 'characteristics of a community' (Williams 1982: 340; cf. Gordon 2006). These changes include, but are not restricted to, the importance of constant assessment of men's 'money on the street', the shrinking of settlements, and the tendency of rich moneylenders to live in houses cut off from others and often hidden behind walls. The decline of the importance of strongmen for social organisation is related to, among other things, the increased presence of the state, the collapse of ambulant trade in animals and, in particular, changed modes of moneymaking in the wake of the financialisation of daily life in Bahia (such as the possibility of making money individually through moneylending, of withholding clients' bank cards, which diminishes risks, or of 'hiding' money from the gaze of others in banks).

While people continue to be committed to the same set of values as in the past, the growing importance of money, of financial institutions and of formalised flows of money for a Calon man's capacity to act have altered the content of *força*, a process accompanied by a shift in the meaning of *vergonha* (cf. Graeber 1996: 7). For instance, from my experience, rich Calon families, whose women no longer read palms on the street and have limited interactions with *Brasileiros*, are more explicit about demonstrating the modesty of women than families living in tent settlements, for whom *vergonha* is made 'apparent' in quotidian relationships (Ferrari 2010). Rich men's greater containment of women within houses and their concern over their wives' and daughters' sexuality allows these men to appropriate the social value of *vergonha* realised by women, and thereby to demonstrate their commitment to 'Calonness'. Although describing these dynamics would require a separate study, it confirms both Turner's and Graeber's observation that 'the most important political struggles in any society will always be over how value itself is to be defined' (Graeber 2001: 115). It is no wonder, then, that Eduardo's relatives sometimes blamed Eduardo's wife for his shamelessness.

Acknowledgements

I would like to thank those Calon of the Bahian coast who let me into their lives. I thank Manuela Ivone Cunha, Florencia Ferrari, David Graeber, Iulia Hasdeu and Mario Schmidt for their reading and helpful comments. The research for this work was funded by an EU Marie Curie Ph.D. fellowship and a Wenner-Gren Dissertation Fieldwork Grant.

NOTES

1. Calon refer to non-Gypsies as *Gajons, Gaje, Juróns* or *Brasileiros*.
2. The Brazilian currency is the reais (R$). At the time of my fieldwork, €1 was worth about R$3.

REFERENCES

Fajans, J. 1983. 'Shame, Social Action, and the Person among the Baining', *Ethos* 11(3): 166–80.
——. 1993. Introduction, in J. Fajans (ed.), *Exchanging Products: Producing Exchange*. Sydney: University of Sydney, pp.1–13.
Ferrari, F. 2010. 'O mundo passa. Uma etnografia dos Calon e suas relações com os brasileiros', Ph.D. diss. São Paulo: Universidade de São Paulo.
——. 2011. 'Figura e fundo no pensamento Cigano contra o estado', *Revista de Antropologia* 54(2): 715–45.
Fotta, M. 2012. 'The Bankers of the Backlands: Financialisation and the Calon-Gypsies in Bahia', Ph.D. diss. London: Goldsmiths College, University of London.
——. n.d. 'Settlements and Violence Among Calon Gypsies in Bahia, Brazil: Clastrian Reflections'. Unpublished manuscript.
Gay y Blasco, P. 1999. *Gypsies in Madrid: Sex, Gender and the Performance of Identity*. Oxford: Berg Publishers.
——. 2004. 'Love, Suffering and Grief among Spanish Gitanos', in K. Milton and M. Svašek (eds), *Mixed Emotions: Anthropological Studies of Feeling*. Oxford: Berg, pp.163–78.
Gordon, C. 2006. *Economia selvagem. Ritual e mercadoria entre os índios Xikrin-Mebêngôkre*. São Paulo: Editora Universidade Estadual Paulista.
Graeber, D. 1996. 'Beads and Money: Notes toward a Theory of Wealth and Power', *American Ethnologist* 23(1): 4–24.
——. 2001. *Toward An Anthropological Theory of Value: The False Coin of Our Own Dreams*. New York: Palgrave Macmillan.
——. 2009. 'Debt, Violence, and Impersonal Markets: Polanyian Meditations', in C. Hann and K. Hart (eds), *Market and Society: The Great Transformation Today*. Cambridge: Cambridge University Press, pp.106–32.
——. 2010. 'On the Moral Grounds of Economic Relations: A Maussian Approach'. Open Anthropology Press, Working Papers Series No. 6. Retrieved 10 October 2012 from: http://openanthcoop.net/press/2010/11/17/on-the-moral-grounds-of-economic-relations/.
Guyer, J.I. 2006. 'Prophecy and the Near Future: Thoughts on Macroeconomic, Evangelical and Punctuated Time', *American Ethnologist* 34(3): 409–21.
Hart, K. 2009. 'The Persuasive Power of Money', in S. Gudeman (ed.), *Economic Persuasions*. New York: Berghahn Books, pp.136–58.
Holbraad, M. 2005. 'Expending Multiplicity: Money in Cuban Ifá Cults', *Journal of the Royal Anthropological Institute* 11(2): 231–54.
Kaprow, M.L. 1992. 'Celebrating Impermanence: Gypsies in a Spanish City', in P.R. DeVita (ed.), *The Naked Anthropologist: Tales from Around the World*. Belmont, CA: Wadsworth Publishing, pp.218–31.

McCallum, C. 2003. *Gender and Sociality in Amazonia: How Real People Are Made.* Oxford: Berg Publishers.

Muldrew, C. 1998. *The Economy of Obligation: The Culture of Credit and Social Relations in Early Modern England.* London: Macmillan.

Munn, N.D. 1977. 'The Spatiotemporal Transformation of Gawan Canoes', *Journal de la société des océanistes* 33(54/55): 39–53.

———. 1992. *The Fame of Gawa: A Symbolic Study of Value of Transformation in a Massim Society.* Durham, NC: Duke University Press.

Robbins, J., and D. Akin. 1999. 'An Introduction to Melanesian Currencies: Agency, Identity, and Social Reproduction', in D. Akin and J. Robbins (eds), *Money and Modernity: State and Local Currencies in Melanesia.* Pittsburgh, PA: University of Pittsburgh Press, pp.1–40.

San Román, T. 1975. 'Kinship, Marriage, Law and Leadership in Two Urban Gypsy Settlements in Spain', in F. Rehfish (ed.), *Gypsies, Tinkers and Other Travellers.* London: Academic Press, pp.169–99.

Stewart, M. 1997. *The Time of the Gypsies.* Boulder, CO: Westview Press.

Tauber, E. 2006. *Du Wirst keinen Ehemann Nehmen! Respekt, die Bedeutung der Toten und Fluchtheirat bei den Sinti Estraixaria.* Münster: LIT Verlag.

Turner, T. 1979. 'Anthropology and the Politics of Indigenous People's Struggles', *Cambridge Anthropology* 5(1): 1–43.

———. 2003. 'The Beautiful and the Common: Inequalities of Value and Revolving Hierarchy among the Kayapo', *Tipití: Journal of the Society for the Anthropology of Lowland South America* 1(1): 11–26.

———. 2006. 'Kayapo Values: An Application of Marxian Value Theory to a Non-commodity Based System of Production'. Unpublished manuscript.

———. 2009. 'Valuables, Value, and Commodities among the Kayapo of Southern Amazonia', in F. Santos-Granero (ed.), *The Occult Life of Things: Native Amazonian Theories of Materiality and Personhood.* Tucson: University of Arizona Press, pp.152–69.

Williams, P. 1982. 'The Invisibility of the Kalderash of Paris: Some Aspects of the Economic Activity and Settlement Patterns of the Kalderash Rom of the Paris Suburbs', *Urban Anthropology* 11(3/4): 315–46.

Martin Fotta received his Ph.D. from Goldsmiths, University of London, and has held a post-doctoral fellowship at the Research Training Group 'Value and Equivalence', Goethe University, Frankfurt/Main. He is currently Lecturer in Social Anthropology at the University of Kent, and his research focuses on moneylending practices of Calon Gypsies of Bahia, Brazil.

Chapter 11

 'Give and Don't Keep Anything!'
Wealth, Hierarchy and Identity among the
Gypsies of Two Small Towns in Andalusia, Spain

NATHALIE MANRIQUE

> Anthropology is about developing theories concerning the human species. The only kinds of theories we can have are ultimately about the human species in general. Ethnography is a different business. It's about getting to know certain people in certain places, getting to know what makes them tick and their own way of thinking. So these are really very, very different enterprises ... It's in the tradition of anthropology to try to combine these two different enterprises. I think there has been a point in trying to combine them, but it's always difficult because one is talking in general and scientific terms when doing anthropology and one is doing interpretation when doing ethnography, i.e. trying to situate people in the contexts in which they live, trying to get at what makes them act in the way they do.
> – Maurice Bloch, 'An Extraordinary Fact'

The towns of Morote, with 9,000 inhabitants, of whom approximately 800 are Gypsies, and San Juan, with nearly 4,600 inhabitants, including almost 450 Gypsies, are located in the south of Spain, near Granada. In the past, Gypsies from these two small towns mainly practised trades connected with horses, donkeys and mules. Today, this particular population, like the majority of Spanish Gypsies (Gitanos), is sedentary (Leblon 1985), although their main economic activity as farm labourers obliges them to travel frequently. When they are at home, they supplement their income by selling handmade wicker baskets, either door to door or through orders placed by non-Gypsy neighbours.

Gitanos have never fitted easily into the strongly hierarchical nature of Spanish society. Here, as elsewhere in Europe, the once dominant ideology primarily based social hierarchy on territorial ties, status inherited by descent and the accumulation of wealth.[1] Spanish Gypsy identity is constructed from opposite qualities: mobility and, most importantly, the refusal to accumulate goods, or to transmit the symbols of power and wealth. Indeed, they even practise the destruction of a person's material and symbolic goods in the case of their death. All these practices entail the destruction or transfer of goods. The latter implies donors and receivers of the goods in question, and for the Gypsies of Morote and San Juan, it classifies and hierarchically differentiates people and groups according to the presupposed superiority of donors. This process[2] also classes individuals or groups in the world by means of inherited categories – non-humans, human beings, Gitanos, *Payos*, men, women and so on – which are hierarchically related depending on the supposed intensity and direction of relations between groups and individuals.[3] I shall use here the term 'gift' to denote this movement of goods, as this transfer does not imply a counter-transfer, and furthermore it is not conceivable in that context.[4] Within each inherited category, equality is supposed to reign – donors can become receivers and vice versa. Here, we can refer to counter-transfers as 'sharing gifts', even if they are not desired by the potential receiver because the status of receipt implies a position of inferiority. Precisely because of this, such counter-transfers are a part of the internal dynamics of exchange or reciprocity inside a category.

The burial practices of the Gitanos of these two small towns, through their destruction and forgetting of a deceased person's material and symbolic goods, highlight the lack of inherited wealth and status, and favour an ideal of equality: among Gitanos, goods are not intended to be accumulated, but are rather a tool for people to perform their capacity to give, and in this way to achieve a higher status level.

'Natural' Classifications

According to Robert Hertz, '[e]very social hierarchy claims to be founded on the nature of things, φύσει, οὐ νόμῳ it thus accords itself eternity, it escapes change and the attacks of innovators' (Hertz 2013 [1973]: 335). For the Gypsies of Morote and San Juan, certain categories are thought to be 'natural' and permanent because they distinguish individuals and groups according to criteria acquired by birth. These innate characteristics legitimise and are legitimised by the process of gift giving, or, as Gypsies say in Spanish, *ser generoso* (to be generous). In Gypsy cosmology, groups and individuals are ranked according to a mechanism that, in some respects, is very similar to the general process of gift giving developed by Mauss, in which the donor is superior to the recipient when the latter is not in a position, for socio-economic or ideological reasons, to give back what they have received: 'The unreciprocated gift still makes the person who has accepted it inferior, particularly when it has been accepted with no thought of returning it' (Mauss 1925: 160). In sum, the act by which a person gives a symbolic or material good to another puts the former automatically in a higher position. Thus, everyone feels obliged to give back. Indeed, another gift made to the original donor rebalances the situation. This is what Mauss (ibid.) refers to as a 'counter-gift', and Lévi-Strauss (1949) describes with the notion of 'balanced reciprocity'.

This obligation to give back, which is fundamental to Mauss's theory, does not apply to exchanges between persons of different categories within the Gitano 'natural' classification of beings, since this classification is supposed to be permanent and sealed, and no change of its hierarchical order is theoretically possible.[5] This classification is first based on the generosity (that is, the inclination to give and not to receive) that everyone is expected to possess, albeit to differing degrees. In this way, human beings are held to be superior to animals, men to women, and so on. Their status is based on the intensity of the presupposed propensity of each to give: in Gitano terms, to be 'generous'. Indeed, Gitanos actually highly value the generosity that distinguishes groups and individuals from each other.[6]

In this manner, for Gitanos, social organisation appears to be structured according to what I call 'super-categories' and 'categories' that link each individual in a 'natural' way – that is, anyone can be classified in terms of a particular super-category or category in terms of 'nature', which is to say by birth or through the passage of time.[7] Super-categories are logical reconstructions from my own data gathered during my fieldwork; although they were not used explicitly by the Gypsies of these two small towns, I noticed in their speech and habits that they make distinctions between them. For example, according to them, Gypsies from other areas are 'all savages', as they are all supposed to be drug addicts and thieves, or '*Payo*-like' (*apayaos*), that is, Gitanos who are adopting a common non-Gypsy lifestyle. So, since to the local Gypsies they are 'not like us', the former do not have any relations with the latter. Categories are functional entities, and their borders are created through the circulation of goods.[8] Exchanges take place regularly within these categories and with local Gypsies from other categories, but the latter movements of goods are often completely denied (generally by higher classified people) in their speech. This can be taken to indicate precisely the limits and rank of each category (see Figure 11.1).

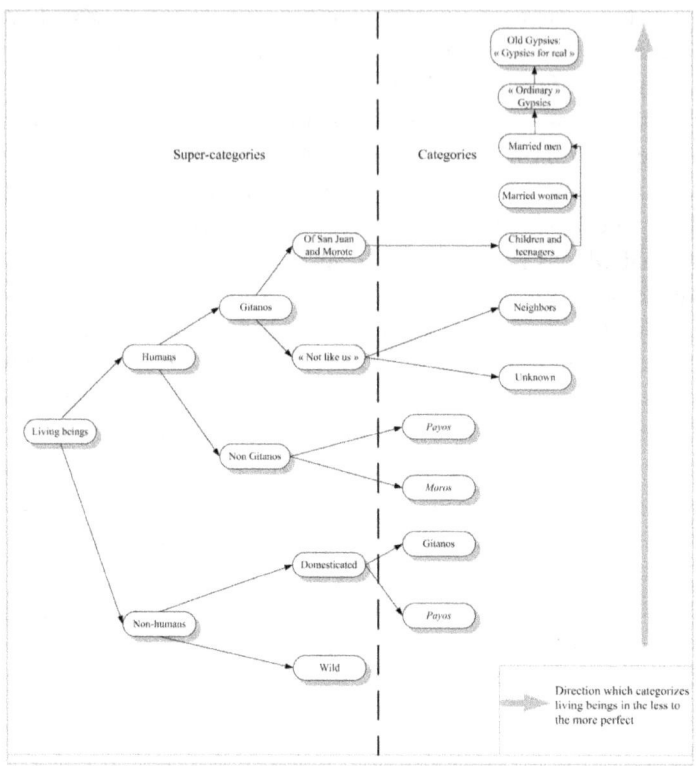

Figure 11.1: Inherited classification.

For Gypsies, the less inclusive categories more closely approach the Gypsy ideal; the image is rather like that of filtration or distillation. At the most 'refined' level, almost divine, is the identity of the Gitano. This Gypsy 'quintessence', the 'real' Gitanos (in some sense the 'purest'), is best reflected for them in the paramount category of the gift, that is, the category inhabited by donors par excellence, which subordinates all the others without integrating them; it is constituted by older gypsy men of the community. These men are, in sum, the 'real' Gypsies – Gypsies say that they are the 'Gypsies for real' (*Gitanos de verdad*), those who are Gypsies both by 'nature' (by birth, filiation and age criteria) and by their valorising attitude – that is to say, those who more closely approximate the ideal Gypsy. Indeed, Gypsy identity is quantified according to this presupposed propensity of each to give: the more generous you are, from the Gypsy point of view, the more you are 'Gypsies for real' – in fact, the closer you are to an accomplished human being, and the further you are from wildness (see Figure 11.1).

I realised this quantifiable character of Gypsyness during a conversation with Antonio, a Gypsy of around forty years of age and father of seven young children. One day I told him to enlist with the local Gypsy association in order to receive food aid from the Red Cross. Suddenly, he looked offended and said, 'I am myself *enough* Gypsy not to have to ask for help from another [meaning from another Gypsy, referring to the much-discredited president of the association]'. Apparently, to accept such assistance might cut into or reduce his identity, that is, the degree of Gypsyness that he has based on his age, sex, community belonging and so on.

It seems that only men have the capacity to achieve this highest status: with maturity, they are supposed to have demonstrated their generosity and become, in some ways, perennial donors. In fact, this generosity is essentially based on marriage alliances, which, for Gypsies of Morote and San Juan, is the most important starting point of several ties that will activate the circulation of goods between peers. Thus, it legitimises the status of old men, as every man of a certain age is supposed to have married off several of his children, and therefore to have actively participated in a series of gifts – mainly by procreation (Manrique 2013), but also by hosting marriage banquets, the sumptuousness of which is often a matter of discussions long afterwards. Actually, old men personify a higher value level of 'Gypsyness' and are those that best represent the ideal status inside the Gypsy community. Thus, they are the ones who can wear the widely respected hat or cap, sport a moustache and carry a stick (*vara* or *garrote*) without risk of being the target of ridicule. I remember the case of Manuel, a stocky man in his early forties, who endured much criticism as president of the local Gypsy association already mentioned. One day, he appeared with the hat, moustache and stick generally reserved for older Gypsy men. After being subjected to an incredible amount of jeering and mockery,[9] he quickly removed all such marks of prestige.

In order to be an 'absolute donor' – which, as we have seen, depends on one's way of living, filiation, age and sex – others should be, 'by nature', one's perpetual recipients. This is the case, for example, with the *Payos* or *Castellanos* (non-Gypsies who are thought by Gypsies, whatever the circumstances, to be the object of their actions). José tells me that the ancients told that the first Gypsies arose from the excrement of a horse, ejected when God administered a kick to the horse while it simultaneously broke wind.[10] On the other hand, *Castellanos* are descended from a raisin. 'We are of different castes' (*Somos de castas diferentes*), he concludes.[11] In this story, the colourful imagery alludes to the respective economic activities that Gypsies and *Payos* are expected to exercise. The latter are visibly placed on the side of agriculture and sedentarism: those who receive their goods from the land that they exploit, and who can also accumulate them. Meanwhile, the Gypsies are here associated with occupations related to horses and nomadism, and so they cannot easily accumulate wealth.[12]

Working on Social Relations

For Gypsies, in contrast to *Payos*, subsistence activities do not emphasise the transformation of nature through labour (or 'production') but rather the control of social relations, especially in exchanges. In fact, to be vigorously active is highly valued by these Gypsies. This is expressed in by the Castilian word *trabajo* (work) and its verbal form *trabajar*, but also by the verb *hacer* (to do), accompanied by a qualifier or a periphrasis that emphatically underlines the effort involved. It relates generally to all forms of activity that are difficult to accomplish, whether due to complexity, physical strength or endurance. I recall a conversation between neighbours, when Rubén, a small eleven-year-old boy who wished to present a positive image of his maternal grandfather, insisted on his grandfather's incredible capacity for work in spite of having had one of his legs amputated.

This understanding of agency is also consistent with Gitano representations of procreation, which is thought to be carried out by men's effort who 'plant the seed in women's bodies', and so is seen primarily as a gift of sperm (whether the intention is to procreate or not).[13] Sexual intercourse is imagined as a succession of 'blows' a man makes in the vagina. This act is seen as work done on a woman's body, which the man progressively modifies in the process. Since as genitors men are seen as transmitting their identity to their children, the 'blows' also result in the increasing control of men over their offspring's identity, or, in fact, of their offspring's appearance (see Manrique 2004).[14]

In Morote and San Juan, Gypsy marriages are practised by abduction, and, unlike the case with most other Spanish Gypsies, do not involve ritual defloration by a professional Gypsy woman. Here, Gypsies of Morote and San Juan differ from other Gypsies in Spain who practise the ceremony of the *pañuelo* (handkerchief) to verify the virginity of the young woman.[15] Through abduction of a bride, what becomes highlighted is not only the fortitude and courage of the young man, but above all his knowledge of the network. This demonstrates his competence to control social ties, in this instance his good knowledge of those linked to the morality of the young woman who, to be abducted, must ideally be a virgin. In fact, young men should make inquiries within their network (usually involving their relatives) about a particular girl they like. Sometimes men take young girls that 'are already open'. But as Lucas said, 'the one who takes a girl who is not anymore a virgin cannot complain because he already knows that'. So, understandably, despite the jeers, it is difficult for him to complain about what might demonstrate his lack of knowledge of local networks.

Women are aware of categorisations based on the intrinsic link between work (hard activity) and social control. In Morote and San Juan, they make a point of demonstrating their ability to work. Thus, Alicia, an eighteen-year-old girl, fulminated one day against her friend Piedad, who was disconcerted. It turned out that Piedad's brother, a Gypsy from Asturias (in the north of Spain), had written a letter to Alicia in which he declared his passion for her and described how he wanted to find a well-paid job in order to prevent her from working. 'Who does he think he is?' she protested. 'I want to work. I will not remain idle while he's working'.

This perception of female activity is obviously not shared by all Spanish Gypsies. In San Juan and Morote, women are required to demonstrate their ability to work by their dynamism and by doing the most arduous tasks without wincing (no matter what they achieve),[16] while men are often defined by their active character and are not required to justify what they are, a situation similar to that described by Lagunas Arias (2000a) for Gypsies from Catalonia, except in cases of disability (see below).

Gypsy relations with *Castellanos* are also intricate in the context of this 'natural' classification. The latter are by birth 'receivers' with respect to Gypsies,[17] despite their economic capital often being greater than that of the Gypsies.[18] Indeed, the *Payos* are spontaneously ranked among those who are acted upon (that is, they are classified as passive beings). By not giving, and by seeking to maximise their assets through hoarding, they seem to endorse the Gypsies' perception of the position of receivers.

Generosity, which implies the distribution of goods, the spending of time or the performing of work for the benefit of Gypsy individuals or groups, is highly valued,[19] and is used to underline the general 'low stature' of the *Payos*. Thus, as Caterina Pasqualino notes, 'the Gypsy ideal is to live in a world of truth where money is banished' (Pasqualino 1998: 32), where only generosity forges links between individuals. She adds: 'Paco, who returned home without paying for drinks for others, was considered a cheapskate. He was nicknamed *el Gaché*, an expression which, like *el Payo*, designates a non-Gypsy' (ibid.: 35). Similarly, Nancy Thède explains, 'One value underlies and guides Gypsy behaviour and puts them, in their own eyes, in a position of superiority over *Payos*, and that value is generosity' (Thède 2000: 177).[20]

The movement of goods, seen as generosity, is therefore the sign of full Gypsyness. But, what about situations where Gypsies gain something from members of lower categories? I will argue that, through an act I call 'catching' (in the sense that the giver is by definition not aware of the action, and therefore cannot approve of it before it occurs), Gypsies, who occupy superior categories, transmute their position as receivers into that of catchers, which, by its dynamic nature, appears to be equivalent to that of donors.

'Catching' Is Not Stealing

Payos are often in a better economic situation than Gypsies, but are nevertheless considered by Gypsies to be their 'recipients'. This negation of the Gypsy status of receiver is performed under the equity method which transmutes the 'naturally' passive nature of the act of receiving (the *Payo* position) into a voluntary and active act of 'catching'.[21] Then, through the immoderate valorisation of the Gypsy activity, itself contrasted with 'natural' non-Gypsy passivity, the subordinate position of receiver becomes, in the Gypsy social hierarchy, equivalent of that of donor, which also often implies strenuous activity or 'work'.

In sum, I argue that in the Gypsy mind, a Gypsy does not receive, they 'catch'. The positions of 'catchers' and donors are equivalent. Therefore, *Payos* cannot, under any circumstances, occupy donor positions with respect to Gypsies. While some (Gypsies) constantly renew their social morphology and ensure equality between (potential) peers, others (*Payos*) retain the prerogatives of their ancestors and strive to create and perpetuate status differences through the accumulation of wealth. Wealth is not desirable for Gypsies, because it may cause an imbalance of 'natural' statutes within each category. 'Natural' categories based on the concept of generosity legitimise this hierarchy, allowing Gypsies to act in a *Payo* world while maintaining their self-defined superiority and Gypsy integrity (see above). Gypsy superiority is therefore ensured, whatever relations they maintain with non-Gypsies and regardless of the interactive situations 'committed' with *Castellanos*.

'Catching' not only prevents Gypsies from being categorised as 'receivers' but is also for them a transformative act that puts relationships in their proper order: on a beautiful sunny afternoon, while I was walking alongside a field of sunflowers with Remedios, Elena, Dulce, Encarna and

María, five young Gypsy girls from Morote, Remedios suddenly rushed into the plantation, immediately followed by three other young women. Maria was amazed at my reluctance and told me they used to take only one sunflower each to sample the tasty seeds. Noting that I was still reluctant, she explained patiently that the owner of the sunflowers was very rich, that his plantation was huge, and it was normal to take some flowers, on the condition that the amount taken did not exceed what they considered equitable. She explained to me that in some way it was the duty of this man to supply these excessive quantities, too great for his own consumption. In fact, their 'catch' is somehow a way to avoid the storage of goods, and forces the owner of the plantation to be unwillingly generous too (Manrique 2013). By these remarks, it appears to me that Maria expressed the idea that the act of 'catching' was somehow a way of putting things in order. I felt that the young women laughed gently at my ignorance. Maria had also commented to me a few days earlier that she had strongly criticised Manuel because some people had caught him several times trying to steal significant quantities of almonds (too much for just his family) from a *Payo* farmer. She concluded with the following judgment: 'he's a thief'. For them, it is the *Castellanos* who are more usually the thieves, who, by not allowing the mobility of goods, and taking them instead for their own enrichment and empowerment, dispossess the Gypsies of their prerogative: to be able to move goods. In sum, according to Gypsy 'natural' classifications, Gypsies are superior to *Payos*. As we will now see, however, men are also considered superior to women.

Women Behind a Smokescreen

Gypsy women seem to have a role as significant as men in their community. Like their fathers, brothers, husbands and sons, they are farm labourers and contribute to the family economy; some old women are highly respected, and are guardians of the family's money and so on. In reality, women are excluded from any mechanical effect on the hierarchy which could allow them to capitalise on symbolic prestige within the Gypsy community. It is as if women, who might otherwise become men's competitors for high status inside the community, are excluded at birth from any socially significant transaction at the community level, such as passing of their nicknames onto their daughters and granddaughters and blood transmission (Manrique 2004, 2009), and the circulation of food and prestigious goods.[22] They can be donors, but for their peers only; they cannot disturb the hierarchy of men.

Performing Classifications

Within each category, equality is supposed to reign (see Figure 11.1). This is the result of the effect of the reciprocal gift, which is here conceivable but not obligatory. Everyone has the ability to accumulate social capital by demonstrating generosity: the highest status is in fact achieved through acts of giving material possessions.

But, since any act of giving places the recipient in a subordinate position, absolute equality between peers does not exist. It is transitory and performative: it depends on the direction of new gift transactions within the category. In this sense, nothing is gained; within each generation, everyone needs to raise some wealth (always with effort) in order to be able to redistribute it. Thus, not only are the concepts of work or energy highly valued in transactions, but more importantly, every man must increase his opportunities to give (and not to receive), which will allow him to expand his social capital, and so achieve higher status among his peers. In fact, to give away one's goods has the effect of rebalancing wealth transactions, and this is conducive to a temporary equality of status among peers.[23] According to Maurice Godelier:

> if the counter-gift does not erase the debt, it is because the given 'thing' was not completely separated, not completely detached from the one who gave it. The thing was given, without really being 'alienated' by the one who gave it. So the given thing carries with it something that is part of the person, of the identity of the one who gave it. (Godelier 1996: 61)

I suggest that if we interpret this concept of a 'given thing' as meaning a 'shared thing', we can better understand the difference between the movements of goods with or without the possibility of the counter-gift. In fact, outside any given 'natural' category, the 'given thing' moves in only one direction, from the top to the bottom, as it were. Therefore the debt cannot be repaid. Each individual or group should preserve their position with respect to the other. On the other hand, within each category, the giving of a gift becomes sharing: the 'given thing' can be modified by a counter-gift (see the case of Antonio mentioned above). Perhaps this is one of the reasons why Gypsy men of San Juan and Morote marry only by abducting their prospective brides (even if it is usually feigned): an abduction denies the unappreciated and compromising 'givenness' that is inherent in any gift, since marriage by abduction cannot be in any way interpreted as the receipt of a 'gift of a woman'. In reality, we can see it as a sort of *mise en scène* of the act of 'catching', that is, as a restatement of the status of giver of the young man and his family (postmarital residence, which is patri-virilocal, is consistent with this logic).

Rape – that is, when abduction takes place against the will of the young woman – is condemned, however. Denying the transient and reversible equality between peers, it excludes de facto the links of solidarity (alliance) between the families of the individuals involved, as neither has an opportunity to demonstrate their generosity. Thus, the reconciliatory banquet is denied. Having become predatory inside the community, the rapist's family is then barred from taking part in alliances and gift exchange. Indeed, the gift makes an identificatory relationship of one with the other. As in the saying 'birds of a feather flock together', it is considered that to be in a relationship with someone is to be like them. So, to have gift transactions with the rapist and his family – if the rapist has not been excluded, which means that they continue to have relations – is unwanted. Therefore, cases of real abductions become family traditions: they are the only way for male members of families of past rapists to find a spouse. Ostracised from other networks, which try to prevent real rape from happening inside them, they repeatedly perpetrate the same offence against their own very close allies – that is to say, within their kin networks: a son's wife, a niece, the sibling of a first spouse, and so on; in short, people who are already kin. By their excessive behaviour (gifts which take place after each marriage to create links of solidarity become superfluous in these cases, although they may occur), these individuals are pushed to the borders of the community, and therefore also of local Gypsy identity, which is based on memory exchanges between the various networks that compose it (see Manrique 2008, 2015). We can now examine what regulates gift movements.

Gift Control

Essentially, for the Gypsies of Morote and San Juan, the gift is the main way of controlling situations by initiating all interactions: to give is to start or renew relations.[24] In fact, there are several ways by which to avoid being indebted to the other (by becoming a 'receiver') while moving goods: by the circulation of money (such as buying and selling), and by theft or 'catching' (depending on the speaker's mind). However, the gift is the only way for the continual creation of new interactions or the update of old ones, which may lead to new more-or-less sustainable alliances, and so contribute to an individual's ability to manage the morphology of the networks in which they are embedded: those giving the gift – that is, those who initiate the social link – assign the position of receivers to their new recipients.

In the same way, the status of a 'catcher', which does not involve sharing anything, but only the initiation of an action, becomes thereby equivalent to that of the giver. Furthermore, as we have seen, 'catching' can be interpreted as a means to put things in order (according to Gypsies' perceptions of order).

We might wonder why one finds this constant quest for control. Indeed, as these people are a minority, the power they are able to gain can only be very restricted. To have power and/or authority in the larger society, it would be better for them to adopt the behavioural habits of other Spanish people (such as the transmission of wealth, social advancement through education, the pursuit of a political or religious career, and so on). But despite a policy of positive discrimination towards them throughout the Andalusia for many years, and even if other Spanish Gypsies have moved in this direction, the Gypsies of Morote and San Juan have not: in 1998, nearly all of the Gypsies of more than twenty years of age had left school before the age of sixteen, and almost all of those over forty were illiterate.

It may seem that Gypsies seek to control everything in order to avoid losing their Gypsyness (in other words, to be as perfect and far from animality as possible), but there is one thing they can never overcome: death. How, then, do they cope with this unsolvable problem?

The Death of the Gift

Not to accumulate wealth becomes most apparent in the case of an individual's death. After the death of a Gypsy of San Juan or Morote, transmission of his goods is unthinkable.[25] In fact, it appears that when somebody dies, the mechanics of gift relations are believed to be able to cause the death of close consanguines or affines of the deceased. Indeed, when a death is about to occur, great agitation shakes the whole community: all Gypsies who have (had) links of kinship, marriage, trade and so on with the dying person rush sometimes from several hundred kilometres away in order to 'demonstrate their respect for the dying' and, in my words, to undo any engagement they had with the deceased before death.

Actually, everything possible is done to break all links (in whatever form) with the deceased and to deprive them of any function in gift exchange networks (this is true especially when the deceased was an important man). To confirm this break with the society of the living (the dead individual, it is believed, may remain among the living or come back from the world of the dead), goods associated with the deceased cannot be kept, and are burned or buried and officially 'forgotten', including their personal belongings (such as their clothes, knife, stick, motorcycle), and their home furnishings are burnt if their home is a cave (*cueva*).[26] In this way, the hierarchy that oversees the entire Gypsy social organisation, that is, the classification into 'natural' categories, as well as equality between peers established at birth, is maintained: categories and individuals of low status cannot accumulate assets acquired by previous generations. Thus, Gypsies' statutes, which are not conveyed by the notion of inheritance of wealth but only by gifts (whether material or symbolic goods), are not transmissible.

In short, the Gypsies of San Juan and Morote distinguish living beings according to the principle of gift giving, in which some are integrated in the mechanism of sharing (with dues and duties to give) while others are outside community rules. This dynamics in reality concerns only humans as animals and plants cannot be donors (see Manrique 2008: 151). The further a category is from the top one, the more differentiated it is from the wholeness of mankind. To be rich is then like a symptom of 'wildness', which is the opposite of 'ideal Gypsyness', because it reveals one's disinclination to give and one's preference for the accumulation of wealth. So, even if the death is always felt as a terribly dramatic event, it is in a sense the chance for the community to move or destroy all those goods that have been accumulated by an individual during his life. In the Gypsy perception of social links, death represents the perspective of anomie – that is to say, the loss of control of the social field of the living (the dead can do what they want; for example, they may come back) and so of their Gypsy identity. In these circumstances, it is better to sever all connections with the dead.

Acknowledgements

I am endebted to Martin Fotta, Micol Brazzabeni and Manuela Ivone Cunha, whose many comments and suggestions allowed me to deepen and improve several aspects of this chapter.

NOTES

1. Several historical and anthropological studies of Europe highlight the close link between identity and heritage through matrimonial practices (e.g. Bourdieu 1980; Zonabend 1980; Segalen 1985; Bestard Camps 1986).
2. In this chapter, I try to reveal the model by which the Gypsies of Morote and of San Juan, with whom I spent almost two years between 1996 and 1998, and then four months in 2000, perform their identity, and by means of which speeches and observed behaviour are made meaningful by the anthropologist in more abstract terms. I postulate that this model (generosity/gift) is and must be continually redefined, and in that the Gypsies of Morote and San Juan (and all Spanish Gitanos, for that matter) do not act every time according to this model. A person who consistently ignores this ideal is said to be *apayao* (those who have become closer to *Payos*), or, one who steps out of line occasionally, to lack respectability and, ultimately, Gypsyness. Regarding Herzfeld's arguments about nationalism (Herzfeld 2005), I propose that this adherence to an apparent static cultural ideal permits and encourages the subversion of norms which, *in fine*, legitimates and feed this ideal.
3. The term *Payos* means non-Gypsy in Caló, the Para-Romani of Spain. In Morote and San Juan, Gitanos (Spanish Gypsies) usually speak in Spanish. Only the older people use Caló, primarily using the words related to kinship and/or death.
4. I do not have space here to fully discuss anthropological discussions of the gift, which go back to Malinowski (1922) and Mauss (1925), including the compulsory or reciprocal nature of the gift (Godelier 1996; Graeber 2010; Testart 2013) and its role in the market economy (see Polanyi 2001; Graeber 2010). Actually, as no one covers all the representations of the Gypsy gift, I have not completely adopted any of these definitions, although analyses of relations of alterity in Amazonian anthropology seem relevant, in particular to the notion of predation (see e.g. McCallum 2003; Viveiros de Castro 2009; Descola 2011).
5. This is not completely true. Indeed, within each 'natural' category, some individuals, in some circumstances, can, due to their great generosity, be considered part of the category is immediately above. Thus, the categories are theoretically embedded together with an option for some individuals to be treated 'in the manner' of individuals in the immediately superior category. But this is related to only some particular contexts (people have to 'know' the person in question), and then may only be circumstantial (see Manrique 2015).
6. The valorisation of generosity often became explicit when individuals assessed the civilities of others when talking to me. Without being directly expressed, I detected a certain contempt towards those who had shown their asocial character towards the complete foreigner that I was at first in their community. Such behaviour was equated with savagery (*son unos salvajes*). By this behaviour, individuals in a certain sense dehumanise themselves. I later learned that the refusal of all or part of this generosity humanised me instead.
7. In Gitano parlance, 'it's natural' (*es natural*).

8. No goods shall be kept. This is also the case with money that is lent, sometimes even to *Payos*, in this case at high interest.
9. Young Gypsies from these two towns are accustomed to compose and sing (sometimes with a guitar) songs with words that glorify or sometimes criticise aspects of other people's behaviour, the latter to the delight of listeners, who guffaw and laugh uproariously. In fact, it is not really transgressive as the victims are those who have already been denigrated because of their family reputation (based on behaviour deemed unacceptable by one or more of their relatives) or their own past behaviour.
10. At first I thought that this story was a joke (Gypsies enjoy teasing foreigners, as I was initially for them, with fables recounted as historical facts), but several Gypsy men told me the same story. I later found that Courthiade (2004) says that very similar stories are told amongst Carpathian Roma groups. This story is, in Morote and San Juan, actually a reinterpretation of the act of procreation, with the male seed (seen as a fart) as the sole active contribution to the process (see Manrique 2004, 2009).
11. José expresses a distinction 'of nature' without referring to kinship. Other Spanish Gypsy groups commonly use the word *raza*, which refers to descent (see San Román 1976; Ardévol Piera 1986; Gay y Blasco 1999; Lagunas 2000a).
12. According to the parochial archives of Morote and San Juan, Gypsies of these two towns have traditionally exercised trades directly related to horses (equine grooming at cattle fairs, and horse trading). In this remote and mountainous region, where distances between towns and villages often exceed several tens of kilometres of roads, frequently with steep and very rough passages, the movement of people, goods and agricultural equipment was usually done with beasts of burden. Moreover, historically, the local economy depended mainly on agricultural work. The transaction in such beasts was therefore of paramount importance: it allowed local farmers to work their land, to transport agricultural commodities, to move more easily and so on. Having no land – in the past, different royal laws (*pragmaticas*) prevented Gypsies from owning land and exercising professions connected with it (see Sánchez Ortega 1977; Leblon 1985) – this activity allowed them to meet their needs and those of their families while creating an ongoing basis for trade networks involving the making of wicker objects useful in everyday peasant families and activities related to the trade in horses.
13. Malinowski (1922) and Mauss (1925) also suggest that sexual relations have to be considered as a type of gift, even if their perception of the gift (pure or not) are different. Indeed, unlike Malinowski, for Mauss, a 'pure gift' – 'that is, an offering for which nothing is given in return' (Malinowski 1922: 176) – cannot be invoked for sexual relations between a couple (Mauss 1925: 172). When a woman becomes pregnant, women say 'she has her belly full' (*tiene la panza llena*), but this expression is also used to refer to a woman who has just had sexual intercourse (see Manrique 2004).
14. Men consider themselves to have an active influence on the physical appearance of their offspring. Indeed, according to them, the greater the intensity of

the 'blows' (*golpes*) a man makes in the vagina, the greater the extent to which the child will resemble him. See Manrique (2009, 2015).

15. For the Gitanos of Barcelona, see San Román (1976) and Lagunas Arias (2000a, 2000b); for those of Madrid, see Gay y Blasco (1997, 1999); for those of Jerez, see Pasqualino (1998); and for those of Granada, see Gamella (1996) and Manrique (2008).
16. People who demonstrate willingness and courage to face a difficult task can be variously excused when the task is not completed or incorrectly completed.
17. Even if Gypsies consider all *Payos* to be their receivers, the former control the level of generosity they actually offer to the latter. For instance, I remember that at the very beginning of my fieldwork, when I visited a Gypsy family, there was always a Gypsy woman or girl to ask me what they had offered to me to eat in someone else's home. After my answer, they usually gave their opinion, openly or more discreetly, of the generosity of my host. Moreover, this opinion then gave rise to more or less agitated conversations in the neighbourhood to evaluate the more or less good level of generosity shown towards me. After a time, one of my hosts commented to me on how this or that person was ungenerous to me and, on the other hand, shared her convictions about hospitality. She always concluded by ranking people, using statements such as 'she/he is a good person, she/he is generous' or 'she/he is not a good person at all', with a face showing her disapproval. Then she would say, 'better you never go to their house again, you know', or words to that effect, adding several comments about this person and their family to demonstrate to me that they were not good Gypsies.
18. In a more general context, the Roma (and not only Gitanos), are aware of this situation and take full advantage of their relationships with the non-Roma. This is what Piasere calls '*Gağikano* capital' (Piasere 1984: 139–46).
19. Among the Xoraxané located in Verona (Italy): 'the accumulation of goods exists only as a function of distribution. Though the forms are different (celebration of birth, of the first haircut, of marriage, daily offers of food and drink to friends, etc.) the aims of distribution are to increase the prestige of the head of the family and to preserve the subalterns' consensus' (Piasere 1987: 118 n.4).
20. In my case, a *Castellano* of Morote, quite amazed, explained to me how respected I was by the Gypsies of the town. He told me that one day, as I was walking in one the town's streets, he heard a Gypsy woman saying that I was a very respectable person because I had helped several Gypsies in the city, and above all that I was very generous to spend so much time helping them. I was very surprised because, with the exception of my Gypsy friends, I never felt that the Gypsies appreciated my work.
21. This analogy between acts of receiving and 'catching' by giving can be, I think, assimilated to the notion of gathering that Piasere (1987: 113) uses for Xoraxané activities in order to associate begging and taking (theft): to give and to gather are active rather than passive behaviour in situations of relationship.
22. Examples of the latter include horses, canaries and hunting game (especially hares): see Manrique (2008, 2015).

23. This concept of wealth appears to be widespread in the Gypsy world. Thus, a Romani proverb has it: 'If you have nothing, the Rom will give to you; if you have much, the Rom will take from you' (Courthiade and Méritxell 2006: 37).
24. We can here take the comparative example of Hungarian Rom, who buy and sell horses and trade with (non-Gypsy) peasants. According to Stewart: 'In this game (the market) ... it seems to me that it is in order to enjoy the pleasure of creating a deal, as much as for any remuneration, that Gypsies play the role of *cincár* (i.e., a middleman)', which makes him a 'true Gypsy' (Stewart 1992: 107, 108).
25. See Williams (1993) for a similar description among the Mānuš.
26. If it is not a cave, all the family move to another home without burning it. But only *Payos* would agree to live in it afterwards.

REFERENCES

Ardévol Piera, E. 1986. 'Vigencias y cambio en la cultura de los Gitanos', in T. San Román (ed.), *Entre la marginación y el racismo. Reflexiones sobre la vida de los Gitanos*. Madrid: Alianza Editorial, pp.61–108.

Bestard Camps, J. 1986. *Casa y familia. Parentesco y reproducción doméstica en Formentera*. Palma de Mallorca: Institut d'Estudis Baleàrics.

Bloch, M. 2013. 'An Extraordinary Fact', Anthropology of This Century. Retrieved 1 June 2013 from: aotcpress.com/articles/extraordinary-fact.

Bourdieu, P. 1980. 'Le capital social: notes provisoires', *Actes de la recherche en sciences sociales* 31(31): 2–3.

Courthiade, M. 2004. 'Kannau3 on the Ganges, Cradle of the Romani People', in D. Kenrick (ed.), *Gypsies: From the Ganges to the Thames*. Hertfordshire: University of Hertfordshire Press, pp.105–26.

Courthiade, M., and S. Meritxell. 2006. *Sagesse et humour du peuple rom. Proverbes bilingues romani–français*. Paris: L'Harmattan.

Descola, P. 2011 [2005]. *Par-delà nature et culture*. Paris: Editions Gallimard.

Gamella, J. 1996. *La población gitana en Andalucía. Un Estudio Exploratorio de sus condiciones de vida*. Seville: Consejería de Trabajo y Asuntos Sociales, Junta de Andalucía.

Gay y Blasco, P. 1997. 'A "Different Body"? Desire and Virginity among the Gitanos', *Journal of the Royal Anthropological Institute* 3(3): 517–35.

———. 1999. *Gypsies in Madrid: Sex, Gender and the Performance of Identity*. Oxford: Berg Publishers.

Godelier, M. 1996. *L'énigme du don*. Paris: Fayard.

Graeber, D. 2010. 'Les fondements moraux des relations économiques. Une approche maussienne', *Revue du MAUSS* 36(2): 51–70.

Hertz, R. 2013 [1973]. 'The Pre-eminence of the Right Hand. A Study in Religious Polarity' (Translated by Rodney and Claudia Needham, reprint), *HAU: Journal of Ethnographic Theory* 3(2): 335–57.

Herzfeld, M. 2005. *Cultural Intimacy: Social Poetics in the Nation-State*. New York: Routledge.

Lagunas Arias, D. 2000a. 'Dentro de "dentro". Estudio antropológico y social de una comunidad de gitanos catalanes', Ph.D. diss. Jaén: University of Jaén.

———. 2000b. 'Rethinking Gitano Kinship: The Calós of Catalonia', Europæa 6(1/2): 159–93.
Leblon, B. 1985. Les Gitans d'Espagne. Paris: Presses Universitaires de France.
Lévi-Strauss, C. 1949. Les structures élémentaires de la parenté. Paris: Presses Universitaires de France.
McCallum, C. 2003. Gender and Sociality in Amazonia: How Real People Are Made. Oxford: Berg Publishers.
Malinowski, B. 1922. Argonauts of the Western Pacific: An Account of Native Enterprise and Adventure in the Archipelagos of Melanesian New Guinea. London: Routledge.
Manrique, N. 2004. 'La lune pétrifiée. Représentations parthénogénétiques dans une communauté gitane (Grenade)', in F. Héritier and M. Xanthakou (eds), Corps et Affects. Paris: Odile Jacob, pp.205–20.
———. 2008. '"Sois généreux!" Du don comme principe structurant de l'organisation sociale des Gitans de deux petits bourgs andalous (Espagne)', Ph.D. diss. Paris: École des Hautes Études en Sciences Sociales.
———. 2009. 'Corpo-real Identities: Perspectives from a Gypsy Community', in J. Edwards and C. Salazar (eds), European Kinship in the Age of Biotechnology. Oxford: Berghahn Books, pp.97–111.
———. 2013. 'Vocabulaire de parenté gitan: une terminologie marquée par le don', L'Homme 205: 35–54.
———. 2015. 'Sois généreux!' Don et hiérarchie chez les Gitans de deux petits bourgs andalous (Espagne). Paris: Petra.
Mauss, M. 1925. 'Essai sur le don. Forme et raison de l'échange dans les sociétés archaïques', L'année sociologique 1: 30–186.
Pasqualino, C. 1998. Dire le chant. Les Gitans flamencos d'Andalousie. Paris: CNRS Éditions/Éditions de la Maison des Sciences de L'Homme.
Piasere, L. 1984. 'Mare Roma. Catégories humaines et structure sociale. Une contribution à l'ethnologie tsigane', Ph.D. diss. Paris: École des Hautes Études en Sciences Sociales.
———. 1987. 'In Search of New Niches: The Productive Organization of the Peripatetic Xoraxané in Italy', in A. Rao (ed.), The Other Nomads: Peripatetic Minorities in Cross-cultural Perspective. Kohl: Böhlau, pp.111–32.
Polanyi, K. 2001. The Great Transformation: The Political and Economic Origins of Our Time. Boston: Beacon Press.
San Román, T. 1976. Vecinos gitanos. Madrid: Akal Editor.
Sánchez Ortega, M.H. 1977. Documentación selecta sobre la situación de los Gitanos españoles en el siglo XVIII. Madrid: Biblioteca de Visionarios.
Segalen, M. 1985. Quinze générations de Bas-Bretons. Parenté et société dans le pays bigouden sud, 1720–1980. Paris: Presses Universitaires de France.
Stewart, M. 1992. 'Gypsies at the Horse-fair: A Non-Market Model of Trade', in R. Dilley (ed.), Contesting Markets: Analyses of Ideology, Discourse and Practice. Edinburgh: Edinburgh University Press, pp.97–114.
Testart, A. 2013. 'What Is a Gift?', HAU: Journal of Ethnographic Theory 3(1): 249–61.
Thède, N. 2000. Gitans et flamenco. Les rythmes de l'identité. Paris: L'Harmattan.
Viveiros de Castro, E. 2009. Métaphysiques cannibales. Lignes d'anthropologie post-structurale. Paris: Presses Universitaires de France.

Williams, P. 1993. *Nous, on n'en parle pas. Les vivants et les morts chez les Manouches*. Paris: Maison des sciences de l'homme.

Zonabend, F. 1980. *La mémoire longue. Temps et histoires au village*. Paris: Presses Universitaires de France.

Nathalie Manrique received her Ph.D. from the École des Hautes Études en Sciences Sociales (EHESS) and is currently affiliated with the Laboratoire d'Anthropologie Sociale, Paris. She has carried out ethnographic fieldwork over a period of five years in various Gypsy communities in Andalusia, Spain. Her current work concerns comparative research on representations of death and burial practices among Roma, Sinti and Gypsies as part of the research network Comparative Research on Representations of Death among Roma. Her publications include *'Sois généreux!' Don et hiérarchie chez les Gitans de deux petits bourgs andalous (Espagne)* (2015).

Afterword
KEITH HART

The Promise and Limits of Ethnography

I feel lucky to have witnessed what a lively bunch of young anthropologists are capable of today and to reflect on Gypsy economy as a lens through which to consider the human predicament that we all share at this time. This Afterword is based on a speech I made at the end of the meeting in Lisbon. Its theme was the strengths and limitations of the ethnographic method, and how anthropologists' professional standby of fieldwork might be inserted into a new approach better suited to the world we live in. I anchored these remarks on method in something I wrote almost three decades ago, a Malinowski lecture given at the London School of Economics on money (Hart 1986). There I argued that ethnography should come after an attempt to locate oneself in our moment of history and within a body of specialist ideas concerning the topic. In the present case, this would mean relating the study of Gypsy economy to neoliberalism today, and then to some relevant bodies of thought outside anthropology as well as in it.

It bothers me when I observe how unreflectingly my younger contemporaries identify anthropology with 'ethnography', and listening to the essays presented here did not alleviate these concerns. Yet it is not a mistake for anthropologists to claim that our greatest achievements of the twentieth century were based on the ethnographic revolution. The move to join people where they live in order to find out what they do and think was revolutionary. It is still the case that the administrative and intellectual classes generally talk about people without encountering them directly. So the first thing that ethnography is for is to report on this experience. Second, many disciplines use the term 'ethnography', but not in the way that anthropologists do. I feel that anthropologists have been very poor at articulating why what we do is different from and superior to what other disciplines call ethnography. Sociologists, institutional economists, nurses and all the others equate ethnography simply with making qualitative observations on the spot. In other words, if you go somewhere and record your observations, you are doing ethnography.

Third, as Tim Ingold (2008) says, anthropology is not ethnography. The reason that anthropological ethnography is different is that we bring to it at least the aspiration to generalise about the human condition as a whole or to place our findings in the widest possible framework of comparison. The challenge we face, however, is to overcome the academic legacy of our discipline's modern foundation. A century ago our predecessors needed to institutionalise the ethnographic revolution by finding a place in the universities – in order to reproduce ethnographers. In the intellectual climate of the day, we had to pretend that what we do is science. 'Scientific ethnography' was the banner under which we sought to establish ourselves, and this drew attention away from what makes anthropology different. Our trademark is our commitment to living with a people in a particular place for a long time with the aim of internalising society by participating in it (as Durkheim taught us). This generates a kind of knowledge which cannot be reduced to objective research material (fieldnotes). It is a sort of intuitive knowledge.

Let me explain this with an anecdote from my own experience. When I went to work with development economists around 1970, the big crisis of the day was thought to be Third World urban unemployment. The cities were growing very fast and there did not seem to be many real jobs available. I lived for two-and-a-half years in Ghana, mainly in Accra; but it actually took me quite a long time to work out why I did not like how the economists described the contemporary crisis of the cities. It took me a year to realise what the problem was: these people were not unemployed, they were working. This was not based on fieldnotes that I wrote down; it was based on living there. I had to excavate this idea from my half-buried experience. This is why anthropologists get it right more often than the others, because we have made a more whole-hearted commitment to living in another society and we do not fetishise the more tangible features of what we have learned.

Anthropological ethnography is also a fully paid up member of the genre known as realism. This was a key concept for the British Marxist critic, Raymond Williams (e.g. 1976), from whose voluminous writing on the subject my memory extracts the following. He makes three points. The first and most important is that realism reveals a new class, at least to the middle-class readership for the media that we are generating. Thus Irvine Welsh's novel *Trainspotting* (1993) reveals Edinburgh drugs-users to an audience that has never seen them before. Second, realism is contemporary; it enables readers to be part of what is going on now; and it differs from most stories, at least from the genres that preceded it, because they were usually situated in the past and involve a different kind of dialectic. Linked to this is a third point, that these narratives are secular; they are not sacred myths. He argues that an unequal society depends on sacred stories to reproduce itself, and realism is a democratic genre because it tries to blow away these myths of an unequal society.

If you take these three points and apply them to *Argonauts of the Western Pacific* (Malinowski 1922), it is immediately apparent that Malinowskian ethnography is realist in Williams's sense. Malinowski is saying: this is something you have never seen before – complex international trade without money, markets or states, and even without the principle of buying cheap and selling dear. Second, let us ditch the evolutionist idea of 'primitive societies' illustrating what the civilised world might once have been; let us study rather who they are now as contemporaries in our world. Finally, the point of this is to blow up *Homo economicus*, which is one of the sacred myths of our own version of unequal society. Perhaps the relationship between ethnography and ideology deserves more critical inspection.

Ideology is the premise that ideas are more important than life. Thus the priest says to you, 'Don't worry, I'll get you to heaven; just stick with the system'. The man who controls the ideas has the key to happiness, to life after death and so on. Ideology, as Marx (1867) says, is the *camera obscura* which turns the image upside down and makes it appear that life is derived from ideas and depends on them. Malinowski then turns the *camera obscura* upside down and says that ideas come from life. In other words, anthropologists can go into the field without any ideas, they come back and somehow they have discovered all their ideas through doing fieldwork. There is no attempt made to place the fieldwork tradition within intellectual history. I hated this feature of my education in the discipline: my teachers were very well-educated people who knew all about Marx, Freud and the rest, but they did not want to tell me where they got it all from. Instead, it was 'go off to the field and do your work, it's where good anthropology comes from'.

This is the main problem with a version of ethnography which I fancifully call the *synthetic a posteriori* (Grimshaw and Hart 1993). Kant has two sources of knowledge, the *synthetic a priori*, which consists of the ideas that our minds bring to encounters with the world, and the *analytical a posteriori*, which are the sense impressions we have of the world that we have to sort out afterwards. Our task is to bring these two together in a dialectic, according to Kant. Malinowski is saying that we get the synthetic ideas we have from our experiences in the field. This is clearly impossible. There was a time in the early twentieth century, however, when the object, theory and method of social anthropology formed a unity. The object was to study 'primitive' or simple societies as a way of understanding the mechanisms underlying more complex societies. The theory was functionalism: find out what they do and see how it fits together. The method of doing fieldwork in such places was entirely congruent with this. We knew who we were studying and why, from what theoretical perspective and with what method. It was a whole. That is why the British school was so powerful and produced permanent classics of ethnographic description and analysis in the interwar period.

It all became very different later. Anthropologists first got rid of the object: the collapse of empire did that; they were not around anymore, these so-called 'primitive' societies. The theory was dumped and replaced by the latest fashions from France and America. But we retained the method; fieldwork-based ethnography makes us professionals. But once you have decided that your professional identity hinges on ethnography, ideas inevitably take a back seat. Anthropology has now become a species of writing. It is not the case that what anthropologists mainly do is fieldwork. This is concentrated in the early phase of their careers. The main activity is cranking out useless papers for publication in journals, books and conferences. But the authority of the writer still rests on fieldwork. All the ideas incorporated into this style of writing are made to fit the ethnographic argument. The ethnographers believe that they can actually choose what the ideas mean, depending on whether they help the empirical analysis or not. The notion that the ideas and their authors have a history that should be respected has no place in the ethnographic tradition. We pay lip service to 'the literature', but reduce that to sound bites, clips from sources that just happen to be useful for the ethnographic narrative. And this means that we lack a coherent theoretical universe to work in.

Heads or Tails?

Martin Fotta referred to a lecture of mine on money when suggesting a title for the meeting: 'Heads or tails? Two sides of the coin' (Hart 1986). The lecture is actually a methodological commentary. If you want to write about something important like money, you cannot just sit there and say 'The X do it this way'. I claimed that you cannot start with ethnography, you should end with it. The argument has three parts. First, like it or not, we are informed by the history of the moment we are living through. The questions we pose and the way we go about answering them depend heavily on present times. So we should be quite explicit about how our research is shaped by contemporary social forces. The 1980s were a period when neoliberal economics was beginning to dismantle the Keynesian macroeconomics that had organised the postwar boom. I wanted to talk about how state and market relate to money, but the context was that people who said the state makes money were being overthrown by others who said sound money is based on leaving it to the market.

So you do not have to be a genius or a regular reader of the *Financial Times* to realise that the questions we are posing about Gypsies here are in some way a reflection of the times we are in. It is always good to keep that in mind, otherwise you are an automaton who does not have a clue why you are doing what you do. It is the same Durkheimian notion that we internalise social experience by immersing ourselves in it, but it takes a lot of work to excavate this existential soup and turn it into analytical objects that we can share with others. This is the first, preliminary step.

The second section of the lecture argued that we cannot talk about a topic like money without addressing at some level what the specialists have written about it. Anthropologists tend to subscribe to weak, oversimplified abstractions from economic thought like *Homo economicus*, so that they can say 'The Trobrianders are not like that, so we don't need to know any more about economics'. I doubt if, in the case of this volume, I would say 'Go away and immerse yourselves in the history of political economy'. What strikes me is how many different intellectual traditions inside anthropology, but more often outside it, have been referred to at various points in our discussions. I will return to that. The third part of my lecture is a reanalysis of Malinowski's Trobriand ethnography drawing on the first two sections. If Malinowski had taken the trouble to be more aware of the context in which he was writing and had familiarised himself a bit more with some of the theories that were available to him, he would have done a better job of analysing the Trobriand economy than he did.

My general line was as follows. Look at a coin – it has two sides, heads and tails. It has two sides for the good reason that both are indispensable. Heads represents political authority, top-down control, the state; tails represents the idea that the coin has an objective value in trade and can purchase commodities. What ruins contemporary monetary theory, especially in the anglophone world, is that policy flips from one extreme to the other, while ignoring their dynamic interrelationship. One major problem is that the state/market pair is not self-sufficient, it is not the whole story. Both sides privilege impersonal social organisation; they each operate by depersonalising people. In long-distance trade, money had to be impersonal because the participants did not know each other, while state bureaucracies are supposed to treat citizens equally. A French economist, Bruno Théret (2008), makes substantial use of my argument, but he adds that coins are three-dimensional, they have thickness, an edge. The third dimension of money, he says, is institutional. Between the top-down state and bottom-up market provision of money, social institutions organise what people really do.

In my later work I acknowledge this point, but approach it somewhat differently. We need impersonal society, the idea that all people should be subject to the same rules, independently of who they are and who they know. The twentieth century was based on impersonal society – state bureaucracy, capitalist markets and scientific expertise (including economics, to which most people had no real access). Yet we also believe that modern societies give all of us a chance to develop a unique personality, and that achieving this identity is essential. There is a huge contradiction between this drive for personality and the impersonal conditions of our participation in mainstream society. But I have argued elsewhere that the digital revolution in communications is altering rapidly and profoundly the terms of interaction between the personal and impersonal dimensions of social life, chiefly through a radical cheapening of the cost of transferring information (see Hart 2000). The circulation of large amounts of data surrounding the participants in long-distance transactions is transforming our experience of economic life. Mobile phones take all this further, since we now carry around miniaturised computers in our pockets, making our interactions with digital worlds even more directly personal. The internet does not have a payment system built into it and relies on archaic and clumsy methods, whereas mobile phones allow us to have directly personalised and objectified relations with the market; and this will make a huge difference to how we encounter markets and money – and state bureaucracies – in future.

So applying some of the lessons of this lecture to the present case of Gypsy economy should not rest with the question of states and markets, which is to define the problem in a way that you are not all that expert in. But if what is missing is the need to repersonalise these impersonal constructions of the economy, an ethnography of Gypsies, who do stand as a remarkable example of personalised economy, could make a major contribution to that project.

Why Study Gypsy Economy?

Looking at the assemblage of contributions to this volume, I would pick out four themes: the first is money transfers (begging, credit, loans, state grants); the second is economic strategies – a more dynamic and proactive look at what people are up to in market situations; the third focus is on performance, examining closely how people interact with each other; and the last concerns wealth and value in its different forms. So this collection adds up to quite a lot as a set. It is always important, if you want to know what someone thinks, to pay attention to the content of their writing rather than just the headlines. Thus Max Weber says he wishes to promote a subjective sociology, but 90 per cent of *Economy and Society* (Weber 1978) is a structural historical analysis with no people in it. This is because his sources were records written by the administrative classes, and people as such did not appear in these documents. So his material evidence did not support a *Verstehendesoziologie*. It is one thing to set out to do something, but you also need to analyse what you did.

To recapitulate, how should ethnographers take account of our moment in history and of theoretical strands relevant to Gypsy economy? Somehow you must make a link to neoliberalism. One obvious precedent for this is the Comaroffs' recent book, *Theory from the South* (Comaroff and Comaroff 2012), in which they claim that South Africa reveals a form of neoliberalism towards which the global North is evolving. This is a stimulating thought experiment, but we should not get carried away by it. Neoliberalism is an ideal type and the South African economy is more than that. For example, 25 per cent of the South African government's expenditure goes on state grants; so that however you want to characterise the country's political economy, the redistributive system of the ruling party, the ANC, is an enormous part of it. For many anthropologists, but not the Comaroffs, 'neoliberalism' has become a convenient tag, like *Homo economicus* for an earlier generation, an excuse for not thinking. There are some things that we all think we know about neoliberalism, but they are often just slogans taken in isolation. Many of us thought that the financial crisis would deal a death blow to neoliberalism, but, as Philip Mirowski (2013) has shown brilliantly, the neoliberal project has been strengthened by the crisis.

For our purposes, the most important aspect of neoliberalism is its promotion of the free market as a form of statelessness, the dream of money without politics which is shared by the techno-utopian movement that generates crypto-currencies like Bitcoin. This plays into an old and good standby of anthropology. How did anthropology get going? Because people in the nineteenth century wanted to know how permanent and universal Western industrial capitalism was, what alternatives there were – liberal, anarchist, communist or socialist? We went out to study people who were not part of the capitalist system in order to throw critical light on what we had left behind. Why did we study societies without the state? Because we wanted to show that the assumptions of state-made societies could be challenged. The theme of statelessness is absolutely central to the study of Gypsy societies everywhere. We no longer pretend that we are studying stateless peoples, but we are studying people with a history of statelessness who interact with states, global capitalism and the rest.

One theme is neoliberal governance, and it was most clearly evident in a paper on begging in Italy that unfortunately did not make it into this volume. Why suddenly is begging a problem? Why do they start giving the police bogus administrative instruments with which to harass Gypsy beggars? Because they infringe the dominant narrative of responsibility and autonomy; they provide a bad symbol of the free-market society that must be presented as inevitable. Other themes associated with neoliberalism are privatisation – the dismantling of the public sphere – and precarity. The Western middle classes, including most students, now discover that they are indebted and with precarious employment. If you think you know precarity, try being an Inuit, waiting for the whales to turn up. In fact, the hit movie the year Malinowski's *Argonauts* was published, 1922, was Robert Flaherty's *Nanook of the North*, a celebration of the resilience of an Inuit individual faced with almost insurmountable difficulties. And whatever neoliberalism is supposed to be, state transfers to the indigent are very important. The neoliberal state is also a very coercive one. It readily throws people into jail in large numbers.

Even if its demise has been too readily assumed by its opponents, neoliberalism has been facing for years now a huge legitimation crisis. Especially in the years of the Arab Spring and Occupy Wall Street, anthropologists made direct reference to the growing level of insurgency, agitation and revolt. These would seem to be the inevitable political consequence of the demons that have been released. For all these reasons, it seems to me that a collection of studies of Gypsy economy offers an opportunity to investigate questions that have tremendous resonance at this historical moment.

Finally, more exciting in some ways than pointing out the parallels with the neoliberal crisis, anthropologists have an opportunity to use and play with some of the bodies of theory that address the more performative and interactive aspects of our ethnographies and of the social situations in which we live. It is a great might-have-been of intellectual history that anthropologists generally missed the chance to learn from and draw on the achievements of social psychology. You may not know that Erving Goffman was seconded (between 1949 and 1951) as a Chicago doctoral student to the new Department of Social Anthropology at Edinburgh University, which was his base for fieldwork in a Shetland Islands hotel, and that he published *The Presentation of Self in Everyday Life* through Edinburgh's Social Science Research Centre in 1956. Social psychology (which could pass itself off as either anthropology or sociology) was the greatest contribution of the United States to modern thought, stemming from the work of G.H. Mead, the founder of symbolic interactionism. This was because the massive migration from Europe to the United States in the decades before the First World War threw strangers together in huge cities like New York and Chicago, speaking different languages and given the task of building society from scratch. That is what generated not only the Chicago School of sociology, but the social psychologists also. They were compelled to ask how it was that people who do not know each other and are thrown together in large numbers can make society.

This was Kant's question in *The Perpetual Peace* (1795), based partly on fieldwork down in the docks, where he would ask Portuguese and Dutch sailors how they made society on the open seas, well beyond the reach of states. We all know about states that organise societies within territorial boundaries and apply laws, punishments and the rest of it; but what happens outside those boundaries? People tend to think Kant was not funny, but he took his title from a Dutch pub sign that offered amnesia in this life (rather than after death) based on getting blasted with gin. This pub sign was a metaphor for a world society that exists beyond states. Gypsies are another striking example of the same thing. Most of the contributors to this volume are discussing boundary crossing, the refusal of nomads to be pinned down and the rest of it.

The crisis of our times is the contradiction between life on the move and institutions that tie us to the ground. More specifically, politics is still based mainly on nation-states, but the money circuit has gone global. Unless we can find, hopefully short of world war, the means of making a global society that is more effective than the framework erected after the Second World War (the Bretton Woods institutions, United Nations and so on), which is now clearly decadent, there will not be a twenty-second century. So anthropology, which once used ethnography to raise questions about the legitimacy and permanence of Western industrial society, could reinvent itself as the study of how people make society beyond the boundaries of existing states. This is a question that goes far beyond mere critique of free markets and the neoliberal dismantling of public provision, deregulation and all the rest. Far from going away, it more pertinent than ever today to ask how we can organise society without states. Gypsy ethnography and the comparative history of Gypsies offer rich opportunities to explore those questions.

Is ethnography concerned with what is particular about the Gypsies? No it is not. The objective cannot possibly be to document the Gypsies for their own sake and then move on. Clearly we are studying a sophisticated set of interactions at many levels that all of the chapters assembled here are already addressing in one way or another.

In conclusion, anthropologists have to be more self-aware about what we bring to the table in the form of ethnographic method. We cannot afford to rely on our theoretical premises emerging piecemeal from ethnographic descriptions. There has to be another level somehow. The present volume is a valuable exercise pointing in that direction, and I have been glad to be part of it.

REFERENCES

Comaroff, J., and J.L. Comaroff. 2012. *Theory from the South: Or, How Euro-America is Evolving toward Africa*. Boulder, CO: Paradigm Publishers.
Goffman, E. 1990 [1956]. *The Presentation of Self in Everyday Life*. New York: Penguin.
Grimshaw, A., and K. Hart. 1993. 'Anthropology and the Crisis of the Intellectuals'. Prickly Pear Pamphlet No. 1. Cambridge: Prickly Pear Press.
Hart, K. 1986. 'Heads or Tails? Two Sides of the Coin', *Man* 21(4): 637–56.
———. 2000. *The Memory Bank: Money in an Unequal World*. London: Profile Books.
Ingold, T. 2008. 'Anthropology Is Not Ethnography', *Proceedings of the British Academy* 154: 69–92.
Kant, I. 1795. Perpetual Peace: A Philosophical Essay (Read by D. E. Wittkower), trans. W. Hastie. Retrieved 1 September 2014 from: https://librivox.org/perpetual-peace-by-immanuel-kant/.
Malinowski, B. 1922. *Argonauts of the Western Pacific: An Account of Native Enterprise and Adventure in the Archipelagos of Melanesian New Guinea*. London: Routledge.
Mirowski, P. 2013. *Never Let a Serious Crisis Go to Waste*. London: Verso.
Marx, K. 1867. *Das Kapital: Kritik der politischen Oekonomie*, Vol. 1. Hamburg: Otto Meissner.
Théret, B. (ed.) 2008. *La monnaie dévoilée par ses crises*, Vol. 1. Paris: Editions EHESS.
Weber, M. 1978 [1922]. *Economy and Society*, ed. G. Roth and C. Wittich. Berkeley: University of California Press.
Williams, R. 1976. *Keywords: A Vocabulary of Culture and Society*. London: Croom Helm.

Keith Hart is Centennial Professor of Economic Anthropology at the London School of Economics and Political Science and Professor Emeritus of Anthropology at Goldsmiths, University of London. He is also International Director of the Human Economy Programme in the Centre for the Advancement of Scholarship at the University of Pretoria. His recent books include *The Memory Bank: Money in an Unequal World* (2000), and he is a co-editor (with Jean-Louis Laville and Antonio David Cattani) of *The Human Economy: A Citizen's Guide* (2010) and co-author (with Chris Hann) of *Economic Anthropology: History, Ethnography, Critique* (2011).

Index

A

abundance, 5, 114, 158–59, 175
   the logic of, 20, 147
Agamben, Giorgio. *See homo sacer*
agricultural work, 54, 69, 73–74, 77, 83, 221. *See also* fruit picking
Alentejo (a region in Portugal), 68, 72–74, 76, 78, 80, 83
alertness/complete presence, 13, 133, 138, 204. *See also* opportunities 'on the wing'; social navigation; *soro*
ambulant/itinerant trade
   and calendar of horse fairs, 76
   demise of, 74, 218
   practices of Ciganos, 19, 69, 77–78, 83 (*see also* mobility and rooting of Ciganos)
   See also door to door sale; nomadism; peripatetics
anomie, 52, 233
anthropology and capitalism, 247
anti-Gypsyism, 6, 10, 11, 115, 122. *See also* Gypsy stereotypes
antiquities trading, 150, 153
assymetrical relation, 174. *See also* misunderstanding: as controlled equivocation
authorities, 131
   interaction with, 17, 37
   Italian, 107–8, 113–14, 116, 119–20
   mistrust of, 12
   Portuguese and Cigano spatial dynamics, 69–70, 74–75, 80–81, 84
   See also police
autonomous work/employment, preference for, 91–92

B

Bahia (a state in Brazil), 17, 21, 24, 201, 204, 207, 211, 213, 218
banda/extended family (Hungarian Gypsies concept), 49–51, 53, 57
bank loans, 34, 37, 39, 55–57, 90
barvalo/rich (Gabori concept), 157. *See also Rom baro*
Bastos, Jose Gabriel Pereira, 71
Bateson, Gregory, 168
baxt. *See* luck
baxtale. *See* luck: Roma as lucky
begging, 13, 78, 93, 109, 113, 116, 123n8, 182, 186–87, 194–96, 236n21
   manglimos (Cortorari concept), 186
   manghel (Sinti concept), 13, 179n4
   and neoliberal governance, 247
Beres, Tibor, 52
Berland, Joseph, 70
Berta, Peter, 198n2
big man. *See Rom baro*
bişniţari (Spoitori concept)
   and entrepreneurialism, 131
   as entrepreneurs, 128, 138, 141
   as traders, 130, 138–39
Borsod (a region in Hungary), 49, 53, 59–60
Bosnian Gypsies (non-Roma concept), 115–16
Bourgois, Philippe, 136
Brazil, 3, 17, 21, 201, 211. *See also* Bahia; Sao Paulo
Brazzabeni, Micol, 15–16
Britain. *See* United Kingdom
brotherhood. *See* brothers
brothers, 58, 60, 135
   economic cooperation with, 110
   and inheritance, 190, 198n4

and mutual help, 51, 133, 136
and non-brothers, 56
as in Stewart, 17, 204, 143n6
See also sociability; solidarity
Bucharest, 20, 127–29, 131, 140–41
Budilova, Lenka, 40
Butler, Judith, 15

C
Callon, Michel, 17
Calo (Spanish Romani), 234n3
Calon, 3, 17, 21–22, 24n6, 163–78
    passim, 201–18
    settlements, 202–3
    use of the ethnonym, 178n1
capital
    economic, 82, 97, 155, 157, 227
    Gagikano (as in Piasere), 114–15,
      152, 236n18
    relational, 152, 155
    social, 4, 23n4, 57, 83, 99, 230
    symbolic, 83, 122
'catching', 228–29, 231
    and marriage by abduction, 230
    as transformation of the receiver
      status, 228, 232
categories, social, 224, 227, 229–30,
    233
    seen as inherited ('natural'),
      223–26
Catholicism, popular, 167–68, 177
chalices
    their association with the old,
      189, 195
    definition of, 198n2
    as heirlooms, 184, 189–90
    invisibility of, 189, 197
    their role in social reproduction,
      191
    as wealth, 189
    See also marriages
Charta 77, 10
chefe (Calon concept), 203, 205, 214,
    216
    and Calon settlements, 212–13
    compared with 'men of respect'
      (Gitano concept), 213

as strongmen, 209, 215, 217–18
See also respect; *Rom baro*
Chibi (Calon form of Romani), 166,
    171, 175, 178n1
'*Cigana*'s curse', 168, 175, 177
Ciganos (Portugueses)/Portuguese
Ciganos, 3, 9, 15–16, 19, 68–85
    passim
    use of the term, 84n2
    sedentarisation of, 73–76
Cigany, 65n1. *See also* Gypsy
    community in Hungary
circulation of objects, 203, 205,
    223, 225, 229. *See also* money: in
    circulation; 'traffic'
civilisation, 127, 132, 134
civilised, 56, 75, 133–35 (*see also* raj)
    compared to uncivilised, 55, 116,
      120–21
classification, social. *See* categories,
    social
client(s), 31, 40–43, 56, 59–60, 63, 77,
    83, 114, 151–55, 176–77, 206, 208,
    210, 217–18. *See also* moneylenders:
    porous boundary between and their
    clients; patronage
collaboration, 134, 136, 139, 141
    principles of, 137
    See also mutuality
Comaroff, Jean, 246
Comaroff, John, 246
combination, 137–39, 142
    principles of, 137
construction, employment in, 54, 81,
    94–97, 103
consumption, 20, 148, 149, 184, 189,
    193, 229
    communal, 6
    conspicuous, 89, 89, 183, 194
    temporal orientation of, 171, 194,
      197
    See also chalices; houses;
      sociability: and spending;
      visibility
control
    through gift exchange, 226,
      231–33

and importance of movement, 205
over oneself, 135–36
over one's environment, 21, 128, 133, 136–38, 141–42, 179n4, 215, 205–7, 213, 226–27, 232–33
over one's time, 158, 170
over transactions and its relation to age, 195, 212
and work, 227
See also exchange: and personal control; *força*; misunderstanding: as controlled equivocation
coppersmithing, 142n2, 185–86, 196
Cortorari, 21, 181–98 passim
neighbourhood, 188, 192
sedentarisation of, 185–86
use of the ethnonym, 185
cosmology, 1, 21, 122, 172–73, 211, 217, 223
Courthiade, Marcel, 235n10
'culture of poverty', 148
and moneylending, 52–53
Czech Republic, 38, 95–97
Czechoslovakia, 10, 94–95

D
Day, Sophie, 5, 122
Deans, Fran, 56
death, 64, 243n3 (*see also* respect: towards the dead)
and destruction of property, 170, 201, 222, 233
and inheritance, 232–33
debt(s), 10, 60–63, 149, 154, 156, 191, 210, 212, 230
its centrality for life in segregated settlements, 19, 32, 35, 45, 55
and hierarchy, 36, 223, 230
its impact on social relations, 35–36, 40, 52
and indebtedness, 5, 10, 52, 97
relationship, 41, 44, 63, 208
deserving poor, 56, 58

diline Roma/ 'fool Gypsies' (Slovak Roma concept), 41–44
divine favour, 100, 108, 116–22
domestic mode of production (DMP), 20, 148–50, 157–59. *See also* households
door to door sale, 74, 221. *See also* street: vending
dowry, 171, 190, 198n3, 212–13
its relationship to chalices, 189–90
See also money: and dowry
drug(s), 75, 82, 127–28, 130–33, 139, 141, 223, 242
Durkheim, Emile, 52

E
economic practices, 1–3, 6, 18, 90, 181, 197 (*see also* Gypsy economy)
during communism, 93, 186
and marginality, 9, 80–83, 91, 122, 148 (*see also* marginality; interstitial: spaces)
and mobility, 9, 69–70, 76–77, 83, 110–11, 151, 183 (*see also* ambulant trade; migration; transnational mobility)
and identity, 43, 91, 108, 152, 158 (*see also* identity; performance)
as performative, 16–18 (*see also* performance)
and sociality, 8, 13, 24n6, 147, 158 (*see also* debt: its impact on social relations)
and values, 13, 157 (*see also* value; values)
See also informal activities; informal economy; interstitial economy; marginality
effective intelligence, 151. *See also* 'thinking up': inventively
efficacy, 17, 21, 117, 172, 176–78. *See also* luck
encompassment, 13, 22, 71, 109, 172, 205, 207, 209–10
'enduring'/endurance, 91, 99–101, 226. *See also* labour: endured

England. *See* United Kingdom
English Gypsies, 7, 14, 118–19, 164
equality, 6, 75, 134, 201, 204, 207, 222, 228, 230–31, 233
    and food sharing, 57, 214, 216–17
    and hierarchy, 22, 118, 156, 210–12, 234
    and mutual aid, 51, 57–58, 137, 204 (*see also* brothers; generosity; mutuality; solidarity)
    See also exchange: and equality
equivocation. *See* misunderstanding
ethnography, 240, 249
    anthropological, 241–42
    fieldwork-based, 243
European Union, 6, 8, 10, 54, 90, 101–2, 115
    enlargement, 89, 98, 108, 184
Evans-Pritchard, E.E., 165
Evora, 19, 68–69, 71, 73–74, 76, 78–80, 83–84, 85n10
exchange, 55, 63–64, 76, 81, 84, 96, 129–30, 148–49, 188, 190
    of affections, 178
    and equality, 142, 207, 214, 222 (*see also* equality)
    forms of, 129, 137–39, 142 (*see also* collaboration; combination)
    as in Graeber, 54
    importance of, 147, 188, 204, 207
    means of, 21
    networks, 77, 147, 232
    and personal control, 196, 207, 210, 212–13, 226 (*see also* control)
    See also value: exchange; gift; wealth: circulation of

F

factory work, 11, 17, 20, 89, 91–92, 94, 98–99
farming, 96, 150
Ferentari, 127–28. *See also* Bucharest, Țiganie
Ferrari, Florencia, 205–6

ferrivecchi, 109–15, 118–19, 121–22, 123n5. *See also* scrap metal
fieldwork, 9, 18, 32, 45n1, 53, 65n1, 73, 94, 109, 130, 133, 142n2, 164, 186, 217, 223, 236n17, 241–43
    and ideas, 242
financialisation, 17, 207, 218
Finland, 10
'fixing up', 88, 95, 100–103
    as learned disposition, 90, 101
    money, 20, 89, 97
food sharing, 192, 214, 236n17 (*see also* equality: and food sharing)
fool/*fraier*/*prost* (Romanian), 128, 136, 138, 141. *See also diline Roma*
força (Calon concept), 201–2, 204–6, 213–14
    realisation of, 206
    as reputation, 206
    See also control; *vergonha*: and *força*
fortune telling, 164–65, 168, 179n2
    and deception, 168–69, 177–78
    as production of the future in the present, 169
    and psychoanalysis, 165, 176
    truth of, 169
    See also '*Cigana*'s curse'; palm reading
Fotta, Martin, 171, 243
frame, 119, 166–69
    capturing within, 175, 178
    of fortune telling, 174, 177–78
    metacommunication through, 168–69, 176
framing, as determination of boundaries in exchange, 16–17, 208
France, 10, 18, 188, 234
fruit/herb picking, 33, 55, 68, 77, 92
    tomato harvest, 69, 77
fušky (Slovak Roma concept). *See* informal: one-off jobs
future. *See* time, conception of

G

Gabori Roma, 10, 20, 108, 104n3, 117, 145–60 passim, 185, 192n2

Index   255

Gadje
  Brasileiro(s), 163, 171, 203–4, 206,
    208, 210, 212, 216–18, 219n1
  Castellano(s), 225, 227–29, 236n20
  Gadzo/Gadze, 31, 43–44, 88, 103
  Gadzso, 65n1
  Gago/Gage, 8, 23n6, 114, 116–21
    passim, 123nn9–10, 179n4
  Gajon(s)/Gajin(s)/Gaje, 21, 24n6,
    163–65, 168–78, 205–10, 212–14,
    219n1
  Garron(s)/Garrin(s), 166, 178n1
  Gazo/Gazi/Gaze, 145–47, 149–59,
    160n1, 185, 193, 194, 198
  Gazos, 8, 16, 24n6
  Gorgio(s), 14, 165
  Juron(s), 208, 219n1
  Magyar, 65n1
  Payo(s), 222, 225–29, 234nn3–4,
    235n8, 236n17, 237n26
  Rarlon(s), 178n1
  Romanies' attitudes to, 11
  use of terms throughout the
    book, 23n6
Gamella, Juan, 236n15
Gawa (Papua New Guinea Island), 207
Gay y Blasco, Paloma, 117, 210–11, 213,
  236n15
  on gendered personhood, 13, 15
gender, 2, 7, 8, 13, 24n8, 189
  division of economic activities,
    24n8, 94, 104n5, 148–49, 155,
    186, 187
  hierarchy in gift giving, 224–25,
    229
  and personhood, 13, 15
  and procreation, 189, 226
generation(s), 21, 24n8, 109, 147, 170,
  194–96, 201, 230, 233
  replacement of, 196–97
generational cycles. See chalices;
  houses; households
generosity, 22, 36, 136, 157, 204, 223,
  225, 227, 230–31, 234n2, 234nn5–6,
  236n17
  and 'Gypsyness', 228

  See also gift; mutuality;
    reciprocity; solidarity
Germany, 10
ghetto, 9, 19, 20, 32, 54, 127. See also
  segregated communities
gift(s), 22, 138, 190
  and counter-gift/transfer, 222–23,
    230
  giving and legitimisation of
    social classification, 222, 224
  and relationships between donor
    and receiver, 222–33
  as sharing, 230
  See also control: through gift
    exchange; hierarchy: through
    gift giving
Gitanos/ Spanish Gypsies, 15, 22,
  24n6, 84n3, 121, 204–5, 210–11, 213,
  217, 221–37 passim
  'de verdad'/'Gypsies for real', 224
  apayaos/'Payo-like', 223, 234n2
gleaning, 97
Godelier, Maurice, 230
'God's help'. See divine favour
Goffman, Erving, 248
good price/ lașo prețo (Gabori concept),
  146, 153–55, 157
  and profitability, 153
Graeber, David, 54, 57, 62, 201, 205,
  208, 218
  on debt, 35
  on money, 214
  on moral reasoning, 51
  on power, 54, 62, 214
  on value, 201
Greece, 71
guttering, 148, 150, 156. See also
  tinsmithing
Guyer, Jane. See niches: Guyer, Jane on
Gypsies
  comparison of with futures
    traders, 12–13
  exclusion of from formal
    economy, 3
  integration of, 11, 107
  non-Gypsy stereotypes of, 2, 8,
    14–16, 43–44, 46n9, 75, 82, 84,

104n7, 119–21, 152, 165, 173, 178n1
   as scapegoats, 6
   use of terms throughout the book, 23n2
Gypsy (Cigany) community in Borsod county (Hungary), 49–65 passim
Gypsy economy, 13, 152, 240, 246, 247
   double meaning of, 3, 5–6, 129
   and market economy, 1–2, 122, 159, 246
   as personalised economy, 245
   use of the term, 23n1
   variety of practices within, 2, 10
'Gypsy work'/*ciganska robota* (Slovak concept), 92

H
Hart, Keith, 3–5, 22
   on impersonal society, 3–4, 245
   on informal economy, 3
Hayden, Robert M., 70
Hertz, Robert, 222
Herzfeld, Michael, 121, 234
hierarchical redistribution, 19, 58, 63
hierarchy, 21
   and behaviour, 211, 217, 234n2
   contested through consumption, 194
   through gift giving, 222–24, 227
   as in Graeber, 54, 62
   between Gypsies and non-Gypsies, 54, 91, 152, 186, 194, 227
   and maturity, 225
   and power, 211
   between Romani communities or individuals, 58–59, 71, 75, 93, 96, 118, 152, 156, 223, 234n2 (*see also* categories, social; *diline Roma*; *malta*; *pele*; recursive hierarchisation; *Rom baro*)
   workplace, 98, 104n7
   See also equality
hire-purchase, 34

Holbraad, Martin
   on quality of multiplicity of money, 209
   on truth, 169
home
   kher–al (Cortorari concept), 185
   as in *khere*/'at home' (Gabori concept), 157
   as in *nossa casa*/'our home' (Cigano concept), 69, 79
Homo economicus, 160, 242, 244, 246
homo sacer, 20, 108–9, 119–20, 122
horse(s), 16–17, 77, 237n24
   fair or market, 16–17, 68, 76–77, 83
   trade, 9, 16–17, 19, 68–69, 73–76, 81–84, 91–92, 186, 221, 226, 235n12, 237n24
   traders, 12, 69, 73, 77–78
Horvath, Kata, 92
house(s), 21, 35, 37, 39, 45n2, 181–98 passim
   architectural style of, 156, 181–82, 192
   their association with the youth, 194, 195, 197
   as co-constitutive of marriages, 195–96
   as collateral in loans, 60
   construction of and migration, 88–89, 95–96, 100, 131, 183
   fascination with Romanian Gypsy houses, 182
   as *Gaze*-oriented projects of civilisation, 191, 193–94 (*see also* visibility)
   incompleteness of, 196
   transformations of, 192–93
   See also home; household; marriages
household(s), 37, 153, 159, 160n6
   centrality of, 7, 131, 134–35, 204, 213
   daily subsistence of, 42, 148–49, 155
   and lifecycle, 21, 201, 212, 215
   See also house; marriages; street: and household

Hungary, 49, 51, 53, 55, 57, 62–63, 65nn2–5, 130, 151, 157
  during state socialism, 2, 6, 8, 16, 54
  See also Borsod; Miskolc
husbandry, pig, 186, 196

I
identity, 69, 117–21, 224, 226, 231, 234, 245
  collective, 108, 117
  construction of, 2, 15, 90, 92, 104n3, 108, 194
  personal, 215, 225
  politics of, 10, 187
  shifts in conceptualisations of, 45, 103, 222
  and the state, 69, 109, 119
  See also performance: of ethnicity; performance: performative character of 'Gypsyness'; *Romipen*
ideology, 91–92, 122, 152, 155, 157, 204, 221, 242
  androcentric, 189
  socialist, 95, 103
illicit activities, 72, 128, 139–42
independence, 91, 117, 152, 155
  symbolic, 20, 108–9, 122, 147
informal
  activities or practices, 38, 61, 81, 90–91, 128, 186 (*see also* illicit activities)
  economy, 3–4, 12, 35, 53, 56, 75, 96, 109, 121
  moneylending. *See* moneylending, usury
  one-off jobs/*fušky* (Slovak Roma concept), 89, 96, 99, 105n8
  strategies, 90, 96, 130
informality, 9, 11, 122, 128, 130, 137
Ingold, Tim, 241
interstice(s), 1, 9, 19, 70, 72, 74–76, 82, 84. *See also* niche
interstitial
  economy, 6, 9, 70, 83–84, 141–42

spaces/domains, 72–73, 82, 84, 90, 102, 104, 109, 128, 131
Italians, 110, 112, 115, 116, 119–20, 122
Italy, 8, 10, 20, 23n6, 71, 107–9, 113, 115, 120, 122, 123n2, 130, 145, 188, 247.
  See also Rome

J
Jakoubek, Marek, 40
James, Deborah, 32, 36, 38
job agency, 91, 98, 101

K
Kalderas Rom, 12
Kant, Immanuel, 242–43, 248
Kayapo (Amazonian People), 211
'know-how', 148, 150–51, 158–60
Kosice, 94

L
labour, 88–105 passim
  endured (Slovak Roma concept), 88, 99 (*see also* 'enduring')
  and 'fixing up money' (Slovak Roma concept), 90, 97, 100–101, 103 (*see also* 'fixing up')
  hard/*phari butji* (Slovak Roma concept), 89–90, 99, 105n9
  under socialism, 10–11, 94–96, 103
  wage, 2, 3, 33, 54, 81, 91, 92, 99, 103–4, 151, 158
  See also agricultural work; factory work; precariat; Romani *butji*
Lagunas Arias, David, 227, 236
Lemon, Alaina, 23n5
Levi-Strauss, Claude, 223
Liebow, Elliot, 5
Lisbon, 16
loan shark(s). *See* moneylender(s); usurer(s)
luck, 20, 21, 102, 112, 138, 174, 178
  as *baxt*/*bacht*, 17, 100, 108, 116–22, 153, 159–60, 160n8, 172
  Roma as lucky/*baxtale*, 16–17, 108, 118–19, 160, 172
  See also efficacy
Lukacs, Gyorgy, 52

living for the present/moment, 13, 170
    and exclusion, 5
    as future-oriented, 5
    See also precarity

M
mahala, 127, 142n2
Malinowski, Bronislaw, 234n4, 235n13, 242–44, 247
malta/maltêses (Cigano concept), 73, 78, 84n5
Manus, 18, 191, 237n25
marginality, 9, 73, 148
    and entrepreneurship, 12, 116–17
marime, 175
market economy, 149, 192, 234n4
    as milieu of interstices, 1
    recent changes of, 3, 5, 183
marriage(s), 145, 189–90, 212, 236n19
    by abduction/capture, 226–27, 230–31
    alliance, 225, 232
    payments. See dowry
    processuality of, 189, 194–96
    status isogyny in, 75, 80, 83
    See also chalices; houses; households
Marx, Karl, 242
Mauss, Marcel, 159, 222–23, 234n4, 235n13
meștero/craftsman (Gabori concept), 151–53, 155
metal dealers, 110, 112, 122
migration, 8, 20, 21, 248
    of Bosnian Xoraxane Roma, 109
    labour, 94, 98–101, 104n7
    of Romanian Roma, 108, 115
    of Slovak Roma, 88, 97–104
    See also transnational mobility
Miller, Daniel, 193
Miskolc, 54
misunderstanding, 154, 172–75
    as controlled equivocation, 173–75, 177, 178
    productivity of, 21, 119
mobility and rooting of Ciganos, 69–71, 75, 79–80, 83–84

Moldova, 130, 143n7
money, 2, 4, 8, 17, 35, 38, 194, 210, 213, 227, 229, 232, 243–55
    in circulation, 209, 213, 231 (see also circulation of objects)
    conceptualisations of, 13, 20–21, 148–49, 156–57, 160, 244
    as double medium, 209
    and dowry, 190–91, 198n3, 212, 215
    as hidden, 202, 204, 209–10, 212, 215, 218
    'on the street', 163, 205, 206, 208–10, 212, 215, 218
    within palm-reading interaction, 164, 167–69, 175
    and respect, 12, 21–22, 147, 156
    See also exchange; 'fixing up': money; Graeber: on money; Holbraad: on quality of multiplicity of money
moneylender(s) (unofficial), 50–51
    'fair' vs. 'vulturous', 59–60, 63
    as 'helper of the poor', 59, 62, 64
    porous boundary between and their clients, 32, 38–41, 44–45
    views of, 19, 41–42, 59, 62
    See also usurer(s)
moneylending (unofficial), 17, 19, 21, 35, 51–52, 64, 77, 82, 97, 139, 235n8
    of Calon to Brasileiros (non-Gypsies), 171, 204, 206–7, 214
    interest rates in, 32, 35–41, 51, 55, 58–60, 62, 97, 149, 160n4, 208
    and kinship, 40, 52–53, 57, 59 (see also mutuality; solidarity)
    views of, 19, 32, 37–38, 51, 53, 63, 65n2
    as way to escape poverty, 31, 39, 42, 44, 46nn11–12, 52, 56
    See also 'culture of poverty': and moneylending; usury
Munn, Nancy, on intersubjective space–time, 207
mutuality, 77, 137, 139, 141–42, 210.
    See also brothers: and mutual help; collaboration; equality: and

Index

mutual aid; generosity; reciprocity; solidarity

N
neoliberalism, 33, 240, 244, 246–47, 249. *See also* begging: and neoliberal governance
niche(s)
    as adaptation, 7–8, 72
    economic, 7–8, 23n2, 71–73, 82, 90, 97, 101–3, 207
    Guyer, Jane on, 8
    and interstices, 9, 19, 72
    as sociotechnical *agencement*, 17 (*see also* framing)
    See also interstice; interstitial
Nomad camps (*campi nomadi*) in Italy, 107–8, 109, 120–22
Nomads' camp (*Parque Temporário de Acampada para Populações Nómadas*) in Portugal, 20, 69, 73, 76, 78, 80–84, 85n10
nomad(s), 6, 68, 81, 248
    as a political and legal category, 68–70, 74–75, 80, 84, 85n8, 107, 119
nomadism/nomadic lifestyle, 32, 75, 85n8, 148, 185–86, 226. *See also* ambulant trade; peripatetics
non-Gypsies, non-Roma. *See* Gadje

O
Okely, Judith, 2, 7, 12, 24–25n9, 72, 118–19, 164–65, 176, 198n1
    on performance of ethnicity, 14
Olivera, Martin, 104n3, 108, 117, 185
ontological turn in anthropology, 165
opportunities 'on the wing', 93, 97, 103. *See also* alertness; social navigation; *soro*

P
palm reading, 21, 163–68, 172, 174, 176–78, 179n4, 186, 218
    as giving luck/*dinhá bahje* (Calon concept), 164

    See also '*Cigana*'s curse'; fortune telling; money: within a palm-reading interaction
Papataxiarchis, Evthymios, 5, 122
Pasqualino, Caterina, 227, 236n15
patego(s)/*patio*(s) (Cigano concept), 81–82
patronage/ patron-client relationship, 54–55, 64, 73
patrono/boss (Gabori concept), 152
pawnshop(s), 34–35, 58
peasant(s), 4, 17, 24n6, 65n1, 96, 148–49, 154, 192–95
    as antithesis of a 'good *Gazo*', 154–55
    interactions with, 54–55, 93, 184, 186, 189, 235n12, 237n24
pele(s) (Cigano concept), 78, 85n9
performance, 14–18
    arts, 14
    as enactment, 16–17, 175, 178
    of ethnicity, 14–15, 25n9, 104, 115, 119–20, 164, 166, 173, 234n2
    as in performative character of Gypsyness, 13–15, 117–18
    as in performativity of economic practices, 8, 16
peripatetics/peripatetic populations, 2, 7, 9, 70, 148 (*see also* ambulant trade; nomadism)
    limitations of the concept, 7, 71–72
person(s), social
    attributes of, 15, 21, 90, 133–36, 171, 184, 194–95
    creation of, 15, 94–95, 131, 141, 175, 204, 207, 210–11, 215, 217
    distribution of attributes of, 22, 212–13, 215
    value attributed to, 15, 128, 133–34, 136–37, 139, 141–42, 143n4, 189
    See also gender; identity
personhood, social. *See* person(s), social
perspectivism, 173

Piasere, Leonardo, 2, 7–8, 11, 23n6, 46n3, 71–72, 92, 114, 123n8, 236nn18–19, 236n21
   on circumstance approach, 18
   See also capital: *Gagíkano*
police, 10, 17, 36, 63, 68–70, 78, 83, 107–8, 110, 114, 116–17, 120, 132–33, 138, 141, 164, 166, 176, 247. *See also* authorities
Portugal, 3, 71, 74–75
poverty, 2, 4, 9–10, 34, 50, 52, 57, 61, 75, 84, 89, 96, 100, 127
   economic uncertainty, 53, 55
   generational, 32–33, 37, 39, 44
   See also 'culture of poverty'; moneylending: as a way to escape poverty; precarity
precariat, 4
precarity, 4, 6, 9, 73, 81, 89, 247
   as 'the time of the Gypsies', 4
   See also poverty
present. *See* time, conception of

R
Rao, Aparna, 2, 7, 70
raça(s) (Cigano concept), 69, 73–74, 77, 79, 84n3. *See also* raza
raj/gentleman (Cortorari concept). *See* civilised; house: as *Gaze*-oriented project
rationality and irrationality, 37, 164–65
raza(s) (Gitano concept), 211, 213, 235n11. *See also* raça
reciprocity, 157, 158
   balanced, 223
   generalised, 35–36, 40, 159
   kinship-based, 77, 81
   negative, 152, 160n5
   See also collaboration; gift; mutuality; solidarity
recursive hierarchisation, 212–13. *See also* hierarchy
religious syncretism, 167
   and Gypsy spirits, 177
   See also Umbanda

respect, 61, 115–16, 135–36, 138, 142, 147, 210, 212
   towards the dead or dying, 13, 232
   'men of respect' (Gitano concept), 211, 213
   symbols of, 213, 225
   See also chefe; money: and respect
respectability, 79, 117, 127, 133–34, 152, 154, 156, 186, 234
respectable. *See* respect; respectability
risk, productivity of, 12
Rom baro/big man, 156. *See also chefe*
Romanes (the Rom way), 91, 147, 149, 156, 158, 160n3
Romanes (language), 123n13, 151
Romani butji (Rom/a work), 2, 17, 20, 90, 92, 97, 103, 108, 148–58
   as know-how, 151
Romania, 9–10, 21, 108, 115, 129, 142n2, 143n7, 146, 150, 158, 160n3, 182–83, 185, 190, 198n5
   during postsocialism, 128, 131, 138, 184
   See also Bucharest; Transylvania
Romanian Gypsies (non-Roma concept), 115–16
Romanian Roma, 93. *See also* Cortorari; Gabori; Spoitori
Romanies, 23n2, 10
Rome, 9, 108–10, 113–15, 120, 123nn8–14
Romipen (Roma identity), 43–44
Romungro Roma, 54
Rumuni (Romani concept), 108, 110, 115–16, 118, 120–21

S
Sahlins, Marshall, 20, 147–49, 152
   on domestic mode of production, 148, 159
Salo, Matt, 71
San Roman, Teresa, 72, 205, 236n15
Sao Paulo (city), 163, 166
scarcity, notions of, 5, 21, 157
Scheffel, David, 46n11
scrap metal, 132, 139, 141

buying and selling of, 110, 112, 129
collection of, 9, 33, 55, 92, 109–17, 119–22
as 'going for iron', 20, 110, 113, 116–18
separation of, 110–11
See also waste
secret, 164
segregated community or settlement, 10, 19, 32, 45n1, 45n11
communist attempt at destruction of, 95
'Gypsy village' (Hungary), 53
in Hungary, 52– 55
osada (Slovakia), 45n2
taboris (Slovakia), 31, 33–41, 44, 45n2, 93, 96
See also ghetto
self-representation, 115–16, 119–20, 204. *See also* performance: of ethnicity; person: creation of
shame, 21, 193, 205. *See also vergonha*
shameless, 173, 203, 214, 216, 218
Sinti, 11, 13, 113, 179n4, 191
Slovak Roma, 10, 17, 19, 20, 31–46 passim, 88–106 passim
during state socialism, 94–96
centrality of kinship relations, 33
Slovenska Roma (disambiguation of ethnonyms), 32, 46n3
Slovakia, 10, 19–20, 31–33, 35, 45nn1–2, 46nn4–12, 88–90, 97–98, 100–102
Slovensko (Slovenian) Roma, 8, 11
snail collecting, 92
sociability, 51, 148 158
'protected', 131
and spending, 155–56
social mobility, 19, 44, 45n2, 56, 88, 95
social navigation, 138
solidarity, 52, 57–59, 62, 132, 231
kinship, 33, 35, 45, 40, 51–52, 57, 64
mechanical, 159
See also brothers; mutuality
sorcery, 176–78

soro (Romani concept) 117–20, 121. *See also* divine favour
space(s)
appropriation of, 70, 79, 82–83, 113–16 (*see also* territoriality)
'in-between' (*Zwischenräume*), 4, 7
patterning of through exchanges, 207, 210
See also interstitial: spaces/domains
Spain, 22, 69, 129–30, 130, 205, 221, 226, 234n3
Spoitori Gypsies, 20, 129–43 passim
Stan, Sabina, 137
Stewart, Michael, 2, 4–6, 8, 11–22, 16–17, 24n6, 72, 91–92, 105n9, 108, 117, 119, 122, 143n6, 147, 157, 160, 170, 172, 198n1, 204, 237n24
street
conceptualisation of, 129, 131, 142n3
economy, 129–31, 133, 137, 141–42
and household, 128, 130–31
life, 133–35, 137, 140
and 'school of life', 129, 138
vending, 75, 81, 84–85n7, 119, 129
See also money: 'on the street'
Sweden, 10

T
Tauber, Elisabeth, 2, 13, 113, 179n4
taxtaja. *See* chalices
territoriality, 19, 69–71, 74, 78–80, 113
territories
stigmatised urban, 130, 132
working, 20, 111, 113–15
Thede, Nancy, 227
Theodosiou, Aspasia, 24–25n9, 71
Theret, Bruno, 245
'thinking up', inventively, 93 (*see also* effective intelligence)
Ţigan/Ţigani, 142n2, 150, 152, 194
Ţiganie/ 'Gypsy area', 127, 141
time, conceptions of, 170–72
tinsmithing, 150–51, 153
'traffic', 20, 129–30, 133

transnational mobility, 96–97, 157, 183, 197. *See also* migration.
Transylvania (a region in Romania), 20–21, 150, 160n3, 185, 187, 189
travelling traders. *See* ambulant trade
trust, 36, 56, 77, 79, 131, 133–34, 142, 154, 164, 204, 208
Turkey, 97, 130
Turner, Terence, 11, 211–13
    on value, 211

U
Ukraine, 96
Umbanda (Afro-Brazilian religion), 167, 176. *See also* religious syncretism
undeserving poor. *See* deserving poor
unemployment, 10, 33–34, 54, 56–57, 88, 96, 241
United Kingdom, 20, 88–90, 95, 98–104, 104nn4, 104–5n7, 165
Umbres, Radu, 12, 24n7
usurer(s), 31–32
    appreciation of, 36
    'band of usurers' (Hungarian Gypsy concept), 49
    dependence on, 35, 38, 52
    interešar (Slovak Roma concept), 46n5
    and state authorities, 44 (*see also* usury: as criminal offence)
    their views of lending as risky, 36–37, 40
    See also moneylender
usury, 19, 41–42, 51–53, 58, 59, 63
    as criminal offence, 39, 41, 50, 56, 65n3

V
value, 20–21, 91, 118–19, 152–53, 155, 189–90
    of actions, 201, 205
    anthropological theory of, 202, 217 (*see also* Graeber: on value; Turner: on value)
    appropriation of, 211–12, 218
    conversion of, 203–4, 207, 209, 216
    creation of, 128, 131, 175
    exchange, 148–49, 157
    material and non-material, 128, 131, 138–39, 141
    media of, 206–7, 213
    monetary, 157, 208
    objectification of, 215
    template, 205
    use, 21, 148–49, 157, 160
    See also person, social: value attributed to; wealth
values, 13, 15, 17, 20, 24n6, 33, 51–52, 81, 165, 229–28
    hierarchy of, 134
    paired sets, 205
    shame and strength (Calon), 201, 215, 218
Veblen, Thorstein, 194
vergonha (Calon concept), 174–75, 205–7, 212
    realisation of, 206, 209, 214–15, 218
    in Ferrari, 205
    and *força*, 201, 205, 213, 217–18
    laje, 175, 205
    See also força; shame
violence, 41, 44–45, 77, 79, 81, 131, 134–36, 142, 201, 206–7
    and non-violence, 133
    state, 103, 108
visibility, 187
    and invisibility of wealth forms, 184
    as political statement, 187–88
Viveiros de Castro, Eduardo, 173–74
Vlach Rom, 2, 6, 8, 11, 16, 24n6, 91–92, 108, 157, 170, 172, 204, 237n24

W
Wacquant, Loïc, 4
wage labour. *See* labour: wage
Wagner, Roy, 173–74
waste, 110, 118–20, 122. *See also* scrap metal

wealth, 19, 21–22, 152, 186, 203, 214, 230
  (non-)accumulation of, 157, 222, 226, 228, 232–33
  circulation, 156, 204, 209, 223 (*see also* circulation of objects; money: in circulation)
  cosmologies of, 1
  display of, 89, 100, 157, 196 (*see also* visibility)
  and scarcity, 158, 160
  See also chalices
Weber, Max, 160, 246
welfare/state benefits/payments, 4, 10, 19, 33, 37–39, 41–43, 55, 57, 61–62, 69, 75, 78, 81–82, 84n4, 90, 96, 101, 149, 158, 182
  and public works, 55–56
  and work activation programmes, 46n6
welfare reform in Slovakia, 33
Williams, Patrick, 2, 12, 18, 198n1, 237n25
Williams, Raymond, 241

X
Xoraxane Roma, 9, 11, 20, 109–22 passim, 236n19, 236n21

Z
Zaloom, Caitlin, 12–13
Zatta, Jane Dick, 23–4n6, 92

www.ingramcontent.com/pod-product-compliance
Lightning Source LLC
Chambersburg PA
CBHW070916030426
42336CB00014BA/2430